D1520632

Speaking in Tongues and Dancing Diaspora

Race and American Culture

General Editors:
Arnold Rampersad and Shelley Fisher Fishkin

Speaking in Tongues and Dancing Diaspora

Black Women Writing and Performing

MAE G. HENDERSON

OXFORD
UNIVERSITY PRESS

OXFORD
UNIVERSITY PRESS

Oxford University Press is a department of the University of Oxford.
It furthers the University's objective of excellence in research, scholarship,
and education by publishing worldwide.

Oxford   New York
Auckland   Cape Town   Dar es Salaam   Hong Kong   Karachi
Kuala Lumpur   Madrid   Melbourne   Mexico City   Nairobi
New Delhi   Shanghai   Taipei   Toronto

With offices in
Argentina   Austria   Brazil   Chile   Czech Republic   France   Greece
Guatemala   Hungary   Italy   Japan   Poland   Portugal   Singapore
South Korea   Switzerland   Thailand   Turkey   Ukraine   Vietnam

Oxford is a registered trademark of Oxford University Press
in the UK and certain other countries.

Published in the United States of America by
Oxford University Press
198 Madison Avenue, New York, NY 10016

© Oxford University Press 2014

All rights reserved. No part of this publication may be reproduced, stored in a
retrieval system, or transmitted, in any form or by any means, without the prior
permission in writing of Oxford University Press, or as expressly permitted by law,
by license, or under terms agreed with the appropriate reproduction rights organization.
Inquiries concerning reproduction outside the scope of the above should be sent to the
Rights Department, Oxford University Press, at the address above.

You must not circulate this work in any other form
and you must impose this same condition on any acquirer.

Library of Congress Cataloging-in-Publication Data

Henderson, Mae.
Speaking in tongues and dancing diaspora : black women writing and performing / Mae G. Henderson.
pages cm
Includes bibliographical references and index.
ISBN 978–0–19–511659–5
1. American fiction—African American authors—History and criticism.   2. American fiction—Women
authors—History and criticism.   3. American fiction—20th century—History and criticism.   4. African
American women entertainers—History—20th century.   5. African American women—Intellectual
life—20th century.   6. African Americans in literature.   7. African American women in literature.   I. Title.
PS374.N4H47 2014
810.9'928708996073—dc23
2013039953

1 3 5 7 9 8 6 4 2
Printed in the United States of America
on acid-free paper

In memoriam
For Mz Inez and daughter Josephine
Aunt Essie and my great aunt Evelyna:
All southern black women who surely knew what it meant
to "cut the rug" and definitely knew how to tell a story

And in celebration
For my new niece and namesake, Toni Mae:
May she pass on the steps and the stories

CONTENTS

ACKNOWLEDGMENTS

I am, most of all, thankful for black women writers—novelists, poets, and critics—whose *words* have opened new *worlds* to their readers, and whose intellectual and artistic gifts have modeled for me the passion of language, the pleasures of reading, the beauty of knowledge, and the joys of the imagination. The voice and vision of the authors treated in this volume create for me what I can only describe as an experience of *sublimity*, emanating from the gift of discourse, and defined by the Ancient Longinus as the power of great conceptions, vehement and inspired passion, the due formation of figures, noble diction, and dignified and elevated composition. I am especially indebted to Toni Morrison for her masterful performance of the art of *periphrasis* (what she describes as "circling the subject"), which the Ancient regarded as the most delicate and dangerous of figures. I offer this volume as critical testimony bearing witness to the experiences of awe, astonishment, and revelation I discover in engaging the high art of letters associated with these writers—and to their power to transport the reader and hearer into an experience of sublimity that, in the words of Longinus, "flash[es] forth at the right moment scatter[ing] everything before it like a thunderbolt and at once display[ing] the power of the orator in all its plenitude."

Virginia Woolf wrote that woman needs a room of her own in which to write, but I have found that my own production as a scholar has depended more on a rhizomatic space without walls, a space of multiple entryways and exits, a space governed by the principles of interconnectivity and heterogeneity. In 1996, upon the occasion of her award of the medal for Distinguished Contribution to American Letters from the National Book Foundation, Morrison opened her acceptance speech with the following remarks, suggesting the relationship between the writer and the reader:

> There is a certain kind of peace that is not merely the absence of war. It is larger than that. The peace I am thinking of is not at the mercy of history's rule, nor is it a passive surrender to the status quo. The peace I am

thinking of is the dance of an open mind when it engages another equally
open one....

Closing, she continues, the "real life [of the book] is about creating and producing and distributing knowledge; about making it possible for the entitled as well
as the dispossessed to experience one's own mind dancing with another's." This
image of the dancing mind invokes the appeal of Piedade's song and Consolata's
empathetic listening in the coda to Morrison's *Paradise*. It is also an image that summons the Self's encounter with the Other (even when that other is the self)—in
the discursive spaces where knowledge gets produced, exchanged, transmitted, and
disseminated: around the kitchen table; in the seminar room, the lecture hall, the
academy, the conference center, the athenaeum, the salon, the public sphere; and
across the global space of the Internet and other telecommunications networks.
And it is an image that calls forth the fruits, blessings, rewards, riches, and peace
flowing from the sacred encounters occurring in these open and fluid spaces of
conjunction and connectivity—these *rooms without walls*—within a community
that is at once both hospitable and respectful of difference and diversity. It has been
in this kind of rhizomatic space, without enclosures—the opposite of the Farsian
notion of *pairidaeza*—that I have encountered a community of scholars, colleagues,
and friends, with whom I have had the pleasure of "tripping the light fantastic": to
George Cunningham who has, on many occasions, served as my ideal lead in the
pas de deux, lifting me *à l'aire*; to Cheryl Wall, whose impeccable poise, timing, and
technique always work to restore my balance, keeping me *en pointe*; to Charlene
Regester, JoAnna Mann, Régine Latortue and Cherry Muhanji—each of whom has
given me a gentle push, and sometimes, a hard shove, when I was inclined to leave
the dance floor; to Gene Melton who, on more than one occasion, has kept me from
falling *à terre*; to the many others, including Henry Louis Gates, Jr., Houston Baker,
Jr., Hortense Spillers, Ann duCille, and other dance partners who would remind me
of the old steps and inevitably taught me new moves so that I could begin my own
improvisations; to Patricia Hill Collins, Thadious Davis, Valerie Lee, Wahneema
Lubiano, and multiple others who have introduced new positions and added moves
that forever changed the dance; to the younger dancers, Katherine Bassard, Jennifer
Devere Brody, Daphne Brooks, Silvia del Pilar Castro Borrego, Cathy Cohen, Brent
Edwards, Farah Jasmine Griffin, Sharon Holland, Robert Reid Pharr, E. Patrick
Johnson, Maria Isabel Romero Ruiz, and others who have syncopated the dance; to
my graduate and undergraduate students—whose exercises kept me stretching and
flexing; to those lapsed partners (who shall remain unnamed) with whom I may
have been out of step but who have nonetheless continued the dance; and, finally,
to Brendan O'Neill, my editor at Oxford University Press, whose choreography has
sustained the dance into a structured series of movements—making it all of a piece.

    And I would be remiss if I did not thank the Rutgers Institute for Research
on Women; the Stanford Humanities Center; the National Endowment for the

Humanities; the Schomburg Center for Research in Black Culture-New York Public Library; the New York Public Library for the Performing Arts; the Yale University Beinecke Rare Book and Manuscript Library; the Emory University Manuscript, Archives, and Rare Book Library; the Stanford University Eugene Lerner Josephine Baker Collection; and the University of Minnesota Center for Advanced Feminist Studies—all open-air dance studios and grand ballrooms that feature, promote, and reward the dance of open minds encountering one another.

The author notes that in some instances minor changes (unless indicated otherwise) have been made to earlier versions of these essays for purposes of correction and clarity. And while the essays contained herein should be regarded as the authoritative version, in no way do these changes alter the meaning or intent of the original essays.

"Alice Walker's *The Color Purple*: Revisions and Redefinitions" originally appeared as "*The Color Purple*: Revisions and Redefinitions" in *Sage: A Scholarly Journal on Black Women* 7 (Spring 1985). Reprinted by permission of Mae G. Henderson.

"(W)Riting *The Work* and Working the Rites" originally appeared in *Black American Literature Forum* 33, no. 4 (Winter 1989). Copyright © 1989 Mae G. Henderson.

"Speaking in Tongues: Dialogics and Dialectics and the Black Women Writer's Literary Tradition" originally appeared in *Changing Our Own Words: Essays on Criticism, Theory, and Writing by Black Women*, ed. Cheryl Wall. Copyright © 1989 by Rutgers, the State University. Reprinted by permission of Rutgers University Press.

"Toni Morrison's *Beloved*: Re-Membering the Body as Historical Text" originally appeared in *Comparative American Identities: Race, Sex, and Nationalities in The Modern Text*, ed. Hortense Spillers. Copyright © 1991 Routledge Press/Taylor & Francis Group. Reprinted by permission of Routledge Press/Taylor & Francis Group.

"The Stories of (O)Dessa: Stories of Complicity and Resistance" originally appeared in *Female Subjects in Black and White: Race, Psychoanalysis, Feminism*, ed. Elizabeth Abel, Barbara Christian, and Helen Morgan. Copyright © 1997 by the Regents of the University of California. Published by the University of California Press. Reprinted by permission of the University of California Press.

" 'Seen But Not Heard': A Poetics of Afro-American Women's Writing" originally appeared as the Response to Chapter 5: "There Is No More Beautiful Way: Theory and the Poetics of Afro-American Women's Writing" by Houston A. Baker, Jr., in *Afro-American Literary Study in the 1990s*, ed. Houston A. Baker, Jr., and Patricia Redmond. Copyright © 1989 by The University of Chicago. All rights reserved. Reprinted by permission of The University of Chicago Press.

"Gayl Jones's *White Rat*: Speaking Silence/Silencing Speech" originally appeared as the "Foreword to the 1991 Edition" of *White Rat* by Gayl Jones (Boston: Northeastern University Press, 1991). Reprinted by permission of University Press of New England.

"The State of Our Art: Black Feminist Theory in the 1990s" originally appeared as "The State of the Art" in *The Women's Review of Books* 8, no. 5 (February 1991): 23–26. Reprinted by permission of *The Women's Review of Books*.

"What It Means to Teach the Other When the Other Is the Self" originally appeared in *Callaloo* 17, no. 2 (Spring 1994): 432–438. Copyright © 1994 Johns Hopkins University Press. Reprinted with permission by Johns Hopkins University Press.

"Authors and Authorities" originally appeared in *The Women's Review of Books* 12, no. 9 (June 1995): 22–24. Reprinted by permission of *The Women's Review of Books*.

"Nella Larsen's *Passing*: Passing, Performance, and (Post)modernism" originally appeared as the "Critical Foreword" to *Passing* by Nella Larsen (New York: Modern Library, 2002). Copyright © 2002 by Mae Henderson. Reprinted by permission of Mae G. Henderson.

"Josephine Baker and *La Revue Nègre*: From Ethnography to Performance" originally appeared in *Text and Performance Quarterly* 23, no. 2 (April 2003): 107–133. Copyright © 2003 by National Communication Association. Reprinted by permission of Routledge Press/Taylor & Francis Group.

"Dancing Diaspora: Colonial, Postcolonial, and Diasporic Readings of Josephine Baker as Dancer and Performance Artist" originally appeared as "Colonial, Postcolonial, and Diasporic Readings of Josephine Baker as Dancer and Performance Artist" in *The Scholar & Feminist Online* (*S&F Online*) *Double Issue* 6, nos. 1 & 2 (Fall 2007/Spring 2008). Copyright © 2008 by Barnard Center for Research on Women. Reprinted by permission of Mae G. Henderson.

"About Face, or, What Is This 'Back' in B(l)ack Popular Culture?: From Venus Hottentot to Video Hottie" originally appeared in *Cultural Migrations and Gendered Subjects: Colonial and Postcolonial Representations of the Female Body*, ed. Maria Isabel Romero Ruiz and Silvia Pilar Castro Borrego (London: Cambridge Scholars Publishing, 2011), 125–156. Copyright © 2011 by Silvia Pilar Castro Borrego and Maria Isabel Romero Ruiz and contributors. Reprinted by permission of Silvia Pilar Castro Borrego, Maria Isabel Romero Ruiz, and Mae G. Henderson.

"Sherley Anne Williams (1944–1999): 'Someone Sweet Angel Chile'" originally appeared as "In Memory of Sherley Anne Williams: 'Some One Sweet Angel Chile' (1944–1999)" in *Callaloo* 22, no. 4 (Fall 1999): 763–767. Copyright © 1999 Johns Hopkins University Press. Reprinted with permission by Johns Hopkins University Press.

"Bebe Moore Campbell (1950–2006): 'Literature as Equipment for Living'" originally appeared as "Bebe Moore Campbell: 'Literature as Equipment for Living'" in *Girls' High Alumnae Magazine,* Spring 2007. Reprinted by permission of *Girls' High Alumnae Magazine.*

Speaking in Tongues and Dancing Diaspora

Introduction

Black Women Writers Speaking, Listening, and Witnessing

I. Sisters Speaking the Spirit

There is...a certain spirituality I feel from black women writers. Spirituality to me is a belief in the animated world—a world that has a life force, that permeates all of it, and a unity....A force that is in the trees, in each of us, in the air. A force that is available for us to go to, to learn from, to be nurtured by, nourished by, and most important, to be responsible to.
—Gwendolyn M. Parker, from *I Know What the Red Clay Looks Like*

[The] Black woman, silent, almost invisible, in America, has been speaking for three hundred years in pantomime or at best in a borrowed voice.
—Josephine Carson, *Silent Voices: The Southern Negro Woman Today*

But no *man* can tame the tongue.

—James 3:8 (emphasis added)

Mah tongue is in mah friend's mouf.
—Zora Neale Hurston, *Their Eyes Were Watching God*

And they were filled with the Holy Ghost, and began to speak with other tongues, as the spirit gave them utterance.

—Acts 2:4

Perhaps more than any other African American novel, and in spite of a title that would seem to interpellate the *visual* rather than the *oral* as its dominant literary modality, Zora Neale Hurston's *Their Eyes Were Watching God* has become foundational to theorizing a model for reading African American narrative that privileges speech, orality, voice, and storytelling—and this paradoxically in marked contrast to the prevailing aesthetics of a poststructuralist moment privileging *writing and textuality* in the interpretation of literary texts.[1] And with the notable exceptions of Mary Helen Washington's pioneering essay, "I Love the Way Janie Crawford Left Her Husbands: Zora Neale Hurston's Emergent Hero," which argues that Janie, the novel's protagonist, remains narratively silenced, and Carla Kaplan's "The Erotics of Talk," which, in ironic assent, proposes that the protagonist adopts self-silencing as a strategy to evade the incompetent listener, the preponderance of critical readings (including my own) of this by-now-classic novel has focused on the assertion of *voice*.[2] Such readings—linking freedom and voice, storytelling and subjectivity, testimony and recognition—continue to shape contemporary African American literary criticism and an evolving theoretical tradition that remains rooted in *orality*.

A brief backward glance at what many would consider a formative period in the development of modern African American literary theory and criticism suggests an alignment between contemporary sonic literacies and subjectivities and prior theoretical models and paradigms grounded in colloquial language, speech, voice, orality, storytelling, and singing. The association of African American writing with a culture and tradition that has invoked the vernacular trope of the "talking book" and generated critical tropes such as the "speakerly text" and the "talking text" further signals a continuity between the oral and written forms of black American expressivity. Other tropes—ranging from Robert Stepto's "call and response," to Henry Louis Gates's "signifyin'," Houston Baker's "bluesman," Geneva Smitherman's "talkin' and testifyin'," bell hooks's "talking back," Cheryl Wall's "worrying the line," to my own "speaking in tongues"—all affirm the power of voice and sonance in the African American literary tradition.[3] Significantly, the critical focus of these literary scholars demonstrates the liberational and salvific impulses attached to the assertion of voice in a culture in which African Americans have been victim, historically, not only to vocal suppression, but victim, in some instances, to self-silencing as well. Such tropes continue to form critical grist for the theoretical mill propelling contemporary readings of black women writers in which narrating and storytelling, along with their musical equivalent, singing (blues and spirituals), become instrumental to securing freedom from slavery, reconstituting damaged and fractured subjectivities, and reconstructing personal narratives and communal histories. As signified by my title, the chapters here contribute to the tradition of theorizing the preeminence of voice and narration (and the consequences of their absence) in the literary performances of black women. As a trope, "speaking in tongues" is intended to invoke both private, privileged, inspired utterance and publicly performed formal speech; as a sign, it is intended to speak to the discursive diversity of black women. Further, speaking in tongues is meant to invoke the oral and oracular attributes that I associate with black women's voices. The opening chapters, in particular, propose an interpretive model that seeks to demonstrate the interlocutory, dialogic, intertextual, and revisionary character of black women's literary and cultural performance.

In my personal history, tongue-speaking is deeply intertwined with trace memories of growing up in the Pentecostal, or Holiness, church. My aim here is to reclaim and reconstruct a fundamentally *spiritual rite* and *cultural practice* as a *critical praxis* and *theoretical trope* for reading black women's literary performance. For although the Apostle Paul's epistles to the first-century Christians in Corinth caution, "Let your women keep silence in the churches: for it is not permitted unto them to speak," attributing the gift of tongues to "men and angels," in my own memory and imagination, this extraordinary Pentecostal rite is inextricably bound to women—black women—shouting and dancing up and down the aisles of a quaintly rural meeting house in my native Fayetteville, a southern town known principally for its military installation, Fort Bragg, and located in the heart of the Bible Belt in southeastern Carolina.[4] Pentecostalism itself, according to several historians, is rooted in black culture, and embraced particularly by black women who have long been accorded evangelical status in the Pentecostal or (as it is sometimes called) the Sanctified Holiness Church.[5] This title trope, then, theorizes a practice uniquely associated with black women's spiritual communication, shaped as it is by a conjunction of private and public orality and performance. In Scripture, speaking in tongues has been aligned not only with "unknown," but also "known," tongues. It is a practice linked with intimate, familial, and ecstatic as well as diverse, foreign, and public discourses. And it invokes a notion of discursive diversity that speaks both to the "other" within as well as across borders and boundaries of difference—in discourses that are both testimonial and adversarial, empathetic and confrontational, collaborative and competitive, reflexive and dialogical—and, at once, polyglottal, polysemous, and polyvocal. As such, the title ultimately reclaims and re-signifies a spiritual rite and cultural practice as literary praxis and critical trope—by way of appropriating and reconstructing a profoundly personal and collective experience associated with my girlhood, my mother, and the community of black women whose voices pervade the texts that I have read and taught.

While the tongue, as James 3:5 reminds us, is "a small part of the body," references to it abound throughout the Old and New Testaments. It is both praised and cursed, exalted and demonized ("With the tongue we praise our Lord and Father, and with it we curse men" [James 3:8]). "Tongues" has myriad connotations in the Scriptures—ranging from "an organ of taste and speech" to "foreign languages" to "people" and "nation" to "ecstatic utterance," or intimate, privileged speech. The most common biblical usage of the term, however, is in the context of the allusion to Pentecost. "Speaking in tongues" is the English transliteration for what is often referred to as "glossolalia," a term originally used in Pentecost (Acts 2:1–4) that has its roots in the Greek noun *glossa* (tongue) and verb *lalein* (to speak). Those who speak in tongues are known as *glossolalists* or *glossolalics*, and tongue-speaking, according to Pentecostal doctrine, is regarded as a genuine manifestation of the Spirit, a charismatic gift, and a "second blessing." In the Southern, Protestant, evangelical tradition in which I grew up, devotion and witnessing characteristically expressed themselves in visions, the laying on of hands, spirit possession, speaking in tongues, and other charismata, or "gifts of the Spirit." The ability to speak in tongues represents, then, only one—but perhaps the highest and most preeminent—of the nine gifts of the Spirit identified by the Apostle Paul:

> To one there is given through the Spirit the message of wisdom, to another the message of knowledge by means of the same Spirit, to another faith by the same spirit, to another gifts of healing by that one Spirit, to another miraculous powers, to another prophecy, to another the ability to distinguish between spirits, to another *the ability to speak in different kinds of tongues*, and to still another, the interpretation of tongues. (1 Corinthians 12:8–10, emphasis added)

These were the gifts gloriously manifested by the sisters in the Sanctified Holiness Church. For, in spite of Paul's misogynistic injunction forbidding women to speak in the church, these women dreamed dreams, beheld visions, and gave expression to inspired utterances. They were teachers, preachers, pastors, prophets, evangelists, healers, and tongue-speakers. And while the gifts of the Spirit were multiple in manifestation, it was, above all, speaking in tongues that gave evidence and bore witness to an outpouring of the Spirit. These sisters speaking (in) the Spirit made visible the invisible, expressed the inexpressible, and spoke the unspeakable.

As a trope, speaking in tongues is further meant to designate a race- and gender-specific paradigm privileging "otherness" and "difference" in relation to broader, more totalizing, interpretive models for reading African American women's literary performance. It also seeks to reclaim a tradition thematized in early black women's spiritual autobiographies. Even in the nineteenth century, black women revivalists and evangelists were able to achieve some measure of personal expression and liberation through the recording of religious and conversion experiences that became, for them, a means by which to secure personal autonomy and limited mobility in a society that offered few opportunities for status or advancement either to blacks or women. As Katherine Bassard maintains in *Spiritual Interrogations*, it was "in the public forum of oratorical performance" that these women spoke "the most private communications—between self and Spirit." Indeed, it was through the public utterance of private communication, "a communication with Spirit [that] is dialogical, a give-and-take signified by its interrogative nature," that these women "often experienced a conferral of personhood denied by larger social constructions of African American and female subjectivity." Thus, maintains Bassard, "It is with this divine dialogue that black women's subjectivity is produced even as her agency is acknowledged and affirmed. The 'I' that hears the interrogative in the conversion account becomes the empowering 'I' who is 'able.'"[6] Further, these early black women's spiritual autobiographies, as Sue Houchins notes, were a form "particularly suited to, and a logical extension of, these women's vocation to preach, teach, pray publicly, and testify. It retained the orality of both their homiletic exhortations…and their prayers [in a] 'consecration of words.'"[7]

If, as Robert Stepto has argued, the quest for literacy and freedom constitutes the African American pre-generic myth set in motion by the secular slave narratives,[8] I would argue that the quest for voice, authenticity, and authority constitutes a unique and distinct difference defining the nineteenth-century spiritual narratives of black women authors such as Maria W. Stewart, Jarena Lee, Zilpha Elaw, Julia A. J. Foote, Amanda Berry Smith, and Rebecca Cox Jackson, a cohort that Carla Peterson would describe as "doers of the word."[9] It is the link between a spiritual and secular ethos and the spoken and the written word that, I propose, continues as one of the salient and defining aspects of black women's writing.

II. "Pennycostalism"

When the day of Pentecost had come, they were all together in one place. And suddenly a sound came from heaven like the rush of a mighty wind, and it filled the house where they were sitting. And there appeared to them tongues as of fire, distributed and resting on each one of them.
—Acts 2:1–3

The whole movement of the Sanctified Church...has brought in a new era of spiritual making....The Saints, or Sanctified Church, is a revitalizing element in Negro music and religion.
—Zora Neale Hurston, *The Sanctified Church*

[During Sunday morning service] the sisters in white, heads raised...the white caps of the women seeming to glow in this charged air like crowns...the women all seemed patient...the Power struck someone...they cried out, a long, wordless crying, and, arms outstretched like wings, they began the Shout.... then the tambourines began again, and the voices rose again, like fire, or flood, or judgment.
—James Baldwin, *Go Tell It on the Mountain*

Most histories of Pentecostalism affiliate the movement and its origins with urban migrants and the "illiterate masses" of the South. Yet others associate Pentecostalism with the religious practices of the American slave.[10] In the 1950s, when waves of postwar Southern immigrants—including families like mine from North Carolina—flooded into Northern cities in search of jobs and better opportunity, it was the church that offered structure and continuity for countless numbers confronted with disruption, displacement, and dislocation. My own faith and practices, begun in a tiny Southern "pennycostal" (as I have always called it) church at a time almost before conscious memory, were subsequently groomed and nourished in a more urban venue by the deacon and sisters in a corner storefront Pentecostal Holiness Church, located near 33rd and Ridge, just one block down from the three-room, first-floor flat—formerly a single-family row house that had seen better days—where I lived, along with my mother, brothers, and sisters. It was in this North Philly neighborhood, Strawberry Mansion, historically a heavily Jewish settlement bordered by Fairmount Park and the Schuylkill ("Surekill") River, that I eagerly anticipated at the beginning of each week, the Sunday morning worship service at the Pentecostal Holiness Church. Typically, some among the church sisters would meet early, before the arrival of the congregation, to adorn the makeshift pulpit, unfold and arrange the oak wood chairs, and prepare to "make a joyful noise unto the Lord" by singing, clapping, praying, and shouting (sometimes in tongues), before stepping forward, at the end of service, to answer the altar call. And although I have long since ceased formally to observe its doctrine and rites, "pennycostalism," characteristically embraced by the dispossessed and underprivileged, continues to be a part of my heritage.

Currently identified with the revival of the neo-Pentecostal movement and the emergence of the non-Pentecostal "charismatic" movements dating back to the 1950s and early 1960s, contemporary Pentecostalism traces its origins to the convergence, in 1906, of antebellum black spirituality and the Holiness Movement in Los Angeles.[11] The Azusa Street Revival, as it was called, was led by a one-eyed African American preacher and son of former slaves, William J. Seymour, whose Sunday sermons at the Apostolic Faith Gospel Mission preached the New Testament message of Pentecost, which describes the Holy Ghost descending upon the gathering of disciples like "tongues of fire." Known for its diverse (African American, Hispanic, white, and Asian) following, the Holiness movement embraced the beliefs of faith healing, sanctification, and, most especially, speaking in tongues as evidence of baptism in the Holy Spirit. And it was known especially for its embrace of women in leadership and other participatory roles. Notable black women in the Holiness-Pentecostal movement included not only legendary gospel singers like Sally Martin, Sister Rosetta Tharpe, and the inimitable Mahalia Jackson, but women leaders like Elder Lucy Smith, founder of All Nations Pentecostal Church in 1918, a church largely administered by women, and Mary Magdalena Lewis Tate, founder of the House of God, who convened the first great Pentecostal revival. In 1908, "Mother Tate," as she was affectionately known, was reputed to have contracted an incurable disease, but "spoke in tongues and declared that she was 'healed and sealed and baptized of the Free and Holy Ghost.'"[12] Like the present-day charismatics, the "holy rollers" (as the Pentecostals were sometimes derisively called), a small sect often set apart as too emotive and excitable in their religious zeal and public worship, have since grown from a relatively obscure presence into a massive, worldwide movement.

What I recollect most vividly about our Sunday morning services were the church saints (and sinners), moved by the "Holy Ghost" to jubilant and ecstatic forms of witnessing and worshipping. Even though I was not then—nor am I now—a tongue-speaker, these services always held me enthralled. Silent, voiceless, tongue-tied, and denied authority and recognition in public and secular life, these women—like my mother, they were typically domestics, maids, and "day workers" during the week—arose on Sunday mornings and found their voices at the altars and in the pulpits, choirs, and pews of the church. Accompanied by the rhythms of gospel singing, foot-stomping, hand-clapping, head-shaking, and the percussion from the tambourines, organ, and cymbals, these women in white sang, shouted, and testified for hours on end. It could be a trial of patience awaiting the arrival of the Spirit at evening "tarrying service," but when the Holy Ghost entered, there was joy and jubilation, praise and adoration. Touched by the Spirit, these sisters and mothers and daughters of the Sanctified Church spoke and sang in what English theologian and hymnist Charles Wesley once described as "a thousand tongues." And speaking *to* or *in* the Spirit not only accorded authority to the glossolalic, but relegated to secondary status a patriarchal doctrine that granted entitlement to the church *fathers*. It is precisely women's role in the Sanctified Church, argues religious historian Cheryl Gilkes, that "has been part of a larger historical role of black women, a role that emphasizes independence, self-reliance, strength, and autonomy and that contradicts the dominant culture's expectations and demands of women."[13] At the same time, the experiential nature of their "talkin' and testifyin'" allowed these women to combine authority with witnessing and self-reliance with empathetic identification.

However, the practice of glossolalia is not simply a speech act; nor is it simply a performance. Rather, it is a *performative speech act*, and in the Holiness Pentecostal Church, glossolalia is a "sign" not only in the semiological sense, but also in the sense that it becomes a mark of holiness and membership in the Beloved community ("Wherefore tongues are for a sign...to them that believe not").[14] It was our belief that speaking in tongues was the first and greatest of the gifts of the Holy Spirit, and that these women—the "Saints"—had an honored role and special standing in the church because of their possession of a rare and precious gift—a second blessing, entitling them to privileged communication. Their first-person testimony bore witness to an experience of illumination that was accessed only by those who possessed the gift of tongues, and their interpreters. At times these glossolalics were themselves both mediums and interpreters of the Spirit; at other times, the presence of an interpreter was required to understand and translate inspired communication. And because of its reliance on personal experience and biblical authority, Pentecostalism has stressed not only oral forms of ritual and worship, but also the importance of education and literacy. An emphasis on orality and literacy, speaking in tongues, spirituality, textual authority, personal testimony, and female participation are all characteristically associated with the values and rituals of worship in the Sanctified Holiness Church. But, again, the singular and distinguishing mark of Pentecostalism is speaking in tongues. For black women writers, then, the spoken and written Word occupies a near sacred place. The invocation of tongues is a strategy by which I attempt to use a rite and figure of spiritual discourse to create a theoretical trope for black women's praxis and literary discourse.

As noted above, the practice of tongue-speaking embodies a form of expression and communication that privileges individual, firsthand experience over doctrine and theology. And, in contrast to Judaism and Western Christianity, notes Ghanaian church historian John Pobee, pre-literate cultures (such as those of the pre-industrialized American South and indigenous black Africa) are perceived to have produced no "theological treatises and tomes," nor "systematically worked out volumes which stand on the shelves of libraries"—so what has come to be known as "oral" or "living" theology has depended heavily on preaching, praying, hymns, songs, testifying, witnessing, and storytelling in the transmission of theological values.[15] Moreover, as cultural anthropologist Michael Rynkiewich notes, oral cultures "are marked by the use of ceremony, dance, art, poetry, and so on."[16] In such cultures, orality and performance thus become vehicles for passing on social, cultural, and moral values. Yet, as Toni Morrison reminds us, because African Americans (unlike many Third World indigenous groups) no longer "live in places where we can hear . . . stories any more, the novel is needed by African Americans in a way it was not needed before."[17] What Morrison suggests here is that what oral tradition was to an earlier pre-literate African American culture, the novel is to a modern and literate African American culture. And this project's underlying premise is that what tongue-speakers (and prophets and interpreters of tongues) were to an earlier period, so novelists (and poets and critics) are to contemporary culture.

While, in my experience, the practice of glossolalia is specifically associated with the Holiness and Pentecostal Church, it is notable that the historical and religious antecedents of glossolalia date back to the classical and early Christian periods. While in the history of Christianity, glossolalia has emerged during periods of "revival and spiritual renewal," it has also been practiced by groups experiencing repression and persecution.[18] Even earlier, however, during the classical period, ecstatic speech was held to be intrinsic to oracular prophecy. For Plato the poets were coupled with women oracles—including the prophetesses and priestesses at Delphi, the priestess at Dodona, and the prophetess Sibyl on the isle of Delos.[19] The practice of glossolalia is also paralleled in the practice of spirit possession associated with certain forms of shamanism among the North American Indians as well as with the indigenous religions of West Africa and black Atlantic diasporic culture. Further, this speech practice has an analogue or visual equivalent in traditions that art historian Robert Farris Thompson describes as "ideographic writing" and poet-critic Harryette Mullen designates as "spirit-writing" or "textual glossolalia," a practice that she defines as "[a] unique illegible script produced in a trance-like state [that] functions as a graphic representation of spirit possession."[20] Like oral glossolalia, textual glossolalia is associated with spiritual empowerment and cultural authority, but also, I'd like to think, with a discursive diversity linking the oral and written to the spiritual and secular traditions of black women's writing. Speaking in tongues, then, is a term I associate with black women in the Pentecostal Church, but more broadly with traditions of classical, Christian, African, and black diasporic spirituality.

III. Ermeneglossia, or Listening Matters

My choices of language (*speakerly, aural, colloquial*), my reliance for full comprehension on codes embedded in black culture, my effort to effect *immediate co-conspiracy and intimacy* (without any distancing, explanatory fabric), as well as my (failed) attempt to *shape a silence* while breaking it are attempts (many unsatisfactory) to transfigure the complexity and wealth of Afro-American culture into a language worthy of the culture.
—Toni Morrison, Afterword to *The Bluest Eye* (emphasis added)

Child learn a lot of things sitting between some grown person's legs, listening at grown peoples speak over they heads. This is where I learned to listen, *right there between mammy's thighs, where I first learned to speak, from listening at grown peoples talk....*
—Sherley Anne Williams, *Dessa Rose* (emphasis added)

Only when someone else listens to me can I listen to myself.
—Kelly Oliver, *Witnessing: Beyond Recognition*

The absence of an addressable other ... who can *hear* annihilates the story.
—Dori Laub, "Bearing Witness, or the Vicissitudes of Listening"
(emphasis added)

If you don't have to hear, if your humanity isn't somehow involved in hearing, you don't. Hearing has to be essential. You have to be able to hear other people's voices and you have to be able to hear your own voice.
—Gayl Jones from "Gayl Jones: An Interview [with Michael Harper]"

It is important to note that the paradigms for reading so far discussed are predicated on the presence of narrators who move from silence to speech. Yet Morrison has described storytelling—one of the distinguishing characteristics of black literary expression—as "the ability to be both print and literature: to combine those two aspects" so that one can both "hear" the stories as well as be able to "read [them] in silence."[21] Morrison's remarks regarding *silence* and the *hearing* (and *reading*) positions, along with her remarks above emphasizing the *speakerly* and *colloquial* character of black expressivity, constitute what might be described as *an aesthetics of the oral and aural.*

In one of his perhaps lesser-known publications, a collection of dialogues entitled *The Ear of the Other: Otobiography, Transference, Translation,* Jacques Derrida, in a lecture entitled "Otobiographies" (from the Greek *oto,* meaning "ear"), considers (within the context of a broader discussion of Nietzsche and the status of autobiography) the function and structure of the ear as a visible and discrete auditory organ that is "involved in any autobiographical discourse that is still at the stage of hearing oneself speak." Noting the slippage between "auto" and "oto," Derrida reflects,

I am telling myself my story ... here is the story that I am telling myself; and that means I hear myself speak.... I speak myself to myself in a certain manner, and my ear is thus immediately plugged into my discourse and my writing. . . . But the necessity of passing onto and by way of the ear is not just this. . . . To be more precise, it is . . . *the difference in the ear.* . . . the larger the ear . . . the more finesse it lacks in its attention to difference. . . . A keen ear is an ear with keen hearing, an ear that perceives differences. . . . between apparently similar things.[22]

Addressing the beginning and origin of the text "in terms of a relation between the one who signs (the author) and the one who reads . . . or hears," Derrida insists that the signature of a text, or the proper name attached, "becomes effective—performed and performing—not at the moment it apparently takes place, but only later, *when ears will have managed to receive the message.*" What is interesting in his remarks is not only the dialectical and dialogical interplay between speaking and hearing the self speaking but also the slippage between *reader* and *hearer.* Derrida maintains the primacy of the addressee "whose ear will be keen enough to hear my name . . . or to understand my signature, that with which I sign." For Derrida, the ear that receives is what finally validates, or "signs," the text of the speaker: "When . . . the other will have perceived with a keen-enough ear what I will have addressed or destined to him, or her, then my signature will have taken place."[23] Derrida's claims suggest that a text can only be understood, validated, or honored, as it were, when the speaker is allied with and his text is received by the hearer (even when that hearer is the speaker). Without an addressee, he implies, there would be no addresser.

In contrast to Derrida, Roland Barthes, in an essay entitled "Listening," differentiates between "hearing," "a physiological phenomenon" and "listening," a fundamentally "psychological act." If hearing, for Derrida, authenticates and validates the signatory of the text, listening, for Barthes, connotes a "psychoanalytic relation [that] is effected between two subjects," and entails the receiver's "recognition of the other's desire." The recognition of the other's desire "implies that one enters it [and] ultimately that one [finds] oneself [in the space of that desire]." Maintaining that "listening" can be a delicate matter, fraught with danger (and potential reward) in the sense that one enters into and surrenders oneself to the desire of the other, Barthes concludes that it "will exist only on the condition of accepting . . . risk."[24] Thus, for Barthes, listening can be risky business, a proposition surely confirmed in Freudian theories of transference and counter-transference between analyst (listener) and analysand (speaker). Significantly, then, if the Derridean hearer is positioned to become a guarantor of the speaker's text, then the Barthesian listener functions as witness to and participant in the production of the speaker's text. In both instances, however, the speaker's story remains unfinished until it is read and rewritten in the "ear of the other." Even so, one must acknowledge and distinguish within the range of listeners' subject positions— from resistant to fusionist, from incompetent to deserving. Addressing precisely this issue, Jean-François Lyotard, in his "testimonial pact," defines the listener, or addressee, as one who is "worthy of being spoken to" as well as "willing to listen and accept the reality of the referent."[25] His testimonial pact would suggest that listening carries with it an ethical response or obligation. For Lyotard, then, the contract would exclude the "nonqualified"—that is to say, the non-engaged or "absent"—participant from the addressee position.

Considering the role of hearing or listening in relation to Hurston's *Their Eyes Were Watching God*, the reader cannot fail to note how Janie Crawford, as speaker, is empowered by her thoughtful and engaged addressee, Pheoby Watson. And while scholars generally acknowledge Pheoby's role as listener and even interlocutor, most do so only to return the critical gaze—and ear—to Janie, the protagonist and privileged narrator. What I propose is a critical turn in reading Hurston's novel. Rather than focusing exclusively on Janie as storyteller or "tongue-speaker," I submit here (for purposes of argument) a reading that centers on the luminous Pheoby, whose feminine name, like that of her masculine counterpart *Phoebus* (the Latin name of the Greek sun god, Apollo), connotes both *radiance* and *oracularity*.[26] As empathetic listener or hearer (whose presence complements that of Janie, the storyteller and first narrator), Pheoby—a character given only passing nod by critics—nevertheless plays a subtle, but pivotal, role in Hurston's narrative as *earwitness*. Her function, as signified by a name connoting prophet and inspiration, highlights not the *aesthetics of the oral*, but the *aesthetics of the aural*. And, significantly, her textual posture invites the reader to deliberate further on a character whose name associates her with "letters," signifying biblically on the female "benefactor" who delivers Paul's message—in the form of his epistles—to the Church of Cenchrea in Romans 16:1.[27]

In the narrative's opening frame, the omniscient narrator, with a *perlocutionary* call, summons the reader, along with Pheoby, to become authenticators and witnesses of the tale Janie is about to relate: "It was the time to *hear* things and *talk*... [to become] lords of *sounds* and lesser things."[28] Thus, at the outset, the narrator issues a call that speaks to the effect of the tale on the listener, but also a call that suggests the subsequent interpellation of the listener into the role of storyteller. Emphasizing the importance of "hearing" (the porch-sitters "done 'heard' 'bout you just what they hope done happened"), Pheoby's remark suggests that the reliable hearer, or listener—like the reliable narrator—must willingly and generously open him- or herself to the experience and desire of the other, for, as Pheoby puts it, "[A]n envious heart makes a treacherous ear" (16). In response, Janie assures her "kissin' friend" of twenty years, "Ah depend upon you for a good thought, [and] Ah'm talking to you from that standpoint" (19). Unlike the porch-sitters, Pheoby, positioned as empathetic listener, "[holds] her tongue for a long time," but then takes the risk "to feel and do through Janie" (18). By aligning her listening with "feeling" and "doing," Pheoby demonstrates how listening can become a risky and engaged position. Moreover, Pheoby would seem to possess what feminist theologian Nelle Morton describes as "depth hearing," that is to say, a hearing that "takes place before speaking" and "that is more than acute listening." Depth hearing, Morton maintains, evokes "a hearing that is a direct transitive verb that evokes speech—new speech that has never been spoken before."[29] In this reading, then, it will be left to Pheoby to deliver the text of Janie's tale (just as the biblical Phebe delivers Paul's epistle).

Henry Louis Gates, Jr., in a compelling and oft-cited reading, "Zora Neale Hurston and the Speakerly Text," postulates the relation between narration and subjectivity by positing "free indirect discourse" as the primary strategy of the narrative:

> A convenient way to think about the free indirect discourse is that it appears initially to be indirect discourse (by which I mean that its signals of time and person correspond to a third person narrator's discourse), "but it is penetrated, in its syntactic and semantic structures, enunciative properties, thus by the discourse of a character," and even in Hurston's case by that of characters. In other words, free indirect discourse attempts to represent "consciousness without the apparent intrusion of a narrative voice."[30]

Gates continues, and persuasively, to substantiate his thesis that, in Hurston's text, individual characters speak in the third person, but express the consciousness of a first-person narrator. Yet, although Gates makes an impressive case demonstrating the complexities of bivocalism in Hurston's narrative, his argument regarding free and indirect discourse brings to mind Ptolemy, who devised complex equations and a complicated mathematical system in order to demonstrate that the solar system was geocentric rather than heliocentric.

Rather than following the principle of greatest complexity, I suggest that considering the novel from Pheoby's standpoint as earwitness who gives narrative testimony to her friend's story allows the critic to follow the principle of Occam's razor—by constructing a model of reading with fewer inconsistencies, ambiguities, and redundancies. Indeed, if we take Janie at her word when she says "mah tongue is in mah friend's mouf," advising Pheoby, "you can tell 'em what Ah say if you wants to," it follows that we, as readers, must expand our horizon of expectation and allow for the possibility that it is indeed Pheoby herself who relates the narrative—not in the first person, nor in free indirect discourse, but in her own voice, and appropriately, from a third-person perspective (17).[31] Arguably, then, it is left up to Pheoby to choose how to tell Janie's story—a story that, as she puts it, is sometimes "hard for [her] to understand" ("It's hard for me to understand what you mean, de way you tell it" [19]). But like the Pentecostal glossolalic, Janie possesses not only the gift of speaking in tongues, but the gift of interpretation as well: "[T]ain't no use in me telling you somethin' unless Ah give you de understandin' to go 'long wid it" (19). Responding to Janie's story, Pheoby acknowledges not only the power of speaking, but also the power of listening—from a position of "depth hearing": "Ah done growed ten feet higher from jus' *listening* tuh you" (284, emphasis added). And making good on her promise to the porch-sitters (and the reader), she declares, "if she [Janie] got anything to *tell*, you'll *hear* it," suggesting, arguably, not that Janie will tell them, but that they will hear it from Pheoby herself (13, emphasis added).

Pheoby's remarks give meaning to her function as oracle, benefactor, and deliverer of the letter (text), but they also render her resplendent (thus living up to the Hellenistic etymology of her name) in a response which, in effect, interpellates the listener (or reader) by defining her position proleptically as *narratee*—and, at least hypothetically, as *soon-to-become-narrator*. Moreover, such a reading locates Pheoby both as narratee, occupying the readerly position and as narrator, occupying the speakerly position—thereby allowing the porch-sitters (and reader) to construct both listening and narrating as productive critical strategies and paradigms.

Thus, the alternative reading presented here is meant to suggest that it is the "ear of the other"—or the luminous Pheoby's ear—that finally "signs" or validates Janie's narrative by passing it on to the porch-sitters and to the reader. And to invoke Barthes and Lyotard, it is as an attentive, engaged, empathetic, worthy, and willing listener that Pheoby allows Janie to pursue her deepest desire: "[T]hat oldest human longing—self-revelation" (18). In the end, the testimonial pact between Janie and Pheoby is affirmed, with the latter functioning, in effect, as earwitness to (and soon to become secondary narrator, as it were, of) Janie's tale. And ultimately, like the Barthesian listener, Pheoby is rewarded for her risk, and led to re-examine the text of her own life, exclaiming to Janie, "I ain't satisfied wid mahself no mo'" (284).

While many of the following chapters focus on speaking and storytelling, drawing on the critical reconstruction of the spiritual rite of glossolalia, or what biblical scholars have called the "miracle of *speech*,"[32] I propose in this introduction a more expansive reading of Pentecost, a reading that acknowledges not only the miracle of speech, but also "the miracle of *hearing*"—an approach to reading that embraces an *oral/aural aesthetic* affirming the hearer's/listener's/reader's response to the speaker/narrator/storyteller. Historically, there exists an exegesis of Pentecost that postulates the miracle of communication as that of *hearing*.[33] Acts 2:8 tells us that "each understood, each in his own tongue"—emphasizing the *hearing* rather than *speaking* of tongues. Thus, although popular readings of Pentecost preponderantly support the miracle of speech, the actual biblical passage would seem to locate the moment of understanding in the ear of the auditor as much as in the ability of the speaker. Ermeneglossia (from the Greek *hermeneia*, meaning "explain" or "interpret," and *glossa*, meaning "tongue")[34] is my preferred term for this emphasis on hearing (or what I designate as *aural reading*) and gifted interpretation. Such a reading postulates that the twelve tribes of Israel from various linguistic orientations *both heard and understood*, each according to its own native dialect.[35] According to this interpretation of Pentecost, the meaning of the communication would be determined by the hearers rather than by the speakers. Ermeneglossia, then, reflects the role and position of the hearer/listener (and, by extension, the reader), and the degree to which s/he understands and engages what is being said. Such an interpretation invites the critic to expand the emphasis from the act of speaking (or writing) to that of listening (or reading).[36] And, whether as speakers giving testimony or listeners

bearing witness, black women writers, I propose, occupy multiple and simultaneous positions and positionalities, rendering them both subjects of polyvocality (tongue-speakers) and polytonality (tongue-listeners). In the latter position,
I would suggest that these writers must be attuned to the attenuated and the
amplified, the discordant and the harmonious, the dominant and the muted
voices both in their dialogical engagements as well as in their exotopic representations. In other words, they must be able to listen (to) and hear (in) the multiple
and simultaneous chords, harmonies, and keys of interlocutors—whether in the
form of characters, readers, or authors. These writers, I propose, possess discursive diversity as tongue-speakers as well as a discerning ear as tongue-listeners, a
"keen ear" capable of distinguishing chordal and melodic modulations of form
and meaning.

IV. Bearing Witness, Dancing Diaspora, and Performing Testimony

> Now, watching Beloved's alert and hungry face, how she took in every
> word…her downright craving to know, Denver began to *see* what she
> was *saying* and not just to *hear*.… The monologue became, in fact, a duet
> as they lay down together, Denver nursing Beloved's interest like a lover
> whose pleasure was to overfeed the loved. Denver *spoke*, Beloved *listened*,
> and the two did the best they could to create what really happened, how
> it really was.…
>
> —Toni Morrison, *Beloved* (emphasis added)

> That was why it did not matter to either of them which one did the
> talking, since it was not the talking alone which did it, performed and
> accomplished the overpassing, but some *happy marriage of speaking and
> hearing*.…
>
> —William Faulkner, *Absalom, Absalom!* (emphasis added)

> Someone moved a chair a little to give them room, the rhythm paused,
> the singing stopped, only the pounding feet and the clapping hands were
> heard; then another cry, another dancer.…
>
> —James Baldwin, *Go Tell It on the Mountain*

> Dance movements convey speech-like qualities which contain mean-
> ing beyond the formal, aesthetic shapes and sequences of movement
> detailed by the body in motion. African diaspora dance conveys the
> sense of performative utterance.…Within black social dance construc-
> tions, dancing black bodies express actionable assertions.
>
> —Thomas F. DeFrantz, "The Black Beat Made Visible:
> Hip Hop Dance and Body Power"

> Negro dancing is dynamic suggestion. No matter how violent it may
> appear to the beholder, every posture gives the impression that the
> dancer will do much more.…It is compelling insinuation. That is the

very reason the spectator is held so rapt. [She] is participating in the
performance [herself]—carrying out the suggestions of the performer.
                                    —Zora Neale Hurston, "Characteristics of Negro Expression"

Closely related to tongue-speaking and tongue-listening are the rituals and practices of giving testimony and bearing witness. In many ways, the literary and cultural
performances examined in this volume closely model the processes of testimony
and witnessing. And even though the notion of witness and witnessing in contemporary discourse is overwhelmingly associated with the law and, more recently,
psychoanalysis, it also has a notable presence (both in its juridical and spiritual
connotations) in the Old and New Testaments, and is, in fact, referenced in the
opening of the Book of Acts, just before the Apostle Luke introduces the scene of
Pentecost ("But you will receive power when the Holy Spirit comes on you; and
you will be my *witnesses* in Jerusalem, and in all Judea and Samaria, and to the ends
of the earth").[37] In her remarkable study, *Witnessing: Beyond Recognition*, Kelly
Oliver defines the verb *witness* as "to bear witness, to testify, to give evidence, to be
a spectator or auditor of something" and the noun *witnessing* as "the action of bearing witness or giving testimony." Emphasizing both connotations, Oliver observes,
"We have both the juridical sense of bearing witness to what you know from experience as an eyewitness and the religious sense of bearing witness to what you believe
through blind faith."[38] It is this complex and equivocal sense of witnessing, I propose, that is attested by the literary and cultural practices of black women writers
and performers treated in this volume.

The above quotations from William Faulkner's *Absalom, Absalom!* and Toni
Morrison's *Beloved* reflect the dialogical and intersubjective structures of these classic (post)modernist novels, but they also suggest a model for reading narrative—an
interpretive paradigm based on witnessing as an act that combines the "miracle of
speech" (glossolalia) and the "miracle of hearing" (ermeneglossia). And while both
narratives include plot references to the law, courtroom, or judicial witnessing, each
is also narrated by characters who engage in a process of testimony and witnessing
that requires "a joint responsibility" between an addresser and *an other*.[39] Not only
do the characters in these texts find themselves haunted by what Marianne Hirsch
describes as "postmemory," but through storytelling and witnessing, each character seeks to come to terms with traumatic transgenerational experiences, experiences that have "preceded their birth but that were nevertheless transmitted to
them so deeply as to seem to constitute memories in their own right."[40] And, significantly, the authors' dialogical acts of narration replicate this process, rendering the characters' storytelling equivalent to the authors' narrations of novelistic
events. In the narratives, events are multiply rehearsed as the process of storytelling
and listening is prolonged and redoubled such that with each subsequent recount-
ing, they accrete meaning through what Peter Brooks describes as *dilation*—to
the point at which the stories achieve their proper closure. This process of "active

repetition and reworking of [the] story" endows Faulkner's Quentin and Shreve, on the one hand, and Morrison's Denver and Beloved, on the other, with the responsibility for reconstructing events at which they were not present, in such a way that their dialogical recitations give meaning to the ciphers of the past.[41] Also demonstrated in these quotations are the dynamics of testimony and witnessing in which storyteller and listener participate. More broadly, these stories demonstrate how, through the processes of transference and counter-transference, the characters attempt to "remember, repeat, and work-through" postmemories of traumatic events by re-ordering them into satisfying narratives within which they can integrate their life histories.[42]

In pairing Faulkner and Morrison, I'd like to suggest that the latter's "epiloging" text witnesses the former's precursor narrative. [43] In doing so, however, the contemporary black woman writer, in effect, revises and rewrites her white male precursor. Quentin Compson's testimony (to Shreve's witnessing)—essentially the testimony of a white son of the South traumatized by the specter of a past that he seeks to escape—is reconfigured in the testimony of Denver, a black girl survivor of slavery who attempts to recreate and reclaim that past in order to satisfy the "hunger" of another, Beloved, a sacrificial victim to that violent history. Such a model of reading narrative moves the writer and critic (and, as we shall see, the performer) beyond the aural/oral *aesthetics* proposed above into the deeper and vastly more complex realm of *ethics*. Arguing that witnessing is the essential condition of human subjectivity, Oliver identifies the positions of "giving testimony" and of "bearing witness" to the witness (the speaker or one who gives testimony). If the first position suggests the role of *speech* (and, in the context of bodily performance, *spectacle*), then the second position invites us to consider the role of *auditor* (and *spectator*). Oliver maintains not only that speaking and listening are interdependent, but that speaking is fundamentally an act of witnessing, just as listening is fundamentally an act of bearing witness (to the witness). Theorizing the importance of witnessing to those (individuals or groups) whose subjectivities have been "othered" or undermined through objectification, Oliver argues that witnessing "relies on address and response"—and what she further defines as the dual and simultaneous processes of "address-ability" and "response-ability":

> Through the process of bearing witness to oppression and subordination, those othered can begin to repair damaged subjectivity by taking up a position as speaking subjects. What we learn from beginning with the subject position of those othered is that the speaking subject is subject by virtue of address-ability and response-ability. Address-ability and response-ability are the roots of subjectivity, which are damaged by the objectifying operations of oppression and subordination.[44]

As Oliver suggests, witnessing is associated both with *subjectivity* (how the subject gets constituted) and *subject position* (how the subject sees or experiences the world from the vantage point or vector of social location). In the instance of black women writers, in particular, both the subject and subject position—along with the speaking and listening positions emanating from their social locations—carry deep ethical implications and obligations. As Oliver explains,

> Subjectivity is founded on the ability to respond to, and address, others— what I am calling witnessing. Insofar as subjectivity is made possible by the ability to respond, response-ability is its founding possibility. The responsibility inherent in subjectivity has the double sense of the condition of possibility of response, response-ability, on the one hand, and the ethical obligation to respond and to enable response-ability from others born out of that founding possibility, on the other....This ethical obligation at the heart of subjectivity is inherent in the process of witnessing.[45]

Elaborating on the ethics of witnessing, Yale psychiatrist Dori Laub offers a framework for considering the relationship between speaking, listening, and witnessing. Referencing his experiences with post-Holocaust testimony and witnessing, Laub identifies three levels of witnessing: (1) being a witness to oneself, (2) being a witness to the testimony of others, and (3) being a witness to the process of witnessing itself.[46] In the context of post-Holocaust testimony, argues Laub, "The survivors did not only need to survive so that they could tell their stories; they also needed to tell their stories in order to survive."[47] Importantly, for Laub, witnessing is fundamentally a dialogic act: "It is the encounter and the coming together between survivor [storyteller] and the listener [analyst] which makes possible something like a repossession of the act of witnessing."[48] And even at the first level of witnessing ("inner witnessing"), a process by which the narrator reconstitutes the internal "thou"—that is to say, the possibility of acknowledging a witness or a listener inside her- or himself—Laub insists that "it is essential...that [that which] *could not be articulated*...*be told*...*be transmitted*...*be heard*."[49] The listener (interviewer), Laub further explains, "takes on the responsibility for bearing witness [to] that [which] the narrator felt [s/he] bore alone."[50] Focusing more explicitly on what he describes as "the vicissitudes of listening," Laub positions the listener as secondary witness and "enabler of testimony"—even to the point of hearing that which is left unsaid, or (as Oliver puts it) that which is "beyond recognition": "He or she must listen to and hear the silence, speaking mutely both in silence and in speech, both from behind and from within speech."[51] And although Laub highlights the speech act of storytelling, he defines witnessing, bearing witness, and even self-witnessing as fundamentally dialogic, intersubjective, and ethical acts in which the subjects participate in a mutual process of narrating and listening.

    As readers we, in effect, witness that sense of ethical obligation affirmed by Oliver and Laub in the relationship between storyteller and listener in Hurston's *Their Eyes Were Watching God* where Pheoby is discernibly affected by Janie's story

in a way that is profoundly personal and intimate. Peter Brooks, in fact, suggests that
the relation between storyteller and listener is often one of "contamination." And,
as a consequence, the listener (reader) often feels the need to re-transmit that contamination, or as Brooks suggests, the reader becomes compelled to pass on "the
virus of narrative," an act that results in "the creation of the fevered need to retell."[52]
In Hurston's narrative, the listener in the framing story, Pheoby, seeks not only to
re-tell—in an urge to narrate—but to re-enact in her own life the closeness that Janie
has shared with her husband, Tea Cake. Without becoming a fusionist listener,
Pheoby desires to re-create with her own husband, Sam, a relationship based on
greater intimacy and reciprocity ("Ah means to make Sam take me fishin' wid him
after this" [284]). And, if Lyotard distinguishes among various kinds of listeners,
Janie likewise cautions Pheoby to distinguish between various forms of listening
and speaking. After assuring her confidante, "Dat's all right, Pheoby, tell 'em" (284),
Janie hastens to admonish against vacuous listening and empty talk, what she calls
"rattle": " 'Course, talkin' don't amount tuh uh hill uh beans when yuh can't do nothing else. And listenin' tuh dat kind uh talk is jus' lak openin' yo' mouth and lettin' de
moon shine down yo' throat" (285). In other words, it is not just the aesthetics of
listening and speaking that is important; rather, it is the accountability and obligation entailed in the exchange—its address-ability and response-ability—that makes
Pheoby's act of witnessing a fundamentally ethical action.

Up to this point, the focus on Hurston's novel has centered on its oral and aural
modalities; it would be instructive, however, to note that the novel's opening also
calls attention (as does the title) to the *visual* as a modality. And while the title
references the narrative moment in which the characters "seemed to be *staring* at
the dark, but their *eyes* were *watching* God" (236, emphasis added) in the midst
of a devastating hurricane on the muck in the Florida Everglades, the frame of
the story emphasizes the visual as well. Janie, a woman who had "come back from
burying the dead . . . their *eyes* flung wide open in judgment" (9, emphasis added),
finds herself the object of public gaze, as "the porch couldn't talk for *looking*" (11,
emphasis added). Janie, in fact, is rendered an erotic spectacle in the eyes of lusty
male spectators: "The men noticed her firm buttocks like she had grape fruits in
her hip pockets; the great rope of black hair swinging to her waist and unravel-
ing in the wind like a plume, then her pugnacious breasts trying to bore holes in
her shirt. They, the men, were saving with the mind what they lost with the *eye*"
(11, emphasis added). Even her "kissin'-friend" Pheoby is moved to remark on
Janie's looks: "Gal, you . . . *looks* like youse yo' own daughter. . . . Even wid dem
overhalls on, you *shows* yo' womanhood" (14, emphasis added). And Janie herself comments that "y'all ain't *seen* me . . . in a year and a half," later asking "[i]f
they [the porch-sitters] wants to *see* . . . why they don't come kiss and be kissed?"
(18, emphasis added). Without props, backdrop, lighting, or curtains, Janie
nevertheless makes her entrance onto the public stage, subject to the leering,
laughter, and "burning statements with questions" ("She sits high, but she *looks*

low" [emphasis added]) that frame her as spectacle and position her as object of envy, jealousy, ridicule, and lust (10, 12 *passim*). It is precisely these notions of performance and spectacle, suggested in Hurston's narrative, that set the stage for the final chapters of the present volume. Mediating between speech performance and bodily performance is the treatment of Nella Larsen's *Passing,* a novel focusing on the cultural performance of "passing"—a high-stakes performance in which breaking character can be fraught with peril. Staging "whiteness" and "blackness" as public and private performances, Larsen's characters enact and reverse scripts that render the miscegenous body a social cipher in the theater of racial masquerade. It is this notion of cultural performance that forms the focus of the latter chapters in this volume.

In the chapters on transatlantic performer Josephine Baker, as well as on the contemporary hip-hop music video performer (sometimes called the "video vixen"), the locus of critique tilts, as it were, from "word to flesh," from voice to body, from "speaking in tongues" to "dancing diaspora"—that is to say, from performative speech acts to embodied performance as forms of aesthetic expression and, I would argue, testimony and witnessing. Yet, although the early chapters focus on how black women's bodies are imprinted by discourse, my readings construct Alice Walker's *The Color Purple,* Sherley Anne Williams's "Meditations on History" and *Dessa Rose,* Toni Morrison's *Beloved,* and Gayl Jones's *Corregidora* as narratives of speaking and witnessing in which characters like Celie, Dessa, Sethe, and Ursa give testimony— through letter-writing, storytelling, and singing—to the traumatic and sometimes intergenerational experiences of slavery and domestic abuse. The later chapters, however, address how black women performers give embodied testimony—through parody and traumatic re-enactment—to the experiences of oppression and subordination. Dance critic Thomas DeFrantz argues that "black expressive cultures value the process of signification over the signified, the performance of spirituality over scriptural exegesis, talking *by* dancing over talking *about* dancing."[53] In addition to emphasizing the formal quality of black expressivity, DeFrantz specifically addresses black performativity, which he defines as "gestures of black expressive culture, including music and dance, that performs actionable assertions":

> In terms of black social dance, these performative assertions do not "describe" dancing, rather, they are the physical building blocks of a system of communication we may term *corporeal orature.... Corporeal Orature* aligns movement with speech to describe the ability of black social dance to incite action. In this articulation, social dance may contain performative gestures which cite contexts beyond the dance. These citations are read and acknowledged by other dancers who respond in kind with actions or decisions about, at least, the efficacy of the dance gesture. Black social dance thrives within a structure of corporeal orature that presumes the possibility of efficacious performative gesture.[54]

And although DeFrantz privileges the conversation that exists between and among dancers, calling into question the interpretative competency of mere observers who exist "without" the dance in a "society in which bodies can be objectified and marketed as 'black,'" I will plead a case here for the reading and interpretive competency of the observer/spectator who is located culturally and historically "within the dance."[55]

Dance, like speech and narration, is not only a performative utterance and profoundly testimonial act, but a deep spectacle as well—and as such, requires an audience which, in some capacity, responds to performance, testimony, and spectacle. As Hurston notes in "Characteristics of Negro Expression," the spectator is "held…rapt" and "[participates] in the performance himself—carrying out the suggestions of the performer."[56] What Hurston does not say, but implies, is that the spectator gives witness to the narrative performance of the dancer. And although Oliver argues that testimonies from the victims of slavery, torture, and the Holocaust seek to "witness to the horrors beyond recognition," I would also emphasize the demand, especially in the case of Josephine Baker, to be *seen* and *recognized* by the Other—even when it is evident that this recognition remains what Jacques Lacan describes as misrecognition, or *méconnaissance*. In performance testimony, the body, as Pierre Nora might suggest, becomes a "site of memory"—*embodied* memory, as it were—and functions performatively as a "container" figuratively inscribing and literally *incorporating* memory. In this performance of testimony, most especially in that of the so-called "video vixen," I argue that it is the black feminist critic and scholar who must bear critical witness and provide theoretical testimony to what may be regarded as the public "misperformances" of women who are (wittingly and/or unwittingly) somatically re-enacting the body's traumatic history. In performing critical witnessing and testimony, I am proposing that the black feminist critic and scholar can begin, in the words of Oliver, to "reconceive of what it means to be a self, a subject, to have subjectivity, to consider oneself an active agent… by virtue of our dialogic relationship with others." In assuming this role, we perform "a responsibility to response-ability" and exercise "the ability to [critically] respond…in a way that opens up rather than closes off the possibility of response by others"—and I would add to this, a way that opens up new and more empathetic and less objectifying responses by those who fail to recognize the fundamental humanity and pathos underlying what can only be understood as false witnessing and flawed performance.[57]

V. In Retrospect

> Without an addressee, without a witness, I cannot exist.
> —Kelly Oliver, *Witnessing: Beyond Recognition*

In addition to what I regard as certain "fugitive" pieces on black women writers in the present volume (including chapters on book reviewing, pedagogy, the state of black women's art and theory), I have chosen to conclude with chapters that are more memorial than critical—in an effort to provide literary testimony to two writers who have transitioned, Sherley Anne Williams and Bebe Moore Campbell. I do so as a way of offering testimony—personal testimony—to the literature and lives of writers who, in different ways, witness my own story. Telling stories about these writers allows me, as critic, both to resolve issues posed by cultural loss and to use cultural memory as a means of relinquishing grief over personal loss. And so, in the conclusion, I invoke the sound of the name and the sign of the letters of these writers.[58]

At the outset of this introduction, I noted that the Apostle Paul enumerated nine gifts of the Spirit. Among these were the gifts of revelation: wisdom, knowledge, and the discerning of spirits; the gifts of operation: faith, healing, and the working of miracles; and the gifts of inspiration: prophecy, known and unknown tongues, and the interpretation of tongues.[59] It is this last gift, the gift of interpreting glossolalia, that is regarded as "a special ability, in fact, a spiritual gift of value equivalent to tongue speaking [*sic*] itself."[60] The tongue-speaker requires an interpreter of tongues, and the gift of interpretation complements and corresponds to the gift of tongues. Of course, some tongue-speakers are themselves interpreters; others, however, require interpretation. The Scriptures suggest not only that the one is essential to the other, but that, in fact, it is the combination of tongues and interpretation (glossolalia and ermeneglossia) that creates an act of ethical witnessing and, further, achieves the highest manifestation of the inspired Word—the gift of prophecy.[61] The following chapters represent my efforts to interpret and witness to those whom I regard as metaphorical "tongue-speakers"—black women writers and dancers whose performative utterances constitute testimony. It is my hope that this gesture combines with their gift of speaking in tongues and dancing diaspora to provide prophetic inspiration for the reader as witness. And, finally, it is from the perspectives of glossolalia and ermeneglossia that I would propose that you (the reader/ critic) bring to the following chapters a speaking, listening, and witnessing that will complement and dialogically engage these tongues and bodies.

Alice Walker's *The Color Purple*

Revisions and Redefinitions

Alice Walker's *The Color Purple* subverts the traditional Eurocentric male code that dominates the literary conventions of the epistolary novel. As a genre, the English epistolary novel, a form invented by men writing about women, embodies male control of the literary images of women.[1] By appropriating a form invented and traditionally controlled by men, but thematicizing the lives and experiences of women, Alice Walker asserts her authority, or her right to authorship. Signing herself as "A.W., author and medium," Walker suggests that her purpose has been not only to create and control literary images of women, and black women in particular, but to give voice and representation to these same women, who have been silenced and confined in life and literature. *The Color Purple* is a novel that deals with what it means to be poor, black, and female in the rural South during the first half of the twentieth century. In an interview in *Newsweek* in June 1982, Walker explains that Celie, the protagonist of *The Color Purple*, is modeled after the author's own great-grandmother, who was raped at the age of twelve by her slaveowner (and Walker's grandfather). Celie's fate, however, is brighter. "I liberated her from her own history," remarks Walker, "I wanted her to be happy." Walker hopes that "people can hear Celie's voice. There are so many people like Celie who make it, who came out of nothing. People who triumph."[2] For Walker, then, art is liberational and life-saving; it is also an act for the reconstruction and reclamation of self, of past, of women, and of community.

As an epistolary novel, *The Color Purple* employs a narrative technique singularly appropriate to the author's subject. The portrayal of women's friendships in literature is formally linked to the development of the epistolary novel that can be traced back to the beginnings of the modern novel in eighteenth-century England. As Janet Todd argues in *Women's Friendship in Literature*, "the fictional friendship between women grew out of the idea of the confidant—the correspondent in the epistolary novel."[3] Moreover, recent feminist scholarship has recovered and reclaimed letters, diaries, journals, and similar forms of expression associated with the culture of women who have been historically denied access to the popular and commercial print media. Black and Third World women of color, in particular, have begun to appropriate the epistolary form, as represented, for example, in Cherríe Moraga and Gloria Anzaldúa's *This Bridge Called My Back*.[4] By choosing an epistolary style and structure, Walker, like these authors, is able to draw on a form that places her work within a tradition associated with women, allows a feminine narrative voice, and establishes a bond and intimacy between women.

Although there are a number of letters to Celie from her sister Nettie, the story is told primarily from the point of view of Celie, who addresses her letters first to God, and later to Nettie.[5] Such a form is uniquely suited to Walker's subject in that it allows an uneducated, black, Southern woman to speak for herself. The form also allows Walker to link a formal and Western tradition to an oral and distinctly Afro-American folk expression. Celie's letters transpose a black and oral mode into a Western epistolary tradition (a form also adapted effectively by modern African writers such as Camara Laye and Ferdinand Oyono, whom Walker acknowledges as influences). Walker's use of the vernacular (sometimes called Black English) has invested an old and somewhat rigid form with new life.

In adopting the epistolary form, the vehicle for the eighteenth-century novel of sentiment, Walker draws on certain codes and conventions of the genre, but revises them in such a way as to turn the sentimental novel on its head.[6] Like the "Pure but Betrayed Maiden" of the sentimental story, Walker's heroine is a victim of sexual abuse. At age fourteen, Celie is raped by her stepfather. Forcing himself on her, he warns Celie, "You better not never tell nobody but God."[7] Consequently, Celie's early letters are written to God.

After bearing him two children, who are taken away from her, Celie is married off by Alphonso, her stepfather, to an older widower. Saddled with farm work as well as the care of four "rotten" kids and domestic chores, she is overworked, beaten, and reduced to virtual bondage by her husband. Celie's status is suggested as her stepfather negotiates her marriage to Albert:

> She ugly. He say. But she ain't no stranger to hard work. And she clean. And God done fixed her. You can do everything just like you want to and she ain't gonna make you feed it or clothe it.... She can take that cow she raise down there back of the crib. (9–10)

When Albert, whom Celie calls "Mister," returns for a second inspection, the transaction is completed:

> He say, Let me see her again.
> Pa call me.... Like it wasn't nothing. Mr. _____ want another look at you.

I go stand in the door. The sun shine in my eyes. He's still up on his horse. He look me up and down.

Pa rattle his newspaper. Move up, he won't bite, he say.

I go closer to the steps, but not too close cause I'm a little scared of his horse.

Turn round Pa say.

I turn round. (12)

The arrival of Mister represents an ironic reversal of the fairy tale in which the steed-mounted knight in shining armor arrives to save the damsel in distress. Resonating through this passage are not the chimes of medieval chivalry, but the echo of the slavers' auction block in the sale and bartering of human commodity in a quasi-feudal Southern economy. Celie's status as slave, or chattel property—subservient to father and later to husband (and to God)—expected to perform domestic, field, and sexual labor, is confirmed when Albert is assured that the "cow [is] coming" (12).

The inscription of slavery is critical to understanding Walker's intentions. If Mister has inherited from his father, Old Mister, the farm that belonged to his grandfather, the white slaveowner, he has likewise inherited from Old Mister the values of ownership, mastery, and domination bequeathed by the white slaveowner. He attempts, in turn, to impose these values on his own son, Harpo. For Walker, the institution of slavery and its legacy are largely responsible for setting into motion the oppressive mode characterizing relations between men and women, white and black, powerful and powerless.

The indirect impact of white violence on black women and children is suggested by Walker in her treatment of Celie's (biological) father, owner of a prosperous dry-goods store, who is lynched by local white businessmen threatened by his success. While this episode exposes the economic basis of racial oppression, it also suggests the far-reaching consequences of violence directed toward black men. It is the murder of Celie's father that results in her mother's mental derangement and subsequent marriage to Alphonso—the stepfather who violates Celie. Even subtler, perhaps, are the relations of violence initiated by a racial episode that sets the pattern for other forms of racial and sexual violence throughout the novel. The message, however, is an elaboration rather than a restatement of that in *The Third Life of Grange Copeland* in which Walker links the sexual oppression of black women by black men to the racial oppression of black men by white men.[8] What Walker demonstrates in *The Color Purple* is the necessity for each person to struggle against unjust oppression, whether it is in the home, in the community, or in a racially hostile society. As she has written elsewhere, "freedom should force us to stop relating as owner to owned."[9]

Marriage perpetuates Celie's plight. Like the central character in the novel of sentiment, Celie finds herself beleaguered and victimized by what Todd describes as the "scheme of patriarchy." Laying claim to the "right" of *paterfamilias*, Albert attempts to impose a pattern of dominance and submission on his wife and children. "He beat me like he beat the children," writes Celie, "It all I can do not to cry" (22). Advising his son Harpo, Albert declares, "Wives is like children. You have to let 'em know who got the upper hand. Nothing can do that better than a good, sound beating" (34).

The model for the patriarchal scheme in the novel has already been established by Albert's father, who has dissuaded his son from marrying the only woman he has ever loved, Shug Avery ("She black as tar, she nappy headed. She got legs like baseball bats" [49]). Like his father before him, Albert attempts to prevent his own son from marrying Sofia, the woman of his choice and the mother of his child: "No need to think I'm gon let my boy marry you just cause you in the family way. He young and limited. Pretty gal like you could put anything over on him" (30). Although Harpo, in defiance of his father, finally does bring home Sofia and his baby, he tries to beat her just as his father beats Celie.

Yet, the women in *The Color Purple* represent a radical departure from the "sentimental friends" who, Todd argues, "lead conventional lives." Walker's women transform their lives. In the sentimental novel, the women frequently expire or ultimately succumb in form—if not always in spirit—to the patriarchal condition. The women in Walker's novel, however, reform the essential bases of the relationships, codes, and values of their world, and at the same time, strengthen and extend the bonds of female friendship.

When Nettie escapes from her stepfather, she comes to live with Celie and Albert. Because she rebukes Albert's amorous attentions, however, she is forced to leave, and is not heard from for many years. Celie later discovers that Albert has been intercepting Nettie's letters from Africa, where she has gone with a missionary couple, Samuel and Corrine, who have adopted Celie's two children. Albert's unsuccessful attempts to expropriate or conceal Nettie's letters suggest, again, Walker's intention to subvert male efforts to suppress black women in life as well as letters. Thus, if on a formal level, Walker subverts white and male literary codes and conventions, on the level of plot and theme, she subverts the codes and conventions that dominate social and sexual relationships.

Over and over again, Celie accepts abuse and victimization. When Harpo asks her what to do to "make [Sofia] mind," Celie, having internalized the principle of male domination, answers, "Beat her." When Celie next sees Harpo, "his face [is] a mess of bruises" (34–35). Sofia, then, becomes Celie's first model of resistance to sexual, and later, racial subjugation. Cheeky and rebellious, Sofia is described as an "amazon" of a woman. She scorns rigid gender definitions and prefers fixing the leaking roof to fixing the evening dinner. Moreover, as Harpo quickly learns, Sofia gives as good as she takes. "All my life I had to fight," Sofia explains to Celie, "I had to fight my daddy. I had to fight my brothers. I had to fight my cousins and my uncles. A girl child ain't safe in a family of men" (38). Not only does Sofia resist Harpo's attempts to impose submission, but she is also jailed for "sassing" the mayor's wife and knocking the mayor down when he slaps her for impudence.

Unlike Sofia, however, Celie submits to a system of beliefs and values that reinforce conventional and received notions of race, class, and sex—and relegate her to a subordinate status. Celie submits to male authority because she accepts a theology which requires female subjugation to father and husband. Having been taught to "honor father and mother no matter what," Celie "couldn't be mad at [her] daddy because he [her] daddy." She suffers Albert's abuse for the same reasons: "Well, sometime Mr._____ git on me pretty hard, I have to talk to Old Maker. But he my husband. I shrug my shoulders" (39).

"Old Maker" is, for Celie, "big and old and tall and graybearded and white" (165). In linking her notion of divinity to a white, male figure, Celie accepts a theology of self-denial. It is a theology that validates her inferior status and treatment as a black woman in a racist and sexist culture. Not only does she devalue herself, but she attaches little value to a world which reflects her image as "black...pore...[and] a woman...nothing at all" (176).

If Albert separates Celie from Nettie, he introduces her to Shug Avery, his former mistress. Celie moves from a relationship with a stepfather who is sexually abusive to a relationship with a husband who exploits her labor and sex, and finally, to a relationship with Shug Avery, who loves her and teaches her the reverence and mystery of her body, as well as the means of earning a livelihood through her own industry and creativity.

Afflicted with what one character describes as "the nasty woman's disease," Shug, a blues singer, arrives in a covered wagon one afternoon (40). Just as Celie has internalized Albert's principle of patriarchy, so Shug internalizes his demeaning attitude toward Celie. Upon first meeting Celie, Shug "looks [Celie] over from head to foot and cackles, 'You sure *is* ugly....' like she ain't believed it" (42).

Opposite Celie in every way, Shug has the reputation of a high-living, adventurous, independent blues singer, whose lifestyle gives her greater freedom than Celie's more conventional status. Yet when Celie nurses and coaxes Shug back to health, the two women become intimate friends instead of rivals. Unlike the men who have subjugated Celie, Shug seeks neither to control nor to possess her. Celie subsequently forms a relationship with Shug that evolves from a maternal, to a sororal, to an erotic attachment.

Shug initiates Celie into an awareness of her own sexuality and an appreciation of her body—for despite the fact that she has had two children, Celie remains a "virgin" in that she has never shared a loving relationship. Until Shug introduces her to the beauty of her own body, Celie remains devoid of any sense of self-esteem or self-value:

> [Shug] say, Here take this mirror and go look at yourself down there,
> I bet you never seen it, have you?

Naw....

She say, What, too shame even to go off and look at yourself? And you look so cute too, she say laughing....

You come with me while I look, I say.

And us run off to my room like two little prankish girls.

You guard the door, I say.

She giggle. Okay, she say. Nobody coming. Coast clear.

I lie back on the bed and haul up my dress. Yank down my bloomers. Stick the looking glass tween my legs. Ugh. All that hair. Then my pussy lips be black. Then inside look like a wet rose. (69)

Celie's passivity and self-indifference are transformed into receptivity and responsiveness, first to Shug, then to herself:

It a lot prettier than you thought, ain't it? She say from the door.

It mine, I say. Where the button?

Right up near the top, she say. The part that stick out a little.

I look at her and touch it with my finger. A little shiver go through me. Nothing much. But just enough to tell me this the right button to mash. Maybe.

She say, While you looking, look at your titties too. I haul up my dress and look at my titties. Think bout my babies sucking them. Remember the little shiver I felt then too. Sometimes a big shiver. (69–70)

Though her body has been devalued by the men in her life, Celie not only discovers her own sexuality in the relationship with Shug, but she also learns how to love another. The recognition of herself as beautiful and loving is the first step toward Celie's independence and self-acceptance. As Celie, however, becomes more self-reliant, Shug becomes more nurturing and caring. In the course of the friendship, both women are transformed.

Unlike Celie, who derives her sense of self from the dominant white and male theology, Shug is a self-invented character whose sense of self is not male-inscribed. Her theology allows a divine, self-authorized sense of self. Shug's conception of God is both immanent and transcendent:

God is inside you and inside everybody else. You come into the world with God. But only them that search for it inside find it. And sometimes it just manifest itself even if you not looking, or don't know what you looking for....I believe God is everything...Everything that is or ever was or ever will be. (166–167)

Shug rejects the scriptural notion of God: "Ain't no way to read the bible and not think God white....When I found out I thought God was white, and a man, I lost interest" (166). Describing her god as "it," Shug explains that "god ain't a he or a she." God, for Shug, is not only someone to please, but to be pleased: "I think it pisses God off if you walk by the color purple in a field somewhere and don't notice it" (167).

Celie begins to revise her own notions of God and man and her place within the scheme of patriarchy when she discovers, through the agency of Shug, the cache of letters that Albert has concealed from her. Not only does she discover that her sister and children are in Africa, perhaps separated from her forever, but also that her real father had been lynched and her mother driven mad. These calamities and misfortunes shatter Celie's faith in the "big...old...tall...graybearded" white man to whom she has been "praying and writing." "He act just like all the other mens I know," writes Celie, "trifling, forgetful, and lowdown" (164). Resisting the authority of a patriarchal god as well as that of her husband, Celie learns to assert herself both in writing and speaking. When she recognizes that "the god [she] has been writing is a man" who does not listen to "poor colored women," she begins to address her letters to sister Nettie (164).

Writing thus becomes, for Celie, a means of structuring her identity—her sense of self—in relationship to her sister, and by extension, a community of women. The subsequent letters between Celie and Nettie stand as profound affirmation of the creative and self-creative power of the Word. Because the letters, due to Albert's expropriation, are never answered, it is apparent that they function primarily for the benefit of the writer, rather than the recipient. The dedication of the book ("*To the Spirit*: Without whose assistance / Neither this book / Nor I / Would have been / Written") suggests that to create a book is to create a life. Celie (like her creator, Walker) writes herself and *her*story into being. Moreover, the transformation in the character and style of the letters represents and parallels, to some extent, the growth and change in the lives of the writers. Not only do Nettie's letters become more formal and didactic in style as she is educated in the manners and mores of the Olinka tribe, but Celie's letters become longer and more sophisticated as she articulates a more reflective and complex sense of self. The correspondence between Celie and Nettie attests to the power of literacy and, at the same time, reinforces the motifs of community and female bonding that underlie the novel.

Celie's defiance of Albert is both a mark of increasing literacy, as well as a milestone in her journey toward maturity and independence:

> Mr. _____ start up from his seat. . . . He look over at me. I thought you was finally happy, he say. What wrong now?
>
> You a lowdown dog is what's wrong, I say. It's time to leave you and enter into the Creation. And your dead body just the welcome mat I need. (170)

Just as the power of literacy affirms Celie's relationship with Nettie, and moves her close to a sense of self-in-relationship, so the power of voice severs her dependency on Albert, and moves her toward a more autonomous sense of self. If writing demonstrates the creative potential of the Word, then conjuration gives powerful testimony to its destructive possibilities:

> I curse you, [Celie] say.
> What that mean? he say.
> I say, Until you do right by me, everything you touch will crumble.
> He laugh. Who you think you is? he say. You can't curse nobody. Look at you. You black, you pore, you ugly, you a woman. Goddam, he say, you nothing at all.
> Until you do right by me, I say, everything you even dream about will fail. I give it to him straight, just like it come to me. And it seem to come to me from the trees.
> Whoever heard of such a thing, say Mr. _____. I probably didn't whup your ass enough.
> Every lick you hit me you will suffer twice, I say. Then I say, You better stop talking because all I'm telling you ain't coming just from me. Look like when I open my mouth the air rush in and shape words.
> Shit, he say. I should have lock you up. Just let you out to work.
> The jail you plan for me is the one in which you will rot, I say.
> Shug come over to where us talking. She take one look at my face and say Celie! Then she turn to Mr. _____. Stop Albert, she say. Don't say no more. You just going to make it harder on yourself.
> I'll fix her wagon! say Mr. _____, and spring toward me.
> A dust devil flew up on the porch between us, fill my mouth with dirt. The dirt say, Anything you do to me, already done to you.
> Then I feel Shug shake me. Celie, she say. And I come to myself.
> I'm pore, I'm black, I may be ugly and can't cook, a voice say to everything listening. But I'm here.
> Amen, say Shug. Amen, amen. (175–176)

Not only does the Word have a transformative effect on Celie, but in the form of conjuration, it has the power to change, or at least deflect, the hostility and negativity emanating from an ill-wisher—or, as Zora Neale Hurston describes the power of a curse, to place "damnation and trouble...on the head of [her] enemy and not on [her] head."[10] Moreover, as conjure woman, Celie not only has the power to free herself from unjust oppression, but also the potential to release Albert from the burden of his own oppressiveness.

Ultimately, it is Celie's sewing that saves Albert's life. With "a needle and not a razor in [her] hand," Celie channels her anger and violence into creativity (125). Later, in Memphis, Celie's skill with the needle and her talent for designing pants provide her with the means of earning a comfortable livelihood. Thus, if Walker emphasizes the importance of popular culture (singing) in the character of Shug, she stresses the centrality of material culture to women's creativity and survival in her depiction of Celie.

Sewing and quilting are occupations in the novel in which women—and sometimes men—participate. Sofia, Shug, and Celie all share in the art of quilting. Both Sofia and Shug contribute to making a quilt ("Sister's Choice") by donating patching material to Celie. Quilting is both a utilitarian and decorative art; equally important, it represents the collective and collaborative labor of women. Although associated with women and women's culture, quilting is an art particularly associated with the culture of rural, black, working-class women. It is a fitting emblem of the bonding between women.

Sewing is an enterprise, however, which is sometimes performed by men. The Olinka [African] men are known for their "beautiful quilts which are full of animals and birds and people" (159). Moreover, at the end of the novel, Albert significantly begins to make tops to accompany Celie's pants. Thus, textile culture not only forges a bond among black women, but also serves as a link between Africans and Afro-Americans as well as between women and men.

Just as Walker's use of the epistolary form allows her to transpose a formal tradition into a vehicle for expressing the folk voice, so her emphasis on material and popular modes of expression allow us to revise conventional and received notions of "high" art and culture. The significance of these expressions of folk culture is particularly compelling for black women whose creativity has had a direct relationship to personal expression and political survival. Walker uses the quilt, then, as a metaphor for the black and female aesthetic, as well as an emblem of bonding.

Both Celie and Shug have doubles in the novel. Celie and "Squeak," Harpo's mistress, replicate each other in some measure: both are victims of rape and incest by black and white men, respectively. Sofia and Shug also function as doubles: both resist the socially prescribed roles of submission and obedience expected of women, thus subverting the system of patriarchy. Tiring of Harpo's attempts to control and dominate her, Sofia leaves and Harpo takes up with Squeak, who is as submissive to him as Celie is to Albert. When Harpo begins to lose interest, however, Celie, under Shug's tutelage, realizes that Squeak has surrendered her right to self-entitlement by giving up her name. Celie advises Squeak to make Harpo address her by her real name, Mary Agnes.

The women in the novel forge bonds in other ways as well. Celie accedes to the violation of her body in order to protect her sister Nettie from the sexual advances of their stepfather. Squeak (Mary Agnes), with her own body, secures Sofia's release from jail. When Squeak decides to pursue a career as a blues singer and leaves with Shug, it is Sofia who promises to care for Squeak's daughter while her mother is in Memphis. Even Eleanor Jane, daughter of the white mayor's wife (for whom Sofia has been forced to work as a maid), prepares special foods as a curative for Sofia's youngest child, who is victim to a rare blood disease.

Each of these relationships, however, forms part of a larger network of communal relationships in which female bonding is the dominant and connecting link. Challenging the hierarchal power relations exercised between men and women (and by implication, whites and blacks) are the relationships among the women based on cooperation and mutuality. Women share the children, the labor, and even, at times, the men. Ultimately it is the female bonding that restores the women to a sense of completeness and independence. The relationships between Celie and Shug, on the one hand, and between Celie and Nettie, on the other, exemplify the power and potential of this bonding.

Although blacks in the American South as well as the Olinka tribe in Africa are impacted by the presence of whites and function, to some degree, as satellites in a white sphere of influence, it is the black (American/African) community which provides the central focus for the action of the novel. Nettie's letters educate Celie and the reader on the customs and rituals of West Africa. Reportorial rather than expressive, they illuminate the similarities between the condition of black women in the American South and black women in Africa.

As Celie is degraded and devalued as a black woman in the American South, Nettie discovers that, as an unmarried female, she is regarded with pity and contempt by the Olinka. She also learns about scarification and clitoridectomy, rituals of female mutilation in a patriarchal society.[11] Tashi, the young Olinka woman whom Celie's son, Adam, marries, submits to both these rites in order to preserve some vestige of tribal culture and identity in the face of white encroachment upon traditional village life.

Tashi's choice suggests, of course, the conflict between the demands of race and the demands of sex confronting black women. With these rituals, black patriarchal culture replicates the historic Occidental relationship between whites and blacks. Scarification and clitoridectomy both externalize the historic victimization of black women and symbolize gender debasement in patriarchal culture.

In Africa, however, Nettie discovers among the Olinkas the value of female bonding in a polygynous society. "It is in work that women get to know and care about each other" (141), she writes to Celie. Moreover, in the missionary household where she lives with Samuel, a black minister, and his wife, Corrine, Nettie shares the responsibility of rearing the children and administers to the spiritual and medical needs of the Olinka.

Yet, it is Celie and Shug who epitomize the complementarity as well as the autonomy of the women—which extend to include not only other women, but also the men. While developing an individual sense of self, Celie nevertheless respects Shug's rights. Although heartbroken that Shug has run off with Germaine, a young musician in her band, Celie recognizes that "[Shug] got a right to look over the world in whatever company she choose. Just cause I love her don't take away none of her rights. . . . Who am I to tell her who to love? My job just to love her good and true myself" (228). Albert's feelings for Shug, together with his desertion by Shug and Celie, constitute the catalyst for a similar recognition in his life: "I have love and I have been love. And I thank God he let me gain understanding enough to know love can't be halted just cause some peoples moan and groan. It don't surprise me you [Celie] love Shug Avery.... I have love Shug Avery all my life" (228). Finding consolation in each other's company, Albert and Celie become friends for the first time, and spend their evenings sharing interests and reminiscing about Shug.

By the end of the novel, we see that Walker has developed a new model for relationships based on new gender roles for men and women. Not only do Albert and Harpo extend their interests to include activities such as sewing and cooking but, perhaps more important, they begin to relate more affectively to each other. When Albert is nearly dying, Harpo bathes and nurtures his father back to health. Walker suggests here that less rigid and oppressive roles are necessary in order for men and women to live together and fulfill their individual potential. Further, Celie's notions of "manliness" and "womanliness" challenge rigid gender categories and allow for individual variations and preferences:

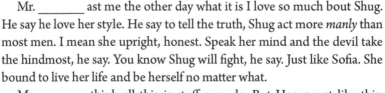

Mr. _____ ast me the other day what it is I love so much bout Shug. He say he love her style. He say to tell the truth, Shug act more *manly* than most men. I mean she upright, honest. Speak her mind and the devil take the hindmost, he say. You know Shug will fight, he say. Just like Sofia. She bound to live her life and be herself no matter what.

Mr. _____ think all this is stuff men do. But Harpo not like this, I tell him. You not like this. What Shug got is *womanly* it seem like to me. Specially since she and Sofia the ones got it. (228, emphasis added)

Walker not only redefines male and female roles, but also suggests a new paradigm for relationships. During the course of the novel, Shug leaves Albert and returns married to Grady, "a skinny big toof man" (93). She later runs off with the youthful Germaine. The intimacy between Celie and Shug, however, survives and incorporates each of these relationships.

In Memphis the initial triad of Shug, Celie, and Albert gives way to a triad consisting of Celie, Shug, and Grady (or alternately, Squeak, Shug, and Grady). When Shug takes up with Germaine, a new triad develops—Celie, Shug, and Germaine. Other triads in the novel include Squeak, Harpo, and Sofia and Nettie, Corrine, and Samuel. The final triad in the novel, formed when Shug returns to Celie, is, in fact, a reconstitution of the first—Shug, Celie, and Albert—with *radically redefined roles*.

Walker's final paradigm, then, is neither the male/female nor the female/female dyad, but a variation on the eternal triangle in which women complement rather than compete with each other, and at the same time, share an equal status with the men. Thus, the novel moves from a male/female coupling in which the woman is subjugated, to a female/female coupling based on mutuality, to a female/male/female triad based on new and redefined roles. In Walker's new model, conventional heterosexual relationships and nuclear families give way to a triad that radiates outward into an extended family network linked by women. Walker's paradigm is confirmed by the work of feminist scholars such as Nancy Chodorow and Elizabeth Abel, who hold that primary bonding exists between women.[12] Moreover, like Chodorow, Walker's resolution to sexual inequality depends on fostering an increased sense of male self-in-relationship and a greater sense of female autonomy. If Harpo learns to "mother" his father, Celie learns to earn her own livelihood. Walker's women, through their unconventional lifestyles, gain greater access to the public sphere. Celie replaces her real father as owner of a dry-goods store, while both Shug and Squeak, as blues singers, perform in public. Both Harpo and Albert, on the other hand, in their enjoyment of cooking and sewing, as well as their heightened sense of nurturance and connectedness, move further into the private or domestic arena.

The novel concludes on a theme of reunion between lovers, family, and friends— symbolizing, on a personal level, the psychic reintegration of personality differences and, on a social level, the reconciliation of gender differences. Having enrolled Germaine in Wilberforce, Shug returns to join Celie, now the successful owner of a house and business, and Albert, who is content to sit back and learn "to wonder" (239). Finally, drawing again on the conventions of the sentimental novel, Celie is reunited with her two children, who have returned with her long-lost sister from Africa.

Embracing and consecrating all forms of existence on the planet, Celie's final letter—addressed, once more, to God—expresses her new concept of the deity: "Dear God. Dear stars, dear trees, dear sky, dear peoples. Dear Everything. Dear God" (242). Her letter is not only a private prayer of thanks for the reunion of her family, but a liturgical lection affirming the rites, rituals, and experiences of the black community. Significantly, the occasion for the reunion and the setting for the closing letter is the Fourth of July—the day on which "white people [are] busy celebrating [their] independence" and "black folks...celebrating each other" (243). Walker's emphasis, once again, is on the psychic reintegration of the self and the reconciliation of community (as opposed to social integration).

Yet, finally, *The Color Purple* is a novel about the right to *write* (oneself) and the right to *right* (a wrong). Not surprisingly, the form Walker chooses is one that confers not only literary authority, with its emphasis on the written word, but moral authority in its rewriting of the Scriptures. In a refiguration of the Apostle Paul's Letter to the Philippians, Celie addresses her epistles not to the church, but to God. If Paul wrote from prison to affirm his belief in death as a blessing for the faithful, Celie writes to affirm her faith that "[t]his life soon be over. Heaven last always" (39). Like Paul, she writes in the midst of persecution and in the hope of divine deliverance. In Philippi, Paul's church was formed as a result of the efforts of a small group of women. Lydia, a dealer in purple cloth, was his first convert, followed by his jailer. If Celie (like Paul) ultimately succeeds in the conversion of her jailer

(Mister), she herself is converted by the dealer in purple (Shug) and a small group of women. In rewriting Paul's letter to the Philippians, Walker, in effect, subverts his more popular Letter to the Ephesians in which Paul prescribes in detail the duties of wives and servants to husbands and masters.[13]

Walker's accomplishments in her third novel are considerable. Not only does she liberate her women from the narrow confines of male-inscribed roles in the literary sphere and male-prescribed roles in the social sphere, but perhaps more important, Walker celebrates the centrality of black women in the reclamation of the past and the transformation of the notion of community. Further, Walker creates a new literary space for the black and female idiom within a traditionally Western and Eurocentric form. In the process of merging two forms and two traditions, *The Color Purple* extends both.

2

(W)Riting *The Work* and Working the Rites

Sherley Anne Williams's "Meditations on History"

[I]f it is true that at the heart of power relations and as a permanent condition of their existence there is an insubordination and a certain essential obstinacy on the part of the principles of freedom, then there is no relationship of power without the means of escape or possible flight. Every power relationship implies, at least *in potentia*, a strategy of struggle.

        —Michel Foucault, "How Is Power Exercised?"

One day this ole slave name John was walkin' through the woods; and he sees this, this here skeleton...laying there in the sun...He don't pay them dry bones no mind...he done see plenty of them bones in his time...he sits down on that rock to rest his weary self; and the next thing you know, he hears somebody eerie say: "Tongue is the cause of my being here." John leaped up and ran back to the Master....."Massa... Massa" he say, "there's a talking skeleton in the woods!" Old Master say, "I don't believe that John, you're not trying to make a fool of me are you?" John say: "No Massa, dem bones is *really* talking." So the Master called all of his friends from all of the nearby plantations....White folks came from all over; and when they arrived at the place of the skeleton—the place of the talking bones—they said to John: "Make him speak." But the skeleton wouldn't talk....So, and then, they beat John to death with anything that they could get their hands on....And left him beside the other skeleton....As the sun set redly, the buzzards was tearing into John's liver, and as the waning sun shined through his vacant sockets...the bones laying beside him commenced to shake and rattle, and then, chillen, them bones spoke....They said: "Tongue, yes, tongue brought *us* here, and tongue brought you *here* too."

        —Old Folk Tale, cited by Larry Neal in
        The Glorious Monster in the Bell of the Horn

It would seem that one must be acquainted with darkies from one's birth in order to fully understand what passes for speech amongst them.

        —Narrator, in Sherley Anne Williams's "Meditations on History"

There is no doubt about it. White people often undo themselves by such running off at the mouth, and God only knows how many nigger triumphs have been won in total silence.

        —William Styron, *The Confessions of Nat Turner*

And unlike white Americans who could assume literacy and familiarity
with existing literacy models as norms, the slave found himself without a
system of written language—"uneducated" in the denotative sense of the
word. His task was not simply one of moving toward the requisite large-
ness of soul and faith in the value of his experiences. He first had to seize
the word.... Only by grasping the word could he engage in the speech
acts that would ultimately define his selfhood.
—Houston A. Baker, Jr., *The Journey Back*

"Meditations on History," Sherley Anne Williams's novella about discourse and
struggle, achieves much of its meaning through its own struggle with previous
modes of discourse.[1] Engaging works by William Styron and Thomas Gray, Williams
explores the discourses of history and fiction. And, although Williams makes reference neither to Styron nor his work in "Meditations," her title signals not only that
Styron's *Confessions of Nat Turner* is the primary anterior text for her work, but that
her purpose is to produce a text which engages Styron as a kind of literary interlocutor.[2] Williams's title, "Meditations," suggests a formal and thematic revision of
Styron's *Confessions of Nat Turner* (that title appropriated from Thomas Gray's earlier document of the same name). Significantly, both titles turn on the notion of discourse (or its absence), silence and utterance, contemplation and revelation, private
thought and public language. Williams takes her title from the "Author's Note" in
Styron's *Confessions*, where he describes his novel as "less a 'historical novel' in conventional terms than *a meditation on history*."[3] By unmasking Styron's work as more
nearly a personal and authorial "meditation" than the "confessions" of his subject,
Williams's title constitutes an ironic affirmation of Styron's stated intentions. For
both Williams and Styron, the notion of "meditation" not only implies the priority of the author's imagination and consciousness, but also an ordered reconstruction of history. In the sense that both authors interpose their literary *meditations*
into a historical episode, both works of historical fiction constitute acts of *mediation* as well. Williams's work suggests, however, that Styron's interventions result
in the misreading of his historical subject, while her own work represents not only
an attempt to reconcile the literary treatment to the historical subject but, in the
process, to deconstruct her predecessor's methods. "Meditations," then, becomes a
gesture of what Henry Louis Gates, Jr., calls "critical parody," in that Williams revises
and thus problematizes the structuration of Styron's *Confessions*.[4]

Styron structures his *Confessions* in terms of an antithesis curiously appropriate to his subject: freedom and bondage. He declares his intention to "re-create a
man and his era," allowing himself as author "the utmost *freedom* of imagination in

reconstructing" the early life and motivations of his protagonist, while remaining "within the *bounds* of what meager enlightenment history has left us about the institution of slavery."[5] Although many critics argue that the novelist, even the historical novelist, is entitled to some literary license, others allege that Styron has created a fictional character who reflects the historical Nat Turner less than he represents the author's highly personal and imaginative reconstruction.[6] In her implicit critique of Styron, Williams suggests that the priority of the imagination—especially when it is distantly removed from the historical subject (object) of meditation by race, gender, class, and culture—creates a peculiar dilemma for the writer.[7]

Williams is concerned not only with the problematics of historical fiction, but also with the relationship between discourse, power, and resistance. She explores the critical relationship between power relations and discourse, and the struggle to dominate as well as to resist domination. The central issue for her is not merely the functions, but also the forms, of discourse. The tension between the vernacular discourse of the slave heroine and the formal discourse of the unnamed white male interviewer who narrates her story raises the issue of spoken versus written language, and their political and ideological functions in racial, sexual, class, and cultural interrelationships.[8]

Williams and Styron employ similar techniques in constructing their works. Both writers take their subjects from an intermediary and create a complex literary personality based upon a historically constituted subject. Styron's narrative is based upon an account told to Thomas R. Gray, who recorded the original *Confessions of Nat Turner* as the convicted slave awaited execution in 1831 for leading a rebellion in which he and his followers killed fifty-five whites. Williams's character, on the other hand, is modeled after a historical figure recorded in Angela Davis's "Reflections on the Black Woman's Role in the Community of Slaves."[9] It is also instructive to note in what ways these two readings of the slave experience are influenced by the work of contemporary historians of slavery. Interpreting the dynamics of the slave community and the character of Nat Turner through Stanley Elkins's controversial work on slavery, Styron concludes that Turner, as a slave rebel, is exceptional in that he initiates "the only effective, sustained revolt in the annals of American Negro history."[10] Williams, on the other hand, reads the experiences of her heroine ultimately through Herbert Aptheker's pioneering work on slave resistance, the source for Angela Davis's work on the slave community. Aptheker argues that the Nat Turner event "was not an isolated, unique phenomenon, but the culmination of a series of slave conspiracies and revolts which had occurred in the immediate past."[11]

Within "Meditations," Williams's unnamed fictional interviewer, whose narrative role parallels that of Thomas Gray, functions as an amanuensis for the slave Dessa (as Williams's heroine Odessa calls herself). However, as author-to-be of *The Roots of Rebellion and the Means of Eradicating Them* (otherwise referred to as *The Work*), his role also corresponds to Styron's. The narrator in Williams's text is thus a kind of composite character who fulfills the functions of both Gray, as historical

Table 2.1 **Subject/Investigator/Interpreter Relationships**

Subject	Historical Investigator	Interpreter
Nat Turner	Thomas Gray	William Styron
Slave Woman	Angela Davis	Sherley Anne Williams
Dessa	Unnamed Narrator	Author of *The Work*

investigator/interviewer, and Styron, as literary interpreter. In figuring the Styron/ Gray fictional composite within her text, Williams sets up an author-character relationship which gives her the same control over Styron and Gray that they possess over their subject, Nat Turner. Table 2.1 illustrates the parallel relationships suggested above between author, Styron; his intermediary, Thomas Gray; and his subject, Nat Turner. It also structures the parallels between author, Williams; her intermediary, Angela Davis; and her subject, the unidentified female slave rebel. Finally, it suggests the relationship in Williams's narrative between the composite Unnamed Narrator/Author of *The Work* and his subject, Dessa.

I am concerned, however, not only with Williams's replication of Styron's process of composition, but also with her critique of Styron. Like the triptych in Table 2.1, the elliptical diagram in Figure 2.1 illustrates the Turner/Gray/Styron and the Slave Woman/Davis/Williams relationships, along with their fictional equivalents in Williams's "Meditations."

Obviously, no schematization can reproduce the complexity of these relationships, but Figure 2.1 is meant to suggest some of the interrelationships examined in the course of this chapter. The nature and function of these several relationships are indicated through unbroken lines of influence, or replication; broken lines of difference and subversion, or *re*reading; and broken/dotted lines of influence and subversion, or *mis*reading.[12] The periphery of the diagram inscribes the *inter*textual relationships between Styron/Gray and Williams/Davis, and the center, the *intra*textual relationships depicted in Williams's "Meditations." In the top left of the diagram, Nat Turner, the original historical subject, is misread (or constituted and subverted) by Thomas Gray, whose representation is, in turn, appropriated and subverted by William Styron as a literary figure in his novel. In a parallel process of composition, the slave woman in the top right of the diagram is cited by Angela Davis to exemplify her thesis and, in a further development, appropriated by Sherley Anne Williams as a literary subject in her novella. The characters in Williams's text are represented at the center of the diagram in a configuration that both repeats the Styron/Williams technique of composition and, at the same time, plays the dual role of both authenticating Williams's method and revising (subverting) Styron's. In this instance, Dessa is the historical subject falsely constituted (misread) by the historical investigator who is writing a book on the suppression of slave rebellions,

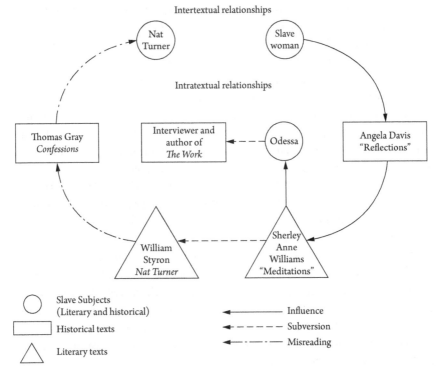

Figure 2.1 Intra/Intertextual Relationships.

a work which (like Styron's) will be shown to illuminate more about the writer than about his subject.

One finds telling similarities and differences between Williams and Styron in presentation as well as perspective. Both address (implicitly) the discourse of historical fiction, and both assume the role of literary interpreters who meditate on history. Styron's work, however, is meant to be a meditation, or reflection, on history itself, whereas Williams's can perhaps be more aptly understood as a meditation on historiography—in the sense that it provides the reader a guide to the contemplation of historical and literary-historical works such as Styron's and Gray's. If, then, Styron's work is a fictional meditation on history, Williams's is a meta-fictional meditation on history (that is, a fictional meditation on a fictional meditation on history), as well as a fictional elaboration of a historical incident cited by Angela Davis. Williams's text thus gestures toward intertextuality, not only in its relationship to Styron's literary antecedent, but also in its relationship to Davis's historical citation.

Styron's protagonist narrates the events of his life from the first person, inviting a judgment from the reader on Turner as subject/narrator, whereas Williams's heroine is presented primarily in the third person from the perspective of the white narrator, inviting the reader to distinguish between the narrator's judgment of the subject and the subject (Dessa) herself. When Dessa speaks in her own vernacular voice, she *interdicts* the narrator's discourse. At the same time, the contrast between Dessa's spoken language and the white narrator's written language allows Williams as author, in Gates's apt term, to "signify" upon her precursors, Styron and Gray.[13] One should perhaps note in passing that the narration of Dessa's story by a white male narrator resolves a technical problem for the author, who must discover a way to present a character who is a victim of an illiteracy enforced by a system that made teaching slaves to read and write a criminal offense. Moreover, it is with a certain appropriateness that Dessa's story is narrated by a white male, representing the class that has historically controlled the print media. It was the historical records of this class (diaries, plantation records, ledgers, and so forth) that, until the emergence of modern revisionist scholarship based on the slaves' folklore and narratives, provided the primary source materials for the study of slavery.[14]

Williams's concern with signification suggests that the reader must approach the discourse of the "real" as well as the discourse of the "imaginary" with a sense of skepticism, based on a recognition of the cultural myths inscribed in language and consciousness. It might also suggest that we can assume the truth claim of historical narrative no more than that of literary narrative.[15] Thus, as readers we must be wary of what Barbara Johnson describes as the "interpretive malpractice" to which writers (both creative and historical) are subject.[16]

Because Williams's text repeats in structure but subverts in meaning the Turner/Gray/Styron dynamic, let us begin by examining the role of Styron's intermediary, Thomas Gray, whom Styron describes as "a somewhat enigmatic lawyer...who published the *Confessions*...and then vanished from sight."[17] In his address "To the Public" in *The Confessions of Nat Turner*, Gray tells us that what he is about to present is a "faithful record" of his interview with the subject:

> I have had ready access to him, and, finding that he was willing to make a full and free confession of the origin, progress and consummation of the insurrectionary movements of the slaves of which he was the contriver and head; I determined for gratification of public curiosity to commit his state-ments to writing, and publish them, with little or no variation, from his own words. That this is a faithful record of his confessions, the annexed certificate of the County Court of Southampton, will attest. They certainly bear the stamp of truth and sincerity.[18]

Although Gray's assertions suggest that he locates the authenticity and value of his account in discourse that is presumed to be objective and value-free, a close read-ing of his prefatory comments would indicate a more complex motivation at work. Turner's actions have, in effect, created moral and social chaos for the narrator and his world. By presenting Turner's story as a cautionary tale, the narrator attempts to restore by simple reaffirmation his own sense of moral and mental order, prerequisite to the re-establishment of the social order that Turner has threatened:

> His [Nat Turner's] own account of the conspiracy is submitted to the public, without comment. It reads an awful, and it is hoped, a useful lesson, as to the operations of a mind like his, endeavoring to grapple with things beyond its reach. How it first became bewildered and confounded, and finally corrupted and led to the conception and perpetuation of the most atrocious and heart-rending deeds. It is calculated also to demonstrate the policy of our laws in restraint of this class of our population, and to induce all those entrusted with their execution, as well as our citizens generally, to see that they are strictly and rigidly enforced. Each particular community should look to its own safety, whilst the general guardian of the laws, keep a watchful eye over all.[19]

The contradiction between the profession of factual objectivity ("without comment") and the editorial imposition of meaning that immediately follows signal Gray's real intentions to the reader. Turner becomes for his amanuensis a symbol of disorder and irrationality. Gray's representation of the events surrounding Turner's activities becomes "a useful lesson," or rather an instrument or device for restoring psychic order. Furthermore, the policy of restraint and repression that he advocates is aimed at re-establishing public order. His comments also suggest that his findings (like those of the scholar and scientist) have implications for both the formulation of public policy and the machinery designed to enforce that policy.

The ambiguous relationship between Styron and his source, Gray, serves to intensify a clearly problematic relationship between Styron and his subject, Turner. In his essay, "This Quiet Dust," Styron discounts as "virtually worthless" the newspaper accounts of the period, which he describes as "sketchy, remote, filled with conjecture." On the other hand, he appears to affirm the authenticity of Gray's original *Confessions of Nat Turner*, "a brief pamphlet of some five thousand words, transcribed from Nat's lips as he awaited trial.... There are several discrepancies in Gray's transcript but it was taken down in haste, and in all major respects it seems completely honest and reliable."[20] Yet, in his exchange with Herbert Aptheker, published in *The Nation* sometime later, Styron suggests a qualification, if not an actual retraction:

> I have never questioned [the] authenticity [of Gray's *Confessions*], whatever semantic emphasis is placed on that word....What I do question...is the *accuracy* of the "Confessions," the overall fidelity to the circumstances of Nat's life and career which Gray maintained during the course of what must have been, considering the hysteria of the moment, an exceedingly difficult and prickly interview.[21]

Continuing, Styron suggests that his primary source, Gray, has in fact subverted and misread his subject:

> The entire pedantic, impossibly elevated and formal tone of the "Confessions" makes me believe that they were *not* recorded with "little or no variation" from Nat's words, as Gray states in his prologue; and so how much during that tense encounter was subtly bent and twisted by the interrogator? Gray was a man of his time, a Southern racist, and as a functionary of the Commonwealth it may well have been to his advantage (and in spite of his disclaimer to the contrary) to distort many things that the helpless prisoner told him, to add things, to leave things out.[22]

Clearly, Styron's remarks here are motivated, at least in part, by the criticism of detractors who accuse him of inauthenticity, distortion, and historical falsification in his treatment of Turner. Styron's critics have leveled, among others, the charges that the author portrays the slave revolutionary as a weak and irresolute figure; that he associates Turner's liberational impulse to sexual repression, pent-up passion for white women, and latent homosexuality; and that he ignores Turner's wife and the role of his family in the shaping of his character.[23] Styron and his apologists have defended both his artistic and historical integrity on the basis that Styron "takes liberties with fact, as every novelist does, but he does not do violence to the historical record."[24] Quoting the Marxist critic, Georg Lukács, Styron argues that "'the novelist must be at liberty to treat [historical facts] as he likes, if he is to reproduce the much more complex and ramifying totality with historical faithfulness.'"[25]

If Styron's most severe critics indict him for perpetuating "white Southern myths, racial stereotypes, and literary clichés," his most astute critics suggest that what is at issue is not Styron's literary license, but his preference for his own imagination over the historical facts of Turner's life.[26] Responding to this issue, Ralph Ellison, for example, would limit the autonomy of the novelist who chooses to write historical fiction. "The freedom of the fiction writer, the novelist, is one of the great freedoms possible for the individual to exercise," says Ellison, "but it is not absolute.... you don't have the freedom to snatch any and everybody, and completely recreate them."[27]

Although at a considerably greater remove, Gray is to Styron's *Confessions* what Angela Davis is to Williams's "Meditations." And what Turner is to Gray, the unnamed slave woman is to Angela Davis. Dedicating her novella to Davis, Williams opens with a quotation from Davis's "Reflections on the Black Woman's Role in the Community of Slaves":

> The myth [of the black matriarchy and the castrating black female] must be consciously repudiated as myth and the black woman in her true historical contours must be resurrected. We, the black women of today, must accept

the full weight of a legacy wrought in blood by our mothers in chains...as heirs to a tradition of supreme perseverance and heroic resistance, we must hasten to take our place wherever our people are forging on towards freedom.[28]

The dedication and quotation contextualize the Williams/Styron dialogue within a tradition of political insurgency and literary revisionism, as a fuller consideration of Davis's original article will show. At the outset, Davis informs us that her work is a repudiation of the myths of the black woman embodied, for example, in the *Moynihan Report*. Referring to "the paucity of literature on the black woman," she writes: "we must contend with the fact that too many of these rare studies must claim as their signal achievement the reinforcement of fictitious clichés. They have given credence to grossly distorted categories through which the black woman continues to be perceived."[29]

Davis argues that we must examine the biases and presuppositions that the scholar brings to the study of black social structures, warning the reader that the putatively objective discourse of the social scientist and researcher can perpetuate negative stereotypes of black women. She cites the following historical event, upon which Williams bases her story, to demonstrate that black women have been leaders in the struggle for liberation of the black community:

> [A] group of slaves, being led from Maryland to be sold in the South had apparently planned to kill the traders, and make their way to freedom. One of the traders was successfully done away with, but eventually a posse captured all the slaves. Of the six leaders sentenced to death, one was a woman. She was first permitted, for reasons of economy, to give birth to her child. Afterwards, she was publicly hanged.[30]

Examining the historical record, Davis concludes that the black woman has been central in the black community from slavery to the present as the "custodian of resistance." Davis thus provides Williams with a connecting link to the historical event within a continuum of political insurgency, establishing a continuity of purpose between Davis, Williams, and Dessa—as opposed to the discontinuity between Turner and Gray, Styron and Turner, and even Styron and Gray.

Williams, in effect, gives dramatic expression to Davis's thesis, while simultaneously providing the anonymous historical figure with literary identity.[31] The violence done to the image of the black slave woman by historians corresponds to the violence done to her literary voice by male (black and white) authors. Just as Davis, in her article, seeks to free the black female from historical libel, so Williams seeks to create a text to liberate her protagonist from literary libel as well as social captivity. If Williams combines the roles of historian and literary interpreter in the character of the narrator, she represents the black woman's struggle against misrepresentation and misreading in the character of Dessa. What is significant in Williams's treatment is her emphasis on the personal and physical struggles, as well as the social and literary struggles, of the black woman. Dessa is *literally* imprisoned in a social system controlled by the slaveholders and *literarily* imprisoned in a text controlled by the defenders of the institution of slavery.

Williams introduces her story not from the narrator's perspective, but from Dessa's. The main narrative is preempted by a prologue that takes the form of a reverie by Dessa. Unlike Styron's Turner, whose early "meditations" center on his experiences as a house slave pampered by an indulgent master, Dessa's "meditations" depict her relationships within the slave community, and, more specifically, her relationship with husband Kaine. Dessa's reveries of Kaine allow her a temporary imaginative retreat from the confines of corporeal imprisonment in the root cellar ("It was gone as suddenly as it had come, the memory so strong, so clear it was like being with him all over again" [208]). Situated before the main text, narrated by the historical investigator, Dessa's reveries, expressed in the language of private reflection, establish her as a *speaking* (rather than *spoken*) subject and provide the reader with a subjective and participatory point of reference for understanding the revelation of events which follow. By opening the text with Dessa's reflections, Williams establishes the reader's narrative expectations, promotes identification with her protagonist, and provides the clues on how to *read*, or decode, the real meaning of the narrator's ostensibly reportorial journal entries.

In the traditional slave narrative, the prologue or preface to the slave's tale was frequently written by a white guarantor, usually an abolitionist, who assured the reader that the story s/he was about to read was truthful and reliable.[32] If the prologue was a device for authenticating and validating the traditional slave narrative, then Williams replicates but, more significantly, reverses this function. The effect of Dessa's prologue in "Meditations" is to subvert the authority and authenticity of the main narration, while, more traditionally, Gray's prologue functions to authenticate Turner's account.

Williams's story, however, inverts not only the structure of the conventional slave narrative but its social and rhetorical strategies as well. If the original slave narrative had as its goal the condemnation and destruction of the "peculiar institution," Williams's narrator (like Gray) attempts to use narrative as justification for the suppression of resistance and rebellion. Ironically, despite the narrator's intentions, Dessa's narrative does, in fact, conform in structure to the traditional slave narrative, which culminates in freedom for the ex-slave narrator. Unlike Styron's Turner, Williams's Dessa not only is liberated from the fate of her historical precursor, but assists in the liberation of her fellow slaves.

More subtle perhaps is Williams's subversion of the formal discourse of the nineteenth-century slave narrative. The slave narratives, which inaugurate the black formal and narrative tradition, appropriate the discourse of the dominant white and male culture and, like Gray's *Confessions*, depend for authenticity upon a highly

charged public rhetoric in which the slaveholder and the slave system represent a
threat to the moral and social order. In *Give Birth to Brightness*, Williams writes,

> It is…clear from these narratives that whatever descriptions of Black
> traditions or "field of manners" are given are there either to point up the
> effects of slavery, or are unintentional by-products. The major impetus of
> these men as writers was the need to call attention to the plight of Black
> people in this country, to point out the inequities and horrors of America's
> caste system, to provide answers and questions and solutions to America's
> dilemma.[33]

Williams's insertion of the black vernacular into this discourse, in effect, writes into
history the voices of slaves like Dessa who did not, like Turner for example, have the
benefit of literacy, but who nevertheless gained some measure of personal autonomy and, not infrequently, physical freedom despite enforced illiteracy.[34]

The main story, as I have indicated, takes the form of a series of journal entries
recorded by the amanuensis, emphasizing the authority of written discourse for the
narrator. His style, reflecting a "scholarly" posture, is impersonal and "objective," based
upon scientific inquiry, reason, logic, cause and effect. In short, his narration represents
white, male, formal discourse. He is author of *The Complete Guide for Competent Masters
in Dealing with Slaves and Other Dependents*, a work that he dismisses as "a mere business venture." More important to the narrator is his forthcoming *magnum opus*. The
slave uprising in which Dessa participates, he believes, will make a "splendid opening"
to his contemplated project: "she will be brought to re-create that event [the uprising]
and all that led up to it for me. Ah! the work, *The Work* has at last begun" (212).

It is the full title of *The Work*—*The Roots of Rebellion and the Means of Eradicating
Them* (also referred to as *Roots*)—which reveals the motivations of the narrator. The
ironic allusion to Alex Haley's historical novel *Roots* suggests a concern not so much
with *roots* as with *eradication*.[35] Assuming the posture of a historical investigator,
the narrator sets out to "discover and analyze the motivating factors which culmi-
nated" in what he regards as "this outrage against the public safety" (222). *The Work*,
then, is projected as a kind of blueprint for the exercise of power and control by
the dominant and privileged over the dominated and subjected, and thus becomes
part of a technology of representation which ensures the ideological dominance
and physical suppression of the slave. Undoubtedly, the rather nice subversion and
parody invoked by the conflation of the abbreviated titles (*Roots* and *The Work*)
will not be lost upon the close reader. As the narrator "writes" *The Work* (*Roots*),
so Dessa "works" the "rites of roots."[36] Based upon trial records, the narrator reconstructs the following incident:

> Wilson picked up a consignment of slaves in Charleston at the end of
> March. While in the area, he attended a private sale where he heard of a

wench, just entered upon childbearing age, and already increasing, that was being offered for sale on the plantation of Mr. Terrell Vaungham. He inquired at the plantation and was told that the wench was being sold because she had assaulted Vaungham.... Wilson paid three hundred eighty-five dollars species for her: she would fetch at least twice that much in New Orleans.... In the early morning hours of April 29, the wench and the four bucks in her chain group managed to free themselves.... Two of these went to subdue the guards and drivers while the other three attacked Wilson and Darkmon [the slave traders], searching for the keys which would free the rest of the coffle. The negress attacked Darkmon and it was his death screams which awakened Wilson.... The darkies then took the horses and pack animals, some provisions and all the firearms and other weapons.... A posse was quickly formed and set out in pursuit.... After a fierce gun battle in which seven of the posse were wounded..., the slaves were finally subdued in hand-to-hand combat at a cost to the posse of three dead and numerous minor injuries....

Thirty-three blacks were tried (all adults above the age of fifteen): six were hanged and quartered because of the ferocity with which they fought the posse (of these last two totals, six were females); three were whipped only; seven were branded only and three were whipped and branded.... The negress still awaits her fate. (217–221)

Significantly, neither the trial record nor the narrator's text reveals anything of the poignant personal dimension of Dessa's experiences. Although both Dessa and the narrator recount similar experiences, the former's reading is from the perspective of a participant in struggle, while the latter's is from a position of power.

To understand the narrator's text, we must understand his psychic processes, his profession, his values. The narrator opens his journal with the conviction that "[i]t will be a curious process to delve into the mind of one of the instigators of this dreadful plot" (211). Ironically, the author's journal reveals more about the narrator's imagination and his sense of self and being-in-the-world than it does about the "negro savagery" which he proposes to examine. In his journal, Dessa's interrogator explains his intentions:

Each day I become more convinced of the necessity, the righteousness even of the work I have embarked upon. Think, I say to myself as I sit looking into the negress's face, think how it might have been had there been a work such as I envision after the Prosser uprising of 1800. Would the Vesey conspiracy and all the numerous uprisings which took place in between these two infamous events, would they have occurred? Would this wretched wench even now be huddled before me? No, I say. No, for the evil deed which blossomed forth in her and her companions would never have been planted. (212–213)[37]

What is interesting here is not only the objective of discourse for the narrator—to restore order by codifying measures of social control—but also the function of his discourse, which is to organize the narrator's world. Like Gray, the narrator believes that the moral and "natural order of the universe" have been violated by those who do not recognize "their place":

> Is it merely the untamed, perhaps even *untamable* savagery of their natures which causes them to rise up so treacherously and repudiate the natural order of the universe which has already decreed their place, or is it something more amenable to human manipulation...? (211)

The narrator's text is motivated as much by a sense of outrage as it is by a desire to discover whether or not "some disciplinary measure or restraining *word*" (211, emphasis added) might not avert further black uprisings. Moreover, the importance attached to *The Work* not only clearly privileges writing for the narrator, but assumes an added significance in that his prescriptions represent a kind of Nietzschean "will to power" through the agency of formal discourse, giving credence perhaps to Claude Lévi-Strauss's contention that writing "seems to be associated with...the exploitation of man by man."[38] The "necessity" of his work indicates the compulsion with which the narrator approaches his task, while its "righteousness" suggests his conviction of acting in accordance with divine law. Indeed, in taking Dessa out of doors from the root cellar in which she is incarcerated, the narrator seeks to free himself under the open sky "from the oppressive sense of her eyes casting a spell, not so much upon me (I know that should it ever come to a contest, God will prove stronger than the black devils she no doubt worships). No, not upon me is the spell cast, but upon the whole of the atmosphere from which I must draw breath" (213). Like Gray's report, the narrator's discourse (through the invocation of the notion of the "evil eye" causing harm or injury) allows him to impose a kind of Manichean vision on his notion of Self and "Other," organizing the world according to the dualisms of God/devil, righteousness/evil, order/disorder.

The objectivity implied by a discourse based upon a presumed neutrality is further undermined by the narrator's white, male, upper-class presumptions. Exploiting all the prevailing stereotypes of the black woman, he describes the fifteen- or sixteen-year-old Dessa as "this wench scarcely more than a pickaninny," "the virago," "this darky," and "the negress." Comparing her to "a wild and timorous animal," "a beast [crouching] in its lair," and "a raging nigger bitch," he sees her as "a cat...spitting, biting, scratching, apparently unconcerned about the harm her actions might bring to her child." More subtle perhaps than these qualities which suggest that the subject is sub-human (animal-like) are others which depict her as non-human (monstrous). She is the embodiment of evil, a "she-devil" who "casts spells" and "worships...black devils" (211–213 *passim*). Incapable of acknowledging courage or intelligence in one who is "but a female and darky at that," he challenges both her humanity and femininity: "Who would think a female so far gone in the breeding process capable of such treacherous conduct?" (222). Yet, despite his attempts to defeminize and dehumanize Dessa, her femininity, for the reader, has been established in her reveries of Kaine and their lovemaking; her motherhood has been affirmed by her pregnancy; her courage has been demonstrated through her role in the slave revolt; and her intellect, as we shall see, is evidenced in her manipulation of the interrogator/narrator.

It is the narrator's representation of Dessa as Other which enables the reader to understand the complex and fragile psychic structure upon which he erects his self-identity. What is apparent is that the narrator's conception of "otherness" serves to define, through a process of negative identification, his own self-concept. The narrator projects his irrational, submerged self onto the Other, defining himself in opposition to the projected image. Erik Erikson explains how this process of negative identification works:

> Identity formation normatively has its dark and negative side, which throughout life can remain an unruly part of the total identity. Every person and every group harbors a *negative identity* as the sum of all those identifications and identity fragments which the individual had to submerge in himself as undesirable or irreconcilable or which his group has taught him to perceive as the mark of fatal difference: in sex role or race, in class or religion.[39]

Thus we see that it is the narrator's effacement and degradation of Dessa which defines his own sense of self-superiority. It is her "savagery" which confirms his "civilization," her "bestiality" which ensures his "humanity," her "evilness" which confirms his "virtue." Erikson's comments also illuminate the subjective source and destructive outcome of the moral outrage expressed by both Turner's and Dessa's interrogators. Such a response is motivated, Erikson suggests, by the threat of losing one's "wholeness"—that is, one's sense of harmony and order—and can "serve the efficient destructiveness of the machinery of oppression and war."[40]

Williams structures her "Meditations" around the struggle between Dessa and the narrator for control of the text. But this literary or rhetorical struggle is only the linguistic equivalent of the other struggles occurring in the text: racial struggle (black vs. white), class struggle (slave vs. master), and sex-gender struggle (female vs. male). Dessa seeks to avoid imprisonment in formal discourse as well as in society. Just as she rebels against her social bondage, so Dessa rebels against her metaphorical bondage within text. She disrupts the text, just as she disrupts the social system. Indeed, it is because she has threatened both social and literary structures—because she refuses to be confined in either the narrator's text or the social order imposed by whites—that she must be "eradicated."

The prologue, as well as Dessa's interpositions into the narrator's journal, are expressed in vernacular discourse. Contrasting his own more direct, linear, formal discourse with Dessa's allusive, discursive, oral discourse, the narrator observes, "[S]he answers questions in a random manner, a loquacious, roundabout fashion—if, indeed, she can be brought to answer them at all" (225). It is her dialect that masks Dessa's true intentions from the narrator, and, at the same time, allows the reader to gain what Williams elsewhere describes as "limited access into the private and personal worlds of the slaves."[41] It is precisely Williams's affirmation of the "speech act" that links Dessa with what Houston Baker describes as "the domain of experience constituted by the oral-aural community of the slave quarters," making Dessa an "authentic voice" of the slave community.[42]

In "Meditations," the meaning of the events resides in the nature of representation, determined largely by the perspective from which they are presented. As Dessa's story unfolds, the reader discovers that Kaine, whose name ironically invokes his biblical precursor, has been murdered by his master:

> when Emmalina meet me that day, tell me Kaine don took a hoe at Mas and Mas don laid into him wid a shovel, bout bus' in his head, I jes run and when the hoe gits in my way, I let it fall, the dress in my way and I holds that up. Kaine jes layin there on usses pallet, head seepin blood, one eye closed, one bout gone. (224)

The pregnant Dessa, falsely accused by her mistress of carrying the master's child, is subsequently sold to a slave trader and becomes one of the leaders in an attempt to free her comrades. Along with her fellow slaves, Dessa manages to escape, but is recaptured and placed in confinement, where she awaits execution after the birth of her child. But Dessa refuses to be either killed in the text or "killed into text," because to do so would be to surrender the control of her life to *an-other*.[43]

If the plot of the narrative revolves around an act of insurgency, its structure is shaped by what I call "narrative insurgency." The narrator's control over his journal is subverted by a series of "interventionist" acts by Dessa that disrupt the narrator's account. Not only does Dessa refuse to give a full confession, but she circumvents the narrator's persistent attempts to extract information concerning other participants in the revolt. Unlike Turner, who enters into a kind of covenant with his interrogator, Dessa rejects such an implicit contract or consensual arrangement—which would limit the boundaries of her struggle. Despite the narrator's persistent attempts to loosen her "reluctant tongue," Dessa chooses when she will speak, what she will say, and when she will remain silent. If she preempts the narrator's story in the prologue, she continues to employ strategies of narrative insurgency—silence, non-acquiescence, evasion, and dissemblance—throughout the narrative.

Repeatedly, the narrator expresses his frustration in attempting to elicit information from Dessa:

> Oh, she may be sullen and stubbornly silent. (211)
> She refused on two occasions to speak with me. (214)
> My latest attempt to have speech with her was this morning.... (215)
> We will try what a little pressure can accomplish with her reluctant tongue. (216)
> I do not make the mistake of putting her silence down to modesty or even fear but...stubbornness. (216)
> And she turned her head and would not speak with me anymore. (225)
> I grew more than a little impatient with the response—or lack thereof—which I have thus far elicited.... (225–226)
> I had phrased this question in various ways and been met with silence. (226)
> But aside from that offensive flicking of the eye, she would not respond. (226)
> I knew when she turned her head from me that for this day, anyway, I had gotten all from her that I could. (238)
> And when I called to her she would not respond. (243)

At other times, Dessa hums and sings in order to avoid responding to the narrator's overtures:

> I admit to being at a loss as to how to begin, but...was about to order her to cease her noise. (215)
> [S]he would hum, an absurd, monotonous little tune in a minor key, the melody of which she repeated over and over. (226)
> The humming became so annoying, I was forced to ask her to cease. (235)
> I asked quickly, perhaps too quickly...and...[t]he humming started again. (238)

Dessa not only exercises control over the narrator's text through her silences and evasions, but emerges in her own voice through a series of "recitals," refusing, as it were, to allow the narrator to inscribe her. The journal entries allow Dessa to emerge at several points in the narrative, displacing the formal discourse of the writer with her own vernacular voice. Her first words, in fact, are not at all in response to the narrator, but rather constitute a speech act of existential self-affirmation, which she delivers in a "loud...even exultant note":

> "I bes. I. And he [Kaine] in air on my tongue the sun in my face. The heat in my blood. I bes he; he me. And it can't end in this place, not this time. Not this. But if it do, if it do, it was and I bes. I bes." (215–216)

If the narrator is motivated by a desire to destroy, Dessa's initial response suggests a determination "to be."

The key to her identity, however, is not in her relationship to the narrator, but in her relationship to Kaine ("'He chosed me. Mas ain't had nothing to do wid that. It Kaine what pick me out and say I be his woman'" [233]).[44] Her love for him—and his death—prompts her rebellion. Dessa recalls that Kaine's final words are "'Nigga and my [Dessa's] name, my name and Nigga.... Nigga *can* do'" (224, emphasis added). Significantly, his words empower Dessa, who *responds* to his *call* to action: "'I kill that white man cause the same reason Mas kill Kaine. Cause I *can*'" (225, emphasis added). With the death of Kaine, she senses herself as part of a network of purposeful—not arbitrary—power and struggle. The social and personal inform one another as Dessa gains knowledge of herself and access to larger social issues. Ultimately, it is through her own exercise of power and will to act that Dessa achieves the subversion of the system that oppresses her and her fellow slaves.

Similarly, it is the exercise of her rhetorical power to control her own voice and image that enables Dessa to subvert the narrator's text. She senses that formal discourse—which works for the narrator—works for her no better than the system does. She understands that part of the problem is language and representation—and, most important, who controls it. As a writer, the narrator has the power to control reality by controlling social imagery. It is because his language has the power to dispossess Dessa of humanity (just as the system has the power to dispossess her of freedom) that Dessa must challenge the narrator's representation. Her challenge to the narrator's historical record preserves between them an adversarial relationship and, at the same time, expresses Dessa's rejection of a formal discourse that excludes or misrepresents her. In the following exchange, significantly one of the few true dialogues taking place in the text ("She spoke to me of her own accord today, spoke to me, rather than the hot windless air, as had been her custom"), Dessa expresses her rejection of a language that can only perpetuate her imprisonment:

> [DESSA:] That writin what you put on that paper?...you be writin down what I say?...What you gon do wid it?
> [NARRATOR:] I told her cautiously that I would use it in a book I hoped to write.
> [DESSA:] Cause why?
> [NARRATOR:] Girl, what I put in this book cannot hurt you now. You've already been tried and judged.
> [DESSA:] Then for what you wanna do it?
> [NARRATOR:] I told her that I wrote what I did in the hope of helping others to be happy in the life that has been sent them to live...
> [DESSA:] You thank...you thank what I say now gon hep peoples be happy in the life they sent? If that be true...[w]hy I not be happy when I live it? I don't wanna talk no mo. (230–234 *passim*)

Thus, we see that Dessa, who has physically already become a part of a collective struggle, achieves class consciousness in her personal identification with others. The physical autonomy toward which she struggles finds an equivalent expression in her protest against the transposition of her voice into the racist and patriarchal white male discourse that assigns to her and others "their place," both in discourse and society.

As the story progresses, the narrator discovers himself to be increasingly haunted by Dessa. His journal entries begin to display an ambivalence, if not a change of attitude, toward his subject. After an earlier session in which he appears moved by Dessa's personal grief over the loss of her husband, the narrator comments, "It is curious...how the negress, well, how she looks in the sun. For a moment today as I watched her I could almost imagine how Vaungham [her previous owner] allowed her to get close enough to stick a knife between his ribs" (229). Hoping to cajole Dessa into disclosing more information by capitalizing upon her feelings, the narrator employs the strategy of "fram[ing] all of his questions in such a way that Kaine can be referred to in some manner." Although acknowledging, finally, that "her attachment to this Kaine appears quite sincere," he nevertheless attributes it to "the basest of physical attraction" (236–237). (One suspects that he is, in fact, describing his own feelings rather than Dessa's.) The narrator, however, apparently begins to consider the humanity of his subject, and in doing so, is driven to rationalize his own actions:

> I cannot summon up all the same sense of contempt with which I first viewed this liaison. I must confess also that I feel some slight twinge— Not of guilt, rather of *compassion* in using her attachment to the young darky as a means of eliciting information from her. But the fact is that my stratagems—while not perhaps of the most noble *type*—are used in the service of a greater good and this consideration must sweep all else before it. (237)

In their meeting of June 27, the narrator "[looks] down at the pages of [his] note-book, blank save for the day's date, or at her [Dessa]" (231). In juxtaposing the blank page and Dessa, Williams symbolizes the futility of the narrator's effort to *capture* Dessa in his text. With perhaps ironic awareness, the narrator ruefully laments at "how limited [his] vision had become" (231). Indeed, the limitations of his vision are nowhere more evident than later, during that same session, when he acknowledges the superficiality of his earlier perceptions of Dessa:

> But now I know that the thick-lipped mouth, so savage in its sullen repose, can smile and even utter small jests, that lurking behind her all too often blank gaze is something more than the cunning stubbornness which, alone, I first perceived, even noted that her skin, which appeared an ashen

black in the light of the root cellar, is the color of strong tea and that even
in the shade it is tinged with gold. (239)

Not only does the "girl" become the "woman" in his notes, but the narrator, who
has not referred to his charge by name throughout his story (suggesting his refusal
to recognize her humanity), calls her by name not less than twenty-two times in his
last four journal entries. (Significantly, Dessa drops the "O" from her given name,
Odessa, exercising not only the power, in the words of Mary Helen Washington,
"to name one's own experience" in the telling of her own story, but also the power
to name oneself.[45] She thus asserts her own identity in opposition to that imposed
by the narrator.) Indeed, as the narrator leaves to join a posse in pursuit of a group
of slave fugitives, he reflects, "We have much to talk about, Odessa and I, when we
resume our conversation" (244). Later, he continues to "look forward to resuming
my conversations with Odessa. She has a subtle presence, almost an influence which
I have only become aware of in its absence" (244). Ultimately, rather than *possessing*
his subject, the narrator himself becomes *possessed* by Dessa ("[the sheriff] charged
that I acted like one possessed" [248]).

It is finally with some irony that upon his return in the early morning of July
4 (a date the narrator notes with "wearied surprise" in his journal), he discovers
that Dessa is absent—vanished without any traceable clues to her route of escape.
The narrator learns not only that Dessa's companions have eluded the posse giving
chase, which has combed the countryside in vain pursuit of the fugitives, but that
they have managed to return and "spirit away" Dessa. Thus, in the conclusion, Dessa
is liberated from bondage as well as from the narrator's text.

The narrator's final representation of Dessa, more than anything else, threatens
the system that the narrator seeks to preserve and defend in *The Work*. Gradual
changes in the narrator's perception confirm that Dessa "works roots" on the narrator and, in so doing, succeeds in reappropriating her voice and image in what is
essentially an act of self-(re)possession. Dessa has escaped from *Roots* and the root
cellar—leaving the narrator obsessed by her absence:

She is gone. Even the smallest clue—but there was nothing, no broken
twig to point the direction, no scent which the hound could hold for more
than a short distance. Gone. *And I not even aware, not even suspecting, just—
just gone.* (248, emphasis added)

The last line suggests that meaning, for the narrator, has been determined exclusively by his own preconceptions. For this reason, he has been a misreader from the
very beginning, and Dessa's actions only confirm his misreading. Her escape means
freedom for Dessa and her unborn child and, with it, the failure of the narrator's
effort. It creates a disruption in the system and a rupture in the preparation of the
narrator's text. His sexist, racist, and classist presumptions have obscured for him

the character and motivations of his subject. Too late, the narrator realizes that he has underestimated his subject's will and intelligence: "And to think that she—*she* was so deep as to give never an indication that they [her rescuers] were then lurking about" (246, emphasis in original).

In fact, had the narrator been more attentive to Dessa's speaking (singing) text, he might have discovered some clues to her intentions. If Dessa refuses to communicate with the narrator, she does communicate with her fellow slaves in a language devised to mask her meaning. On the morning of her escape, Dessa converses with her soon-to-become emancipators through the lyrics of a spiritual:

> *Tell me, sista tell me, brotha how long will it be?*
> *Tell me, brotha tell me, sista how long will it be?*
> *That a poor sinner got to suffer, suffer here?*
> *Tell me, sista tell me, brotha when my soul be free?*
> *Tell me, oh, please tell me, when I be free?*
> *And the Lawd call me home?* (241)

Although the narrator recognizes Dessa's voice and is able to "[figure] out [the] words" (241), he understands neither the meaning nor the motive of Dessa's song. Nor does he even suspect the significance of the response of her "sistas and brothas":

> *Oh, it won't be long. Say it won't be long.*
> *Poor sinner got to suffer here.*
> *Soul's goin to heav'n, soul's gon ride that heav'nly train.*
> *Cause the Lawd have called us home.* (241)

In his failure to discern the secular significance of the spirituals, the narrator misreads them as "only…quaint piece[s] of doggerel which the darkies cunningly adapt from the scraps of scripture they are taught" (236). At best, he regards them simply as "close harmonic part singing" which he finds "rather interesting and pleasing to the ear" (241). For Dessa and her interlocutors, however, the spirituals constitute a code necessary to disguise their communication from the whites. Dessa both represents and draws on an enabling tradition of black folk and vernacular discourse, epitomized in the spirituals. According to Geneva Smitherman, "the oral tradition [in Black America] has served as a fundamental vehicle for gittin ovuh"—which she defines as spiritual and/or material survival. "That tradition," continues Smitherman, "preserves the Afro-American heritage and reflects the collective spirit of the race."[46] In other words, it is the oral tradition which has embodied the collective consciousness necessary to the struggle of the race. Historically, the consciousness and collectivity of the race, engendered by the potent oral tradition, have constituted the principal weapons by which blacks have been able to defend themselves against the technologically superior force of the media and arms controlled by the dominant class.

Significantly, both these concepts, collectivity and consciousness, are key to understanding the function of the spirituals and the secular songs. The call-response dynamic that has shaped the black oral tradition is based on a process of mutuality which "requires that one must give if one is to receive, and receiving is actively acknowledging another."[47] As an "interactive system," the call-response "seeks to synthesize speakers and listeners in a unified movement," embodying "communality rather than individuality," and emphasizing "group consciousness, cooperation, and the collective common good."[48] Unlike the narrator, who uses written language as a means by which to define, control, and establish domination over others, Dessa uses spoken language as a means of interaction and struggle. It is through oral discourse that Dessa, with the help of her companions, plots a successful escape. In the third stanza, Dessa and her companions sing in unison, expressing a unified consciousness and affirming a unity of purpose:

> *Good news, Lawd, Lawd, good news.*
> *My brotha got a seat and I so glad.*
> *I hearda from heav'n today.*
> *Good news, Lawdy, Lawd, Lawd. Good news.*
> *I don't mind what Satan say*
> *Cause I heard, yes I heard, well I heard from heav'n today.* (243)

If formal discourse, for the narrator, separates and subjugates those who are different from the privileged, then oral discourse, for Dessa, creates a unifying bond of struggle and resistance among those defined as different in the dominant discourse. Thus, Dessa's accomplishment, as Williams tells the story, is to infiltrate formal discourse not only through interventionist acts, but, indeed, through an "*outcry*" that draws on a wholly separate (oral and folk) tradition.

Language not only enables Dessa to obscure her intentions from the narrator, and oppose the system that he represents; it also functions more positively as a means of personal enrichment and empowerment. It is through Kaine's blues-like songs, which he would play "sweet-soft" on his "banger," that Dessa evokes memories re-creating her life with him ("She knew the words; it was his voice that had been the music" [208]):

> *Hey, sweet mamma, this Kaine Poppa*
> *Kaine Poppa callin his woman' name*
> *He can pop his poppa so good*
> *Make his sweet woman take to a cane.* (208)

> *Lawd, gimme wings like Noah's dove*
> *Lawd gimme me wings like Noah's dove*

I'd fly cross these fields to the one I loves
Say, hello darlin; say, how you be. (226)

The oral and folk tradition, then, provides for Dessa and the slave community (as it does for the author) not only a means of struggle and communication, but an imaginative resource, based on personal and racial verbal memory.

The unposed question, however, remains: What is to be done with the narrator's journal? Will it evolve from a pre-text into a text? Its initial status is that of a working paper or notebook for a longer, more authoritative public document. Yet the blindness of the recorder compromises the truth value of his journal and thus, presumably, its usefulness as a blueprint for the anticipated work. If the narrator's journal were to be transposed into *The Work*, its authenticity would be subverted by his misreading of Dessa's character and motivation. The journal is not a reliable text because its author is not a competent reader; his discourse is produced by a false hermeneutic.

Williams's text is about the complex interplay of power, struggle, and discourse—literary and non-literary, oral and written (and to-be-written), public and private, individual and collective. It functions as a powerful critique of Styron, Gray, and other white scholars and writers who, through their historical domination of the print media, have controlled the images of black women. Williams's story not only renders to speech a powerful precedence over writing, but also calls into question the authenticity of white, male, formal discourse on blacks and women and, in the process, suggests to the reader the limitations of literary-historical (formal) discourse.

Her work, however, raises two issues that cannot be entirely resolved: (1) Has Williams produced what Stanley Fish calls a "self-consuming artifact" in that she herself appropriates a form of discourse that her character (Dessa) implicitly and explicitly rejects?[49] Does the author, in other words, discredit the very form of discourse that makes it possible for her to deliver such a forceful critique? (2) Does Williams suggest in her relationship to Styron and in Dessa's relationship to the narrator that white males and black women cannot share a common language? Is she arguing, moreover, that whites do not know how to *read* black speech—and by extension, blacks and their experiences—making it impossible for the white writer to render an authentic portrayal of blacks?

Certainly there is an element of self-subversion in Williams's story in that the author does, in fact, problematize the very form of discourse that she herself replicates—namely, formal discourse and, more specifically, historical fiction. It would seem, however, that she replicates the form for the purpose of subverting a particular practice. While there may exist a paradox in demanding historical truth from a literary text, in which conventional meaning is regarded as immanent rather than referential, Williams's treatment acknowledges the elusiveness of her subject. In her characterization of Dessa, Williams represents an ambiguity and indeterminacy that suggest the essential "otherness" of any subject, a quality that must ultimately elude any author who bases his or her fictional character on a historical model. It is the impossibility of *knowing* that quality of otherness, explored by the author in her characterization of Dessa, that distinguishes Williams's representation from Styron's.

Moreover, in her own intervention and *"outcry"* to an alternative tradition, Williams's strategy, in a sense, replicates that of her heroine. Williams's treatment, in effect, redefines what has been traditionally regarded as "historical fiction." Less a personal and imaginative reconstruction based on the "official records" of what has happened, historical fiction as a genre becomes, for Williams, a reconstruction based on other "non-official" sources of past experience—the oral and folk tradition. It is a process that shifts emphasis from the authority of the written, closed, solip- sistic text (that is, the official record) to the oral, open, collaborative text. In other words, for Williams, the historical fiction *writer* enters into a dialogue with an *oral tradition* in a process that not only parallels the call-response pattern in Dessa's spiri- tuals, but that redefines historical fiction itself as a kind of call-response operation. Interestingly, Ralph Ellison addresses this very issue in the context of a forum held at the thirty-fourth annual meeting of the Southern Historical Association in 1968:

> If you project in fiction your version of history, then you have an obligation to think about [the] other feed-ins from the common experience which are going to put to question your particular projection of history. I don't think that history is Truth.... Here in the United States we have had a political system which wouldn't allow me to tell my story officially. Much of it is not in the history textbooks. Certain historians and untrained observers did their jobs, often very faithfully, but... the story they recorded was altered to justify racial attitudes and practices. But somehow, through our Negro American oral tradition... these reminders of the past as *Negroes* recalled it found existence and were passed along. Historical figures continued to live in stories of and theories about the human and social dynamics of slav- ery, and the effects of political decisions rendered during Reconstruction. Assertions of freedom and revolts were recalled along with triumphs of labor in the fields and on the dance floor; feats of eating and drinking and of fornication, of religious conversion and physical endurance, and of artis- tic and athletic achievements. In brief, the broad ramifications of human life as Negroes have experienced it were marked and passed along. *This record exists in oral form and it constitutes the internal history of values by which my people lived even as they were being forced to accommodate them- selves to those forces and arrangements of society that were sanctioned by official history. The result has imposed upon Negroes a high sensitivity to the ironies of historical writing and created a profound skepticism concerning the validity of most reports on what the past was like.*[50]

In response to the second issue—that is, whether or not whites can render a convincing and truthful representation of blacks—one can arguably conclude that Williams makes a case that whites will be able to decode neither black speech nor black life unless they first challenge the motives served by the dominant discourse. In one respect, the author provides a model of transformation by herself employing the (formal) discourse of domination in order to resist that same domination. In the process, she confronts the challenge faced by contemporary black writers who wish to preserve the strengths of vernacular discourse and the folk tradition within what has evolved into a formal, literate tradition. Like other modern black writers, Williams has inscribed the vernacular voice within a formal text, thereby transforming both the oral and formal traditions.

While Dessa's narrative interventions and subversions undermine some of the prevailing cultural myths and received notions about black women, Williams's "Meditations" suggests that we must revise our expectations of white- and male-authored literary and non-literary texts about blacks and women; that we must learn, in the words of Adrienne Rich, to enter "an old text from a new critical direction"; and, furthermore, that the act of "seeing" an old text "with fresh eyes" is "an act of survival." As Rich puts it, "We need to know the writing of the past, and know it differently than we have ever known it; not to pass on a tradition but to break its hold over us." In the sense that Rich uses the term, "re-vision" allows us to reclaim authentic historical and literary models and, in doing so, to liberate ourselves from old stereotypes.[51]

The major significance of Williams's text is that it draws the reader's attention to the representational and interpretative strategies of those who dominate formal discourse. It becomes a decoding device for reading texts by those who control social and literary structures. In this regard, Williams not only reveals the presumptions and pitfalls of racial- and gender-inflected cultural misreadings but, perhaps more importantly, she provides the reader with a model of how to read formal texts in which black and women's voices have been muted, suppressed, or misunderstood.[52]

3

Speaking in Tongues

Dialectics, Dialogics, and the Black Woman Writer's Literary Tradition

I am who I am, doing what I came to do, acting upon you like a drug or a
chisel *to remind you of your me-ness, as I discover you in myself.*
                                    —Audre Lorde, *Sister Outsider* (emphasis added)

There's a noisy feelin' near the cracks
crowdin' me...slips into those long, loopin' "B's"
There's a noisy feelin' near the cracks
crowdin' me...slips into those long, loopin' "B's"
of Miss Garrison's handwritin' class;
they become the wire hoops I must jump through.
It spooks my alley, it spooks my play,
more nosey now than noisy,
lookin' for a tongue
lookin' for a tongue
to get holy in.
Who can tell this feelin' where to set up church?
Who can tell this noise where to go?
A root woman workin'...a mo-jo...
                                    —Cherry Muhanji, "Popsicle Sticks"

Some years ago, three black feminist critics and scholars edited an anthology entitled *All the Women Are White, All the Blacks Are Men, But Some of Us Are Brave*, suggesting in the title the unique and peculiar dilemma of black women.[1] Since then it
has perhaps become almost commonplace for literary critics, male and female, black
and white, to note that black women have been discounted or unaccounted for in
the "traditions" of black, women's, and American literature as well as in the contemporary literary-critical dialogue. More recently, black women writers have begun
to receive token recognition as they are subsumed under the category of woman
in the feminist critique and the category of black in the racial critique. Certainly
these "gendered" and "racial" decodings of black women authors present strong and

revisionary methods of reading, focusing as they do on literary discourses regarded as marginal to the dominant literary-critical tradition. Yet the "critical insights" of one reading might well become the "blind spots" of another reading. That is, by privileging one category of analysis at the expense of the other, each of these methods risks setting up what Fredric Jameson describes as "strategies of containment," which restrict or repress different or alternative readings.[2] More specifically, blindness to what Nancy Fraser describes as "the gender subtext" can be just as occluding as blindness to *the race subtext* in the works of black women writers.[3]

Such approaches can result in exclusion at worst and, at best, a reading of part of the text as the whole—a strategy that threatens to replicate (if not valorize) the reification against which black women struggle in life and literature. What I propose is a theory of interpretation based on what I refer to as the "simultaneity of discourse," a term inspired by Barbara Smith's pioneering work on black feminist criticism.[4] This concept is meant to signify a mode of reading that examines the ways in which the perspectives of race and gender, and their interrelationships, structure the discourse of black women writers. Such an approach is intended to acknowledge and overcome the limitations imposed by assumptions of internal identity (homogeneity) and the repression of internal differences (heterogeneity) in racial and gendered readings of works by black women writers. In other words, I propose a model that seeks to account for racial difference within gender identity and gender difference within racial identity. This approach represents my effort to avoid what one critic describes as the presumed "absolute and self-sufficient" *otherness* of the critical stance in order to allow the complex representations of black women writers to steer us away from "a simple and reductive paradigm of 'otherness.'"[5]

I. Discursive Diversity: Speaking in Tongues

What is at once characteristic and suggestive about black women's writing is its interlocutory, or dialogic, character, reflecting not only a relationship with the "other(s)," but an internal dialogue with the plural aspects of self that constitute the matrix of black female subjectivity. The interlocutory character of black women's writing is, thus, not only a consequence of a dialogic relationship with an imaginary or "generalized Other," but a dialogue with the aspects of "otherness" within the self. The complex situatedness of the black woman as not only the "Other" of the Same, but also as the "other" of the other(s) implies, as we shall see, a relationship of difference and identity with the "other(s)."

It is Mikhail Bakhtin's notion of dialogism and consciousness that provides the primary model for this approach. According to Bakhtin, each social group speaks in its own "social dialect"—possesses its own unique language—expressing shared values, perspectives, ideology, and norms. These social dialects become the "languages" of heteroglossia "intersect[ing] with each other in many different ways....As such they all may be juxtaposed to one another, mutually supplement one another, contradict one another and be interrelated dialogically."[6] Yet if language, for Bakhtin, is an expression of social identity, then subjectivity (subjecthood) is constituted as social entity through the "role of [the] word as medium of consciousness." Consciousness, then, like language, is shaped by the social environment ("Consciousness becomes consciousness only...in the process of social interaction"). Moreover, "the semiotic material of the psyche is preeminently the word—*inner speech.*" Bakhtin in fact defines the relationship between consciousness and inner speech even more precisely: "Analysis would show that the units of which inner speech is constituted are certain *whole entities...[resembling] the alternating lines of a dialogue.* There was good reason why thinkers in ancient times should have conceived of inner speech as *inner dialogue.*"[7] Thus consciousness becomes a kind of "inner speech" reflecting "the outer word" in a process that links the psyche, language, and social interaction.

It is the process by which these heteroglossic voices of the other(s) "encounter one another and coexist in the consciousness of real people—first and foremost in the creative consciousness of people who write novels" that speaks to the situation of black women writers in particular, "privileged" by a social positionality that enables them to speak in dialogically racial and gendered voices to the other(s) both within and without.[8] If the psyche functions as an internalization of heterogeneous social voices, black women's speech/writing becomes at once a dialogue between self and society and between self and psyche. Writing as inner speech, then, becomes what Bakhtin would describe as "a unique form of collaboration with oneself" in the works of these writers.[9]

Revising and expanding Teresa de Lauretis's formulation of the "social subject and the relations of subjectivity to sociality," I propose a model that is intended not only to address "a subject engendered in the experiencing of race," but also what I submit is *a subject "racialized" in the experiencing of gender.*[10] Speaking both to and from the position of the other(s), black women writers must, in the words of Audre Lorde, deal not only with "the external manifestations of racism and sexism," but also "with the results of those distortions internalized within our consciousness of ourselves and one another."[11]

What distinguishes black women's writing, then, is the privileging (rather than repressing) of "the other in ourselves." Writing of Lorde's notion of self and otherness, black feminist critic Barbara Christian observes of Lorde what I argue is true to a greater or lesser degree in the discourse of black women writers: "As a black, lesbian, feminist, poet, mother, Lorde has, in her own life, had to search long and hard for *her* people. In responding to each of these audiences, in which a part of her identity lies, she refuses to give up her differences. In fact she uses them, as woman to man, black to white, lesbian to heterosexual, as a means of conducting creative dialogue."[12]

If black women speak from a multiple and complex social, historical, and cultural positionality that, in effect, constitutes black female subjectivity, then Christian's term "creative dialogue" refers to the expression of a multiple *dialogic of differences* based on this complex subjectivity. At the same time, however, black women enter into a *dialectic of identity* with those aspects of self shared with others. It is Hans-Georg Gadamer's "dialectical model of conversation," rather than Bakhtin's dialogics of discourse, that provides an appropriate model for articulating a relation of mutuality and reciprocity with the "Thou"—or intimate other(s). Whatever the critic thinks of Gadamer's views concerning history, tradition, and the like, one can still find Gadamer's emphases—especially as they complement Bakhtin's—to be useful and productive. If the Bakhtinian model is primarily adversarial, assuming that verbal communication (and social interaction) is characterized by contestation with the other(s), then the Gadamerian model presupposes as its goal a language of consensus, communality, and even identification, in which "one claims to express the other's claim and even to understand the other better than the other understands [him or herself]." In the "I-Thou" relationship proposed by Gadamer, "the important thing is . . . to experience the 'Thou' truly as a 'Thou,' that is, not to overlook [the other's] claim and to listen to what [s/he] has to say to us." Gadamer's dialectic, based on a topology of the "hermeneutical experience," privileges tradition as "a genuine partner in communication, with which we have fellowship as does the 'I' with a 'Thou.'" For black and women writers, such an avowal of tradition in the sub-dominant order, of course, constitutes an operative challenge to the dominant order. It is this rereading of the notion of tradition within a field of gender and ethnicity that supports and enables the notion of community among those who share a common history, language, and culture. If Bakhtin's dialogic engagement with the Other signifies conflict, Gadamer's monologic acknowledgment of the Thou signifies the potential of agreement. If the Bakhtinian dialogic model speaks to *the other within*, then Gadamer's speaks to *the same within*. Thus, "the [dialectic] understanding of the [Thou]" (like the dialogic understanding of the other[s]) becomes "a form of self-relatedness."[13]

It is this notion of discursive difference and identity underlying the simultaneity of discourse that typically characterizes black women's writing. Through the multiple voices that enunciate her complex subjectivity, the black woman writer not only speaks familiarly in the discourse of the other(s), but as Other she is in contestorial dialogue with the hegemonic dominant and sub-dominant or "ambiguously (non)hegemonic" discourses.[14] These writers enter simultaneously into familial, or *testimonial*, and public, or *competitive*, discourses—discourses that both affirm and challenge the values and expectations of the reader. As such, black women writers enter into testimonial discourse with black men as blacks, with white women as women, and with black women as black women.[15] At the same time, they enter into a competitive discourse with black men as women, with white women as blacks, and with white men as black women. If black women speak a discourse of racial

and gendered difference in the dominant or hegemonic discursive order, they speak
a discourse of racial and gender identity and difference in the sub-dominant discursive order. This dialogic of difference and dialectic of identity characterize both
black women's subjectivity and black women's discourse. It is the complexity of these
simultaneously homogeneous and heterogeneous social and discursive domains out
of which black women write and construct themselves (as blacks and women and,
often, as poor black women) that enables these women writers authoritatively to
speak to and engage both hegemonic and ambiguously (non)hegemonic discourse.

Janie, the protagonist in Zora Neale Hurston's *Their Eyes Were Watching God*,
demonstrates how the dialectics/dialogics of black and female subjectivity structure black women's discourse.[16] Combining personal and public forms of discourse
in the court scene where she is on trial and fighting not only for her life but against
"lying thoughts" and "misunderstanding," Janie addresses the white male judge,
a jury composed of "twelve more white men," and spectators ("eight or ten white
women" and "all the Negroes [men] for miles around" [274]). The challenge of
Hurston's character is that of the black woman writer—namely, to speak at once to
a diverse audience about her experience in a racist and sexist society where to be
black or female is to be, so to speak, "on trial." Janie not only speaks in a discourse of
gender and racial difference to the judge and jurors, but also in a discourse of gender difference (and racial identity) to the black male spectators and a discourse of
racial difference (and gender identity) to the white women spectators. Significantly,
it is the white men who constitute both judge and jury, and, by virtue of their control of power and discourse, possess the authority of life and death over the black
woman. In contrast, the black men (who are convinced that the "nigger [woman]
kin kill...jus' as many niggers as she please") and white women (who "didn't seem
too mad") read and witness/oppose a situation over which they exercise neither
power nor discourse (225, 280).

Janie's courtroom discourse also emblematizes the way in which the categories of public and private break down in black women's discourse. In the context
of Janie's courtroom scene, testimonial discourse takes on an expanded meaning,
referring to juridical, public, and dominant discourse as well as familial, private,
and non-dominant discourse. Testimonial, in this sense, derives its meaning from
both "testimony" as an official discursive mode and "testifying," defined by Geneva
Smitherman as "a ritualized form of...communication in which the speaker gives
verbal witness to the efficacy, truth, and power of some experience in which [the
group has] shared." The latter connotation suggests an additional meaning in the
context of theological discourse, where testifying refers to a "spontaneous expression to the church community [by whoever] feels the spirit."[17]

Like Janie, black women must speak in a plurality of voices as well as in a multiplicity of discourses. This discursive diversity, or simultaneity of discourse, I call
"speaking in tongues." Significantly, glossolalia, or speaking in tongues, is a practice
associated with black women in the Pentecostal Holiness Church, the church of my

childhood and the church of my mother. In the Holiness Church (or as we called it, the Sanctified Church), speaking unknown tongues (tongues known only to God) is in fact a sign of election, or holiness. As a trope it is also intended to remind us of Alice Walker's characterization of black women as artists, as "Creators," intensely rich in that spirituality which Walker sees as "the basis of Art."[18]

Glossolalia is perhaps the meaning most frequently associated with speaking in tongues. It is this connotation which emphasizes the particular, private, closed, and privileged communication between the congregant and the divinity. Inaccessible to the general congregation, this mode of communication is outside the realm of public discourse and foreign to the known tongues of humankind.

But there is a second connotation to the notion of speaking in tongues—one that suggests not glossolalia, but heteroglossia, the ability to speak in diverse known languages. While glossolalia refers to the ability to "utter the mysteries of the spirit," heteroglossia describes the ability to speak in the multiple languages of public discourse. If glossolalia suggests private, non-meditated, non-differentiated univocality, heteroglossia connotes public, differentiated, social, mediated, dialogic discourse. Returning from the trope to the act of reading, perhaps we can say that speaking in tongues connotes both the semiotic, presymbolic babble (baby talk), as between mother and child—which Julia Kristeva postulates as the "mother tongue"—and the diversity of voices, discourses, and languages described by Mikhail Bakhtin.[19]

Speaking in tongues, my trope for both glossolalia and heteroglossia, has a precise genealogical evolution in the Scriptures. In Genesis 11, God confounded the world's language when the city of Babel built a tower in an attempt to reach the heavens. Speaking in many and different tongues, the dwellers of Babel, unable to understand each other, fell into confusion, discord, and strife, and had to abandon the project. Etymologically, the name of the city Babel sounds much like the Hebrew word for "babble"—meaning confused, as in baby talk. Babel, then, suggests the two related, but distinctly different, meanings of speaking in tongues, meanings borne out in other parts of the Scriptures. The most common is that implied in 1 Corinthians 14—the ability to speak in unknown tongues. According to this interpretation, speaking in tongues suggests the ability to speak in and through the spirit. Associated with glossolalia—speech in unknown tongues—it is ecstatic, rapturous, inspired speech, based on a relation of intimacy and identification between the individual and God.

If Genesis tells of the disempowerment of a people by the introduction of different tongues, then Acts 2 suggests the empowerment of the disciples who, assembled on the day of Pentecost in the upper room of the temple in Jerusalem, "were filled with the Holy Spirit and began to speak in other tongues." Although the people thought the disciples had "imbibed a strange and unknown wine," it was the Holy Spirit that had driven them, filled with ecstasy, from the upper room to speak among the five thousand Jews surrounding the temple. The Scriptures tell us that the tribes of Israel all understood them, each in his own tongue. The Old Testament, then, suggests the dialogics of difference in its diversity of discourse, while the New Testament, in its unifying language of the spirit, suggests the dialectics of identity. And if the Bakhtinian model suggests the multiplicity of speech as suggested in the dialogics of difference, then Gadamer's model moves toward a unity of understanding in its dialectics of identity.

It is the first as well as the second meaning that we privilege in speaking of black women writers: the first connoting polyphony, multivocality, and plurality of voices, and the second signifying intimate, private, inspired utterances. Through their intimacy with the discourse of the other(s), black women writers weave into their work competing and complementary discourses—discourses that seek both to adjudicate competing claims and witness common concerns.[20]

Also interesting is the link between the gift of tongues, the gift of prophecy, and the gift of interpretation. While distinguishing between these three gifts, the Scriptures frequently conflate or conjoin them. If to speak in tongues is to utter mysteries in and through the spirit, to prophesy is to speak to others in a (diversity of) language(s) that the congregation can understand. The Scriptures would suggest that the disciples were able to perform both. I propose, at this juncture, an enabling critical fiction—that it is black women writers who are the modern-day apostles, empowered by experience to speak as poets and prophets in many tongues. With this critical gesture, I also intend to signify a deliberate intervention by black women writers into the canonic tradition of sacred/literary texts.[21]

II. A Discursive Dilemma

In their works, black women writers have encoded oppression as a discursive dilemma, that is, their works have consistently raised the problem of the black woman's relationship to power and discourse. Silence is an important element of this code. The classic black woman's text *Their Eyes Were Watching God* charts the female protagonist's development from voicelessness to voice, from silence to tongues. Yet this movement does not exist without intervention by the other(s)—who speak for and about black women. In other words, it is not that black women, in the past, have had nothing to say, but rather that they have had no say. The absence of black female voices has allowed others to inscribe, or write, and ascribe to, or read, them. The notion of speaking in tongues, however, leads us away from an examination of how the Other has written/read black women and toward an examination of how black women have written the other(s)' writing/reading them.

Using the notion of "speaking in tongues" as our model, let us offer a kind of paradigmatic reading of two works that encode and resist the material and discursive dilemma of the black woman writer. Sherley Anne Williams's *Dessa Rose* and Toni Morrison's *Sula* are novels that emphasize, respectively, the *inter*cultural and *intra*cultural racial and gendered sites from which black women speak, as well as the signs under which they speak in both these milieus.[22] Artificial though this separation may be—since, as we have seen, black women are located simultaneously within both these discursive domains—such a distinction makes possible an examination of black women's literary relations to both dominant and sub-dominant discourse. These works also allow us to compare the suppression of the black female voice in the dominant discourse with its repression in the sub-dominant discourse.[23] Finally, they provide models for the disruption of the dominant and sub-dominant discourse by black and female literary expressivity, as well as for the appropriation and transformation of these discourses.

The heroine of Sherley Anne Williams's novel *Dessa Rose* is a fugitive slave woman introduced to the reader as "the Darky" by Adam Nehemiah, a white male writer interviewing her in preparation for a forthcoming book, *The Roots of Rebellion in the Slave Population and Some Means of Eradicating Them* (or, more simply, *The Work*). The opening section of the novel is structured primarily by notations from Nehemiah's journal, based on his interactions with the slave woman during her confinement in a root cellar while awaiting her fate at the gallows. The latter section, describing her adventures as a fugitive involved in a scam against unsuspecting slaveholders and traders, is narrated primarily in the voice of Dessa (as the slave woman calls herself) after she has managed, with the assistance of fellow slaves, to escape the root cellar. At the end of the novel, the writer-interviewer, Adam Nehemiah, still carrying around his notes for *The Work*, espies the fugitive Dessa.

Brandishing a poster advertising a reward for her recapture and a physical description of her identifying markings (an *R* branded on the thigh and whip-scarred hips), Adam Nehemiah coerces the local sheriff into detaining Dessa for identification. Significantly, Adam Nehemiah, named after his precursor—the archetypal white male namer, creator, and interpreter—attempts not only to remand Dessa into slavery but to inscribe her experiences as a slave woman through a discourse that suppresses her voice. Like the Adam of Genesis, Nehemiah asserts the right of ownership through the privilege of naming. Not only is his claim of discursive and material power held together symbolically in his name, but his acts and his words conflate: Nehemiah not only wishes to capture Odessa (as he calls her) in words that are instructive to the preservation of slavery, but he wishes to confine her in material slavery. Just as the biblical Nehemiah constructed the wall to protect the Israelites against attack by their enemies, so Williams's Nehemiah sets out to write a manual designed to protect the American South against insurrection by the slaves. Ironically, the character of Nehemiah, a patriot and leader of the Jews after the years of Babylonian captivity, is reread in the context of the Old South as a racist and expert on the "sound management" of slaves.[24]

Dessa fears that exposure of her scars/branding will confirm her slave status. As she awaits the arrival of Ruth, the white woman who abets in the perpetration of the scam, Dessa thinks to herself, "I could feel everyone of them scars, the one roped partway to my navel that the waist of my draws itched, the corduroyed welts across my hips, and R on my thighs" (223). What interests me here is the literal inscription of Dessa's body, signified by the whip marks and, more specifically, the branded *R*, as well as the white male writer-cum-reader's attempt to exercise discursive domination over Dessa. Seeking to inscribe black female subjectivity, the white male, in effect, relegates the black woman to the status of discursive object, or spoken subject. The location of the inscriptions—in the area of the genitalia—moreover, signals an attempt to inscribe the sign *slave* in an area that marks her as *woman* ("Scar tissue plowed through her pubic region so no hair would ever grow there again" [154]). The effect is to attempt to deprive the slave woman of her femininity and render the surface of her skin a parchment upon which meaning is etched by the whip/pen of white patriarchal authority and sealed by the firebrand. Together, these inscriptions produce the meaning of black female subjectivity within the discursive domain of slavery.[25] Importantly, the literal inscription of the flesh emphasizes what Monique Wittig, insisting on "the *material* oppression of individuals by discourses," describes as the "unrelenting tyranny that [male discourses] exert upon our *physical* and *mental* selves."[26] Dessa is ordered by the sheriff to lift her skirt so that these inscriptions can be "read" by her potential captors. (Perhaps we should read the *R* on Dessa's thigh as part of an acrostic for *Read*.) The signifying function of her scars is reinforced when Dessa recognizes that "[Nehemiah] wouldn't have to say nothing. Sheriff would see [i.e., read] that for himself" (223). Her remarks also suggest the mortal consequence of such a reading, or misreading:[27] "This [the scars] was what would betray me.... these white mens would kill me" (223).

If Williams's *Dessa Rose* contains a representation of the inscription of *black female* in the dominative white and male discourse, then Morrison's *Sula* contains a representation of *female* ascription in black sub-dominative discourse. If in the context of the white community's discourse Dessa is suppressed as woman *and* black, in the discourse of the black community she is repressed as woman.

Like Dessa, Sula is marked. Unlike Dessa, Sula is marked from birth. Hers is a mark of nativity—a biological rather than cultural inscription, appropriate in this instance because it functions to mark her as a "naturally" inferior female within the black community.[28] The birthmark, "spread[ing] from the middle of the lid toward the eyebrow" (45), is associated with a series of images. For her mother, Hannah, Sula's birthmark "looked more and more like a stem and a rose" (64). Although in European and Eurocentric culture the rose is the gift of love as well as the traditional romantic symbol of female beauty and innocence (lily-white skin and rose blush), it is a symbol that has been appropriated by black women writers from Frances Ellen Watkins Harper, who uses it as a symbol of romantic love, to Alice Walker, who associates it with sexual love.[29]

Jude, the husband of Nel, Sula's best friend, refers to the birthmark as a "copperhead" and, later, as "the rattlesnake over her eye" (89). If the image of the rose suggests female romantic love and sexuality, then the snake evokes the archetypal Garden and the story of Eve's seduction by the serpent.[30] The association is significant in light of the subsequent seduction scene between Jude and Sula, for it is Jude's perception of the snake imagery that structures his relationship with Sula, suggesting not only that the meaning he ascribes to the birthmark reflects the potential of his relationship with her, but that, on a broader level, it is the "male gaze" that constitutes female subjectivity. At the same time, Morrison redeploys the role of Other in a way that suggests how the black woman as Other is used to constitute (black) male subjectivity.

The community, "clearing up," as it thought, "the meaning of the birthmark over her eye," tells the reader that "it was not a stemmed rose, or a snake, it was Hannah's ashes marking Sula from the very beginning" (99). (That Sula had watched her mother burn to death was her grandmother's contention and the community gossip.) If Jude represents the subject constituted in relation to the black woman as Other, the community represents a culture as constituted in relation to the black woman as Other:

> Their conviction of Sula's evil changed them in accountable yet mysterious ways. Once the source of their personal misfortune was identified, they had leave to protect and love one another. They began to cherish their husbands and wives, protect their children, repair their homes and in general band together against the devil in their midst. (102)

Sula signifies, for the community, the chaos and evil against which it must define and protect itself. Convinced that she bears the mark of the devil because of her association with Shadrack, the town reprobate, the community closes ranks against one who transgresses the boundaries prescribed for women.

For Shadrack, the shell-shocked World War I veteran who has become the community pariah, Sula's birthmark represents "the mark of the fish he loved"—the tadpole (134). A symbol of the primordial beginnings of life in the sea, the tadpole represents potential, transformation, and rebirth. Such an image contrasts with the apocalyptic ending of life by fire suggested by the community's perception of Hannah's ashes.[31] As an amphibious creature, the tadpole has the capacity to live both terrestrially and aquatically. Etymologically, Sula's name is derived from the designation of a genus of seabird, again an image associated with a dual environment—aquatic and aerial. These contrasts suggestively position Sula at the crossroads or intersection of life and death, land and sea, earth and air. Thus both the mark and the designation are particularly appropriate for the black woman as one situated within two social domains (black and female) and, as such, implicated in both a racial and gendered discourse.

But it is the black community—the Bottom—that provides the setting for the action in Morrison's novel, and it is the men who have the final say in the community: "It was the men," observes the narrator, "who gave [Sula] the final label, who fingerprinted her for all time" (197). The men in the community speak a racial discourse that reduces Sula finally to her sexuality: "The word was passed around" that "Sula slept with *white* men" (97, emphasis added). It is thus her sexuality, read through the race relation, which structures her subjectivity within the male-dominated discourse of the black community.

The power of male discourse and naming is also suggested in the epithet directed to the twelve-year-old Sula as she, along with her friend Nel, saunters by Edna Finch's ice cream parlor one afternoon, passing the old and young men of the Bottom:

> Pigmeat. The words were in all their minds. And one of them, one of the young ones, said it aloud. His name was Ajax, a twenty-one-year-old pool haunt of sinister beauty. Graceful and economical in every movement, he held a place of envy with men of all ages for his magnificently foul mouth. In fact he seldom cursed, and the epithets he chose were dull, even harmless. His reputation was derived from the way he handled words. When he said "hell" he hit the *h* with his lungs and the impact was greater than the achievement of the most imaginative foul mouth in town. He could say "shit" with a nastiness impossible to imitate. (43)

Not only does the language itself take on a special potency when exercised by males, but the epithet "pigmeat," which Ajax confers on Sula, still has a powerful hold on her seventeen years later, when at twenty-nine, having traveled across the country and returned to the Bottom, she is greeted by the now thirty-eight-year-old Ajax at her screen door: "Sula... was curious. She knew nothing about him except the word he had called out to her years ago and the feeling he had excited in her then" (110).

The images associated with Sula's birthmark connote, as we have seen, a plurality of meanings. These images become not only symbols of opposition and ambiguity associated with the stemmed rose, snake, fire, and tadpole, but they invoke the qualities of permanence and mutability (nature and culture) inherent in the sign of the birthmark, the meaning and valence of which changes with the reading and the reader. At one point, Nel, Sula's complement in the novel, describes her as one who "helped others define themselves," that is, one who takes on the complementary aspect of the Other in the process of constituting subjectivity. As if to underscore Sula's signifying function as absence or mutability, Sula is described as having "no center" and "no ego," "no speck around which to grow" (103). The plurality and flux of meaning ascribed to the birthmark share some of the characteristics of the Sign or, perhaps more precisely, the Signifier. Sula's association with the birthmark gradually evolves, through synecdoche, into an identification between the subject/object and the Sign. Thus her entry into the sub-dominative discursive order confers on her the status of "a free-floating signifier," open to diverse interpretations.

The inscription (writing) of Dessa and the ascription (reading) of Sula together encode the discursive dilemma of black women in hegemonic and ambiguously (non)hegemonic discursive contexts. However, these works also embody a code of resistance to the discursive and material dominance of black women. To different degrees and in different ways, Williams and Morrison fashion a counter-discourse within their texts.

III. Disruption and Revision

In negotiating the discursive dilemma of their characters, these writers accomplish two objectives: the self-inscription of black womanhood, and the establishment of a dialogue of discourses with the other(s). The self-inscription of black women requires disruption, rereading and rewriting the conventional and canonical stories, as well as revising the conventional generic forms that convey these stories. Through this interventionist, intertextual, and revisionary activity, black women writers enter into dialogue with the discourses of the other(s). Disruption—the initial response to hegemonic and ambiguously (non)hegemonic discourse—and revision (rewriting and rereading) together suggest a model for reading black and female literary expression.

Dessa's continued rejection of Adam Nehemiah's inscription suggests that we must read with some measure of credence her claims of being mis-recognized. ("I don't know this master, Mistress," she says. "They mistook me for another Dessa, Mistress" [226–227].) Ultimately, Dessa's insistence on *méconnaissance* is vindicated in the failure of Nehemiah's attempts either to *con*fine her in the social system or *de*fine her in the dominant discourse.

Dessa not only succeeds in rupturing the narrator's discourse at the outset of the novel through a series of interventionist acts—singing, evasion, silence, non-acquiescence, and dissemblance—but she employs these strategies to effect her escape and seize discursive control of the story.[32] Moreover, Dessa's repeated use of the word *track* (a term connoting both pursuit and inscription) in reference to Nehemiah takes on added significance in the context of both her inscription and revision. Tracking becomes the object of her reflections: "Why this white man *track* me down like he owned me, like a bloodhound on my *trail*," and later, "crazy white man, *tracking* me all cross the country like he owned me" (225, emphasis added). In other words, Nehemiah *tracks* Dessa in an attempt to establish ownership—that is, colonization—of her body. Yet tracking also suggests that Dessa's flight becomes a text that she writes and Nehemiah reads. His tracking (i.e., reading of Dessa's body as text) thus becomes the means by which he attempts to capture her (i.e., suppress her voice in the production of his own text).

If the pursuit/flight pattern emblematizes a strategic engagement for discursive control, Dessa's tracks also mark her emergence as narrator of her own story. It is her escape—loosely speaking, her "making tracks"—that precludes the closure/completion of Nehemiah's book. The story of Dessa's successful revolt and escape, in effect, prefigures the rewriting of *The Work*—Nehemiah's projected treatise on the control of slaves and the prevention of slave revolts. The epilogue of the novel, recounted from Dessa's perspective and in her own voice, establishes her as the successful author of her own narrative. Tracking thus becomes a metaphor for writing/reading from the white male narrator's perspective, and a metaphor for revision (rewriting/rereading) from Dessa's. Creating her own track therefore corresponds to Dessa's assumption of discursive control of the novel, that is, the telling of her own story. In flight, then, Dessa challenges the material and discursive elements of her oppression and, at the same time, provides a mode for writing as struggle.

Nehemiah's inability to capture Dessa in print is paralleled, finally, in his failure to secure her recapture. As Dessa walks out of the sheriff's office, Nehemiah cries: "I know it's her...I got her down here in my book." Leaving, Dessa tells the reader, "And he reach and took out that little black-bound pad he wrote in the whole time I knowed him" (231). But the futility of his efforts is represented in the reactions of the onlookers to the unbound pages of Nehemiah's notebook as they tumble and scatter to the floor:

> [SHERIFF] Nemi, ain't nothing but some scribbling on here.... Can't no one read this.
> [RUTH] And these [pages] is blank, sheriff. (232)

Finally, in two dramatic acts of self-entitlement, Dessa reaffirms her ability to name herself and her own experience. In the first instance, she challenges Nehemiah's efforts to capture her—in person and in print: "Why, he didn't even know how to call my name—talking about Odessa" (225, emphasis added). And in the second, after her release she informs Ruth, her white accomplice and alleged mistress, "My name Dessa, Dessa Rose. Ain't no O to it" (232). She is, of course, distinguishing between Odessa, an ascription by the white, male slave master (used by both Nehemiah and Ruth), and Dessa, her entitlement proper. Her rejection of the O signifies her rejection of the inscription of her body by the other(s). In other words, Dessa's repudiation of the O (Otherness?) signifies her always already presence— what Ralph Ellison describes as the unquestioned humanity of the slave.[33] She deletes nothing—except the white, male other's inscription/ascription.[34]

In the epilogue, Dessa once again affirms the importance of writing oneself and one's own history. It is a responsibility that devolves upon the next generation, privileged with a literacy Dessa herself has been denied: *"My mind wanders. This is why I have it wrote down, why I has the child say it back. I never will forget Nemi trying to read [and write] me, knowing I had put myself in his hands. Well this the children have heard from our own lips"* (236, italics and emphasis in original). Yet, as Alice Walker might say, the story bears the mother's signature.[35]

While Dessa, through interventions and rewriting, rejects white male attempts to write and read black female subjectivity, Sula, through disruption and rereading, repudiates black male readings of black female subjectivity. (Significantly, black males, like white females, lack the power to *write*, but not the power to *read*, black women.) If it is her sexuality that structures Sula within the confines of black (male) discourse, it is also her sexuality that creates a rupture in that discourse. It is through the act of sexual intercourse that Sula discovers "the center of…silence" and a "loneliness so profound *the word itself had no meaning*" (106, emphasis added). The "desperate terrain" that she reaches, the "high silence of orgasm" (112), is a nodal point that locates Sula in the interstices of the closed system of (black) male signifi- cation. She has, in effect, "[leapt] from the edge" of discourse "into soundlessness" and "[gone] down howling" (106). Howling, a unary movement of undifferentiated sound, contrasts with the phonic differentiation on which the closed system of lan- guage is based. Like the birthmark, which is the symbolic sign of life, the howl is the first sound of life—not yet broken down and differentiated to emerge as intersubjec- tive communication, or discourse. The howl, signifying a prediscursive mode, thus becomes an act of self-reconstitution as well as an act of subversion or resistance to the network of signification represented by the symbolic order. The "high silence of orgasm" and the howl allow temporary retreats from or breaks in the dominant discourse. Like Dessa's evasions and interventions, Sula's silences and howls serve to disrupt or subvert the "symbolic function of the language." It is precisely these violations or transgressions of the symbolic order that allow for the expression of the suppressed or repressed aspects of black female subjectivity. The reconstitu- tive function of Sula's sexuality is suggested in the image of the "post-coital private- ness in which she met herself, welcomed herself, and joined herself in matchless harmony" (107). The image is that of symbiosis and fusion—a stage or condition represented in psychoanalysis as pre-Oedipal and anterior to the acquisition of lan- guage or entry into the symbolic order.[36]

It is through the howl of orgasm that Sula discovers a prediscursive center of experience that positions her at a vantage point outside the dominant discursive order. The howl is a form of speaking in tongues and a linguistic disruption that serves as the precondition for Sula's entry into language. Unless she breaks the con- ventional structures and associations of the dominant discourse, Sula cannot enter through the interstices.[37] (This reading of *Sula*, in effect, reverses the biblical move- ment from contestorial, public discourse to intimate, familial discourse.)

In contrast to the howl, of course, is the stunning language of poetic metaphor with which Sula represents her lover and the act of love:

> If I take a chamois and rub real hard on the bone, right on the ledge of your cheek bone, some of the black will disappear. It will flake away into the chamois and underneath there will be gold leaf….And if I take a nail file or even Eva's old paring knife….and scrape away at the gold, it will fall away and there will be alabaster….Then I can take a chisel and small tap hammer and tap away at the alabaster. It will crack then like ice under the pick, and through the breaks I will see the [fertile] loam. (112, italics in original)

It is an eloquent passage—not of self-representation, however, but of representation of the male Other. If Sula cannot find the language, the trope, the form, to embody her own "experimental" life, she "engage[s] her tremendous curiosity and her gift for metaphor" in the delineation of her lover. The poetic penetration of her lover through layers of black, gold leaf, alabaster, and loam signals that her assumption of a "masculine" role parallels the appropriation of the male voice, prerequisite for her entry into the symbolic order. (Such an appropriation is, of course, earlier signaled by the association of the birthmark with the stemmed rose, the snake, the tadpole— a series of phallic images.)

I propose, however, in the spirit of the metaphor, to take it one step further and suggest that the imagery and mode of the prose poem form a kind of model for the deconstructive function of black feminist literary criticism—and to the extent that literature itself is always an act of interpretation, a model for the deconstructive function of black women's writing—that is, to interpret or interpenetrate the signifying structures of the dominant and sub-dominant discourse in order to formulate a critique and, ultimately, a transformation of the hegemonic white and male symbolic order.

If Williams's primary emphasis is on the act of rewriting, then Morrison's is on the act of rereading. Perhaps the best example of Sula's deconstructive rereading of the black male text is exemplified in her reformulation of Jude's "whiny tale" describing his victimization as a black man in a world that the "white man running":

> I don't know what the fuss is about. I mean, everything in the world loves you. White men love you. They spend so much time worrying about your penis they forget their own. The only thing they want to do is cut off a nigger's privates. And if that ain't love and respect I don't know what is. And white women? They chase you all to every corner of the earth, feel for you under every bed.... Now ain't that love? They think rape soon's they see you, and if they don't get the rape they looking for, they scream it anyway just so the search won't be in vain. Colored women worry themselves into bad health just trying to hang on to your cuffs. Even little children— white and black, boys and girls—spend all their childhood eating their hearts out 'cause they think you don't love them. And if that ain't enough, you love yourselves. Nothing in this world loves a black man more than another black man. (89)

As Adrienne Munich points out, "Jude's real difficulties allow him to maintain his male identity, to exploit women, and not to examine himself." Sula, she argues, turns "Jude's story of powerlessness into a tale of power." Through a deconstructive reading of his story, Sula's interpretation demonstrates how Jude uses "racial politics [to mask] sexual politics."[38]

If Sula's silences and howls represent breaks in the symbolic order, then her magnificent prose poem looks to the possibilities of appropriating the male voice as prerequisite for entry into that order. Dessa similarly moves from intervention to appropriation and revision of the dominant discourse. As the author of her own story, Dessa writes herself into the dominant discourse and, in the process, transforms it. What these two works suggest in variable, but interchangeable, strategies is that, in both dominant and sub-dominant discourses, the initial expression of a marginal presence takes the form of disruption—a departure or a break with conventional semantics and/or phonetics. This rupture is followed by a rewriting or rereading of the dominant story, resulting in a "delegitimation" of the prior story or a "displacement" that shifts attention "to the other side of the story."[39] Disruption—the initial response to hegemonic and ambiguously (non)hegemonic discourse—and the subsequent response, revision (rewriting or rereading), together represent a progressive model for black and female utterance. I propose, in an appropriation of a current critical paradigm, that Sula's primal scream constitutes a "womblike matrix" in which soundlessness can be transformed into utterance, unity into diversity, formlessness into form, chaos into art, silence into tongues, and glossolalia into heteroglossia.

It is this quality of speaking in tongues—that is, multivocality—I further propose, that accounts in part for the popularity and critical success of black women's writing. The engagement of multiple others broadens the audience for black women's writing, for like the disciples of Pentecost who spoke in diverse tongues, black women, speaking out of the specificity of their own racial and gender experiences, are able to communicate in a diversity of discourses. If the ability to communicate accounts for the popularity of black women writers, it also explains much of the controversy surrounding some of this writing. Black women's writing speaks with what Mikhail Bakhtin would describe as heterological or "centrifugal force" but (in a sense somewhat different from that which Bakhtin intended) also unifying or "centripetal force."[40] This literature speaks as much to the notion of commonality and universalism as it does to the sense of difference and diversity.

Yet the objective of these writers is not, as some critics suggest, to move from margin to center, but to remain on the borders of discourse, speaking from the vantage point of the insider/outsider. As Bakhtin further suggests, fusion with the (dominant) Other can only duplicate the tragedy or misfortune of the Other's dilemma. On the other hand, as Gadamer makes clear, "there is a kind of experience of the 'Thou' that seeks to discover things that are typical in the behavior of [the other] and is able to make predictions concerning another person on the basis of [a commonality] of experience."[41] To maintain this insider/outsider position, or perhaps what Myra Jehlen calls the "extra-terrestial fulcrum" that Archimedes never acquired, is to see the other, but also to see what the other cannot see, and to use this insight to enrich both our own and the other's understanding.[42]

As gendered and racial subjects, black women speak/write in multiple voices— not all simultaneously or with equal weight, but with various and changing degrees of intensity, privileging one *parole* and then another. One discovers in these writers a kind of internal dialogue reflecting an *intrasubjective* engagement with the *intersubjective* aspects of self, a dialectic neither repressing difference nor, for that matter, privileging identity, but rather expressing engagement with the social aspects of self ("the other[s] in ourselves"). It is the subjective plurality (rather than the notion of the cohesive or fractured subject) that, finally, allows the black woman to become an expressive site for a dialectics/dialogics of identity and difference.

Unlike Harold Bloom's "anxiety of influence" model configuring a white male poetic tradition shaped by an adversarial dialogue between literary fathers and sons (as well as the appropriation of this model by Joseph Skerrett and others to discuss black male writers), and unlike Sandra Gilbert and Susan Gubar's "anxiety of authorship" model informed by the white woman writer's sense of "dis-ease" within a white patriarchal tradition, the present model configures a tradition of black women writers generated less by neurotic anxiety or dis-ease than by an emancipatory impulse that freely engages both hegemonic and ambiguously (non)hegemonic discourse.[43] Summarizing Morrison's perspectives, Andrea Stuart perhaps best expresses this notion:

> I think you [Morrison] summed up the appeal of black women writers when you said that white men, quite naturally, wrote about themselves and their world; white women tended to write about white men because they were so close to them as husbands, lovers and sons; and black men wrote about white men as the oppressor or the yardstick against which they measured themselves. Only black women writers were not interested in writing about white men and therefore they freed literature to take on other concerns.[44]

In conclusion, I return to the gifts of the Holy Spirit: 1 Corinthians 12 tells us that "the [one] who speaks in tongues should pray that [s/he] may interpret what [s/he] says." Yet the Scriptures also speak to interpretation as a separate gift—the ninth and final gift of the spirit. Might I suggest that if black women writers speak in tongues, then it is we black feminist critics who are charged with the hermeneutical task of interpreting tongues?

Toni Morrison's *Beloved*

Re-Membering the Body as Historical Text

Now, women forget all those things they don't want to remember. The dream is the truth. Then they act and do things accordingly.... So the beginning of this was a woman and she had come back from burying the dead.

—Zora Neale Hurston, *Their Eyes Were Watching God*

We tell stories because in the last analysis human lives need and merit being narrated. This remark takes on its full force when we refer to the necessity to save the history of the defeated and the lost. The whole history of suffering cries out for vengeance and calls for narrative.

—Paul Ricoeur, *Time and Narrative*

Upon the death of the other we are given to memory, and thus to interiorization... since Freud, this is how the "normal" "work of mourning" is often described. It entails a movement in which an interiorizing idealization takes in itself or upon itself the body and voice of the other, the other's visage and person, ideally and quasi-literally devouring them. This mimetic interiorization is not fictive; it is the origin of fiction, of apocryphal figuration. It takes place in a body. Or rather, it makes for a body, voice, and a soul which, although "ours," did not exist and had no meaning *before* this possibility that one *must* always begin by remembering, and whose trace must be followed.

—Jacques Derrida, *Memories for Paul de Man* (emphasis in original)

I had brought not a child but suffering into the world and it, suffering, refused to leave me, insisted on coming back, on haunting me, permanently. One does not bear children in pain, it's pain that one bears: the child is pain's representative and once it is delivered moves in for good.... [A] mother is... marked by pain, she succumbs to it.

—Julia Kristeva, "Stabat Mater"

There is an "uncanniness" about this past that a present occupant has expelled (or thinks it has) in an effort to take its place. The dead haunt the living. The past: it "re-bites" [*il remord*] (it is a secret and repeated biting). History is "cannibalistic," and memory becomes the closed arena of conflict between two contradictory operations: forgetting, which is not something passive, a loss, but an action directed against the past; and the mnemic trace, the return of what was forgotten.... More generally speaking, an autonomous order is founded upon what it eliminates; it produces a "residue" condemned to be forgotten. But what was excluded... reinfiltrates the place of its origin—It resurfaces,

it troubles, it turns the present's feeling of being "at home" into an illusion, it lurks—this "wild," this "obscene," this "filth," this "resistance" of
"superstition"—within the walls of the residence, and behind the back
of the owner (the ego), or over its objections, it inscribes there the law
of the other.

—Michel de Certeau, *Heterologies: Discourse on the Other*

Describing nineteenth-century slave narratives, Toni Morrison observes, "No slave
society in the history of the world wrote more—or more thoughtfully—about its
own enslavement." Yet, for Morrison, the narratives, with their "instructive" and
"moral" force, are incomplete:

> Over and over, the writers pull the narrative up short with a phrase such
> as, "but let us drop a veil over these proceedings too terrible to relate." In
> shaping the experience to make it palatable to those who were in a position
> to alleviate it, they were silent about many things, and they "forgot" many
> other things....[1]

"Things too terrible to relate" were most often the sexual exploitation of slave women
by white men. Convention allowed, indeed almost demanded, that these violations
be named but not described. Morrison continues, "But most importantly—at least
for me—there was no mention of their [the slaves'] *interior life*."[2] The writer's "job"—
as Morrison sees it—"becomes how to rip that veil drawn over proceedings too terrible to relate," to "find and expose a truth about the interior life of people who didn't
write it," to "fill in the blanks that the slave narratives left, to part the veil that was so
frequently drawn," and, finally, "to implement the stories that [she has] heard."[3]

Morrison's image of the veil revises a DuBoisian metaphor that was originally
intended to suggest the division between blacks and whites in American society.[4]
Rather than measuring a division *between* the races, however, Morrison's veil measures a division *within* the race—a psychic and expressive boundary separating the
speakable from the *unspeakable* and the *unspoken*.[5] Her task as a writer, therefore, is
to transgress these discursive boundaries by setting up a complementary and dialogic relationship between the "interiority" of her own work and the "exteriority"
of the slave narrative.

Morrison, then, aims to restore a dimension of the repressed personal in a
manifestly political discourse. In some ways, the texts of the slave narratives can be
regarded as classic examples of the "return of the repressed," primarily because the
events relating to violence and violation (which are self-censored or edited out)

return again and again in "veiled allusions." To the degree that her work is intended to *resurrect* stories *buried* and *express* stories *repressed*, Morrison's relation to the slave narrators, as well as the relation of her text to its precursor narratives, can be profitably compared not only to the relation of the historian to informant but also to that of the analyst to analysand.

Dedicating her novel *Beloved* to the "Sixty Million and more" who failed to survive the Middle Passage, Morrison sets out to give voice to the "disremembered and unaccounted for"—the women and children who left no written records.[6] The epigraph from Romans 9:25 prefigures the writer's purpose of reclaiming this "lost tribe":

> *I will call them my people,*
> *which were not my people;*
> *and her beloved*
> *which was not beloved.*

By citing a New Testament passage that echoes a passage from the Old Testament, the author not only problematizes the nature of the relation between the past and the present but also thematizes the importance of historical reclamation and repossession. As Jehovah reclaimed the Israelites after their apostasy (figured in Hosea as spiritual adultery), so Morrison seeks to repossess the African and slave ancestors after their historic violation (figured in *Beloved* as physical rape). Further, Morrison reinscribes the tension between Old Testament law and New Testament spirit. Significantly, it is the epistles of Paul (Romans and Galatians, in particular) which announce that the doctrine of justification by deeds under the Old Dispensation of the Law is revised through justification by grace under the New Dispensation of the Spirit.[7] Engaging the Scriptures as a kind of intertext, Morrison enacts in her novel an opposition between the law and the spirit, redeeming her characters from the "curse of the law" as figured in the master's discourse. In her rewriting of Scripture, Morrison ushers in an ironic new dispensation figured not by the law of the (white) Father but by the spirit of the (black and female) child, Beloved. Thus, Morrison challenges the hegemonic status of the (primarily male) slave narratives as well as the "canonical" history embodied in the master('s) narratives in a project that holds both more accountable to the "disremembered and unaccounted for."

Like several of her contemporaries, Morrison seeks to achieve these ends in a novel that both historicizes fiction and fictionalizes history.[8] In the following passage she recollects the events on which the novel was based:

> I...remember being obsessed by two or three little fragments of stories that I heard from different places. One was a newspaper clipping about a woman named Margaret Garner in 1851. It said that the Abolitionists made a great deal out of her case because she had escaped from Kentucky...with her four children. She lived in a little neighborhood just outside of Cincinnati

and she had killed her children. She succeeded in killing one; she tried to kill two others. The interesting thing, in addition to that, was the interviews that she gave. She was a young woman. In the inked pictures of her she seemed a very quiet, very serene-looking woman and everyone who interviewed her remarked about her serenity and tranquility. She said, "I will not let those children live how I have lived." She had run off into a little wood shed right outside her house to kill them because she had been caught as a fugitive. And she made up her mind that they would not suffer the way that she had and it was better for them to die. They put her in jail for a little while and I'm not even sure what the denouement is of her story. But that moment, that decision was a piece, a tail of something that was always around....[9]

Morrison links the above story fragment to another related in James Van der Zee's *The Harlem Book of the Dead:*

In one picture, there was a young girl lying in a coffin and he says that she was eighteen years old and she had gone to a party and that she was dancing and suddenly she slumped and they noticed there was blood on her and they said, "what happened to you?" And she said, "I'll tell you tomorrow. I'll tell you tomorrow...." That's all she would say. And apparently her ex-boyfriend or somebody who was jealous had come to the party with a gun and a silencer and shot her. And she kept saying, "I'll tell you tomorrow" because she wanted him to get away. And he did, I guess; anyway she died.[10]

These newspaper clippings and Van der Zee's photostory provided the historical or "real-life" bases for the novel. "Now what made those stories connect, I can't explain," says Morrison, "but I do know that, in both instances, something seemed clear to me. A woman loved something other than herself so much, she had placed all of the value of her life in something outside herself."[11] Morrison's project, then, is twofold: the exploration of the black woman's sense of self (subjectivity) and the imaginative recovery of black women's history.

Describing her narrative strategy as a "kind of literary archeology," Morrison explains that, for her, "the approach that's most productive and most trustworthy...is the recollection that moves from the image to...text." Her task, as she defines it, is to "[move] that veil aside" in order to penetrate the "memories within." Although these memories—personal and collective—constitute the "subsoil of [her] work," she believes that these alone cannot give "total access to the unwritten interior life." For Morrison, "only the act of the imagination" can provide such access:

[O]n the basis of some information and a little bit of guesswork you journey to a site to see what remains were left behind and to reconstruct the

world that these remains imply. What makes it fiction is the nature of the
imaginative act: my reliance on the image—on the remains—in addition
to recollection, to yield up a kind of truth. By "image," of course, I don't
mean "symbol"; I simply mean "picture" and the feelings that accompany
the picture.[12]

Elaborating on the relationship between picture and meaning, Morrison contrasts
her own literary method (to move from image to text) to that of writers who move
"from event to the image that it left": "My route is the reverse: the image comes first
and tells me what the 'memory' is about."[13]

The notion of "literary archeology"—the imaginative and reconstructive recovery of the past that characterizes Morrison's fictive process—can be usefully compared with R. G. Collingwood's description of the historical process: If the novelist
relies upon the *a priori* imagination to construct the *possible* story in which characters and incidents develop "in a manner determined by a necessity internal to themselves," the historian relies upon the same inferential process to construct his or her
story of the *past*. In the following passage, Collingwood demonstrates that "as works
of imagination, the historian's work and the novelist's do not differ":

> Each of them makes it his business to construct a picture which is partly a
> narrative of events, partly a description of situations, exhibition of motives,
> analysis of characters. Each aims at making his picture a coherent whole,
> where every character and every situation is so bound up with the rest that
> this character in this situation cannot but act in this way, and we cannot
> imagine him as acting otherwise. The novel and the history must both of
> them make sense; nothing is admissible in either except what is necessary
> and the judge of this necessity is in both cases the imagination. Both the
> novel and the history are self-explanatory, self-justifying, the product of an
> autonomous or self-authorizing activity; and in both cases this activity is
> the *a priori* imagination.[14]

This chapter will examine Morrison's novel in the context of contemporary historical theory on discourse and narrativity, and suggest a reading that links historiography and psychoanalysis.

Like Morrison as author, the principal character in *Beloved* struggles with a past
that is part of white/male historical discourse. Lacking a discourse of her own,
Sethe must transform the residual images ("rememories") of her past into a historical discourse shaped by narrativity. These images, however, remain for a time disembodied—without form, sequence, or meaning. The challenge of the illiterate slave is
similar to that of the highly literate contemporary historian or novelist: to discover a
way of organizing memory, of contriving a narrative configuration in the absence of
written records. If it is true, as Henry Louis Gates, Jr., argues, that the sense of self as

defined in the West since the Enlightenment "turns in part upon written records," if "our idea of the self...is...inextricably interwoven with our ideas...of [writing]," then what are the consequences of an absence of written records? Quite simply and perhaps startlingly, as a slave "one's sense of one's existence...depended upon memory." "It was memory, above all else," according to Gates, "that gave shape to being itself."[15] What these remarks do not address, however, is how one formally shapes and derives meaning from disparate memories. In other words, how does one extract a configuration from a cluster of images or diversity of events? How does one, finally, transpose memories from a visual to a diegetic, or narrative, register? Like Morrison, Sethe must learn to represent the unspeakable and unspoken in language—and more precisely, as narrative.

Morrison figures both the interiority and the exteriority of memory, that is, memory as thought and memory as material inscription.[16] In the novel, "Beloved," a word Sethe had remembered from the preacher's funeral eulogy, is the public inscription of a private memorial—seven letters chiseled into the pink headstone of a child-victim of "mother-love." If the inscription of Beloved is the trace ("the mark left behind") that initiates the novel's plot, it is also an image that haunts the text in the multiple guises of the character Beloved. Besides designating an object of affection, the term *beloved* occurs in matrimonial and eulogistic discourse. Both are commemorative, linguistic events: the former prefiguring the future, the latter refiguring the past. The action of the novel, however, attends to the novelistic present—a present problematized by an unresolved past and an unanticipated future, a present that the past does not prefigure nor the future refigure.

At the outset of the novel, Sethe's "future was a matter of keeping the past at bay" (42).[17] Her aim has been to protect her children from "rememory," which she describes as follows:

> Someday you be walking down the road and you hear something or see something going on. So clear....It's when you bump into a rememory that belongs to somebody else. Where I was before I came here, that place [Sweet Home] is real. It's never going away. Even if the whole farm—every tree and grass blade of it dies. The picture is still there and what's more, if you go there—you who never was there—if you go there and stand in the place where it was, it will happen again; it will be there for you, waiting for you. (36)

"Rememory," it seems, is something that possesses (or haunts) one rather than something that one possesses. It is, in fact, that which makes the past part of one's present. Yet, despite her best efforts to "[beat] back the past," Sethe remains, in her words, "full of it," and she reflects that "[e]very mention of her past life hurt. Everything in it was painful or lost" (58). Hayden White's description of Ibsen's Hedda Gabler also seems apt for Morrison's Sethe: she "suffers [from] the incubus [or, in this case, the succubus] of the past—a surfeit of history compounded by, or reflected in, a pervasive fear of the future."[18]

Thus, unable to contrive a meaningful or appropriate configuration for her memories, Sethe finds herself tyrannized by unconfigured and literally disfiguring images. As a consequence of an attempted escape, she receives a savage beating, which leaves her back "a clump of scars" (21). The scars function as signs of ownership inscribing her as property, while the mutilation signifies her diminishment to a less-than-human status. Traces of the past that Sethe represses (but can neither remember nor forget) have been gouged into her back by the master's whip/pen and bear the potential burden of both *history* and *her*story. Like the inscription of Beloved and the pictorial images of the past, the scars function as an archeological site or memory trace.

If the master has inscribed the master('s) code on Sethe's back, a white woman and a black man offer her alternative readings of it. Although initially "struck dumb" at the sight of Sethe's scars, Amy, a runaway white girl who saves the fugitive's life and midwives the delivery of her second daughter, sees Sethe's back as a "chokecherry tree":

> See, here's the trunk—it's red and split wide open, full of sap, and this here's the parting for the branches.... Leaves, too, look like, and dern if these ain't blossoms. Tiny little cherry blossoms, just as white. Your back got a whole tree on it. In bloom. (79)

Amy describes an image that prompts her to wonder "what God have in mind." In her reverie, Sethe's back remains the trace of an event whose meaning, motivation, and consequence are largely unreadable. Alternative readings are provided by Baby Suggs (Sethe's mother-in-law) and by Paul D, the last survivor of the men from Sweet Home, the Kentucky plantation where he and Sethe had met before the war. Baby Suggs perceives her daughter-in-law's back as a pattern of "roses of blood," stenciled onto the bedsheet and blanket (93). Paul D, who arrives after the open wounds have healed (and keloided), remarks on "the sculpture [Sethe's] back had become, like the decorative work of an ironsmith too passionate for display" (17). The distance between these suggestively gendered readings—the chokecherry tree and blood roses, on the one hand, and the wrought-iron maze, on the other—signifies the distance between so-called "natural" and culturally inscribed meanings attributed to the sign.

It is the white man who inscribes; the white woman, the black man, and the black woman may variously read but not write. Because it is her back (symbolizing the *presence* of her *past*) that is marked, Sethe has only been able to read herself through the gaze of others. Her challenge is to learn to read herself—that is, to configure the history of her body's text. If, as Paul Ricoeur contends, "the past survives by leaving its trace," then Sethe must learn how to link these traces (marks of her passage through slavery) to the construction of a personal and historical discourse.[19] Her dilemma is that as an illiterate female slave, she finds herself the written object of a white male discourse and the spoken subject of a black male and white female discourse. Significantly, Baby Suggs does *not speak* of the wounds on Sethe's back ("Baby Suggs hid her mouth with her hand" [93]). Instead, she concentrates on the ritual of healing: "[W]*ordlessly,* the older woman greased the flowering back and pinned a double thickness of cloth to the inside of the newly stitched dress" (93, emphasis added). The presumption is, of course, that black women have no voice, no text, and consequently no history. They can be written and written upon precisely because they exist as the ultimate Other, whose absence or (non)being only serves to define the being or presence of the white or male subject. The black woman, symbolizing a kind of double negativity, becomes a *tabula rasa* upon which the racial/sexual identity of the other(s) can be positively inscribed.

Sethe's back is numb ("the skin on her back had been dead for years" [18]), signifying the repression of the past. (But the return of Paul D, and later of Beloved, signals the return of the repressed.) For Sethe, these scars constitute traces of past deeds too horrible and violent either to forget or to remember, a situation that Morrison describes elsewhere as "a perfect dilemma."[20] The brutal whipping she receives as punishment for her attempt to run away is only part of a cluster of events that Sethe vainly seeks to forget.

If Morrison formalizes and thematizes the operation of imaginative construction, she also dramatizes, in the character of "schoolteacher" (as he is called by the slaves), the consequences of an alternative approach. The scenes with schoolteacher offer a paradigm for reading the methodology of the white male as scholar and master. Arriving at Sweet Home after the death of its previous owner, schoolteacher announces himself "with a big hat and spectacles and a coach full of paper" and begins to "watch" his subjects (197). His methodology—based on numbering, weighing, dividing—suggests the role of the cultural historian (or ethnologist) who is concerned with sizes, densities, details, appearances, externalities, and visible properties ("Schoolteacher'd wrap that string all over my head, 'cross my nose, around my behind. Number my teeth" [191]).[21] Schoolteacher possesses the master('s) text, and as a data collector, cataloguer, classifier, and taxonomist concerned with matters of materiality and empiricism, he divides or dismembers the indivisibility of the slaves' humanity to reconstruct (or perhaps deconstruct) the slave in his text. His physical measurements recall those of Hawthorne's Custom-House Surveyor, whose careful and accurate measurements disclose little except that "each limb [of the letter A] proved to be precisely three inches and a quarter in length." In both cases, putatively scientific techniques prove altogether inadequate. Yet unlike Hawthorne's Surveyor, who discovers himself confronted with a "riddle which...[he] sees little hope of resolving," Morrison's historical investigator remains hopelessly unconscious "of his own infirmity."[22] Sethe tells us,

> He was talking to one of his pupils and I heard him say, "Which one are you doing?" And one of the boys said, "Sethe." That's when I stopped because

I heard my name, and then I took a few steps to where I could see what they was doing. Schoolteacher was standing over one of them with one hand behind his back. He licked a forefinger a couple of times and turned a few pages. Slow. I was about to turn around and keep on my way....when I heard him say, "No, no. That's not the way. I told you to put her human characteristics on the left; her *animal* ones on the right. And don't forget to line them up." (193, emphasis added)

Schoolteacher's historiography encodes the notion and forms of "wild-ness" and "animality." As Hayden White explains, this notion is a "culturally self-authenticating device" intended to "confirm the value of [the] dialectical antithesis between 'civilization'...and 'humanity.'"[23] Like Adam Nehemiah, the historical investigator in Sherley Anne Williams's *Dessa Rose*, Morrison's school-teacher espouses a concept of "otherness" as a form of sub-humanity that serves, through a process of negative self-identification, to confirm his own sense of supe-riority. Sethe's "savagery" confirms schoolteacher's "civilization"; her "bestiality" assures his "humanity." Schoolteacher's sense of history is defined by the struggle between culture and nature, and questions of meaning and interpretation turn upon this opposition.[24]

The dismemberment of schoolteacher's method is the discursive analog to the dismemberment of slavery. Just as his pupils measure and divide Sethe according to schoolteacher's instructions, so schoolteacher himself, speaking with the slave catchers, reveals to Paul D "his worth." Overhearing the men talking, Paul D, who "has always known, or believed he did, his value—as a hand, a laborer who could make profit on a farm...now [discovers] his worth, which is to say he learns his price. The dollar value of his weight, his strength, his heart, his brain, his penis, and his future" (226). As both slaveholder and scholar, schoolteacher is involved with the *dismembering* of slaves from their families, their labor, their selves. Against these forms of physical, social, and scholarly dismemberment, the act of (re)memory ini-tiates a reconstitutive process in the novel. If dismemberment deconstitutes and fragments the whole, then rememory functions to re-collect, re-assemble, and organize the various discrete and heterogeneous parts into a meaningful sequential whole through the process of narrativization discussed below.

The scenes of Paul D's figurative dismemberment both refigure the earlier scene of schoolteacher's anatomical dismemberment of Sethe and prefigure a later scene that Sethe vainly attempts to forget: "I am full God damn it of two boys with mossy teeth, one sucking on my breast the other holding me down, their book-reading teacher watching and writing it up" (70). Like Paul D, who is forced to go around with a horse's "bit" in his mouth, Sethe is forced to submit to the bovine-like humili-ation of "being milked." In this grotesque parody of Madonna and child, Sethe's milk, like her labor and the fruits of her womb, is expropriated. But the theft of her "mother's milk" suggests the expropriation of her future—her ability to nurture and ensure the survival of the next generation. Ironically, Sethe herself has mixed schoolteacher's ink:

> [Schoolteacher liked] how [she] mixed it and it was important to him because at night he sat down to write in his book. It was a book about [the slaves]....He commenced to carry round a notebook and write down what we said. (37)

The image of schoolteacher's ink converges with the expropriation of Sethe's milk in a symbol that evokes Hélène Cixous's metaphor for "écriture féminine"— women writing a language of the body in the white ink of the mother's milk. Not only the pages of his notebook but also the literal inscription of Sethe's back with schoolteacher's whip/pen constitute the perverse fulfillment of Cixous's call.[25] Appropriating Sethe's "milk" through a process of phallic substitution, school-teacher uses the pen—for Sandra Gilbert and Susan Gubar the symbol and instru-ment of masculine "authority"—to "re-mark" the slave woman with the signature of his paternity.[26] Sethe must discover some way of regaining control of her story, her body, her progeny, her milk, her ability to nurture the future.

Schoolteacher's association with "the prison-house of language," figured not only in his private ledger but in the public slave codes as well, refigures the New Testament's personification of the Decalogue. St. Paul tells the churches in Galatia that "the law was our schoolmaster," or (alternatively translated) "we were held pris-oners by the law."[27] It is this white/male construction of the law according to the authority of the master discourse that Sethe must first dismantle in order to con-struct her own story.

For schoolteacher, history is a confining activity; for Sethe, it must become a liberating one. She must "free retrospectively, certain possibilities that were not actualized in the historical past" by detecting "possibilities buried in the...past," just as Morrison does in her project of historicizing fiction.[28] As historian, Sethe must liberate her present from the "burden of the past" constructed in *history*. She must learn to remap the past so that it becomes a blueprint for the future. Her job is to reconstitute the past through personal narrative, or storytelling. Collingwood has argued that the historian is primarily "a story teller," suggesting that "historical sensibility is manifested in the capacity to make a plausible story out of congeries of 'facts' which, in their unprocessed form, made no sense at all."[29] Like Morrison, Sethe uses the memory of personal experience and what Collingwood calls the "constructive imagination" as a means of re-membering a dis-membered past, dis-membered family, and dis-membered community.

If Morrison moves "from image to text," Sethe, too, begins with the image and proceeds to shape "re-memories" of the past, endowing them with form, drama, and meaning through a process of narrativization described by Ricoeur as *config-uration* and by White as *emplotment*. Narrativization enables Sethe to construct a meaningful life story from a cluster of images, to transform separate and disparate events into a whole and coherent story.[30]

For Sethe, the past has the power to make her either captive or free. Her feelings, hopes, desires, perceptions—all colored by past incidents and events—culminate in what remain for her unspeakable acts and actions: physical violation (mammary rape) and infanticide. "Freeing yourself was one thing," Sethe thinks, "claiming ownership of that freed self was another" (95). Her preoccupation with the past makes it impossible for her to process new experiences, except through the distant lens of prior trauma. What Gates describes as "this brilliant substructure of the system of slavery"—the dependence of the slave upon her memory—had the potential to make the slave (and later the ex-slave), in some respects, "a slave to [her]self, a prisoner of [her] own power to recall."[31]

If certain events remain unconfigured, others are overly and inappropriately configured. Thus, an alternative reading of Sethe's dilemma, based on White's model, might be that she has "over-emplotted" the events of her past; she has "charged them with a meaning so intense that…they continue to shape both [her] perceptions and [her] responses to the world long after they should have become 'past history.'" The problem for Sethe, then, is to configure or emplot, on the one hand, but to reconfigure or reemplot on the other. She must imaginatively reconstitute, or re-member, her history "in such a way as to change the *meaning* of those events for [her] and their *significance* for the economy of the whole set of events that make up [her] life."[32] If Gates can assert that "the act of writing for the slave [narrator] constitute[s] the act of creating a public…self," then the act of re-membering, for the unlettered slave, constitutes the act of constructing a private self.[33] As Ricoeur argues, the (re)configuration of the past enables one to refigure the future; such is Sethe's task.

If memory is *materialized* in Beloved's reappearance, it is *maternalized* in Sethe's (re)configuration. Sethe gives *birth to her past and to her future*: first to the baby with no name whose sad and angry spirit comes back to haunt 124 Bluestone Road and later to the incarnate Beloved, the young woman with "flawless skin and feet and hands soft and new" (52). The return of Beloved, therefore, becomes not only a psychological projection but also a physical (rather than spiritual) manifestation. Her "rebirth" represents, as it were, the uncanny return of the dead to haunt the living, the return of the past to shadow the present.

Yet it is the notion of "self-distanciation" that intrigues Morrison in this as in other works: "What is it that really compels a good woman to displace the self, her self?" asks Morrison. What interests her is not only the nobility and generosity of these actions but also that such love ("the best thing that is in us") "is…the thing that makes us [as women] sabotage ourselves, sabotage in the sense [of perceiving] that our life ['the best part of ourselves'] is not as worthy." Her method of characterization is intended to suggest this process of displacement—"to project the self not into the way we say 'yourself' but to put a space between those words, as though the self were really a *twin* or a thirst or a friend or something that sits right next to you and watches you." Morrison has "[projected] the dead out into the earth" in the character of Beloved, so that Beloved becomes the twin self or mirror of Sethe and other women in the novel.[34] The author's critical reflections, however, point to another dimension of Sethe's dilemma—a dilemma that combines the private and public functions of "re-memory." If the individual is defined as a conduit of communal consciousness, then (drawing on Teresa de Lauretis) the events of Sethe's life can be emplotted through historiography; conversely, if the community is defined as a conduit of individual consciousness, then the events of Sethe's psychic life can be encoded in psychoanalytic discourse.[35]

At the point of this intersection between the personal and the social, the psychic, and the historical begin to merge. What I have been describing as social subjectivity emplotted by historiography can also be figured in terms of psychic subjectivity and represented in the discourse of psychoanalysis. Speaking to the relation between psychoanalytical and historical consciousness, Norman Brown observes that "the method of psychoanalytical therapy is to deepen the historical consciousness of the individual ('fill up the memory-gaps') till [she] awakens from [her] own history." Interpreting Freud's notion of "archaic heritage," Brown further develops the link between history and psychoanalysis by recalling that humankind is a "prisoner of the past in the same sense as [quoting Freud] 'our hysterical patients are suffering from reminiscences' and neurotics 'cannot escape the past.'" He concludes not only that all cultures are bound to the past, but that individuals are likewise bound to what Freud describes as "the memory-traces of the experiences of former generations."[36]

The link between history and psychoanalysis, then, permits the events in Sethe's life to be encoded in an alternate plot structure. The sources of her "complex" or "dis-ease" manifest themselves in her endless efforts to avoid the past and avert the future. The events in her past—namely, her own violation and the ensuing decision to take her daughter's life—have become sources of both repression and obsession. Sethe must "conjure up" her past—symbolized by Beloved—and confront it as an antagonist. As in Freud's "recommendations on the technique of psychoanalysis," one might say that Sethe must learn to regard her problematic past as an "enemy worthy of [her] mettle, a piece of [her] personality, which has solid ground for its existence and out of which things of value for [her] future life have to be derived." Her communication with Beloved—and the events of the past that Beloved both symbolizes and evokes—affords Sethe the opportunity "to become . . . conversant with this resistance with which [she] has now become acquainted, to *work through* it, to overcome it, by continuing, in defiance of it, the analytic work."[37] Thus, the psychoanalytic process becomes the means by which Sethe must free herself from the burden of her past and from the burden of *history.*

In fact, as Michel de Certeau's work suggests, psychoanalysis is itself based on the theme that dominates Morrison's novel: the return of the repressed. "This 'mechanism,'" writes de Certeau, "is linked to a certain conception of time and memory, according to which consciousness is both the deceptive *mask* and the operative *trace* of events that organize the present." "If the past...is *repressed*," he continues, "it *returns* in the present from which it was excluded."[38] The figuration of this "detour-return" and its consequences in the lives of individual characters, as well as the community as a whole, structure Morrison's novel.

In the "poetic" chapters of the novel, the reader senses the full implications of Beloved (and the younger daughter, Denver) for Sethe. The retreat of Sethe and her daughters behind the closed doors of 124 Bluestone represents a familial figuration of what Alfred Schutz calls "the succession of generations: contemporaries, predecessors, and successors," associated with the present, past, and future, respectively.[39] The connection of Sethe's present with her past is embodied in her relationship to Beloved, while the connection with her future is embodied in her relationship with Denver. The family thus becomes the site at which to explore notions of "time and being." As a historical field, it represents the complex and intimate interdependence of past, present, and future; as an ontological field, it represents the complexity of the relation between Self and Other. The family, in other words, becomes a historically constituted social site where individual subjectivity is constructed.

Further, Beloved symbolizes women in both the contemporaneous and historical black communities. She represents the unsuccessfully repressed "Other" of Sethe, as well as other women in and associated with the community: Ella, whose "puberty was spent in a house where she was shared by a father and son" (256); Vashti, who was forced into concubinage by her young master; and the girl reportedly locked up by a "whiteman" who had used her to his own purpose "since she was a pup" (235). Beyond this, however, Beloved is associated with her maternal and paternal grandmothers and the generation of slave women who failed to survive the "middle passage." As trace of "the disremembered and unaccounted for," Beloved's symbolic function of otherness connects the individual to repressed aspects of the self as well as to contemporaneous and historical others. In fact, Beloved's implication in the lives of the collectivity of women makes it necessary, as we shall see, that all the women in the community later participate in the ritual to exorcise her.

The reconstitution of Self and Other through re-memory in the act of storytelling is central to Morrison's vision. It is an act that imposes sequence and meaning on the welter of images that shape and define one's sense of self. Yet, Sethe must not only narrativize her life in White's sense of formulating her past into a coherent story; she must also be able to continue the process of metamorphosis by "metaphorizing" her experiences within narrative.[40] Morrison uses the metaphor of maternity to establish an alternative to the metaphor of paternity common in white/male historical discourse. This recurrent structuring metaphor complements and amplifies the images of the female body encoded in the text. In "The Site of Memory," Morrison provides a *cognitive* metaphor for representing her reconstructive methods as a novelist. The images of interiority that she privileges are specifically female, associated with the "interior" rather than the "exterior" life, with the personal rather than the public representation of experience. Ultimately, such a metaphor suggests that the object of our understanding is *inside* rather than *outside* and can be reached only by what Morrison describes as "literary archeology."[41]

Moreover, Sethe's birthing of the past and future appropriately figures Morrison's use of *depictive* metaphor. If the act of birthing represents Sethe's life story in a metaphor of maternity, then the womb functions as an image of corporeal interiority, the counterpart to Sethe's psychic interiority and Morrison's diegetic interiority. As a narrative metaphor, maternity privileges interiority and marks Sethe's entry into subjectivity. Perhaps the best example of this function is found in the scene describing Sethe's reaction upon seeing the incarnate Beloved for the first time:

> [F]or some reason she could not immediately account for, the moment she got close enough to see [Beloved's face], Sethe's bladder filled to capacity. . . . She never made the outhouse. Right in front of its door she had to lift her skirts, and the water she voided was endless. Like a horse, she thought, but as it went on and on she thought, No, more like flooding the boat when Denver was born. So much water Amy said, "Hold on . . . You going to sink us keep that up." But there was no stopping water breaking from a breaking womb and there was no stopping now. (51)

Significantly, Sethe, on second thought, rejects the equine metaphor. In a radical reconception of history and culture, her ritual of birthing figures motherhood as a primary metaphor of history and culture. The postdiluvian connotation of "breaking of the water" historicizes/mythicizes the event and, at the same time, signifies a maternal delivery that becomes a means of "deliverance" from the dominant conception of history as a white/paternal metaphor. Morrison seems to depict here a second immaculate conception, as it were, in which black motherhood becomes self-generative—a process that reconstitutes black womanhood. By shifting the dominant metaphor from white to black and from paternity (embodied in the slavemaster) to maternity (embodied in the black female slave), Morrison has shifted meaning and value. Through this process of destructuring and restructuring, of decoding and recoding, the author redefines notions of genesis and meaning as they have constituted black womanhood in the dominant discourse.

The images of motherhood function *heuristically* to explain or "trace" Sethe's history and that of the community along "motherlines." Her past, birthed from a womb-like matrix, is read back through motherlines tracked through four generations of marked slave women. Beloved's "thirst" for these stories gives her mother "an unexpected pleasure" in *speaking* things that "she and Baby Suggs had agreed without saying so . . . [were] *unspeakable*" (58, emphasis added). In speaking, that is, in storytelling, Sethe is able to construct an alternate text of black womanhood. This power to fashion a counter-narrative, thereby rejecting the definitions imposed by the dominant other(s), finally provides Sethe with a self—a past, present, and future.

Beloved's persistent questions enable Sethe to remember long-forgotten traces of her own mother, traces carried through memory as well as through the body. Sethe remembers that her own mother bore a mark, "a circle and a cross burnt right in the skin" (61) on her rib. It was the mark of ownership by the master who had as much as written "property" under her breast. Yet like Sethe (as well as Hawthorne's Hester Prynne), her mother had transformed a mark of mutilation, a sign of diminished humanity, into a sign of recognition and identity. Sethe recalls her mother's words: "This is your ma'am...I am the only one got this mark now. The rest dead. If something happens to me and you can't tell me by my face, you can know me by this mark" (61). Indeed, it is Sethe's own markings that help her to decode the meaning of her mother's remarks. Sethe tells her own daughters, Denver and Beloved, "I didn't understand it then. Not till I had a mark of my own" (61).

Constructed and metaphorized along motherlines, Sethe's retelling of her childhood story also enables her to decipher and pass on to her own daughter meaning encoded in a long-forgotten "mother tongue." Although Sethe knows that the "language her ma'am spoke...would never come back," she recognizes "the message—that was and had been there all along," and begins "picking meaning out of a code she no longer understood." Like the historian who seeks to configure a probable story out of a plethora of documents, Sethe seeks to reconfigure events based on "words. Words Sethe understood then but could neither recall nor repeat now" (62). Remembering the story told her by Nan—"the one she knew best, who was around all day, who nursed babies, cooked, had one good arm and half of another"—Nan, who spoke "the same language her ma'am spoke," Sethe is able to reconstruct her own story:

> Nighttime. Nan holding her with her good arm, waving the stump of the other in the air. "Telling you. I am telling you, small girl Sethe," and she did that. She told Sethe that her mother and Nan were together from the sea. Both were taken up many times by the crew. She threw them all away but you. The one from the crew she threw away on the island. The others from more whites she also threw away. Without names, she threw them. You she gave the name of a black man. She put her arms around him. The others she did not put her arms around. Never. Never. Telling you. I am telling you, small girl Sethe." (62)

Sethe's name recalls the Old Testament Hebrew name "Seth," meaning "granted" or "appointed." (Eve named her third-born Seth, saying, "God has granted me another child in the place of Abel.")[42] In this instance, the name conferred upon Sethe would seem to signify the child whose life was spared or "granted" by her mother, who did not keep the offspring of her white rapists.

The story about her own mother that she hears as a child from Nan, another mutilated mother, ironically prefigures Sethe's own actions but at the same time challenges her to some accountability. It is a story that enables Sethe to reread or re-emplot her own experiences in the context of sacrifice, resistance, and mother-love. For although Beloved, like Sethe and her mother, bears a mark of mutilation, the scar across Beloved's throat is the mark of Sethe's own hand. And it is the fingerprints on Beloved's forehead as well as the scar under her chin ("the little curved shadow of a smile in the kootchy-koochy-coo place" [239]) that enables Sethe to recognize her daughter returned from "the other side" (203).

In light of her recognition, Sethe reconstitutes a family story of infanticide, a story of repetition but with a marked difference. Sethe's story of mother-love seems to overwrite a story of rejection, and her task as historian is to find a narrative form that speaks to that difference. But it is her mother's story that refamiliarizes her own story. Sethe receives from her mother that which she had hoped to discover with Paul D: "Her story was bearable"—*not* because it was Paul D's, but *her mother's*—"to tell, to refine and tell again" (99). The maternal discourse becomes a testimonial for Sethe. Mother and daughter share protection of their own children—the one by saving a life and the other by taking a life.

But there are competing configurations as well. The first full representation of the events surrounding the infanticide comes from a collective white/male perspective, represented by schoolteacher and the sheriff:

> Inside [the shed], two boys bled in the sawdust and dirt at the feet of a nigger woman holding a blood-soaked child to her chest with one hand and an infant by the heels in the other. She did not kill them; she simply swung the baby toward the wall planks, missed and tried to connect a second time...Right off it was clear, to schoolteacher especially, that there was nothing there to claim. The three (now four—because she'd had the one coming when she cut) pickaninnies they had hoped were alive and well enough to take back to Kentucky, take back and raise properly to do the work Sweet Home desperately needed, were not....He could claim the baby struggling in the arms of the mewing old man, but who'd tend her? Because the woman—something was wrong with her. She was looking at him now, and if his other nephew could see that look he would learn the lesson for sure: you just can't mishandle *creatures* and expect success. (149–150, emphasis added)

In schoolteacher's narrative, Sethe is "the woman [who]...made fine ink, damn good soup, pressed his collars the way he liked besides having at least ten breeding years left." In his words, "she's gone wild, due to mishandling of the nephew" (149). The white sheriff reads these events as a cautionary tale on "the results of a little so-called freedom imposed on people who needed every care and guidance in the world to keep them from the cannibal life they preferred" (151). Stamp Paid, who ferried Sethe across the Ohio River upon her escape from Sweet Home, grants authority to the white newspaper's account, concluding that "while he and Baby Suggs were looking the wrong way, a pretty little slavegirl had recognized [her for- mer master's hat], and split to the woodshed to kill her children" (158). Paul D, who suddenly "saw what Stamp Paid wanted him to see," summarizes events by insisting, "You got two feet, Sethe, not four" (164–165).

Sethe must compete with the dominant metaphors of the master('s) narra- tive—wildness, cannibalism, animality, destructiveness. In radical opposition to these constructions is Sethe's reconceptualized metaphor of self based on mother- hood, motherlines, and mother-love—a love described by Paul D as "too thick." Convinced that "the best thing she was, was her children," Sethe wants simply to stop schoolteacher:

> Because the truth was…[s]imple: she was squatting in the garden and when she saw them coming and recognized schoolteacher's hat, she heard wings. Little hummingbirds stuck their needle beaks right through her headcloth into her hair and beat their wings. And if she thought anything, it was No. No. Nono. Nonono. Simple. She just flew. Collected every bit of life she had made, all the parts of her that were precious and fine and beautiful, and carried, pushed, dragged them through the veil, out, away, over there where no one could hurt them. (163)

"I took and put my babies where they'd be safe," she tells Paul D (164). And in this way, she explains to Beloved, "[N]o one, nobody on this earth, would list her daugh- ter's characteristics on the animal side of the paper" (251).

In effect, Sethe creates a counter-narrative that reconstitutes her humanity and demonstrates the requirements of mother-love. By shifting the dominant white male metaphor to a black maternal metaphor for self and history, Sethe changes the plot and meaning of the story—and finally, the story itself. A story of oppres- sion becomes a story of liberation; a story of inhumanity has been overwritten as a story of higher humanity. This process of destructuring and restructuring the dominant discourse and its organizing tropes enables Sethe (and Morrison) to subvert the master code of the master('s) text. By privileging specifically female tropes in her narrative, Sethe is able to reconstitute her self and *her*story within the context of intergenerational black women's experiences as represented in memory and in narrative. By placing her life history within a maternal family history and, by implication, placing her family history within a broader tradition of racial history, Morrison demonstrates both the strength of mother-lines in the slave community, and the ways in which ontogeny followed black female phylogeny. (The absence of Sethe's two runaway sons leaves Denver as sole heir and guarantor of the family's future.)

In accordance with Collingwood's notion of "history as re-enactment" of past experience, Sethe is able, finally, to "re-enact" a critical moment in her life. Collingwood describes this process, in which knowledge of the self is recovered:

> In thus re-thinking my past thought I am not merely remembering it. I am constructing the history of a certain phase of my life: and the difference between memory and history is that whereas in memory the past is a mere spectacle, in history it is re-enacted in present thought. So far as this thought is mere thought, the past is merely re-enacted; so far as it is thought about thought [or the thought underlying an action], this past is thought of as being re-enacted, and my knowledge of myself is historical knowledge.[43]

Like the historian, Sethe is able to "re-enact" or "re-think" a critical moment from the past and is consequently able to demonstrate her possession *of* rather than *by* the past and to alter her own life history. Sethe's actions, moreover, show that the present is bound to the past and the past to the future, and it is precisely the (re)configuration of the past that enables her to refigure the future.[44]

What has been enacted in the psychic field in the past is dramatically and therapeutically reworked in the social field. The bonds of the past are broken in a climactic scene in which thirty neighborhood women, unable to "countenance the possibility of sin moving on in the house," perform a ritual of exorcism, which "frees" Sethe from the burden of her past:

> Instantly the kneelers and the standers joined [Sethe]. They stopped praying and took a step back to the beginning. *In the beginning there were no words. In the beginning was the sound,* and they all knew what that sound sounded like. (259, emphasis added)

Invoking "the beginning" in which there were "no words"—only "the sound"— black women's voices revise Scripture ("In the beginning was the Word") in a way that associates the semiotic (rather than the symbolic) with creation and creativity. In its revision, this "key," this "code," this "sound that broke the back of words" challenges the dominant white male constitution of black womanhood. Sethe is, moreover, "born again" in her reclamation by the community ("[The voices] broke over Sethe and she trembled like baptized in its wash" [261]) as much as by the community's exorcism of Beloved. The communal voice of black women, then, possesses the power not only to destroy but also to create. In fact, Sethe's "re-birth" is predicated upon the rupture of the master('s) discourse. Thus, not only is Sethe "delivered" from the "errors" of her past, but her discourse is "delivered" from the constraints of the master('s) discourse.

During the communal exorcism, Sethe espies the "black hat wide-brimmed enough to hide [schoolteacher's] face but not his purpose. He is coming into her yard and he is coming for her best thing. She hears wings. Little hummingbirds stick needle beaks right through her headcloth into her hair and beat their wings. And if she thinks anything, it is no. No No. Nonono. She flies. The ice pick is not in her hand; it is her hand" (262). Sethe, in effect, re-enacts the original event—"remembering, repeating, and working-through" the "primal scene" in a process that evokes psychoanalysis. In this re-enactment, however, Sethe directs her response to the threatening Other rather than to "her best thing"—her children. And, significantly, it is not only Sethe but the community itself that re-enacts the earlier scenario. Because the community had failed to send warning of the slave captors' approach the first time, its "sin of omission" makes it no less responsible for Beloved's death than Sethe's "sin of commission." In a scene of collective re-enactment, the women of the community intervene at a critical juncture, to save not Beloved but Sethe. Thus, by rethinking and revising her actions, Sethe is able to preserve the community, and the community, in turn, is able to protect one of its own.

According to Ricoeur's model, prefiguration denotes the temporality of the world of human action; configuration, the world of the narrative emplotment of these events; and refiguration, the moment at which these two worlds interact and affect each other. Sethe's actions constitute the prefigurative aspect; her storytelling, the configurative aspect; and re-enactment, the refigurative aspect.[45] Moreover, Morrison enables the reader to connect with the otherness of these past generations—especially as it relates to the experiences of the slave women—in a process made possible by "the intersection of the world of the text with the world of the reader." Just as Nan's story of the generational mother enables Sethe to (re)configure her past, so Morrison's story of the historical m(other) enables the reader to do likewise. The reader, like Sethe, learns that she must claim and surrender the past in order to refigure the future.[46]

The question of Sethe's accountability, however, remains. Does Morrison, finally, indict or defend Sethe's "too quick" mother-love? Is Sethe truly redeemed from an unspeakable past? If so, by what means? Where precisely lies the source of Sethe's "redemption" from the "sins" of the past—both those perpetuated *upon* her and *by* her? Is grace achieved through the spirit of Beloved (the past generations she symbolizes) or by its exorcism? Characteristically, Morrison draws out the paradoxes and ambiguities of this "perfect dilemma." I suggest, in fact, that she neither condemns nor condones but rather "delivers" her protagonist. For Sethe achieves redemption through *possession* by the spirit as well as *exorcism* of the spirit. Significantly, for Morrison, it is not through the law ("Because the Law worketh wrath") but through the spirit (its reclamation and relinquishment) that the individual achieves "deliverance" from the "sins" of the past.[47] *Beloved*, then, (re)inscribes the conditions of the promise in the New Testament. What is important for Morrison, however, is the mediation between remembering (possession) and forgetting (exorcism). It is the process of "working-through" that the author finally affirms. As in previous novels, Morrison focuses less on "what" and "why" and more on "how." She privileges the journey rather than the destination, the means rather than the end—a process that enables Sethe to achieve resolution through the construction of a cohesive psychoanalytical and historical narrative.

Like Sethe, Morrison herself seeks to achieve some mediation between "resurrecting" the past and "burying" it. Expressing her desire to provide a proper, artistic burial for the historical ancestors figured by *Beloved*, Morrison says:

> There's a lot of danger for me in writing.... The effort, the responsibility as well as the effort, the effort of being worth it.... The responsibility that I feel for...all of these people; these unburied, or at least unceremoniously buried, people made literate in art. But the inner tension, the artistic inner tension those people create in me, the fear of not properly, artistically, burying them, is extraordinary.[48]

Clearly, Morrison intends to pay the historian's debt to the past, in Ricoeur's sense of rendering to the past its due and, in the process, put it to rest.

What, then, is Morrison's final legacy to readers, and what is her own relation to the past? Does Sethe become for the reader what Beloved is for Sethe—an embodiment of the past and the experiences of previous generations? What of the haunting injunction at the end of the novel that it is NOT a story to "be passed on"—that is, to be remembered, to be retold? Must Morrison's story, along with Sethe's past, be put behind? Must the reader rid herself of the burdens of the past by exorcising from historical consciousness the violence and violation experienced by her ancestors? If this injunction is taken seriously, how can Morrison's own commitment to a project of recovery and "re-memory" be explained? Clearly, such an injunction threatens to contradict the motive and sense of the entire novel.

In a 1989 interview, Morrison called *Beloved* a book "about something that the characters don't want to remember, I don't want to remember, black people don't want to remember, white people don't want to remember."[49] The author's remarks speak to the public desire to repress the personal aspects of the story of slavery. Morrison's accomplishment as historian and analyst in the novel, however, is precisely *not* to allow for the continuation of a "national amnesia" regarding this chapter in America's history. For her, the absent (like the historical) is only the "other" of the present—just as the repressed is only the "other" of the conscious. Read in this context, the narrator's final and thrice-repeated enjoinder resonates with ambivalence and ambiguity. Suggesting that what is absent is not necessarily "gone" (leaving behind no "name," no "print," no "trace"), the narrator's closing reflections ensure the novel's open-endedness and subvert any monologic reading of the final injunction. Is it possible that the narrator means, indeed must she mean, that this is not a story to be PASSED ON—not in the sense of being retold but in the sense of being forgotten, repressed, or ignored? Morrison finally seems to vindicate, and is vindicated by, Richard Hofstadter's observation that "[m]emory is the thread of personal identity, history of public identity." If this is so, it would follow, then, that the importance of our private memories becomes, ultimately, the basis for a reconstructed public history.[50]

5

The Stories of (O)Dessa

Stories of Complicity and Resistance

MS. COLLEN STAN: I was blindfolded, gagged, had this thing over my head, my—my hands are handcuffed behind my back, and my ankles are tied together.

RIVERA: This starts a seven-year captivity.

MS. STAN: He put these leather restraints or whatever you want to call them on my wrists. He connected them up on these bars. He grabs this whip, and he starts whipping me and tells me to shut up.

RIVERA: So you're in this, like, torture chamber now.

MS. STAN: Yeah. I just hung there and cried. So, at this point, I thought, 'This guy is going to kill me....'

—Transcript, "Human Bondage:
The Story of a Slave and Her Master"

Prologue

The above dialogue, excerpted from the transcript of an interview aired on The Geraldo Rivera Show, *"Human Bondage: The Story of a Slave and Her Master," recounts in lurid detail the abuse and torture of a woman who was kidnapped and held in "captivity" as a "sex slave." Collen Stan explains in her own words how the perpetrator, Cameron Hooker (since tried and convicted by the State of California), with the assistance of his wife (who turned state's evidence), abducted twenty-year-old Stan, locked her in a basement, bound her wrists with leather restraints, hooked her arms to the ceiling so that she dangled by her feet, removed her clothing, and repeatedly beat her with a whip. Although blindfolded, she could see her captor and his wife having sex on a table in the corner of the basement. Lying on a small table next to her, she saw a magazine displaying a female figure bound in the same position as her own. Such was the beginning of the seven-year captivity from which she finally escaped.*

These events occurred in the late 1970s and early 1980s (she escaped in 1985) in Red Bluff, California, and are paradigmatic for understanding the historic relation between slavery, gender violence, and sexuality. Their narration presents the audience with a powerful kaleidoscope of scenes depicting relations based on the absolute control (of life and death) of one individual over another, a position maintained both by the threat as well as the actual employment of violence. Second, the circumstances of Stan's experience expose the ritualistic and symbolic aspects of power in the highly personal and private domain of sexuality. And, third, the mimetic staging of these relations re-enact woman's sexual subjection and social subordination at the scene of male power, violence, and domination.

For our purposes, it is critical that these scenarios are drawn together in a metaphor that links the sphere of sexuality in modern society to the practices of power and domination constituting what one historian calls the "central symbolic aspect of slavery." Here, Rivera's role as show host and interlocutor allows him to frame the terms ("captivity," "torture," "slave," "master") and setting ("torture chamber") for Stan's recitation. Through her testimony, Stan bears witness not only to her traumatic experiences, but to Rivera's provocative title, "Human Bondage: The Story of a Slave and Her Master." This spectacle of "woman in captivity" codes the specifically sexual subjugation of women in bondage, a fact borne out by the history of women in slaveholding societies where they have been subject to sexual violence as a means of social control.

Transcoding the metaphor of slavery to the sphere of sexuality requires the formulation of a critical feminist discourse that addresses this intersection. Even without the accomplished (although largely uncritical) lead of Rivera, Stan's scene of captivity unavoidably reproduces the relation between pornography and the abuse of women, explicitly fashioned in the magazine photo that models her own bound and captive position. What the excerpt suggests only in part, but the complete transcript makes evident, is the complicity of women who participate in the eroticization of dominance and submission. (Clearly, compliance on the part of the wife—and later, the victim—reflect the extent to which the sexual fantasies and practices of women have been conditioned by an ideology of female submission, thereby perpetuating patriarchal violence and domination.)

Such a testimony on network television poses unsettling questions implicating victim and perpetrator (both of whom spoke on national network television, the latter from the state penitentiary), as well as spectators and producers—in the complicity of reproduction. While Rivera and Stan are engaged in an exposé of sexual atrocity, the media's role in staging desire as production, and sexploitation as entertainment, point to the problematics of representation—even when it is in the service of exposé and critique. Rivera coaxes a willing (for the sake of exposé) Stan into replicating the language and/or visuals of the pornographic scenarios that are meant to be subject to social critique. Here, however, the dilemma posed by Stan and Rivera can be instructive to the critic. Like them, the critic must necessarily reproduce elements of the sexual/textual event in the act of analyzing the representation of erotica/pornography, thereby risking the subjection of the spectator/reader to the seductions of desire—or perhaps more appropriately, violence masked as desire.

Because Sherley Anne Williams's Dessa Rose *embodies a paradigm of race and gender conjoined with slavery and sexuality at precisely the moment when the critical issues of complicity and resistance converge, Rivera's "Of Human Bondage" provides an appropriate introduction to the following discussion of Williams's text. The staging of violence, linked with desire, that underscores his production points to the necessity of a critical analysis of slavery that uncovers its repressed subtext—the pornographic. Of course, the "ob-scene" which confronts the contemporary reader has always existed as part of the story of slavery: Most frequently, this aspect is registered by allusions to the physical abuses of black women's bodies (stories "too terrible to tell") recounted by former slaves and abolitionists. This discursive legacy of slavery (and its persistence in the American sexual imaginary) challenges Williams to literary exposé—without reproducing the structures of desire already encoded in the pornographic scenario. The critic's challenge is to discover a critical method analogous to Williams's literary method—one that illuminates the relationship between slavery and pornography, but that resists manipulating desire.*

I

What I have discovered is that Sherley Anne Williams characteristically invokes an antimodel that highlights, by contrast, her own narrative investment.[1] Yet, in the absence of a designated intertext, the reader must often rely upon "the resources of his or her personal 'library' of literary experience"[2] to appreciate how Williams's intertextual, or "contratextual" discursive context shapes the reading and writing process. My earlier work on Williams predisposes me to take with much seriousness the range of implicit and explicit intertextual references in her work. Her novel *Dessa Rose* provides a unique example of intertextuality—or contratextuality—for it dialogically engages not only Williams's own previous work but, at the very least, two texts outside the African-American literary tradition: William Styron's *Confessions of Nat Turner* (based, in part, on Thomas R. Gray's work of the same title, published in 1831) and Pauline Réage's *Story of O*. Common to all of these works are recurring scenes of political and/or sexual captivity that eroticize relations under the sign of lordship and bondage: white master/slave woman; white interviewer/slave interviewee; writing subject/written object; critic/text. Williams, however, reconceptualizes prior representations of women and blacks at the scene of writing captivity, particularly when the condition of black and/or female subjectivity is their subordination to the writing subject (or interlocutor). Through my reading of *Dessa Rose*, I examine how Williams exposes both Styron's racial masquerade, which appropriates black to white (male) subjectivity, and the racial specificity of Réage's performance of femininity. Through this second, more extended inquiry, I argue that narratives of female masochism must be reconceptualized racially, as Williams rewrites the erotics of white feminine surrender as the politics of black feminist resistance.

II

Dessa Rose appeared in 1987 as an elaboration of Williams's earlier novella, "Meditations on History." Why did Williams, an accomplished poet and short story writer, choose, in her novel, to revisit and revise this earlier work? What issues does the longer narrative engage that distinguish it from the shorter one? How do the problems introduced by Williams in "Meditations" get reworked or worked through in *Dessa Rose*? In addressing these questions, we must look not only to the texts, but also at the historical contexts of their production. In a preliminary examination of the historical referents and perspectives of these two works, I seek to demonstrate how Williams weaves into the novella and the novel strands of competing and complementary historical and contemporaneous discourses.

"Meditations" roughly coincides with the first of three sections in the novel *Dessa Rose*. Set in Alabama in 1829, the action centers on the encounter between an unnamed slavery apologist who functions as interviewer-narrator and a pregnant "rebellious slave girl."[3] Dessa, who has been imprisoned in a root cellar, awaits a hanging that is to be postponed until the birth of her child. We learn that Dessa has attacked her master for having killed her child's father. As a result, she is sold to a slave trader, but manages to escape from the slave coffle, along with several companions, after a fracas in which she kills one of the traders. It is not until after Dessa's recapture, while awaiting her baby's birth (before her scheduled execution), that she is introduced to the reader. The white male who functions as narrator in the novella attempts to interview Dessa and record her story in his journal. His project is to gain information in support of a forthcoming book on how to eradicate slave rebellions. The novella and Part I of *Dessa Rose* conclude with Dessa's second escape, this time from both the social system and the system of literary representation ("the prison house of language").

As indicated by the interviewer-narrator's project, the era of the 1820s was a period of slave unrest, marked by the massive conspiracies led by Gabriel Prosser in 1800 and Denmark Vesey in 1822, events anticipating Nat Turner's 1831 insurrection. In documenting and elaborating the story of a nineteenth-century female slave rebel, Williams, in effect, intervenes into a male story of resistance, and locates her work within a historical and contemporary tradition of race struggle.[4] By dedicating her story to black woman scholar and activist Angela Davis, and prefacing it with a quotation from Davis's article, "Reflections on the Black Woman's Role in the Community of Slaves," Williams links her heroine to a tradition of violent resistance to oppression extending from the nineteenth into the twentieth century.[5]

Beyond this, Williams critiques a discourse of race as it informs both historiographical and literary writing. As I demonstrate earlier, Williams's intention to engage William Styron's *Confessions of Nat Turner*, published in 1967, is initially signaled by the title of her short story, "Meditations of History."[6] In his "Author's

Note," Styron tells the reader that his intention has been to "re-create a man and his era, and to produce a work that is less a 'historical novel' in conventional terms than a *meditation on history*."[7]

When Williams published her own novel two decades later, she changed the setting from 1829 to 1847, thus advancing the temporal frame of the action by some eighteen years. Clearly, the 1840s, with its increased abolitionist activity and militant resistance to slavery, provides a more dramatic backdrop for the events in the novel, as well as the impetus and motivation for much of the character action. Significantly, both the mid-1840s (the historical period of the novel's enactment) and the mid-1980s (the contemporary period of the novel's production and reception) represent periods of retrenchment on the race question. For example, just as the abolitionist movement of the 1840s was undermined by the internal divisions of political pragmatism versus moral suasion, so the leadership of the 1970s and 1980s Civil Rights and Black Power movements was undermined by similar internal strife and dissension. Moreover, just as the issue of women's participation in the abolitionist movement provided the background for the subsequent emergence of the women's rights movement from the 1840s to the 1860s, so the Civil Rights and Black Power movements set the stage for the emergence of second-wave feminism spanning the period from the 1960s to the 1980s. And, significantly, these women's rights movements challenged the priority of race as the privileged locus of dissent. Further, just as the abolitionist movement generated a counter-response from the proslavery faction of Southern ideologues, so the politics of Civil Rights and Black Power generated a backlash from an empowered religious Right.[8] Finally, the decade of the 1980s also saw the emergence of a new academic discourse—the feminist critique, as a counterpart and counterpoint to the racial critique. Like the 1980s, then, the 1840s had been a period of racial turbulence as well as progressive agitation for women's rights.

Accordingly, we can see that Williams's novella and, later, novel draw upon both their fictional/historical settings as well as their contemporary/political settings. "Meditations," written during the 1970s, foregrounds a *discourse of race* in the wake of the Civil Rights and Black Power movements, while *Dessa Rose*, published in the mid-1980s, foregrounds a *discourse of race and gender* during the period that has since become associated with the second wave of American feminism.

In her "Author's Note" (paralleling Styron's), Williams explains that the novel is based on two historical incidents:

> A pregnant black woman helped to lead an uprising on a coffle...in 1829. Caught and convicted, she was sentenced to death; her hanging, however, was delayed until after the birth of her baby. In North Carolina in 1830, a white woman living on an isolated farm was reported to have given sanctuary to runaway slaves.... How sad, I thought then, that these two women never met.[9]

Dessa Rose provides the occasion for such a meeting, an encounter that enables Williams to stage a dialogue between the discourse of slavery and the discourse of nineteenth-century womanhood, reading both through a contemporary dialectic of race and gender. Moreover, in its intervention into the racial critique of the 1960s and 1970s and the feminist critique of the 1970s and 1980s, Williams's novel positions itself at the discursive juncture of two oppositional discourses. In some respects, *Dessa Rose* marks Williams's entry as a *woman* into the racial critique and as a *black* into the feminist critique, making her work as a black feminist writer a site of struggle and affirmation in two historically emancipatory, but all too often competing, discourses.

Directly engaging Styron in her own "Author's Note," Williams "admits to being outraged by a certain critically acclaimed novel…that travestied the as-told-to-memoir of slave revolt leader Nat Turner" (5). In *Dessa Rose*, the white male interviewer-narrator, Adam Nehemiah, like the lawyer in Styron's *Confessions*, functions as an amanuensis for the slave. However, as author-to-be of *The Roots of Rebellion in the Slave Population and Some Means of Eradicating Them* (or more simply, *Roots*), his role also corresponds to Styron's. For Williams, what is problematic in Styron's text is the mimetic relationship between author and subject. Styron's representation of Nat Turner's voice in formal, poetic, religious-inflected prose links the slave rebel not with the vernacular of the other slaves, but with the highly literate author. Thus, although Styron's racial masquerade establishes a homosocial identification with his subject, Nat, it would also appear to cover an oppositional relation between the black male revolutionary and the white male liberal writer. Not only is Nat constructed as weak and irresolute, but his liberational impulses are dissociated from the realm of power and resistance and linked to sexual repression in the form of latent homosexuality and repressed passion for white women. Thus, Styron seeks to establish a rigid distinction between the public and private, thereby dispossessing Nat of his political motivation and constructing him as object of erotic desire rather than subject of political interest. What is at issue here is not only the emasculation of the black male revolutionary, but the ends served by such constructions, as well as the manner and degree to which these constructions articulate the author's subjectivity.

III

If Williams's "Meditations," figured in Part I of *Dessa Rose*, rewrites Styron's controversial *Confessions*, the remainder of the novel rewrites Pauline Réage's equally controversial *Story of O* (originally published in 1954, but translated into English in 1965, two years before the appearance of Styron's *Confessions*). André Pieyre de Mandiargues, who writes an introduction to the original edition of *Story of O*, sees the novel as a mystical allegory of the "Western 'soul'" while Susan Sontag argues that it is a story of erotic desire expressed through religious metaphor. Similarly, Leo

Bersani sees it as a universal allegory of human desire in which the coherent unitary subject is "dismembered" through a loss of self. Jessica Benjamin, on the other hand, sees the narrative as a "fantasy of erotic domination" deriving from a female position of passivity resulting from woman's "tendency 'to experience her continuity' " by " 'merging with the mother.' "[10] My own reading of this novel is through what I take to be Williams's rewriting of a story of complicity as a story of resistance. In part, my reading (like previous readings) is allegorical in that it "reaches outside of the terms of the text in order to explain textual activity."[11] I argue that for the black feminist writer and reader, such a text must be read as an allegory of white female complicity with the patriarchy, an allegory underscored by the recent discovery of the female authorship of this text. The relationship between O and her victimizer constitutes a hazardous alliance in which the scheme of patriarchy is further institutionalized by the integration of the white woman into its fundamental structures—structures ranging from psychoanalytic to literary to political practice.

In the United States, Réage's novel was hailed by some as a "transgressive erotic classic" and literary manifesto of woman's sexual liberation, and by others as a pornographic representation of woman's degradation. Notably, feminist critic Susan Gubar defines pornography as "a gender-specific genre produced primarily by and for men but focused obsessively on the female figure."[12] Réage's text, however, represents an example of a genre produced not *by* a man, but *for* a man. Clearly, female authorship here raises the problematic of women assuming authority in controlling their own images, even—or especially—when those images reproduce male-inscribed images of women. Although some critics may argue that the author's intent is exposé, rather than fantasy fulfillment, the author's own testimony that she wrote the *Story of O* to rekindle the romantic interest of publisher, editor, and lover, Jean Paulhan, would suggest that the text was less "diagnostic" than "symptomatic."[13]

Publication of the *Story of O*, along with that of another French text, the *Portuguese Letters* (originally published in 1669), became the occasion for an extended debate in the early 1970s between American feminist critics Nancy Miller and Peggy Kamuf. Responding to Kamuf, Miller insisted on a patriarchal signature and line of descent for a text that glamorizes "female suffering around a man." Miller writes, "Kamuf doesn't care whether the *Portuguese Letters* were written by a woman or by a man, and I do. Much as I care if the *Story of O* was written by Pauline Réage or Jean Paulhan... I *prefer* to think that this *positioning* of woman is the writing of a masculine desire attached to a male body." Miller concludes, however, that "this preference is not without its vulnerabilities.... It could," she speculates, "one day be proven definitively that the heroines of the [*Portuguese*] *Letters* and the *Story of O* were female creations after all. I would then have to start all over again."[14]

It has now been established that the author of the *Story of O* is indeed a woman, Anne Desclos (*aka* Dominique Aury). Although this was not known to be the case when I began this essay, my assumptions and argument (unlike Miller's) remain substantially unchanged. This text now allows us to consider the consequence when women, occupying the male subject position, produce male fantasies of feminine identity. Réage (as I will continue to identify the author) is, in effect, legitimized by her appropriation of the language, perspective, and vision of a woman who is identified as "male." Nonetheless, whether the *Story of O* was written directly by Jean Paulhan or, as we now know, ventriloquized by his companion writing under the *nom de plume* of Pauline Réage, my task is to address the politics of representation, as well as to show how meaning is produced when the reader/critic brings a black and feminist perspective to such a text.[15] Assuming, then, that Simone de Beauvoir is correct when she writes that some women "still dream through the dreams of men,"[16] I read the *Story of O* not as a female story in which subordination encodes masochism as woman's transgressive erotic desire; nor do I read it as a subversion of male sadistic desire achieved by the heroine's spiritual transcendence over physical degradation. Rather, I seek to deconstruct a surface "female" narrative of submission, exposing it as a cover story displacing a deeper "male" narrative of the manipulation of female fantasy and desire.

The *Story of O* is preceded by Paulhan's prologue citing a specific historical incident relating to slavery (analogous to similar prologues in *Confessions* and *Dessa Rose*). As in the slave narratives, these prologues or "pre-texts" serve to guarantee the authenticity or reliability of the tale that follows. Thus, just as Styron used Gray's document to authenticate his own tale, so the introduction by Paulhan, identified as a member of l'Académie Française, is meant to authenticate Réage's narrative. Yet, as we shall see, Paulhan's prefatory remarks inadvertently serve to establish an identification between guarantor and narrator. (Notably, Williams's own prologue, inscribing Dessa's personal reveries, functions to subvert rather than authenticate Nehemiah's construction of the latter in his journal—a literary move that implicitly subverts both Styron's and Réage/Paulhan's constructions of black and female subjectivity.)

Paulhan's prologue, "Happiness in Slavery," introduces *Story of O* by way of an analogy comparing O's response to her "master" with that of a group of black slaves in Barbados who massacre their master for refusing "to take them back into bondage":

> In the course of the year 1838, the peaceful island of Barbados was rocked by a strange and bloody revolt. About two hundred Negroes of both sexes, all of whom had recently been emancipated by the Proclamations of March, came one morning to beg their former master... to take them back into bondage. An Anabaptist minister, acting as spokesman for the group, read out a list of grievances which he had compiled and recorded in a notebook.... [E]ither from timidity or because he was scrupulous or simply afraid of the law, [the master] refused to be swayed. At which point he was... set upon and massacred... by the Negroes.[17]

Not only does Paulhan's allegory compare the slaves' response to their (former) master with O's relation to her master, it also suggests that Réage's *Story of O* may itself be modeled on the genre of the slave narrative. Further, Paulhan refers to a notebook in which was compiled a list of grievances recorded by an Anabaptist minister, a strategy clearly refigured by Williams in the journal of Adam Nehemiah, the interviewer. The unrecovered notebook, Paulhan speculates, "would seem even more heretical today than it did some hundred and thirty years ago; today," he concludes, "it would be considered a dangerous book" (*Story*, xxii–xxiii). Thus if Paulhan's introduction reconfigures the story of slavery as the story of desire, I argue that Williams rewrites Réage's narrative of desire as a narrative of slavery. By transposing the element of servitude in a narrative of eroticism into a narrative of slavery that reveals the element of the erotic, Williams—in a narrative where eros is inseparable from domination—reminds the reader of the material rather than the metaphorical aspects of slavery.

The association between the story of slavery and the story of desire (masking the pornographic), for me, rests on an affiliation between slavery as an institutionalized system of power—and pornography as a visual and discursive representation of power: both inevitably raise issues of violence and violation. Moreover, in an economy of production and consumption, both slavery and pornography entail issues of control and profit from the commodification of others. Finally, the question remains whether what I call "the stories of (O)Dessa" are narratives of desire/pornography or narratives of slavery.[18]

It is useful here to bridge these two narratives—the story of slavery and the story of desire—by recalling a poignant moment in Frederick Douglass's 1845 *Narrative* when he recounts awakening to the horrors of slavery during a scene where he witnesses the whipping of his aunt by his master (reputed to be his father). I refer specifically to the scene that he describes as "a most terrible spectacle"—namely, his master's "great pleasure in whipping a slave":

> I have often been awakened at the dawn of day by the most heart-rending shrieking of an aunt of mine whom he used to tie up [to a joist] and whip upon her naked back until she was literally covered with blood. The louder she screamed the harder he whipped. And where the blood ran fastest there he whipped longest. He would whip her to make her scream, and whip her to make her hush; and not until overcome by fatigue, would he cease to swing the blood-clotted cowskin.[19]

What this passage, a typical one in the slave narratives, suggests to me is what critic George Cunningham describes as a "world of sadism where the violent and sexual are conflated."[20] Not only an object of exchange in a slave economy, the aunt is also an object of desire within a system unbound by legal or cultural restraints. The sexual imagery encoded in this passage speaks as much to the master's desire for violence as it does to the violence of the master's desire. Such a passage also under-scores the symbolic and ritual function of slavery as an institution based on power and violence.

Further, the image of the female slave subjugated by the lash (a classic porno-graphic female stance) conveys not only the power of male over female, but the power of master over slave and the power of white over black. It is a race- and gender-inflected image that combines images of unchecked power and sexual pleasure. If blacks are frequently portrayed as women in the verbal and visual ico-nography of nineteenth-century slavery, it may not be surprising to learn that the historical origins of slavery are traced by scholars to the enslavement of women.[21] Arguing that slavery had its origins in "sexual stratification," Dorothy Wertz writes that "it seems logical that a major functional equivalent of slavery today is the subju-gation of women." Wertz concludes that "women have comprised the bulk of slaves throughout history" and that "perhaps they still serve some of the slaves' symbolic roles."[22]

In language that, in fact, conflates the discourses of dominance and eroticism with the act of reading, Paulhan warns the reader that "the very act of referring to [such texts] would seem *bound* to make us want to read them and *expose* ourselves to danger" (*Story*, xxiii, emphasis added). Thus the reader is placed in a masochis-tic posture in relation to the text. The "somewhat risky business" to which Paulhan alerts the reader again encodes the dangers of these stories: "From every indica-tion," he writes, "the *Story of O* is one of those books which *marks* the reader, which leaves *him* not quite, or not all, the same as *he* was before *he* read it," an interpellation that would seem to figure the reader as *masculine* (*Story*, xxiii, emphasis added). It is in this context that Paulhan informs us that, "in her own way O expresses a virile ideal, Virile, or at least masculine" (*Story*, xxv). Yet, despite the masculine pronomi-nal referents, the position interpellated is feminized—to the extent that it locates the reader (bound and marked) in a passively masochistic position.

In a curious and telling "slip," Paulhan suggests in the introduction that the role of "dangerous" (that is, erotic) books is to "inform and instruct," "to reassure us on the subject, the way a father confessor does" (*Story*, xxvii). We note that Paulhan's Anabaptist minister, authoring a "lost" text containing an apologia for slavery, is clearly invoked and inverted in Williams's Adam Nehemiah, whose projected book on the eradication of the roots of slave revolts remains similarly incomplete. Nehemiah's journal, refiguring the notebooks of the Anabaptist minister and Thomas Gray, is projected as a book designed not only to relieve the fears of slaveholders, but equally important, it is meant to be instructive to the preservation of slavery.[23]

Like Styron's, Réage's work is structured around "confessions" or "revela-tions": the *Story of O* is described as a "love-letter representing the narrator's desire to reveal the innermost sexual secrets of her being." The seductiveness of the text, figured as a kind of "love letter" to the reader and recipient, is replicated in its illo-cutionary frame: "But to whom is the letter addressed? Who is the speech trying to convince? Who can we ask?" queries Paulhan. Although Paulhan sees O's story as "more of a speech than a mere effusion; of a letter rather than a secret diary" (*Story*, xxiv), he nonetheless describes it as a confession, a mode that confirms the value and authority attached to the Other. The female confession, then, becomes an articulation of male mastery through its manipulation and representation of desire. Like a father confessor, Paulhan declares,

> At last a woman who admits it!...Something that men have always reproached them with: that they never cease obeying their nature, the call of their blood, that everything in them, even their minds, is sex. That they have constantly to be nourished, constantly washed and made up, constantly beaten. That all they need is a good master, one who is not too lax or kind.... [One who] must, when [he goes] to see them, take a whip along. (*Story*, xxv)

Here, the construction of O as willingly and willfully subordinate to male superordination is meant to gratify male desires for power and male powers of desire. Réage/ Paulhan thus conceals what is fundamentally a story of sadistic mastery beneath a story of masochistic submission. Legal scholar Catherine A. MacKinnon would call this the "eroticization of dominance"—and, one might add, "the sexualization of submission."[24]

As a Sadean narrative, the plot of *Story of O* can be briefly summarized as follows: To please her lover, O, a successful fashion photographer, willingly accompanies him to the chateau at Roissy where she is confined to a small, solitary, cell-like room, released only to satisfy the sexual demands of the male guests.[25] The men at Roissy represent the principle of male dominance in physical and psychological relations. As they explain to O, "if the costume we wear in the evening...leaves our sex exposed, it is...for the sake of insolence...so that you may learn that there resides your master." O is also informed, "Your hands are not your own, nor are your breasts, nor, most especially, any of your bodily orifices, which we may explore or penetrate at will." Further, her masters explain that

> in principle [O] would be whipped only on the thighs and buttocks, in other words between her waist and knees...but that in all likelihood one of the four men present would want to mark her thighs with the riding crop. (*Story*, 15)

Not only is O chained, tortured, and whipped, but she is branded as well. If the whipmarks signify traces of white and patriarchal authority, the branding suggests a more personal and precise inscription of sexual ownership. Moreover, like the slave woman who becomes an object of economic exchange, O is circulated in an economy of male desire—not only among the male patrons at Roissy, but also between her lover and his half-brother, whose name is branded into her flesh and whose iron rings bound her labia.

Yet in *Story of O*, these rituals of debasement have the effect of enhancing rather than diminishing the victim. The protagonist, in fact, sees her self-abnegation as an act of spiritual asceticism: The more she is physically tortured, the more her experience is represented as a mystical imitation of the Christian martyrs. Surprised that the whippings leave her in an "untroubled" and "calm" state (*Story*, 23), O can only hope that her endurance is equal to that of other martyrs ("prisoners she had seen in engravings and in history books, who had been chained and whipped...centuries ago" [*Story*, 26]). She perceives that her lover has prostituted her only to enhance her value to him: "The more he surrendered her, the more he would hold her dear.... Thus he would possess her as a god possesses his creatures." Her lover, then, "gave her only to reclaim her immediately, to reclaim her enriched in his eyes, like some common object which had been used for some divine purpose and has thus been consecrated" (*Story*, 32). For this reason, O discovers that "the chains and the silence, which should have smothered her, strangled her, on the contrary freed her from herself." Her ritual defilement becomes the means of her purification: "She felt herself literally to be the repository of impurity, the stink mentioned in the Scriptures.... [A]nd yet those parts of her body most constantly offended, having become less sensitive, at the same time seems to her to have become more beautiful and, as it were, ennobled" (*Story*, 44). O discovers in her degradation a dignity and illumination that affirm her spiritual transcendence. Rather than a site of captivity, the chateau at Roissy thus becomes the liberating "sacrificial site" of a sacred initiation.

IV

If Réage and Styron construct in their respective works the subjectivity and sexuality of white women and black men, Williams's project demonstrates how these fictive discourses are deployed to perpetuate hierarchal differences based on gender and race. If the *Story of O* recuperates the myth of female passivity, *The Confessions of Nat Turner* reinforces the myth of black male emasculation. If, in Réage's novel, psychosexual subordination is the condition of (white) woman's subjectivity, in Styron's novel, psychosexual repression is the condition of black (male) subjectivity. Williams's *Dessa Rose* seeks to deconstruct these antecedent constructions and, at the same time, open up a space for the black female, marginalized in Styron's text and subsumed under the categories of slave and woman in Réage's text.

Williams opens her narrative by deconstructing Paulhan's dialectic of accommodating masters and passive slaves (as well as Styron's dialectic of sexual repression and political revolution). Moreover, she rewrites Paulhan's "happiness in slavery" thematic not only to demonstrate the coercive power relations inherent in slavery, but to represent, more particularly, the coercive relations involved in female sexuality under slavery. Williams's *Dessa Rose*, then, deconstitutes Réage's prior narrative, which attempts to spiritualize a relationship of sexual slavery and submission, reconstituting it as a historical narrative of enforced physical slavery and resistance. Despite Paulhan's repeated allusions to the "ruthless decency" of this very "*decent*" book, Réage's narrative is actually a story of *descent* "from freedom to slavery," while Williams's is a story of ascent "from slavery to freedom." Further, Williams's strategy—to move the politics of sexual domination from the private into the public sphere—locates sexual desire/fantasy within a larger system of social domination and gender hierarchy.

Williams's intent to enter into dialogue with the *Story of O* is suggested onomastically in her protagonist's ritual of self-naming. In two dramatic acts of self-entitlement, Dessa reaffirms her ability to name herself and her own experience. In the first instance, she says of her would-be captor, Adam Nehemiah, "Why he didn't even know how to call my name—talking about O*dessa*" (*DR*, 225). And in the second, she tells Ruth, the white woman who provides sanctuary to runaway slaves in exchange for labor, "My name Dessa, Dessa Rose. Ain't no *O* to it" (*DR*, 232). She is, of course, distinguishing between (O)dessa, an ascription by the white, male slave master evoking her problematic literary ancestress, Réage's O, and Dessa, her self-entitlement. Clearly, her rejection of the "O"—a signifier of "lack"—also signals her rejection of the Other's objectification. Lest there remain any doubt of Williams's intention here, a fellow slave from New Orleans explains to Dessa that in French the term "*blanc*" (creolized as "blank") means white, an allusion surely to the encipherment of O as both "white" and "absence."

Williams, however, signals to the reader another kind of intertextual reference, one aptly defined by Gerard Genette's notion of *architextualité*.[26] By interposing into her own text a series of cameos that signify on the conventions of erotica/pornography, Williams invokes the genre rather than a specific text. The first scene depicts Ruth nursing Dessa's infant son, Mony, thereby juxtaposing the conventions of the pornographic with those of the racial obscene. The image of the white nursemaid and the black infant dismantles a long tradition in American sentimentality naturalizing the ur-image of the black mammy and the white child. Williams signifies on the stereotypical "mammy-child" image by representing its inversion as the eroticized object of the white woman's self-reflexive gaze, one which proceeds from an initial response of repulsion and mortification:

> And only when his cries were stilled and she looked down upon the sleek black head, the nut-brown face flattened against the pearly paleness of her breast, had she become conscious of what she was doing. A wave of embarrassment had swept over her and she had looked guiltily around the parlor...she had felt some mortification at becoming wet nurse for a darky....[But] she herself liked to watch the baby as he nursed, the way

he screwed up his face and clenched his fist with the effort, the contrast between his mulberry-colored mouth and the pink areola surrounding her nipple, between his caramel-colored fist and the rosy cream of her breast. (*DR*, 101–102)

Such a reversal also has the subtle effect of transcoding a traditionally sacred iconographic representation of Madonna and child into an obscene image by re-inscribing it into the context of a suggestively pornographic scenario.

In two subsequent scenes, Williams provides a counterpoint to Réage and Styron by figuring the white woman in an aggressive posture, and the black man in a posture of sexual potency (a combination that could not have existed for either of these earlier writers). This scene provides a series of graphic descriptions of fellatio and cunnilingus between the boy Nathan (a sexually potent refiguration of Styron's emasculated Nat) and Miz Lorraine, his former mistress, who has a penchant for younger slave lovers:

> She knelt before him and took his penis in her mouth. Terrified, he at first tried fumblingly to pry her head away, but already her mouth and tongue were sending such intense waves of pleasure through him that all he could do was hold her head and moan—and try to control the muscle that threatened to leap from his control.... He could hold it no longer. The power of his climax rocked him back onto the bed and he lay there, uncaring. She squirmed onto his still erect penis. Her lips still wet with his come, she sought his mouth. Faintly repelled but already excited by the pull of her vaginal muscles on his penis, he turned his lips towards hers.... the knowledge that he lay in danger [if exposed], not only of his member but of his life, sent him plunging up a peak of *unspeakable desire.* (*DR*, 156, emphasis added)

Not only does this scene speak to the psychic and physical charge of tabooed desire ("If climax, as some men said, was like death, then a nigger died a double death in a white woman's arms" [*DR*, 158]), but to the passion and aggressivity of the white woman: Miz Lorraine is a woman who wanted "to be in control" and in whom "[n]ature was strong" (*DR*, 157). Nevertheless, she refuses to allow Nathan to copulate orally with her. And on the single occasion when he attempted to do so, "she had writhed and kicked" (although "he held on until he felt the thick come against his tongue"). Because she "threatened to yell rape that night, to sell, to have him flayed... [h]e never took the lead in sex with her again" (*DR*, 157). Clearly Miz Lorraine's control here contradicts Réage's script of passive and submissive white femininity, while the representation of the dangers and pleasures of miscegenation (overlaid with undertones of adult-child sexuality) invoke two stock conventions of pornographic representation.

Yet another scene parodies the conventions of pornographic representation by invoking the dichromatic thematics of interracial sexuality—represented here as object of the black woman's gaze. It is Dessa's "startled gasp" that surprises Nathan and Ruth as they are making love:

> Nathan was the color of eggplant, a rich, velvety blueblack; beside him, [Ruth's] skin took on a pearly glow. They sweated and rested, his face buried in her bosom, one leg caught between hers. She stroked his back; his fingers played purposefully in matted pubic hair, teasing the slick lips of her vagina. Supine, she waited for him to enter her again. (*DR*, 158)

In Dessa's eyes ("I never *seed* such a thing!"), the scene before her reprises the earlier scene: "It was like seeing her [Ruth] nurse Mony [Dessa's son] for the first time all over again" (*DR*, 163). The character of Nathan allows Williams to refigure the black man's control of his sexuality, thus again subverting Styron's representation of black male emasculation.

But perhaps Williams's most subtle strategy is to signify upon the relation between O and her lover (a story of white male desire and white female submission) in her representation of the relation between Adam Nehemiah and Dessa (a story of white male desire and black female resistance). Dessa's confinement in a root cellar during the period of her "lying in" refigures O's confinement in a solitary cell. It is during this period that Nehemiah attempts to interview Dessa in preparation for his book on slave rebellions. (The relationship between the two clearly parodies a familiar scene—one that we recognize as the writing scene for that category of slave narratives commonly referred to as "as told to" narratives.) In *Dessa Rose*, it soon becomes apparent that Nehemiah cannot configure a reliable or cohesive story of Dessa in his journal—a manuscript (designed to foster the illusion that slaves can "be happy in the life that has been sent them to live" [*DR*, 231]) that would be analogous to that of the Anabaptist minister in Paulhan's text ("Happiness in Slavery"). Nehemiah is mistakenly convinced that Dessa has been "used" by her master for his own purposes, thus imagining (falsely) a prior scene of sexuality between Dessa and her master. Tellingly, the interaction between Nehemiah and Dessa takes on sexual overtones. Nehemiah discovers himself at times "oddly arrested" by Dessa, "[fancying] he could smell her, not the rank, feral stink of the cellar, but a pungent, musky odor that reminded him of sun-warmed currants and freshly turned earth" (*DR*, 38, 39). Indeed, Nehemiah regrets that he had not the responsibility of "Odessa's *breaking*" (*DR*, 68, emphasis added). In his reading, Dessa (like the slaves in Paulhan's allegory) lacked a "good" master: "What a waste," he rues, "that she should have fallen into hands such as those." While in vain pursuit of a group of slaves who ultimately rescue Dessa, Nehemiah looks forward to "a bed [which would be] most welcome—and, perhaps...something to warm it when we get back" (*DR*, 69). In the earlier "Meditations" version, the narrator notes that the sheriff "charge[s] that [he] acted like one possessed."[27] It is this hidden narrative of repressed erotic desire, signaled in the sexual coding of the language, that provides the basis for the intratextual and intertextual dialogue, linking Williams's to Styron's and Réage's narratives.

Upon recapture, Dessa expresses fear that exposure of her scars and branding will confirm her slave status. The literal inscription of Dessa's body, signified by the whipmarks and branding around the waist, hips, and thighs, precisely refigure O's markings. The location of the scarring in the area of the genitalia inscribes and sexualizes her status as *slave* and *woman* ("Scar tissue plowed through her pubic region so no hair would ever grow there again" [*DR*, 154].) These inscriptions produce, within the domain of slavery, the meaning of black female subjectivity and sexuality.

Just as O must expose her buttocks so that her inscription can be "deciphered" by her master or his surrogates, Dessa is ordered by the sheriff to raise her skirt so that her inscriptions can be "read" by her captors. But unlike Dessa, O internalizes the values and desires that are predicated upon her subordination to a system of male patriarchal privilege. And although both O and Dessa are tortured and abused, O's response to her emotional and psychological bondage differs radically from Dessa's response to social and physical bondage: If O is passive and submissive, Dessa is disruptive and defiant. If O voluntarily surrenders to a system designed to subjugate her, Dessa rebels. If O's bondage seems to be self-imposed and a consequence of her masochistic psychic needs, Dessa's enslavement is imposed from without by those who control the socioeconomic system. If O willingly exposes her scars for all to read and "penetrate," Dessa refuses to reveal hers (her successful concealment literally guarantees her freedom). If exposure and self-revelation structure O's story, concealment and escape provide the structure and motif of Dessa's. Finally, it is O's collusion in the subordination of women that makes possible patriarchal dominance, while Dessa's resistance functions to subvert both racial and sexual domination.

It is significant, then, that Dessa purposefully drops the "O" from her appellation, for unlike her problematic literary predecessor, Dessa refuses compliance in her own exploitation. The rejection of the "O" (signaling cipher, an emblem of non-being) sets Dessa in radical opposition to Réage's heroine. In her insurgency, Dessa interdicts her physical and cultural inscription, while O subscribes to the male cultural script, making her, in effect, an encipherment of male desire.

As a revision of O's story of complicity, Dessa's tale of defiance elaborates on the signifying function of inscription not only in a phallocentric, but in an enthnocentric economy of representation. If Réage's story emphasizes the role of gender difference in relation to signification and the constitution of sexuality and subjectivity, Williams's story reveals the role of sexual *and* racial difference.

Together, the works of Styron and Réage secure the subject as white and male. In the case of Styron, manhood and sexuality are constituted as attributes exclusive to *white* males; in the case of Paulhan/Réage/Aury, aggressivity and self-mastery are constituted as attributes exclusive to white *males*. In the latter instance, the construction of the feminine as passive, masochistic, and exhibitionistic obscures the construction of the masculine as aggressive, sadistic, and voyeuristic. Williams's text, however, displaces notions of feminine passivity and black emasculation by interrogating the ideological structures intrinsic to these works, which instate the subject as white and male.

If historically and psychologically, the passive feminine represents a cover for the sexually aggressive female, the emasculated black male represents a covering image generated by fear of the "Nigger Rapist." Williams challenges these stereotypical constructions of black and female identities, along with the supporting ideologies that reinscribe cultural myths and underwrite public policy decisions. Styron's work, for example, reinforced popular myths of black male emasculation promoted by the *Moynihan Report*, a document influential in determining public policy during the 1960s. Réage's novel, on the other hand, perpetuates an ideology of submission that reinforces widespread essentialist assumptions regarding women's nature as inherently passive and subordinate. Such eroticization of domination, as Susan Gubar points out in another context, "teaches us to see women as the willing, desirous, and even deserving slaves of punitive masters."[28] Both these works become part of what Michel Foucault describes as "the technologies of subjection."[29]

Epilogue

I began this chapter by discussing the risks of (re)production, and the ways in which texts (visual and verbal) interpellate us as readers, critics, interlocutors, and spectators. Styron, Réage, and Williams all, in their own way, produce and reproduce a struggle for meaning and power. The premise of this chapter is that these texts figure scenes of writing captivity; its conclusion is meant to suggest that they also figure scenes of reading submission and conquest. If Styron derives pleasure from the text through an act of mastery of the Other as black, Réage derives pleasure through an act of submission to the Other as male. But there also exists a power relationship between text and critic, one that Ross Chambers describes as a "vertical power relationship" that entails "a question of 'mastery.' "[30] Playing on the "sexual connotations of textual intercourse," Chambers claims that the power/ seduction of fiction (much like the seduction of a television talk show) resides precisely in its ability to inscribe the desires of the Other. But as reader-critics, we must ask ourselves how this process of sexual/textual mastery positions us; what happens when we yield to the mastery of the text? Is it true, as critic Kaja Silverman contends, that texts master us insofar as "they oblige us to re-enact those moments of loss and [false] recovery by which we are constituted as subjects?" Her assumption, arguably, is that, as readers, our pleasure is derived from a position of subjection to the text—a position that re-enacts a Freudian "*cultural narrative of loss and recovery.*"[31] *If Silverman's contention is true, the problematic, then, for the reader who would make reading a "liberatory" rather than "captive" experience, becomes how to avoid the passive position. In other words, how can we avoid being constructed as victims "by texts that master us" as readers who derive our pleasure from a "position of subjection"? How can we avoid victimization when we experience our subjugation as "a pleasurable repetition of [our] own history of loss and recovery?"*[32]

If, on the other hand, we should construct ourselves oppositionally as "resisting readers"—must we experience our textual pleasure from a position of dominance? Must we, in other words, become voyeurs who experience our pleasure in the Other's victimization? How can we avoid redoubling the positions of submission and conquest in the reading process? In some respects, Williams models a mode of reading that addresses these questions.

Dessa Rose is a novel that functions to instruct us on how to read literary as well as social and cultural texts. If Nehemiah suggests that misconstruction is the consequence of (mis)reading from a position of mastery, then Dessa suggests that deconstruction is the consequence of a reading of mastery from the position of victim. It is, in fact, the act of resisting subjugating readings by the master that enables her to achieve self-mastery.

The issue for the politically conscious and morally conscientious reader, as I see it, is how to deconstruct mastery and empower the victim without assuming a position of victimization. Once again, to invoke Chambers, our responsibility as readers is to "free the text from its own limitations," and that is done by identifying the "ideological and cultural constraints that have limited the text's self-conception." In other words, our incumbency as reader-critics is not only the liberation of ourselves from the text, but also the liberation of the text—a task that is accomplished by "identifying both the limitations [the text] puts on itself and the means whereby it does this, so that they can be relativized in the act of reading."[33]

There is, however, another kind of textual power that my own critical reflexivity invites the reader to consider: the power (and seduction) of the critical text—both in its desire to "master" the master('s) text and the critical reader. Chambers distinguishes between the vertical power relationship between critic and text and what he describes as the "horizontal" power relationship between critic and critical reader. In other words, the critical reader is positioned by the critic in ways that are analogous to the positioning of the reader by the literary text. Both relations carry the potential of liberation and constraint, conquest and submission. By engaging such texts—critical and fictive—in our own projects, we will necessarily occupy competing positions—competing insofar as the act of textual criticism both binds us to and liberates us from constraints of the fictive text. I would suggest, however, that as both literary and critical readers, our projects must be to deconstruct literary fictions and social relations of authority and subjugation. To the degree that her novel deconstitutes positions of dominance and submission, I would suggest that Williams's Dessa Rose provides a model for our work.

6

"Seen But Not Heard"

A Poetics of Afro-American Women's Writing

Entering from the garden, pen in hand, I assume a place at the writing table of Phillis Wheatley and Frederick Douglass to pen a response to Houston Baker's theoretic-discursive practice and call for imagistic fields. My form, too, will privilege the autobiographical as I dialogically engage Baker's theory and poetics of Afro-American women's writing. Because my current theoretical and critical work privileges the personal voices and autobiographical experiences of black women, I situate myself for this occasion in the space between discursive practices and imagistic fields.

Baker offers for our consideration the thesis that Afro-American discourse, in its most eloquent and cogent manifestations, is constituted by what he calls an autobiographical "negotiation of metalevels." "The generative conditions of African life in the New World that privilege spiritual [or metalevel] negotiation," argues Baker, "also make autobiography the premiere genre of Afro-American discourse." He concludes that "Afro-American intellectual history, therefore, is keenly theoretical because it pays a compulsory attention both to metalevels of cultural negotiation and to autobiographical inscription.... privileg[ing] the unseen and the intangibly personal."[1]

Afro-American intellectual history is characterized by engagement in the senses of being both committed *and* interlocutory. Metalevel negotiation not only engages theory but praxis as well, culminating, Baker tells us, in actional theory. One of the strengths of such a thesis is that it expands the notion of syncretism—which has, in the past, embraced the domains of folk history and the oral tradition. Baker's thesis is successful in that it produces and privileges syncretism at the level of formal literature. In anthropological terms, his thesis implies a negotiation between two traditions—the hegemonic and non-hegemonic—that results in a change for both. Such an approach constitutes an emerging consensus in poststructuralist Afro-American criticism. We can no longer regard either Afro-American literature or criticism as separate and disengaged from other literary-critical discourses. Nor,

I might add, can other literary-critical discourses any longer be considered in isolation from Afro-American discourse. Finally, Baker's theoretic-discursive model builds on the tradition of studies of the slave community begun by such scholars as John Blassingame who, in effect, rereads slave religion as Afro-Christianity and collective metalevel negotiation.

For the purposes of my response, I interpret Baker's autobiographical act, in its broadest sense, as a particular and personal discursive reading. In the spirit of this project, I would like to engage in an autobiographical negotiation not directly with a precursor but with Baker's reading of the brief excerpt from Phillis Wheatley's "To Maecenas":

> The happier *Terence* all the choir inspir'd,
> His soul replenish'd, and his bosom fir'd;
> But say, ye *Muses*, why this partial grace,
> To one alone of *Afric's* sable race,
> From age to age transmitting thus his name
> With the first glory in the rolls of fame?

Baker's interpretation suggests quite correctly that Wheatley conjures one whom the Western muses do not typically invoke, the African slave-poet Terence. In doing so, Baker tells us that Wheatley writes "her male precursor's African name...and body into the discourse of eighteenth-century heroics"—that she becomes, in effect, "an African embodiment of Terence's precursorial spirit."[2] I would submit, however, that Wheatley accomplishes something over and above a negotiation with the master discourse of Western heroics; she not only writes Terence into literary history, but (similar to her successor Douglass, who writes himself into history) performs the equally important task of writing *herself* and *her story* into *history*. This act of self-inscription is achieved through what I have elsewhere described as a dialogic engagement with both the dominant or hegemonic discursive tradition as well as the sub-dominant or (to use Rachel DuPlessis's admirable term) "ambiguously (non)hegemonic" discourse.[3] What I am proposing is that Wheatley, in the subsequent tradition of black women writers, engages in *multi*-metalevel negotiations with a tradition that privileges not only white but male discourse. Thus, the "partial grace / To one alone of *Afric's* sable race" calls into question not only the exclusion of other African voices, but the privileging as well of "the happier *Terence*" (the expression begs a comparison with the author herself).

It is, after all, *his* name transmitted "from age to age... / With the first glory in the rolls of fame." My point here is that Wheatley's complex autobiographical negotiations are not only racially but sexually strategic. Her situation positions her in a doubly marginalized relation to traditions from which she is excluded by race as a black and by gender as a woman. It is on the basis of this multi-metalevel negotiation—or what I describe as dialogic engagement with the various and multiple discourses of the other(s)—that I affirm Baker's racial reading of Wheatley's discursive dilemma but propose a simultaneous gendered rereading of the same text.

Baker's poetics of Afro-American women's writings is based on the notion of "imagistic fields," generated by Alice Walker's metaphor for the roots of black women's creativity—"our mothers' gardens."[4] Baker argues that the critic's autobiographical negotiation in relation to the imagistic fields inscribed in Afro-American women's writings yields "a unique inscription of the Afro-American self as woman" and "a refiguration of the African body that emerges from the standard male theoretical story."[5] It is noteworthy that the image of woman and the female principle have long been associated in Western thought with "the dark continent." From Freud to Suleiman to Cixous, scholars and critics have conflated the image of Africa with that of the female body, images suggesting the mysteriously unknown: the erotic and exotic, the natural and the spiritual, the primitive and the pristine. Baker, it would seem, reverses and revalorizes the conventional Western metaphorical construction of the female body in terms of the African (continental) body by suggesting that the works of contemporary Afro-American women writers inscribe the African body in terms associated with the female—spirituality, nurturance, and fertility.

Gaston Bachelard's "felicitous poetic image" becomes, for Baker, a generative metaphor for an Afro-American women's poetics. Alice Walker's image of the garden, in her essay "In Search of Our Mothers' Gardens," is a prototype of the "felicitous image" that Baker employs to formulate a poetics of black women's writing. The project is an elegant one which assumes that universal fields or categories such as space and time can only be meaningfully experienced through a culturally specific field of "particular" or vernacular imagery unique to the Afro-American imagination—and, implicitly, the Afro-American woman's imagination.

The significance of this field in the Afro-American woman's imagination is clearly suggested in Robert Stepto's interview with Toni Morrison, "Intimate Things in Place." The interview not only hints at the meaning of place—that is, "geographical landscapes"—but more precisely, the importance of "places ... set in time"—that is, the specificity of place read through time, read through the Afro-American woman's novelistic imagination. In what we might call an autobiographical negotiation of spatiality, Morrison explains to the interviewer what it is like to create a racially defined space ("the community"), and further, what it is like to create a woman's place within that community:

> I felt a very strong sense of place, not in terms of the country or the state, but in terms of the details, the feeling, the mood of the community, of the town. In [my] book, I was clearly pulling straight out of what autobiographical information I had. I didn't create that town. It's clearer in my memory than when I lived there.... Also, I think some of it is just a woman's strong sense of being in a room, a place, or in a house. Sometimes my relationship to things in a house would be a little different from, say, my brother's or my

father's or my sons'. I clean them and I move them and I do very intimate things "in place": I am sort of rooted in it, so that writing about being in a room looking out, or being in a world looking out, or living in a small defi-nite place, is probably very common among most women anyway.[6]

From a somewhat different perspective, Julia Kristeva, in her essay on "Women's Time," takes the position that "when evoking the name and destiny of women, one thinks ... of the *space* generating and forming the human species."[7] The very notion of space, maternal space, in the examples Kristeva cites, is elaborated not only by writers and theorists such as Joyce and Freud, but by Western thinkers extending back to Plato, whose *chora*, or matrix space, "provides a ground for all that can come into being."[8] Moreover, as a spatial trope for a ground of being, a source of nour-ishment and fecundity, Walker's garden is associated with Bachelard's birth and renewal imagery in *The Poetics of Space*.[9]

Indeed, so compelling is this connection between women's subjectivity and space for Kristeva that it modifies her conception of the fundamental categories of time and space as they are filtered through women's perceptions and experiences. Time, for Kristeva, can only be understood within the dimensions of spatiality. She formulates a kind of space-time ratio, "monumental temporality," that conceptual-izes "the problematic of a time indissociable from space"—a notion of time that, as she puts it, "has little to do with linear time" and more with an "all-encompassing and infinite like [*sic*] imaginary space."[10]

I confess to a certain seduction by Baker's theory for all the above reasons. Yet, while Baker is, in some respects, very much in accord with Morrison and Kristeva, the danger is not only that of essentializing but of reinforcing the most conventional constructs of (black) femininity. An equally interesting strategy would be to read these notions of female space and female body in a way that destabilizes the idealiza-tion of women.

I have a second confession—and that is to a certain sense of "dis-ease" with the *specularity* of this rather *spectacular* theory. Both the Arnoldian injunction ("to see 'the' object as in itself it really is"), Pater's revision ("to see 'a' particular, unique object as it is to me"), and Mary Russo's more specific view of woman as spectacle, are problematized for the black woman as a privileged object of discussion in the formulation of a poetics of Afro-American women's writing.[11] The privileging of the visual image, in particular, from the "autobiographical situationality" of the male, poses, for me, certain conceptual and theoretical problems.

My concerns are twofold and interrelated, and involve both the adjectival and the nominal referents in "felicitous image." Baker defines his task as "comprehensive analyses of the guiding spirituality to be discovered in the imagistic fields of black women's writing." In a further delimitation, however, he explains that "the field is decidedly not one where pathological or aversive images dominate." Continuing, he observes that "what are revealed are felicitous images of the workings of a spirit, as so wonderfully captured" by Walker's garden imagery.[12]

It is this meditation on the image (as opposed to negotiation of metalevels of discourse) that raises the problematic of the gaze. The privileging of the image—that which we can see—resides uncomfortably in Luce Irigaray's "dominant scopic economy." "In this logic, the prevalence of the gaze," writes Irigaray, woman is once again "[relegated] to passivity: she will be the beautiful object."[13] In other words, if theoretical activity connotes discursive engagement, performance, and praxis, then "imagistic fields" connotes woman as spectacle—objectified and inscribed by the male activity of scopophilia. Moreover, if black/female subjectivity is constituted by the gaze of the other(s)—just as, I would suggest, the subjectivity of the (black/male) other(s) is constituted by the (black/female) gaze—what happens to those aspects of the (black/female) self from which the gaze is averted? If, as Lacan suggests, "the gaze is the instrument through which light is embodied and through which...I am *photo-graphed*," if what "determines me, at the most profound level, in the visible, is the gaze that is outside," then I am at the mercy of what the other(s) determine is the appropriate "scopic field."[14] It is the appropriate scopic field, the grid separating the "pathological or aversive" from the "felicitous," that constitutes the most disturbing aspect of Baker's approach. What happens, one might query, when the eye is averted from the "nonfelicitous" image?

Parenthetically, and by way of transition from the noun *images* to the adjective *felicitous*, I would like to rephrase Baker's own question to non-Afro-American commentators on Afro-American expressive cultural theory. My question is addressed to those excluded by gender and/or race from the autobiographical experiences of black women: Does an autobiographical condition of existence and authenticity preclude non-Afro-American women commentators from the domain of Afro-American women's poetics? Rephrasing Baker's own response, "*I* must answer a painful No. Painful because the incumbency for the non-Afro-American *woman* critic is to finger the jagged grains of a brutal experience in which—if he or she is *white and/or male*—he or she is...implicated."[15] The non-black feminist critic/theorist who honestly engages his or her own autobiographical implication in a brutal past is likely to provide nuances such as that of the black feminist scholar. What, however, are the preconditions or precautions for the non-black feminist critic/theorist who dares to undertake such a project?

The critical act, for Baker, is "the mapping of position" or the "autobiographical situationality" which allows the "successful theorist" to know "where and how to listen," or in terms of "the poetics of space," "where and how to see."[16] Thus, the first requirement for the critic or theorist of black women's writing must be the deconstitution of the gaze of the other(s)—that is, an alteration of perception, or revision, in the sense of approaching the discursive subject or object from a new perspective or angle of vision. By confronting not only the felicitous in the imagistic fields of women's literature, but the nonfelicitous as well, one is able to "disrupt the male gaze by interrupting the pleasure of the visual."[17]

The real status of black women and their relationship to the rest of society, I would argue, cannot be captured in "felicitous images." Such a representation would suggest that black women inscribe themselves in nonadversarial relation to both the community and society at large. Such images have the potential to maintain and reinforce the status of currently marginalized and sub-dominant groups. The power of black women's writing is precisely its ability to disrupt and break with conventional imagery. If, for example, Walker's mother in the garden symbolizes birth and renewal, then Morrison's mother who burns her son to keep him from reentering the womb evokes death and destruction. If Hurston's Tea Cake can be, for her protagonist Janie, "a bee for a blossom," he is subsequently transformed into a rabid creature whom she must kill in self-defense. If Jessie Fauset's "Old Philadelphians" represent the achievements of the (black/female) middle class, the secular rewards of race uplift, and the values of material redemption, then Gloria Naylor's *Linden Hills* explores at what spiritual and emotional cost their objectives are attained. If Maya Angelou triumphs over rape and near-incest, then Morrison's Pecola succumbs to the madness resulting from the incestuous rape of a young black girl.

What do we readers learn from these *non*felicitous images—positive images that elide into their opposites? What is the danger of a poetics that locates black women within the confines of a prelapsarian Edenic garden, a poetics that does not take account of negative or aversive images? Do we run the risk of concealing from ourselves very real problems resulting from generational, class, gender, color, or racial difference and disharmony by limiting our focus to felicitous images? Dare we risk reducing the complexity and misconstructing (or misconstruing) the totality of our experiences? Although the reading suggested by the felicitous-images approach is critical and descriptive, in some respects, it seems a more sophisticated and refined reformulation of the more prescriptive positive-images approach, one component of the 1960s Black Aesthetic. Black women's lives and literature are much too complex to be limited to the duality of positive and negative images.

These eliding and ambivalent images have the effect of defamiliarizing quotidian experience and producing what Fredric Jameson calls a sense of "dialectical shock," the transitional moment in which, according to William Dowling, the reader is forced "out of customary and comfortable positions and into painful confrontations with unsuspected truths."[18] In conclusion, I would like to address the issue of difference—"critical difference." The black literary-critical tradition, as Baker has demonstrated elsewhere, has been subject to periodic shifts as we discover new critical paradigms to organize and structure our readings.[19] As a result of these sometimes seismic shifts, earlier paradigms lose their immediacy—I do not say value, but immediacy. Older critical and theoretical approaches become wrapped into tradition, as we privilege that which Roland Barthes, in "What Is Criticism?," describes as "a construction of the intelligibility of our own time."[20]

Part of the commitment of the black feminist project, however, is the privileging of difference. It is, after all, the rhetoric of universality that has excluded gender, race, and class perspectives from the dominant literary-critical discourse as well as the sociopolitical centers of power. It is the reduction of multiplicity to undifferentiated sameness that has empowered white feminists to speak for all women, black men to speak for all blacks, and white males to speak for everyone. What I propose is a multiplicity of "interested readings" which resists the totalizing character of much theory and criticism—readings that can enter into dialogic relationship with other "interested readings"—past and present.

We must deconstitute the notion of *the* black tradition. Our literary history speaks to dialogue and debate among various and competing critical camps from at least the Harlem Renaissance to the present. We engage not only in *inter*cultural metalevel negotiations, but *intra*cultural metalevel negotiations as well. Just as we must move away from the hegemony of the dominant discourse, we must move away from the hegemony of the dominant mode(s) of literary criticism within our own tradition. To suggest a pluralist resolution is perhaps too simple; we must, however, promote rival critical paradigms that critique each other's theories and readings, for despite pretensions to wholeness, there will always and forever be inadequacy in models and paradigms. They are, after all, explanations and constructions of reality based on "strategies of containment" and "boundaries of exclusion."[21]

What has sustained us in the past in our attempts to construct a whole tradition has been dialogue among rival and, at times, antagonistic models. It is the differences among these contestorial and critical models—as they speak to and critique each other—that enable us to return again and again to the notion of a black critical tradition. We must continue to recognize and respect that dialogue is necessary to fill in the lacks or deficiencies within and among different and competitive paradigms. In pursuing this critical dialogue, we engage not only our peers but also our predecessors (as Wheatley engages "the happier *Terence*"). This critical connection with both past and present is in the spirit of the Afro-American community. We are a people who have survived through recognizing and respecting each other and the ancestors.

Gayl Jones's *White Rat*

Speaking Silence/Silencing Speech

Silence itself—the things one declines to say, or is forbidden to name, the discretion that is required between different speakers—is less the absolute limit of discourse, the other side from which it is separated by a strict boundary, than an element that functions alongside the things said, with them and in relation to them within over-all strategies. There is no binary division to be made between what one says and what one does not say; we must try to determine the different ways of not saying such things, how those who can and those who cannot speak of them are distributed, which type of discourse is authorized, or which form of discretion is required in either case. There are not one but many silences, and they are an integral part of the strategies that underlie and permeate discourses.
  —Michel Foucault, *History of Sexuality, Vol I: An Introduction*

And in the naked light I saw
Ten thousand people, maybe more
People talking without speaking
People hearing without listening
People writing songs that voices never share
And no one dared
Disturb the sound of silence
  —Simon & Garfunkel, "The Sound of Silence"

As language always points to its own transcendence in silence, silence always points to its own transcendence—to a speech beyond silence.
  —Susan Sontag, "The Aesthetics of Silence"

Gayl Jones comes from a maternal line of writers that includes her playwright grandmother, Amanda Wilson, and her mother, Lucille Jones, who is a short story writer. Her favorite stories as a child growing up in Lexington, Kentucky, were the tales her mother wrote and read to her and her brother. Indeed, from her first stirrings as an author when she was in the second or third grade, young Gayl was drawn to spoken rather than written language. She learned to write from listening to the speech of her mother in particular and the speech of her community in general, demonstrating

Barbara Christian's assertion that black women writers are "immersed into their communities and their communities' ways of making meaning through their mothers."[1] Jones herself explicitly attributes the source of her creativity to her mother and her mother's stories. "If my mother hadn't written and read to me when I was growing up," she says, "I probably wouldn't have even thought about it at all."[2]

If her mother was the formative literary influence on Jones, it was the creative writing program at Brown University, where she enrolled after earning a bachelor's degree at Connecticut College in 1971, that provided her with formal training. There, in the poet Michael Harper, Jones found a teacher and mentor whom she "admired and trusted as [her] 'first' reader." At Brown, Jones also found what every fledgling writer needs—namely, the "time to write."[3]

Jones obviously used that time well, for she produced her first novel, *Corregidora* (1975), while still a graduate student. Her second novel, *Eva's Man*, appeared a year later. An experimenter in various genres, she published the collection of short stories *White Rat* in 1977 and the narrative poem *Song for Anninho* in 1981. By the time she came to the University of Michigan as a Fellow, remaining as a teacher and writer-in-residence, Jones had begun to achieve the status of writer. In 1983 she published a second volume of poetry, *The Hermit-Woman*, and two years later, another volume entitled *Xarque and Other Poems*. After a period of relative silence, Jones published a critical volume, *Liberating Voices: Oral Tradition in African-American Literature* (1991), a publication marking a departure from her earlier creative work as well as continuing an interest in exploring the oral roots of black literary forms.

It is no simple task to summarize the stories and sketches comprising Gayl Jones's *White Rat*. They enact moments and mindscapes that resist not only the narrator's moralization of experience, but ostensibly the reader's quest for "hidden meaning."[4] In part, the difficulty in identifying thematic connections resides in the characteristic absence in her fiction of authorial intrusion and judgment. Jones prefers to write in the first person, giving the impression that "it's just the character who's there." In constructing the interiority—the psychology, or psychic landscapes—of her characters, Jones, in effect, allows them to speak for themselves, sometimes in dialogue and sometimes in interior monologue. At the very heart of her stories are speech and silences that speak eloquently to the pleasure of her text, but also to "that deep well that one can trust... [that] sense of location" that guarantees the storyteller "a certain moral and human perspective" rendering access to the "deep part that [she] knows, that human center."[5] In Pinteresque fashion, Jones's work resonates with both the plenitude and paucity of language in human relationships in the modern world. Yet her stories both thematize and formalize silence as a stratagem that reveals the discontinuities and breaks in the connections and bonds between individuals. Sometimes these silences are expressed by a recalcitrant refusal to speak, and, at other times, by an eruption of speech that displaces or veils that which is left unsaid. Fundamentally, the stories in this collection explore what I might call the inner imaginary—those feelings, passions, emotions, thoughts that get expressed on the "lower frequencies," that are not always subject to observation and rarely to judgment, that sometimes remain inarticulate, but at other times convulse into uncontrollable speech. The reader cannot help but associate these dynamics with a therapeutic process that centers on repression (silence) and dialogue (speech).

The tension between silence and speech, however, is a theme that permeates not only Jones's art, but also her life. "Your Poems Have Very Little Color in Them"— which Jones says is the only story in her collection that "comes close to autobi-ography"[6]—concerns the artist/narrator's problems with communication. This is a story that articulates an anxiety between what Jones describes as "[her] own trouble communicating (talking) and writing as a means of doing that"[7]; here, the narrator muses:

> Some people say things they shouldn't say....It is better to say nothing at all than to say what you shouldn't say....Some people think before they talk. Some people talk before they think. Some people make you say things you don't want to say....I wish I knew someone who could make you say what you do want to say. I suppose that is only yourself.[8]

At the end of the story, the narrator retreats into reticence. Ironically, Jones herself is known to be as taciturn, if not indeed as enigmatic and mysterious, as some of the characters in her fiction. It is telling that, when interviewed, early in her career, by Claudia Tate, who asked Jones, "Do you want to have a reputation, a recognizable name?," the fledging author even then replied:

> The writers whom I would most like to be like are those whose works have a reputation, but the person, the writer, is more or less outside of it. I would want to maintain some kind of anonymity, like J. D. Salinger. That's the kind of reputation I'd like, where you can go on with what you're doing, but have a sense that what you do is appreciated, that there's quality to what you're doing.[9]

With the exception of her poems, which have appeared intermittently, Jones's creative voice went underground during her self-imposed exile in France for sev-eral years. In the late 1990s, she published two well received novels, *The Healing* (1998) and *Mosquito* (1999).[10] Since the appearance of these latter volumes, however, Jones has suffered family tragedy, and has once more retreated from the public eye.[11]

Jones's work, like her personal life, confronts the reader with gaps and silences. In *White Rat,* she creates characters for whom language is frightening (Maggie, in the title story "White Rat," is "a woman scart of words" [10]). Yet, if her writing is pre-occupied with what Susan Sontag, in another context, describes as "the aesthetics of silence," Jones also creates characters who *must* speak. "I often like to have *talkative* people in my stories," she maintains.[12] Silence and its opposite, speech, then, are primary attributes of Jones's work.

Jones, in fact, achieves much of her effect through a technique of writing that is self-reflexive, in the sense that her work is preoccupied with its own fictive processes of creation. In an interview with Charles Rowell, Jones says, "Often themes of communication and taciturnity enter my work."[13] Elsewhere, Jones describes her writing as a way of defining herself. "There was no way I could explain who I was to myself or anybody else except that way," she says, "[p]articularly my silence. I had to say something about it some way." Readers of her work, she believed, "would feel less badly [*sic*] about [her] not talking."[14] Clearly, Jones identifies with women characters such as the mother in her novel *Corregidora*, who cannot speak to her husband ("It was just like my mouth was there, but I just couldn't say nothing"),[15] as well as with male characters such as Jake in "The Roundhouse," who works in silence ("[He] doesn't say anything and people think he can't talk").[16]

A dramatic example of how Jones brings voice and silence into meaningful conjunction, "Your Poems Have Very Little Color in Them" also serves as a model for how the reader might approach the pieces in this collection, a model formulated in opposition to that of the readers/listeners figured in the story. Jones's narrator positions herself as storyteller in relation to her audience. However, when she tells her "funny stories" and sings her "funny songs," her listeners respond with "Is that all? Had us sitting here listening for that?" (20). Like her narrator, the author offers her readers story fragments—texts that subvert our notions of form and structure and meaning—thus frustrating our expectations of the unity and coherence of traditional narrative. When the reader expects plot, the author constructs collage; when the reader expects characterization, the author transcribes dialogue; when the reader expects closure, the text remains open-ended. After reading the stories and sketches in *White Rat*, we may wonder aloud, along with the listeners in "Your Poems," "Is that all?" Jones's technique of de-narrativization, however, is meant to challenge our notions of what constitutes a story by re-inscribing the relation between storyteller and listener, between author and reader. In the process of raising questions that the stories refuse to answer, Jones requires the listener/reader to participate in the production of meaning. It is, thus, up to the reader to supply a measure of coherence by constructing context and identifying patterns of repetition in a form that manifestly lacks either.

Confronted with the voices and silences in which the text speaks, the reader must enter into a kind of dialogue with the writer. Jones positions her "implied reader" in much the same way as the Russian theorist Mikhail Bakhtin might position his active "listener," who must fill in the textual silences and blanks. Inevitably, then, meaning resides neither in what German reception theorist Wolfgang Iser calls "the reality of the text" nor in "the subjectivity of the reader." Rather, it is constituted as a product of the interaction between text and reader. The production of meaning is therefore negotiated, in Iser's words, not as "an object to be defined, but an effect to be experienced."[17] Moreover, the dialogue between text and reader not only subverts the notion of any single, coherent, or determinate meaning associated with the text, but also creates an encounter that has the possibility of yielding multiple meanings. Jones's work, finally, becomes the site of mediation between writer and reader who collaborate in the processes of literary creation and interpretation.

The analogies of speaker to writer and listener to reader are particularly apt in considering Jones's work because of her own emphasis on the importance of spoken language in the construction of these narratives. "I've never written a story without dialogue," Jones remarked in an interview with Harper. "I always have to have people talking. Speech has to be there. I guess you could say my method is improvisational."[18] Clearly, the most striking feature of Jones's work is her emphasis on storytelling and the *orality* of Afro-American narrative. In an early interview, Jones explains the oral foundation of her art:

> I used to say that I learned to write by listening to people talk. I still feel that the best of my writing comes from having *heard* rather than having read... [M]y first stories were heard stories—from grown-up people talking. I think it's important that we—my brother and I—were never sent out of the room when grown-ups were talking. So we heard their stories. I've always heard stories of people generations older than me.[19]

However, not only is the author a storyteller, but she creates characters who are also storytellers. The technique of first-person narration, Jones believes, is "the most authentic way of telling a story" because it implies "direct identification of the storyteller with the story."[20] By creating a narrator who is also the subject of the story, Jones virtually ensures the "erasure" of the author.

"A Quiet Place for the Summer" is another instance of Jones's coded self-reflexivity, in that it speaks to the polyvocality of her work. In the interview with Rowell, Jones affirms the black woman writer's ability to "create language/voices"—to invent a "linguistic world." As a writer, she desires to relate "[her] own voice—[her] other voice(s)...to the voices" of her female characters.[21] In this story about an artist's awakening to her creativity and sexuality, the protagonist, a college student, rents her English professor's country house in Vermont, where she intends to spend her summer writing stories. Here she meets Coleman, a former seaman and caretaker of the grounds. As a gardener and storyteller, Coleman himself is a kind of folk artist. Like other characters in *White Rat*, the protagonist is reticent. Contemplating the stillness and silence of a tree, she apostrophizes, "You must have many voices in you" (158). Understanding her identification with the tree, Coleman tells her that "a tree can be so still and have so much going on inside of it. There are people like that, you know" (157). Later, however, he adds, "[Trees] stand still but everything is happening inside of them. A person shouldn't stand still. A person doesn't have to. You can let as much that's happening inside of you out—whatever you want to"

(166). A man of many places, he tells her, "I still got my accent. Though I've got many voices" (161). His point, of course, is that, as a writer, she must be able to articulate the voices of others while, at the same time, maintaining her "accent"— her difference and individuality. A catalyst to the protagonist's creativity, Coleman tells stories about the professor and his wife that provoke her wonder and imagination. She gets so she can improvise on his stories. "I've got you talking now," Coleman says to her, "You didn't say much when we first met" (166). Together, they collaborate to produce both text and meaning. But this is a story about sexuality as well as textuality. In contrast to the protagonist's admiration of trees in the winter, Coleman, as caretaker, thinks that "the best time" is "in the spring...when the sap runs" (157). Coleman uses the language of nature to express both his desire and her creativity ("I wonder how a tree feels when it lets go a fruit" [166]). His natural imagery figures the sexual act as well as the creative process in a moment of sexual and artistic awakening for the young writer.

The dialectic of silence and speech found in these stories does not, however, elide those moments of mediation we commonly call secrets or, obversely, confessions—moments described by William Andrews, in another context, as "mode[s] of communication betwixt and between."[22] Jones's characters harbor secrets and stage confessions of miscegenation, madness, sexuality, and violence—secrets that do not bind and confessions that may not heal.

In the title story, "White Rat," the narrator, so named because he "come[s] from a family of white-looking niggers" (5), speaks of vows and violations in a barroom "confession" of racial guilt. Rat relates the parables of two priests—one black and one white—who break their vows of celibacy. Both thereby bring curses upon their progeny, symbolized by a club-footed "white" child sired by the black priest and a "nigger" child sired by the white priest. But these parables about the symbolic dangers of violating religious (or racial) taboos are really parables within a parable: the story of White Rat is about what happens when one worships whiteness. His son's "deformity" is the external projection of his own assimilation of the values of the whites, or "hoogies." Rat, finally, is a character imprisoned within the social myth of race, conditioned by a Pavlovian reflexive response to whiteness.[23]

Another story of imprisonment, "Persona" is a tale of unspoken and unspeakable desire. The narrator, a teacher in a women's college, lives and works in an environment where desire between women is either suppressed or relegated to a "stage" in women's development. At the annual freshman lecture, the students are told that they would experience "sexual ambiguity" and feel "uncertain about their womanhood." The school psychiatrist assures them, however, that such attachments are "natural" and part of the "process of growing up" (86). As a young woman, the narrator herself had been told that her feelings for women were "perfectly natural" and "nothing to worry about," that she would outgrow them (86). Her own experience is thus replicated in the lives of the young female students at the college where she teaches. Both the medical and academic discourses suppress what Willa Cather once described as "the inexplicable presence of the thing not named."[24] Concealed behind the persona of a spinster schoolteacher, then, the narrator, imprisoned within the social myths of gender and heterosexuality, dares not speak of her love for women.

Significantly, both the formal discourse and personal dialogue in "Persona" are punctuated by recurrent mid-sentence breaks and ellipses. This rhetorical device, *aposiopesis* (Greek for "to become silent"), functions as a narrative strategy representing the suppression of both the narrator's discourse and her desire. Desire remains unacknowledged not only by the narrator, but also by the other characters in the story. Isolated by secret doubts and anxieties, characters use speech and deed to disguise rather than express their real needs. Yet the narrator's final gesture ("I stared at her. She looked as if she didn't see me. I put my hand in her short hair and made her look at me" [94]) would suggest that she moves toward a moment of recognition as both subject and object of desire.

According to feminist scholar Colette Guillaumin, "When one is materially appropriated, one is mentally dispossessed of oneself."[25] In "Asylum," the narrator, a black woman, is committed to a mental hospital, where she is required to submit to a gynecological as well as a psychological examination in a scene that suggests the link between the control of woman's body and madness. The psychological examination, like the physical examination, is figured as probing and invasive. In prescribing the "talking cure" for the narrator, the doctor instructs her, *"You must tell me what you're thinking."* The narrator's response—*"Is that the only way I can be freed?"* (81)—suggests that the discourse of psychoanalysis confines women in a "prison house of language." The narrator, however, refuses to "show and tell": she submits neither to gynecological nor to psychological probing. If the doctor's speech links him to a discourse of reason, then the narrator's silence links her to a discourse of madness. In her psychological breakdown, the narrator manifests the classic symptoms of the hysteric, but her symbolic aphasia in the conclusion can also be interpreted as an act of resistance. Like Freud's famous patient, Dora, the narrator of "Asylum" refuses to speak, refuses to allow the psychiatrist to construct her as an object in his discourse. Yet, perhaps unknown to her, the narrator's muteness on one level only confirms the psychoanalytic process. Moreover, if silence implies resistance to a white, authoritarian, male discourse constructed upon the suppression of black women's voices and bodies, it also risks conformity, if not passive collusion, with a system of medical and psychiatric practices and a structure of representation (reason and madness) that function to marginalize, confine, and silence black women.

In "The Return: A Fantasy," the narrator, Dora (another Freudian invocation), introduces the reader to Joseph, a prophet-like figure who believes that it is not enough to "conduct your life *as if* you were Christ. You must become Christ" (105). Bearing a legacy of paternal guilt, Joseph is the son of a sexually ambivalent father and a mother who abandons him. The victim of schizophrenic delusions, Joseph acts out the roles of penitent and confessor. If "Asylum" implies a link between psy-choanalysis and confession, then "The Return" conflates the father-confessor and psychoanalyst with the sinner and schizophrenic.

While Joseph's relationship with his father is based on the guilt-ridden ritual of confession-absolution, the relationships between Joseph and the other characters in the story are structured by the rituals of mystical mergence. For example, Joseph's relationship with Steven, Dora's brother, would seem, on one level, to be that of priest to acolyte. Modeling himself after Joseph, Steven grows a beard and later moves into Joseph's living quarters. Steven, it would seem, does not want to live *as if* he were Joseph, but to *become* Joseph. In turn, Joseph, in a mock sacramental meal, mimics the ritual of transubstantiation as he offers bread and wine to Steven and Dora. This ritual suggests the desire of these characters to merge both physically and spiritually.

Further, Joseph's relationship with surrogate siblings Steven and Dora reconsti-tutes the primal family relationship. He is able to reconcile his parents' separation (reflected in his own schizoid personality) in his intimacy with Dora, whose nurtur-ing allows him to play the role of child, and with Steven, whose "discipleship" allows him to play the role of father. But Joseph's relationship with Steven and Dora also allows him to enact his schizophrenia: his "divided self" achieves expression in a "bisexual" relationship of sorts with surrogate brother and sister in a kind of recon-structed "family romance."

Significantly, there are still things about Joseph that neither Dora, who becomes his wife, nor Steven, his "brother" (nor the reader, for that matter), can ever know. Although the homoerotic subtext of the relationship between Joseph and Steven is not lost on the reader, it is clearly suppressed by Dora, whose leading question, "What's going on between you two?" (109) is followed by an elliptical moment in the text. Thus, in some respects, the narrative strategy of avoidance here not only suppresses, but reinforces the leitmotif of homoerotic sexual suppression. The desire to merge into another body—to be one with another person—is, of course, the ultimate sexual fantasy. Yet the desired mergence is always challenged in this fragmented story about fragmented characters who resist, finally, the coherence of fiction and fictional identity.

If in "The Return" Joseph is presented to the reader from the perspective of Dora, a sympathetic and compassionate narrator, in "Version 2," a kind of coda to the entire collection, Joseph is allowed to speak for himself. Although "Version 2" fills in some of the gaps and fissures of the first story, there is much that remains suppressed. Perhaps the most accented piece in a collection that leans into postmodernism, "Version 2" reflects Jones's preoccupation with the relationship between psychol-ogy and form. Jones experiments with "how psychological states [influence] speech and language patterns and the making of stories, the kinds of fragmentation that would occur in such storytelling."[26] This is a technique that the author utilizes in her longer fiction as well.

In the interview with Rowell, Jones says that her "most authentic stories are in first person" when she is able to "enter the characters and tell their stories as they would tell them."[27] This is precisely what she achieves in "Version 2." If, elsewhere in *White Rat*, Jones shows characters on the "borderlines," then in "Version 2" she explores territory beyond the borders by actually entering the "inner landscape" of madness. In place of the closing silence of "Asylum" is the lengthy interior monologue that concludes "Version 2." If in "Asylum" the narrator imposes a self-silencing, in "Version 2" the narrator explodes into a discourse of madness. The collection thus ends not with silence but with the eruption of a subjugated and repressed discourse.

Jones's stories, however, concern not only persons who are regarded as deviant or different; they also focus on ordinary people caught up in extraordinary situations—individuals trapped in personal fictions and social myths. Her fictive universe is populated by characters from her native Kentucky, characters whose stories dramatize experiences of madness, violence, sexuality, isolation, and, sometimes, communion. These themes indicate a regional sensibility that connects Jones with Southern writers like Flannery O'Connor. But O'Connor's stories end with the option of a hard-earned grace and redemption: Jones's open-ended stories leave her characters with no clear solutions. Rather, they share a quality of tragedy, in the modern rather than Aristotelian sense—tragedy in that these are characters whose dreams have been shattered or, conversely, who have been shattered by their dreams.

If in her short stories Jones explores "a range of personalities," she explores "a range within one personality" in her novels, *Corregidora* (1975) and *Eva's Man* (1976).[28] The stories in *White Rat*, written earlier but published after her novels, signal the directions and preoccupations of the later works. In some respects, they are experiments in form and technique as well as variations in motif and theme that anticipate the longer fictions. *Corregidora* concerns a blues singer, Ursa Corregidora, the last in the line of women who trace their origins back to "old man Corregidora, the Portuguese slave breeder" who made whores of his female slaves and "fathered his own breed" (8–9). At the outset of the novel, the pregnant Ursa is knocked down by her husband, Mutt, and, consequently, loses her child and her ability to "make generations"—traditionally the way by which the Corregidora women preserve their history and "leave evidence." Ursa must break the cycle of abuse exercised upon the Corregidora women, a cycle replicated in her relationship with Mutt. She must discover another way of bearing witness, or giving "subjective testimony," to the pain of her past.[29] After her operation and release from the hospital, Ursa discovers that she has achieved a "new voice" in which to express her pain ("a hard voice that hurts you and makes you still want to listen").[30] It is the language and form of the blues that provide for Ursa a way of speaking the memories of her great-grandmother, her grandmother, her mother, herself: "I wanted a song that would touch me, touch my life *and* theirs. A Portuguese song, but not a Portuguese song. A new world song. A song branded with the new world."[31] It is also through the blues, encoded in what

Jones calls "ritualized dialogue,"[32] that Ursa and Mutt achieve communication and communion after a separation of twenty-two years:

> "I don't want a kind of woman that hurt you," he said.
> "Then you don't want me."
> "I don't want a kind of woman that hurt you."
> "Then you don't want me."
> "I don't want a kind of woman that hurt you."
> "Then you don't want me."[33]

After the three-line repetition (a pattern characteristic of the blues as a form), Ursa cries, "I don't want a kind of man that'll hurt me either,"[34] thus bringing Jones's open-ended "blues novel" to a "resolution" of sorts.[35]

Stories such as "Asylum" and "Version 2" suggest Jones's preoccupation with what she calls "psychological obsessions and oppressions,"[36] a concern developed more fully in *Eva's Man*. Here Jones continues her exploration of what she describes as "abnormal psychology" and its relationship to "the psychology of language."[37] While words are liberating for Ursa, Eva's speechlessness would seem to keep her imprisoned. Indeed, the novel opens with its protagonist-narrator in a prison for the criminally insane. Yet, as her story unfolds through a complex interplay of memory and fantasy, the reader (listener) witnesses the reclamation of a woman's past. If *Corregidora* is what Jones calls a "blues novel," then *Eva's Man* is what she describes as a "horror story."[38] The first novel is structured by ritualized dialogue, which turns on repetition, while the second is driven by a kind of hysterical silence that discharges into unruly speech. Eva, who has committed an unspeakable and bizarre act for which she has been confined, constructs for the listener (her cellmate) an "intimate history" in which she recounts her life "in terms of horrific moments."[39]

Ursa speaks in the rhythms and forms of the blues. Eva speaks in a discourse of madness. By shifting the weight and perspective and proportions of certain events and relationships in the course of telling her stories, Jones shows how "abnormal psychological conditions" affect her protagonist's perception of the events of her life and, hence, the form in which Eva dramatizes them. As an "unreliable narrator" who "refuses to render her stories coherently," Eva controls not only what she tells (her speech), but also what she will not tell (her silences).[40] Jones explains, "I wanted the sense of [Eva's] keeping things to herself, choosing the things she would withhold. But I also wanted the reader to have a sense of not even knowing whether the things she recalls are, in fact, true. She may be playing a game with the listener."[41] Like the woman narrator in "Asylum," Eva may (or may not) remain a prisoner of her own conscience, yet her silence not only resists the doctor's power and authority, but also expresses the assertion of her own autonomy, even within a space of confinement.

One is tempted in these stories of psychopathology to link suffering to creativity and madness to art—as did Plato, Freud, Laing, and others. But whether or not these stories speak to the "creative malady" of the characters, they do indeed speak to the relationship between the writer and psychoanalyst. Like the analyst, the writer explores the inner recesses of the mind. Both also deal in "fictions" of normality and abnormality. Jones's characters, however, do not always experience transcendence or the transmutation of illness into art, suffering into sanity, madness into creativity. The redemptive potential of the "talking cure" is problematized by the silence of the woman in the asylum, the delirium of Joseph, and the fantasies of Eva. If anything, Jones's work would seem to affirm that the redemptive power of art is greater than that of psychoanalysis. After all, it is Ursa Corregidora who is potentially "saved" by the transmutative possibilities of the blues, while Eva, along with Joseph and the narrator in "Asylum," would seem finally to remain entrapped in dangerous and self-destructive fictions.

In her interview with Tate, Jones describes the "contradictory emotions that co-exist" in her characters.[42] What is unique about Jones's characters is that they psychically inhabit liminal zones of ambiguity and contradiction. Throughout *White Rat,* Jones explores what author Gloria Anzaldúa describes as "psychological borderlands...sexual borderlands and...spiritual borderlands." Jones's stories, like her fiction in general, traverse the borderlands between speech and silence, reality and fantasy, reason and madness, art and religion, male and female, heterosexuality and homosexuality, black and white, old age and youth. "Living on borders and in margins," writes Anzaldúa, poses the challenge of "keeping intact one's shifting and multiple identity and integrity."[43] Borders and margins are the uncomfortable zones of contradiction that Jones's characters occupy—that all of us occupy—but which, Jones suggests, are "home" as well. Jones's fiction demonstrates, finally, what she describes as "'connections' to home territory—connections that go to one's ideas of language, personality, landscape."[44]

8

The State of Our Art

Black Feminist Theory in the 1990s

[Some years back, Audre Lorde wrote that "The master's tools will never dismantle the master's house." Many feminists have wrestled with the dilemmas encapsulated in that sentence. But for women of color, the tools of the master—or mistress—have been particularly suspect items, while the need to dismantle the master's house and build one of their own has been especially urgent.—*The Women's Review of Books*[1]]

Women's Review: The traditional opposition of theory and practice has come under fire from several directions in recent years. What are your thoughts on the dichotomy and its current critics? Does it have any special resonance for you as a woman of color?

Mae Henderson: The relationship between theory and practice, as I perceive it, is both multiple and specific. Practice in the absence of theory divorces what we do from any meaning or connection to the entire framework of social activity. On the other hand, we have learned to be suspicious of the grand narratives or total- izing theories of writers like Marx and Freud. In the first place, these worldviews tend to exalt theory over practice. Second, these "beautiful theories" fail to explain adequately the lives and work of blacks and women and other marginalized groups. Marxism must subsume the activities of blacks and women under the banner of the working class in order to account for their role in social change; Freud assumes a male paradigm of development within which he constructs a "deficiency model" of female sexuality and identity formation.

By positing a complex and dynamic relationship between practice and theory, I attempt to subvert the kind of totalizing relationship these conceptions encourage. The "multiplicity of relationships" between theory and practice derives from his- torically specific and localized contexts and positionalities—defined by race, class, and gender as constructed in different periods and places. Not only does practice, from this perspective, derive from theory; theory derives from practice.

In his recent book on black women's poetics, Houston Baker argues that "We are always embroiled with theory—even when the word itself is absent." While I agree with Baker that a non-theoretical subject position is impossible, I would equally contend that a non-practicing subject position is undesirable.[2] Barbara Christian argues that "people of color have always theorized." ("My folk...have always been a race for theory.") Yet she goes on to specify that "our theorizing...is often in narrative forms" rather than in "the Western form of abstract logic."[3] I take Christian's term, "theorizing," as one especially appropriate to my own praxis as a "theorizing" critic. My approach to reading, as a colleague describes it, is to *thematize* theory and *theorize* theme in my readings of black women's writing. I conceive of my own work as a response to Christian's call for a narrative enactment of certain theoretical propositions.

As a theorizing critic, I translate the relationship between theory and practice into the way I read and represent texts. My goal is less to use theory as a means of grounding practice or even, for that matter, practice as a means of building theory, but rather to use both theory and practice, and their multiple relations, to create sites of struggle and resistance to dominant practices.

Beyond first readings and intertextual readings lie what black feminist critic Cheryl Wall calls "relational readings," readings that speak to the relation between the verbal text and what is sometimes described as the "social text."[4] In my work on Sherley Anne Williams, for instance, I show how specific black women's texts situate themselves within and influence certain discursive and social formations [see Chapter 2 of this volume]. My aim is to analyze the relationship between a text such as Williams's novella "Meditations," written in the 1970s, and William Styron's *The Confessions of Nat Turner*, published in 1967, and their relationship to a document such as the *Moynihan Report* and its impact on a political discourse that made certain dangerous notions—the so-called black matriarchy and black male emasculation—instrumental in shaping social consciousness and public policy. At some point, then, the theorizing critic must make connections not only within and between texts, but also between the world and the text. She must be a close reader as well as a relational reader; she cannot separate practical criticism from its theoretical implications.

WR: Another current debate turns on the value—political and otherwise—of the poststructuralist/deconstructionist school of criticism. Do you see that school as pernicious, valuable, or what?

MH: What is of value in the poststructuralist/deconstructionist school is that it aims at decentering what is essentially a white and male tradition and, in the process, creating a space for the representation of voices hitherto muted or marginalized. What is questionable is that it is a project that dismantles notions of authorship (Barthes), notions of tradition (Foucault), and notions of subjectivity (Lacan) during a period when blacks, feminists, and other marginalized groups are asserting authorship, tradition, and subjectivity.

Yet I would suggest that there is an integral, if sometimes overlooked, connection between these two phenomena: it is precisely the emergence of these marginalized groups that is responsible for destabilizing Western normative cultural referents by providing alternative loci of authority. In other words, the category of "black woman writer" itself constitutes a challenge to an ideology of author and subject as primarily male, white, Western, middle class, and heterosexual. The danger is that white feminist and black male scholars, who challenge these notions, run the risk of substituting *the* Other (as Black or Woman) as the irreducible and self-sufficient "alterity" in the reconstruction of authorship, tradition, and subjectivity.

What interests me is the way in which the works of black women writers privilege not an artificially created "unified subjectivity" based on a model of denial or repression of "otherness," but a complex (inter)subjectivity acknowledging the differences *within* and *between*—and figured categorically by at least two metaphors of difference or otherness (race and gender). This inevitably deconstructs notions of tradition, unity, and homogeneity associated with Western metaphysics. Arguably, the so-called "crisis of legitimation" implied in notions such as the decentering of the author is, finally, more a problem for the *West* than for the *rest* of us—whose asserted presence/voices have, in effect, dislocated and destabilized Western notions of origin and homogeneity.

WR: What do you feel are the political implications or presuppositions of the critical writing you do?

MH: I think this question raises some of the same issues as the first, about the relationship between literature and the entire framework of social activity within which we work and live. I'd like, however, to deal with this question more locally in terms of the academy. For those of us who write and teach for a living, the academy is a significant part of our world.

As teachers, writers, and critics, we who profess an "intellectual vocation" use words to change the worlds in which we live. What we write and how we write has much to do with the process of canonization—what we read and what we teach. For this reason, we must recognize and take responsibility for the agency of critical and theoretical writing in (re)constructing and (re)figuring the literary canon. These activities constitute the terrain of struggle within the academy.

The role of the critic, I believe, involves more broadly the responsibility of the intellectual. In the May 1961 issue of the *Monthly Review*, an essay appeared entitled "The Commitment of the Intellectual," in which the author, Paul Baran, argued that the intellectual is essentially a social critic.[5] Within the academy, the role of the (progressive) intellectual is most characteristically to oppose the established order. Rather than raising consciousness or enlightening the masses, the role of the intellectual, as I conceive it, is to challenge more traditional and outmoded, though still dominant, ways of thinking; to deconstruct ideologies that lead us into complicity with our own oppression; to dismantle the conventional wisdom; and in the process of problematizing the "obvious," to create alternative ways of conceptualizing the "natural." In some respects, of course, the very categories of "black woman writer" and "black feminist critic/theorist" challenge received notions of authorship and literary authority as conventionally inscribed in Western cultural mythology.

WR: How much do you draw on, or see yourself allied with, the work of Third World, postcolonial critics and theorists? And what kinds of emphases, arguments, or purposes distinguish your work from that of white feminist and black male critics?

MH: Despite certain historical and context-specific differences among blacks, women, and postcolonials, there are similarities in the positionality of these groups: all are marginalized, by race, gender, or economic exploitation, in relation to a dominant or hegemonic culture. The dominating pattern of symbolic representation (and the underlying power relations characterizing the relationship between the dominant and dominated cultural reference groups) turns on what postcolonialist critic Abdul R. JanMohamed describes as "an economy of manichean allegory" that transforms physical difference into moral and metaphysical difference.[6] Moreover, Third World postcolonial critics/theorists as well as black and feminist scholars share the responsibility of the intellectual as social critic to identify and analyze the significance of Western conceptions of otherness: to ask how they function to structure representation and, more broadly, the inter-relationships between politics, ideology, power, and discourse. Finally, these critics and theorists confront similar methodological dilemmas: they must avoid the uncritical appropriation of Western theoretical apparatuses—and, as Henry Louis Gates, Jr., warns, avoid substituting "one mode of neocolonialism for another."[7]

Black feminist criticism stands at the intersection of two discursive formations—the racial critique and the feminist critique, both fundamentally liberating in impulse. Yet white feminist scholars, more often than not, still subsume black women writers under the category of Woman in the feminist critique, and black male scholars continue to subsume black women writers under the category of Black in the racial critique.

My own work is an attempt to intervene and subvert what can be regarded as a kind of cultural imperialism masked as cultural pluralism. I propose a theory of reading based on what I call the "simultaneity of discourse," a concept meant to signify a mode of reading that examines the ways in which the perspectives of race and gender, and their inter-relationships, structure the discourse of black women writers and locate their works in dialogic, revisionary, and intertextual relation to other historical and contemporary discursive formations. I have demonstrated how this process works in a number of critical essays. In a forthcoming article [see Chapter 4 of this volume], I examine the way in which Toni Morrison in her novel, *Beloved*, engages the discourse of slavery as represented in the works of black male slave narrators and white male historiographers. In an essay I am currently working on [see Chapter 5 of this volume], I seek to demonstrate how Sherley Anne Williams places herself at the juncture of a historical debate on slavery and a contemporary debate on women's sexuality in her novel *Dessa Rose*.

This discursive diversity, or simultaneity of discourse in the works of black women writers, I call "speaking in tongues." The positionality of black women writers is complex, revisionary, and dialogic: it engages not only the positions of black (male) and (white) feminist critics and theorists, but also that of Western, white, and male theorists. My own work represents a combination of Mikhail Bakhtin's dialogics of discourse and Hans-Georg Gadamer's dialectical model of conversation, in a model that addresses both the familial, or testimonial, and public, or competitive, discursive engagement in the writings of black women. Yet my interpretive paradigm is, in some respects, as much indebted to the sisters of the Sanctified Church—the church of my mother and the church of my childhood—as it is to continental philosophy.

WR: Where do you see your field developing in the future?

MH: Despite its origins in the critique of the racism and omissions of white feminist literary scholarship and the sexism and distortions of black male literary scholarship, black feminist practice has been driven less by the "feminist critique" than by "gynocritical" inquiry. Critical activity has been directed, in large part, to the reconstruction and formulation of a black feminist tradition and aesthetic. To this end, much work has been aimed at, first, the reclamation of lost and neglected works by black women writers, and second, close and relational readings of past and contemporary writings by black women.

More recently, black feminist scholarship has begun to demonstrate a preoccupation with broader cultural and theoretical concerns, especially as these challenge the more conventional and received notions of what "properly" constitutes literary studies—both conceptually and canonically. Barbara Smith's pioneering formulation that a black feminist approach to literature "embodies the realization that the politics of sex as well as the politics of race and class are crucially interlocking factors in the works of black women writers" also has tremendous significance for reading the works of non-black women writers.[8] The politics of sex and race and class inform not only the works of black women writers, as Smith argues, but also those of white and male writers as well as black and women writers. After all, we have come to recognize that race/gender/class are particularizing attributes of all authors (and characters). To the extent that black feminist readings of these works frustrate transcendent, universalizing notions of the "human condition"— notions characteristically representative of white, male, middle-class, heterosexual norms and values—this approach affirms the complex and heterogeneous nature of human experience.

9

What It Means to Teach the Other
When the Other Is the Self

The radical feminist...teacher must claim her authority if her students
are to claim their own. The power she has resides precisely and paradoxically in the sources of her stigma: her gender or her race, or both.
—Margo Culley, "Anger and Authority in the Introductory
Women's Studies Classroom"

[T]he circumstances of race and gender alone protect no one from the
seductions of reading her own experience as normative and fetishizing
the experience of the other.
—Valerie Smith, "Black Feminist Theory and the
Representation of the 'Other'"

This chapter is based on three premises. The first is that the question of accountability is tied in with the issue of who gets to teach and speak with authority on what.
And in the instance of the multicultural classroom, in particular, this accountability
gets dispersed among institutions, departments, teachers, authors, and texts. It also
gets dispersed among male and female, white and non-white academic participants.

The second premise is based on the consideration that, in recent years, there has
been a shift in scholarship and pedagogy in the academy from the impersonal to
the personal, from objectivism to subjectivism, from author to reader, from product to process, and—of course—from teacher to student. As many have noted, it
has also been a time during which marginalized and excluded objects of discourse
have become subjects, when marginalized and excluded authors have expanded the
canon, and when African-American and women scholars have achieved some measure of authority in academia.

In light of these two premises, my third actually takes the form of a question, and
that is: How can one translate a postmodern perspective into a pedagogical praxis
without compromising the "authority" of the black and woman teacher? That is,
how can we as teachers bring to the classroom a non-authoritarian, open-ended, and
process-oriented approach—and, at the same time, retain the respect and authority of the students for our positions as blacks and women—categories themselves

identified with absence, lack, irrationality, emotion, and sexuality. Positioned outside what Michel Foucault calls "the fellowships of discourse," black women, in particular, have been historically marginalized from centers of power in the halls of academe.[1]

The contemporary "crisis of representation" in the field of ethnography has had a profound effect on academic studies across the disciplines. Postmodern anthropology has challenged the tendency to naturalize and dehumanize those who are regarded as "Other." Like contemporary anthropology, literary studies has also begun to recognize that all attempts to represent the Other must ultimately yield to self-referentiality. That is, our notions of otherness are always constructed in relation to Self. And while this move has general significance in contemporary cultural and literary studies, it has a particular significance for pedagogy. Like Vietnamese theorist Trinh Minh-ha, we have begun to call into question even the possibility of apprehending those whom she designates as "woman, native, other." To what degree, then, can we as scholars represent the Other in our writing, or indeed in our teaching? Minh-ha challenges the assumptions inherent in the dynamic between what she calls "the subject written and the writing subject."[2] Must we likewise interrogate the relation between the "teaching subject and the subject taught"? Doubtless, it is for this reason that much contemporary scholarship—particularly in the areas of Women's and Ethnic Studies—has begun to emphasize the importance of subject positions and positionalities: what Houston Baker calls "autobiographical negotiations."[3]

If, for the ethnographer, questions of epistemology and cultural authority are primary, for the literary scholar and teacher, such questions are compounded by issues of critical authority, social identity and identification, professional ethics and political responsibility. Accordingly, while the problem for the white and/or male teacher and critic of, for example, black and/or women's literature parallels those confronting the ethnographer in the study of the cultural Other, it also raises a range of issues unique to the positions and practices of academics—as both teachers and critics. The subtext here, of course, is the issue of appropriation and what I call "proprietary claims" on the Other—a heavily fraught and enormously complicated issue involving questions of authority and "authenticity," ethics and responsibility, intellectual arrogance and personal narcissism. The challenge for the teacher and critic is how to "read" and represent the Other without reinscribing a tradition of dominance and appropriation. One must especially question the incumbencies of the critic who directs his or her critical gaze to the productions of a group in whose oppression s/he has been historically implicated. (Such a situation obviously differs from that in which the group we study is distanced from the investigator simply by history or geography—e.g., nineteenth-century British women writers.)[4]

Specifically regarding black women's writing as an object of discourse and analysis in the pedagogical situation, how can the non-female or non-black teacher claim an identification with the subject without risking simply another form of universalizing or totalizing? What indeed are the problematics of invoking the experiences and writings of black women in efforts to historically and materially ground the studies of women and African-Americans in literary and cultural studies? How does the conscientious teacher and critic of black women's writing avoid the twin pitfalls of fetishization on the one hand and commodification on the other? Further, what are the professional stakes and risks involved in invoking the pedagogical and critical authority to speak *for* and *about* the Other? Given these problems and problematics, must we conclude that the teacher/scholar must surrender all attempts to read and represent the Other? Is the proper response indeed what Minh-ha calls the "suspension of language" or what Linda Alcoff labels "retreat"—a disengagement "from all practices of speaking for [the Other]?"[5] As we know, one of the consequences of postmodernism is what Foucault calls the eruption of subjugated knowledges and the expropriation or seizure of language by the previously silenced and muted. Certainly, the inauguration of Ethnic Studies and Women's Studies into the academy has been predicated on the necessity of creating a curriculum and encouraging a pedagogy based on the notion of entitlement—the claim and right of the Other to read and represent and speak for herself. It is a claim that has had the effect of moving the Other from margin to center; of moving the *object* of discourse into the position of *subject* of discourse.

What, one might ask, do these issues have to do with black women—a group themselves sometimes characterized as "the other of the other"? Why should the issue of appropriation be of interest to the black female/feminist teacher of black women's studies? While my general concern is with the question of cross-racial and cross-gender appropriation, my specific attention here is directed to the dangers of appropriation when the teaching or writing subject assumes a gender- and race-specific identification with the subject taught or written. In other words, my concern focuses on what it means to teach (and write) the Other when the Other is the Self. Lest we assume that this issue confronts only white and/or male teachers and critics, black feminist critic Valerie Smith reminds those of us belonging to historically marginalized groups that "the circumstances of race and gender [add class and sexuality] alone protect no one from the seductions of reading her own experience as normative."[6] Such an admonition must serve as caveat alerting all of us to the dangers of privileging even the Self as Other in our efforts to read and represent the complex status and condition of the Other in our pedagogy and scholarship.

Clearly what complicates our efforts to address the issue of speaking for and about the Other (even when we ourselves claim membership in a community of otherness) is precisely the intricacy of social identity and identification—that is, how we are defined by position and how position defines us. Because of the complex identities and multiple positionalities that each of us inhabits, our communities are always fluid and mutable. Indeed, it is this heterogeneous identity (always problematized in the instance of the black woman) that allows, even necessitates, our memberships in multiple and, not infrequently, conflicting communities. Such identifications make it difficult clearly to define or to demarcate our various subject positions as blacks, women, mothers, daughters, mates, professors, scholars, activists—and these do not begin to speak to variables such as class, sexuality, regional background, political affiliations, and so on. The issue I am raising here is whether or not even black women should feel a sense of privilege or proprietorship in the act of speaking as an authority on the Other when the Other is textualized as the black woman. To push the problematic further, one might well ask whether anyone (black women included) can ever break free from what appears to be an inescapable solipsism? Are we, indeed, condemned to know only "[our] own narrow individual experience and [our] 'own truth'"?[7] The question I raise, then, is what happens when the critical gaze is self-directed; when the Self objectifies and authors the Self as Other; when the Self must become an Other to the Self? This perspective is meant to question the notion of the black woman teacher as "authenticating" (as opposed to "authorizing") text: it challenges the black woman teacher's role as one who must either verify or contest the reliability or "truth" claims of the classroom text—especially in instances where those texts are authored by or represent the experiences of black women.

To be sure, my intent is not to diminish the additional authority that the black woman teacher brings to a black woman's text—an authority of experience and intellect that has been historically denied as incompatible with blacks and women. After all, as Susan Stanford Friedman argues, "a [white] man stepping into the role of professor has a certain authority granted to him by his students that operates immediately. Women, on other hand, must earn that authority and respect, which is an event often granted with great resentment, even hostility."[8] The problem for the black woman instructor, then, is how to enter the classroom with authority without replicating the "white" and "male" models of power that excluded and marginalized both black women and their texts from the class and curriculum in the first place. Our position in academia speaks to the contradictions born of being a black female/ feminist teacher in a white patriarchal institution.

Unlike the white male teacher whose presence can only reinforce what Margo Culley describes as the "deep structures of privilege," the black woman teacher "must claim her authority if her students are to claim their own."[9] For this reason, white and male teachers—whatever "the amount of knowledge, insight and sensitivity" they bring to the classroom—"cannot be the agents of the deepest transformations" for their black and women students "in a culture where the dominant values are white [and male]." For Culley, the agent mediating transformation is *anger*—anger that is frequently directed toward the instructor. The premise here is that when the black woman instructor enters the classroom "with her authority in question," she is bound to provoke on the part of some a degree of "unexamined anger" through a pedagogy that "initiates a process challenging the world view and the view of self of her students."[10] The paradox of her predicament is that it challenges precisely the "patriarchical authority [that is] conferred by her position."[11]

This authority, however, is not that of the teacher's "standing in" as authenticating text, but rather of privileging the study of black women in such a way that we become the centers and subjects of our own experiences—rather than corollaries of another's. In other words, the presence of the black woman teacher in the multicultural classroom repositions the *location* of blacks and women in the academy and, at the same time, repositions the *texts* of black women in the academic curriculum— moving both from a position of margin to center.

I distinguish here between what I regard as a narcissistic approach based on an authoritarian monologic teaching style, one which sets up the Self as the measure of Truth and Authenticity, and a related, but different, approach that might be regarded as self-reflexive—an approach that focuses not on personal experience, but reads it in terms of a broader social (con)text of difference and identity. Toni Cade Bambara's distinction between the "imperialized eye ['I']" and the "*un*imperialized eye ['I']" connotes, in the context of the African-American oral tradition, a distinction between the styles respectively associated with "preaching" and "testifying."[12] In the first instance, the teaching subject risks a claustral relationship between the Other as Self and the Other as text—an egocentrically bounded and restrictive relationship allowing little room for negotiation or mediation. In the second instance, however, I like to imagine the Other as Self and the Other as text entering into a relation based on mutual acknowledgment and mutual interrogation. I use the term "self-reflexive" to refer not only to the way in which the teacher encodes and/or resists the text, but also to refer to its original meaning, suggesting self-reflection. This link between self-reflexivity and self-reflection directs us to an activity leading not to an "authentic" or "inauthentic" product (in this instance, the text), but rather to a process by which the teacher and text and students simultaneously affirm and challenge notions of self, textual identity, and interpretation.[13] The focus, then, is on process rather than product, and on the mutual interaction between text and teacher and students, rather than on the teacher (or student) as authenticating text.

One way of working against totalizing or essentialist notions of what constitutes black womanhood is to locate oneself in the body—that is, for the teacher to represent herself as *embodied text*—produced by certain personal and historical experiences. In my own classes, I try to achieve embodiment by speaking of my participation in the development of black feminism in the academy, as well as by integrating my critical and theoretical works into the syllabi. In this way, the teacher's role is expanded into that of "resource text"—in the sense of locating the personal and autobiographical within a broader set of sociohistorical and ideological forces. What I seek to avoid (often at the risk, I fear, of inducing a kind of impersonalization or absentism of the self) is a self-indulgently narcissistic practice based on self-revelation or personal confession in the intersubjective space of the multicultural classroom. I should note that these practices are not without a certain political efficacy insofar as they introduce the *body* into a classroom where traditionally the professor is figured as a disembodied *mind*—a possessor of knowledge and power ("one who is presumed to know") who, as Marian Yee writes, "incites hero worship and tends to inhabit the form of a white man."[14] What students are likely to recognize from such embodied performances are personal anecdotes, literal references to the body—size, shape, clothes, color, hair, sexuality—and even references to the literary and historical bodies of black women. While such references lead to the notion of embodiment—literally locating the black woman teacher in the material body—the politics of such a move are arguably undermined as a consequence of (1) re-figuring the traditional and stereotypical embodiments of black womanhood and (2) privileging the personal at the risk of the sociopolitical as a primary category of analysis.

I emphasize the importance of the social and "public" self, fully recognizing that the cornerstone of feminist pedagogy has been its emphasis on the "authority of experience" and its accompanying emphasis on personal narrative as a means of establishing knowledge claims. Surely, many of us have found ourselves in situations that productively conjoin personal experience and theoretical analysis; we must be careful, however, not to allow the personal and self-revelatory to overwhelm or submerge the social and theoretical. Having said this, I am nevertheless reminded of John Schib's observation that "theorizing about any type of instruction sooner or later compels the theorist to drift in one of two directions: toward purity or toward pragmatism."[15]

Yet and still, as one of my students reminded me, the effect of a black woman teacher in the classroom is invariably to point out the unspoken obvious: that a *woman*, a *black* woman, is standing in the role previously occupied by a *man*, a *white* man. From this disruption follows the possibility of discussing the significance of the status quo and change.[16] Importantly, what this student speaks to is the impact of the black woman teacher's presence in modeling a response that resists received notions of classroom and critical authority. The pedagogical scene is thus set for a discussion of how black women's texts can perform in similarly disruptive ways.

Returning to the necessity of the black woman teacher's resistance to the role of "authenticating text," I must emphasize, however, that whether or not the black woman professor determines to use herself as "text," she will indeed be "read" by the students (either consciously or unconsciously)—and in spite of her "authorial intention," so to speak. What will be "read" is her gender and racial performance in the context of the dominant cultural script. I am not advocating here a "non-textualization" of the self—but a conscious self-textualization that will generate neither simple nor reductive, but rich and complex, readings of black women.

I raise these issues with the intent that they should lead not to a position of retreat or silence—although certainly there are moments when "silence" must alternate with "speech" and "retreat" with "intervention," when the "activity" of *"speaking to"* must yield to the "activity" of *"listening to."* It is this *dialectic*, or more appropriately *dialogic*, of speaking and listening that I find most fruitful in the pedagogical situation.

What I am suggesting is that we can learn and teach from positions of authoritative knowledge as well as from positions that challenge authoritative knowledge. It is in sites of ambivalence and exchange frequently where real learning (and teaching) takes place. The teacher herself, then, must listen to the voices of the Other—and I refer here not only to the student as Other, but also to the text as Other. Beyond this, however, she must also listen to the otherness within—that otherness which is defined not in its relation to the Self as Same, but in its relation to the Self as Other.

There is, however, another important element in the teaching/reading process that moves it beyond either an authoritarian monologic or even a reciprocally dialogic encounter between teacher and text—and that is the critical mediation of the third term: what Helen Moglen describes as that "multiplicitous, heterogeneous collectivity" that actually constitutes the class.[17] It is finally by emphasizing "the collectivity—multiple positionings, interactions, collaborations within the classroom" that we can achieve a truly heterogeneous and intertextual pedagogical situation in which teachers and students collaborate in a process of reading and interpretation, a process in which difference is affirmed and the reduction of experience, reading, and interpretation is contested.[18]

I conclude with a quote from the ever remarkable Roland Barthes, who describes "the space of the seminar [as] phalansteric, i.e., in a sense fictive, novelistic."[19] For me, the classroom as novel is an apt metaphor—especially when read in the context of Mikhail Bakhtin's notion of the novel as a dialogic, heteroglossic genre. For Bakhtin, the novel is constituted as a dialogue—a series of dialogues incorporating a multitude of diverse and colliding voices. The space of the classroom, like the novelistic space, is inhabited by heterogeneous voices, speaking from different positionalities. Like the novelist who becomes exemplary in fulfilling the potential of the genre, the teacher can become exemplary in fulfilling the potential of the multicultural classroom. She is able to do so by resisting a reductive and totalizing monologic preacherly discourse, replacing it with a series of dialogic encounters set in motion by the multiple voices and personalities and positionalities that constitute the multicultural classroom as space for "testifying" and interrogating. Like the novelist, the teacher subverts a falsely monologic unity by encouraging students to *speak* and *listen*. In this context, the multicultural classroom (like the polyphonic novel) stages a *"form of knowledge* [that puts] different orders of experience—each of whose languages claims authority on the basis of its ability to exclude others— into dialogue with each other."[20]

Authors and Authorities

> Reviewers have an inordinate amount of power....I've been given too
> much by the reader...and by the listeners. The power to make or break
> somebody is too much power.
>
> —Jill Nelson

In a 1988 essay in the *Georgia Review*, "Fighting Words: Unlearning to Write the Critical Essay," Jane Tompkins compared the violence in popular Westerns to the violence that occurs in the academic arena, noting that

> violence takes place in the conference rooms at scholarly meetings and in
> the pages of professional journals; and although it's not the same thing to
> savage a person's book as it is to kill them with a machine gun, I suspect
> that the nature of the feelings that motivate both acts is qualitatively the
> same. This bloodless kind of violence that takes place in our profession is
> not committed by other people; it's practiced at some time or other by vir-
> tually everyone. *Have gun, will travel* is just as fitting a theme for academic
> achievers [read: reviewers] as it was for Paladin.[1]

Instead of offering a solution, however, Tompkins concludes by calling our attention to "the moment of righteous ecstasy, the moment when you know you have the
moral advantage of your adversary, the moment of murderousness. It's a moment,"
she reminds us, "when there's still time to stop, there's still time to reflect, there's
still time to recall what happened in *High Noon*, there's still time to say: 'I don't care
who's right or who's wrong. There has to be some better way....' "[2]

Tompkins's comments bring to mind Milton's memorable words from the
Areopagitica (1644), expressed in the patriarchal idiom of his day: "As good almost
kill a man as kill a good book: who kills a man kills a reasonable creature, God's
image; but he who destroys a good book kills reason itself."[3] Yet, one might justifi-
ably ask, what, if anything, is the alternative to *textual homicide*? How can one produce a useful, fair review that points out where an author goes astray, or reaches her

limits, without demolishing an entire project, or abdicating the critical function? Are we presented with only the alternatives Tompkins provides, namely either "not caring who's right or who's wrong" or morally righteous "murderousness"?

While it is true that a reviewer can rescue a book from obscurity with a positive (and, sometimes, negative) review—and while I would suspect that most reviews are favorable due to the pre-selection process by which some books are included and others excluded by editorial fiat—it is also true that a harsh review or simple inattention can provide further lubricant to that conveyor belt into oblivion to which most books are inevitably bound. Surely, the potential damage done to an author's reputation and notoriety—by either negative reviewing or a total lack of reviewing—is so extensive and evident as to be beyond dispute.

In extreme instances, unfavorable reviews have been held accountable for death, expatriation, and the failure to continue publishing. Byron's poem "John Keats" (Who Killed John Keats? / "I" says the *Quarterly* / So savage and Tartarly; / "T'was one of my feats.") refers to John Wilson Croker's review of Keats's *Endymion*, published in the *Quarterly Review* in April 1818. At that time, it was widely believed by the general public that harsh criticism had hastened Keats's untimely death. More than a century later, Randall Jarrell, in one of his characteristically rotten, characteristically masterful, reviews wrote of the now-forgotten poet Frederick Prokosch that his poems "pour out like sausages, automatic, voluptuous, and essentially indistinguishable." In response, the devastated Prokosch wrote to the *New Republic* to declare that he would "publish no further verses in America, where they have met with [such] vituperation."[4]

In an essay on reviewing, Virginia Woolf cites the examples of Tennyson and Dickens, among others, to demonstrate the effects of the negative review upon both the author's sales and sensibility. For "the sensitive Tennyson," the reviewer was a "formidable" judge and critic whose negative remarks could not only lead to the alteration of his poems "at the reviewer's bidding," but, indeed, to such a state of despair that he "actually contemplated emigration." Even such a "robust and self-confident" writer as Dickens vowed to overcome his rage at the critics whom he saw as "lice...[discharging] their pigmy arrows...rotten creatures with men's forms and devils' hearts."[5]

Yet and still, if white and male authors are subject to negative reviews, imagine the fate of black and women authors whose works have been subject to criticisms of exceptionalism (Phillis Wheatley), inauthenticity (Harriet Jacobs), trivialization (Zora Neale Hurston), or worse, neglect and suppression (Harriet Wilson). As Henry Louis Gates, Jr., has pointed out, the historical suppression of black women's texts like Harriet Wilson's *Our Nig* and the effective erasure of such authors from the American literary canon have been due in large part to the absence of reviews documenting the work's existence.

My intent here is to explore the possibilities and limitations associated with alternative models for reviewing. In particular, I am interested in the politics and ethics of women reviewing women. If, for Dickens, reviewers are figured as "rot-ten creatures with men's forms and devils' hearts," what happens when the review-ers are women reviewing women? Do we get "sweet creatures with female forms and angels' hearts"? Is it possible to reconcile the authority and discursive power of the woman reviewer to a feminist ethic of responsibility that does not sacrifice the integrity of the reviewing subject or risk insulation from serious and constructive criticism?

Reviewers often disagree; indeed, there are potentially as many judgments as there are critics and readers. These extreme and contrary judgments on the value and authority of any single book constitute the politics of public debate. Yet, while I can agree with critic Steve Weinberg, who wrote that "it is a truism that no two reviewers read the same book in the same way," I cannot concur with his com-ment that "in the end, many of the disputes over 'fairness' and 'ethics' are clashes of opinion, pure and simple."[6] Such a dismissive summary of the consequences of reviewing fails, in my opinion, to take into account the considerable stakes in book reviewing. I would like here to direct attention to the issues of *power, positionality,* and *process* in book reviewing: *the power of the review, the positionality of the reviewer,* and *the process of reading.*

At least since the end of the eighteenth century, the role of the reviewer has been to provide information that would enable a growing reading public to make choices not only as to what books to read but, indeed, how to read them. Like academic monographs and articles, book reviews occupy a space in public culture with which we are all familiar—a space that (according to a 1989 statistic) is rapidly expand-ing to accommodate the more than one thousand books published internationally every day.[7] But whereas the public sphere is supposedly a place for engaged par-ticipation and contestation, there is in fact little room for either dialogue or criti-cal appeal against the reviewer's pronouncements. Rather, the reviewer functions as a kind of privileged first reader, invested with the power to mediate between the author and the reading public. Unlike the interview, which is essentially a "dialogic" or interactive genre, the review tends to allow little space for rejoinder by either author or reader. As traditionally conceived, the review has been both authoritarian and monologic or single-voiced, rarely inviting or eliciting responses representing differences in points of view.

With regard to the academic review in particular, one might ask: What are the benefits and costs of promoting an authoritarian, monologic discourse that often dis-places, suppresses, or competes with the voice of the author? Is reviewing necessarily *critical*—in the sense of being a hostile act of negation? Is there an alternative to the competitive "anxiety of influence" model of academic reviewing, which positions the reviewer in patricidal (or matricidal) opposition to the author? And what are the stakes and consequences involved for the reader, the reviewer, and the author?

The British group "Women in Publishing," which researched the status of women reviewing women, contended in *Reviewing the Reviews: A Woman's Place on the Book Page* that the review remains a "male preserve." In this study of women's book reviews based on twenty-eight British publications, they argue that there is a "pervasive discriminatory pattern that can only serve to heighten the second-class status of women's books in most general readership publications."[8] The study compared the width, length, location, and other material aspects of the book review. The group found a clear bias against women's books, reflected in the fact that, in the publications examined, less space and coverage are devoted to reviewing women's books than books authored by men. Only in women's magazines were the woman author and reviewer regularly featured; outside this venue, "publicity diminish[ed] sharply."[9]

Discovering that general readership publications, as a rule, give more coverage to reviews by and about men, they conclude, "What this means for women authors is that, if they get reviewed at all in [these publications] they can expect to receive a shorter review than their male colleague for no apparent reason other than the fact they happen to be female."[10] These kinds of investigations justify, even demand, the continued existence of publications such as *The Women's Review of Books, Belles Lettres, The Austrialian Women's Book Review*, and other women's review journals.

My own qualified and "interested" reflections on the issue of women reviewing women turns, in part, on an incident involving *The Women's Review of Books*. When Cheryl A. Wall's collection *Changing Our Own Words: Essays on Criticism, Theory, and Writing by Black Women* (1989) was reviewed in this publication by SallyAnn Ferguson in December 1991, my essay [see Chapter 3 in this volume], in particular, was subjected to criticism for its "[successful employment of] a Eurocentric critical method."[11] Although it was clear that the reviewer objected to the stated theoretical premise of the project in general, and to my use of theoretical language in particular, less clear was why the editors chose someone with an anti-theoretical bias to review such a collection. This is not to say that congruity between the reviewer and the subject must be a criterion for the selection of the reviewer, for the point of the review is not to eliminate dissonance between the perspectives of the author and reviewer. Most of us would agree with Toni Morrison, who writes in *Playing in the Dark* that "all of us, readers and writers, are bereft when criticism remains too polite or fearful."[12]

Neither, however, should the review simply present an occasion to voice the reviewer's reflexive animadversions. At the very least, the reviewer's biases and assumptions deserve some preliminary acknowledgment, if not actual interrogation. In this instance, however, the reviewer's point of view was less conspicuous than her disdain for the theoretical presumption. Evidently, the reviewer deemed the application of continental theory to black women's writing to be a sign of complicity, if not collusion, with the dominant discourse. Because it has so often been pressed into the service of the status quo, theory has frequently roused suspicion even among some oppositional critics, who associate it with "whiteness" and "maleness." With little appreciation of how black and feminist scholars have appropriated and, at the same time, interrogated these theories, this reviewer failed to understand the potential subversion inherent in a black and feminist appropriation of contemporary theory.

Linda Kauffman has noted that "the languages of critical theory are difficult because of their foundations in disciplines [e.g., philosophy] that were long isolated from literary studies."[13] Although the degree to which such language can or should be represented in a book review is a subject for debate, there can be no doubt that critical theory has yielded new insights that continue to enrich academic as well as public discourse. Further, this language is available not only to the author, but to informed readers as well, and most especially to the critic who undertakes to review such a text.

Neither the editor nor the contributors to *Changing Our Own Words* felt comfortable in making a public response. This self-imposed "censorship" notwithstanding, some of us were not only confounded by the review, but confused by the selection criteria for the reviewer. Although the editors chose a black woman scholar to review the volume, I would propose that the authors, the reading public, and even the *Women's Review of Books* would have been better served had they recognized the diversity among black women critics and scholars and, in this instance, selected or solicited a reviewer who could have demonstrated more familiarity with the issues at stake in the debate around critical theory, as well as with some of the new directions in black feminist criticism and theory.

Perhaps the real problem here lay in an editorial assumption of the politics of "authenticity"—by which I mean that the journal's commendable intent to enlist a black woman to review this collection on black women (authored for the most part by black women) nevertheless enabled the reviewer, another black woman, to serve as gatekeeper in maintaining the status of theory as a primarily white and male practice and preserve.

I raise this incident not only to call attention to the anti-theoretical presumption of the reviewer and the selection criteria for the reviewer, but also to the reviewer's responsibility to establish her perspective or positionality in relation to the project under review. And, lastly, I am concerned about the silence or "silencing" of the authors that, in this instance, was due to the fact that virtually all the scholars in a position to respond (and that includes the volume editor) were reluctant to do so because we feared being adjudged "self-interested." An opportunity to use the occasion of the book review as a forum for dialogue and exchange around the relation of contemporary theory and black women's writing was irredeemably lost.

While each of these issues certainly deserves attention in its own right, such an incident invites us to consider the motivations and agenda of the reviewer. What, in other words, is at stake—in a case like this—for the academic reviewer? Achieving name recognition; garnering authority; increasing professional visibility; padding one's résumé; ingratiating oneself with the author, or clearing a space for oneself by attacking the author—surely all these represent plausible, but not always professionally ethical, intents and motivations for writing the academic review.

My concern turns upon the responsibilities of the reviewer. I would propose not a *prescription*, but a *protocol*, in writing and publishing reviews, beginning with the provision that the reviewer disclose, at the outset of the review, whatever prejudices and preconceptions she brings to the subject. Some time ago, I received an invitation from *College English* to review several books, and was struck by the (woman) editor's request, which read as follows: "The review would, I hope, reveal your own philosophical positions, as well as those of the author." What is interesting here is that the editor's guidelines neither encourage nor anticipate that the reviewer will try to maintain a neutral or disinterested stance. On the contrary, the editor emphasizes the importance of recognizing the interests, preferences, and values framing the reviewer's perspective and evaluation. Such a position implicitly acknowledges that reviewers (like readers) always bring to the text prior interests that are dictated by their particular social and historical backgrounds, as well as intellectual investment and scholarly training.

Virginia Woolf's distinction between the critic as one who deals "with the past and with principles" and the reviewer as one who takes "the measure of new books as they [fall] from the press" no longer, strictly speaking, obtains.[14] The increasingly prevalent review essay not only evaluates the contributions of new works to the field, but subjects the standard works to re-examination.

Perhaps it is for this reason that the reviews and reviewers too often remain subject to positivist claims of detachment and objectivity. Why, as scholars and critics, do we fail to call into question the discourse of the review, as we have the positivist claims of other kinds of writing? Are we promoting our own professional self-interests when we choose to accord it such power and authority? Certainly, the review potentially advances the reviewer up the professional ladder, whether it assails or panders to published authorities in the field. On the other side of the coin, it may also impede the career of the young scholar whose first book earns peremptory dismissal or ill-considered attacks by the "authorities" in the field. With such stakes at issue, the reviewers need to bring to their task not only the wit and rhetorical skills to engage the reader, but a moral responsibility (and, sometimes, political accountability) to their role as "authority."

Although evidence suggests to me that many, if not most, "bad" reviews are in fact addressed to the author, while "good" reviews principally address the reader, I am assuming that any serious reviewer seeks, on some level, to address both the author and reader, and to explain how and why the text works or does not work for the reviewer. Any serious author, on the other hand, is interested in knowing how or why she has succeeded or failed. Such an exchange between author and reviewer would, I believe, benefit the reader—and serving the reader is, after all, what is most at stake here.

What I propose is that editors consider creating space for the author's response— not for the purpose of granting to the author the last word or final right of refutation, but to dismantle the monolithic status of the review. What I have in mind is a format similar to the "Comment and Response" feature of *College English* or the "Forum" section of *PMLA* in which the readers are invited to comment on articles in previous issues. Both authors and readers would be invited to respond to the reviewer's point of view. It would be difficult to overestimate the consequence of encouraging this conversation among reviewers, authors, and readers during an age when print culture is forced to compete with popular culture and popular culture ideology—both inside and outside the academy—in order to sustain its own vitality.

I should like to conclude by making four recommendations to review journals: (1) that the review editors enunciate and periodically remind their readers of the selection process and/or the criteria by which reviewers are assigned or solicited for their publications; (2) that the reader practice what Paul Ricoeur calls "a hermeneutics of suspicion" that at the very least calls into question the positivist claims to authority and objectivity too often accorded the reviewer and the reviewing process; (3) that the review editors reserve a space for the author's response in the same issue of the publication in which the author's work is reviewed; and (4) that the editors encourage and set aside space in future issues for reader responses to such a dialogue.

To date, the most effective examples of the kind of format I am proposing come not from a women's journal or from an example of women reviewing women. The first appeared in the recently founded *Social Identities: Journal for the Study of Race, Nation and Culture*. In its 1995 inaugural issue, Paul Gilroy's *The Black Atlantic: Modernity and Double Consciousness* is reviewed by multiple and (sometimes) dissenting reviewers.[15] The second appeared in the Spring 1993 issue of *The Journal of the Midwest Modern Language Association*. Located in the book review section, this piece is aptly entitled "Kenneth Warren and Gerald Graff on the Politics of Talking Back: Gerald Graff's *Beyond the Culture Wars: How Teaching the Conflicts Can Revitalize American Education*." Undoubtedly, the model of "critical conversation" that Graff himself proposes in the volume under review provides some inspiration for the dialogic or multivoiced format of the review itself. The exchange opens with a rigorous review of Graff's work by Kenneth Warren, followed by a strong rebuttal in which the author further illuminates his own position and, at the same time, examines the reviewer's assumptions. The review concludes with Warren's outlining specific areas of agreement and difference, and Graff's final rejoinder. Appropriately, the signatures of both reviewer and author signify their co-authorship of the review.[16] As a reader, I followed this provocative dialogue with immense interest—and then proceeded to form my own judgment by turning to the book itself.

Nella Larsen's *Passing*

Passing, Performance, and (Post)modernism

Like other novels of the Harlem Renaissance, Nella Larsen's *Passing* (1929) has been read as an exemplar of African-American modernism, a form linking the aesthetic and political dimensions of this outpouring of work by black artists in the 1920s, and designating literary techniques ranging from the experimentalism of Jean Toomer, to the realism of Rudolph Fisher to the romantic racialism of Claude McKay. In *Passing*, as in other novels of the Harlem School, the city—particularly Harlem—functions as a kind of topos that becomes a site of transformation and, potentially, liberation in that decade of black cultural and social awakening.[1] Although the opening scene of the "Encounter" between Larsen's two central characters occurs in their native Chicago, the main action and denouement of the novel transpires in New York, the mecca of the "New Negro" and locus of the "New Woman." Yet, the geographical location of Larsen's characters in Chicago and New York codes the city itself as a site of ethnic and social diversity in the aftermath of the Great Migration, as well as a space newly open to the "feminine" during an era when women were moving from the domestic sphere into public culture. Larsen's self-conscious engagement with an urban culture of modernity from which her characters derive their social location of marginality—as blacks and women—is particularly pertinent to the narrative theme of racial passing, since, as Werner Sollors aptly notes, a primary condition of passing in the United States has been "social and geographical mobility," especially as it prevails "in environments such as cities...that provided anonymity to individuals, permitting them to resort to imaginative role-playing in their self-representation."[2] Situated during an era of profound cultural change and social transition, Larsen's modern passing characters distinctly "belong to [their] own time." Her "raced" and "gendered" subjects appear to inhabit a social, economic, political, and cultural geography that both affirms and contests arrangements that sustain the "color line" demarcating race and the "separate spheres" defining gender.

As one of several novelists of the period, Larsen is, in some respects, singular in that her novels, unlike those of Renaissance writers such as Jessie Fauset,

Walter White, Claude McKay, Rudolph Fisher, and Wallace Thurman, not only engage the racial thematics of African American modernism but also deploy the formal techniques of Anglo-American and European modernism. Larsen's modernist articulations, mediated from the perspectives of race, gender, and sexuality, are demonstrated by what Rita Felski defines in *The Gender of Modernity* as "aesthetic self-consciousness, stylistic fragmentation, and...[a] questioning of representation" within the context of "a distinctively modern sense of dislocation and ambiguity."[3] In addition, Larsen's figuration of the African-American woman as a racially (un)marked, middle-class subject in both her first novel, *Quicksand* (1928), and her second, *Passing,* privileges the mulatta, or biracial, woman in particular as the site of contradiction and negotiation, transgression and conformity, tradition and modernity. In some respects, the complexity of this image, as we shall see, marks this figure as a signifier—a duplicitous signifier—of the competing impulses, ideologies, and aesthetics characterizing the Harlem Renaissance itself.

But Larsen's latter novel also belongs to a genre, the passing narrative, that some critics maintain has become defunct. Surely it is true, as some have argued, that "passing," in the sense of "passing for white," has ceased to be the social issue that it was in the nineteenth and early twentieth centuries,[4] yet the recent republication of Larsen's novel, along with James Weldon Johnson's *Autobiography of an Ex-Colored Man,* would suggest that perhaps W. E. B. Du Bois was not entirely accurate in his prediction that the "intriguing and ticklish subject" of passing "is all a pretty, silly matter of no real importance which another generation will comprehend with great difficulty."[5] And while, as Gayle Wald has documented, the postwar 1950s witnessed the emergence of what she describes as the "postpassing" narrative in black popular fiction, it is demonstrably evident that this genre has discovered a receptive audience during the late twentieth and early twenty-first centuries.[6] Much of the renewed attention to the genre of the passing novel has emerged from an increased interest in what Werner Sollors has defined as a tradition of "interracial literature" as well as from a more general preoccupation with notions of hybridity, biraciality, and social constructionism as these structure contemporary conceptions of personal and social identity.

Although *Quicksand* has traditionally received the higher critical regard, in light of recent attention, it would seem that a reevaluation of *Passing* is due. Contemporary critics have insisted on according Larsen's novel its "rightful place" in the canons of American, African-American, and women's literature.[7] Historically, however, Larsen's reputation rests less on *Passing* than on her first novel. In a contemporary review of *Quicksand* in *The Crisis,* W. E. B. Du Bois pronounced it a "fine, thoughtful and courageous piece of work," the best that "Negro America has produced since the heyday of Charles Chesnutt."[8] And although Du Bois praised Larsen's second novel as "one of the finest novels of the year," *Passing* has not always fared so well among later critics and scholars.[9] While rating *Passing* as "probably the best treatment of the subject [of passing] in Negro fiction," Robert Bone considers it Larsen's "less important novel."[10] Comparing it to the typical "women's magazine story," Hoyt Fuller describes *Passing* as a "flawed" and "rather banal" novel."[11] Hiroko Sato describes *Passing* as a "slight book," written by a novelist who wrote "only one good book [*Quicksand*]."[12] Nathan Irvin Huggins ranks *Quicksand* as Larsen's "best novel," and *Passing* as her "lesser novel."[13] David Levering Lewis views *Quicksand* as "one of the...best novels of the Renaissance,"[14] and George Hutchinson regards it as "the best novel of the Harlem Renaissance until Zora Neale Hurston's *Their Eyes Were Watching God*."[15] Cheryl Wall comments on the "inevitable melodrama," that "weakens the credibility" of Larsen's second novel."[16] And one of Larsen's biographers, Charles Larson, suggests that "*Passing* is a lesser novel than *Quicksand*," while another, Thadious Davis, considers it "less skillfully developed," although "more carefully structured" than her first novel.[17]

Despite these critical evaluations, *Passing* has established itself during recent decades as a major Harlem Renaissance novel as well as an important contribution to the genre known as the "modernist passing narrative." What is less well-known is that the novel also belongs to a literary pedigree that links the passing narrative to an originary form of African-American literature, the nineteenth-century African-American slave narrative. Elements of the passing narrative and passing plot can be found in several of the slave narratives, including *Running a Thousand Miles for Freedom; or the Escape of William and Ellen Craft from Slavery* (1860), in which two slaves successfully escape from bondage by having the light-skinned Ellen "pass" for the "white" (and male) master of her dark-skinned slave husband, William. Not only does "the passing plot"[18] appear in the narratives of the fugitive slave who sometimes deployed racial passing as a strategy by which to escape the fetters of slavery, but it also resurfaces as a plot element in nineteenth-century African-American fiction, including ex-slave author William Wells Brown's *Clotel, A Tale of the Southern States* (1864);[19] Frank J. Webb's *The Garies and Their Friends* (1857); Francis Ellen Watkins Harper's *Iola Leroy, or, Shadows UpLifted* (1892); as well as Hannah Crafts's recently "discovered" *The Bondwoman's Narrative* (c. 1853–1860), now deemed to be the earliest novel by a black woman in the United States.[20] Richard Hildreth's *The Slave; or, Memoirs of Archy Moore* (1836) and Harriet Beecher Stowe's *Uncle Tom's Cabin* (1852), both Anglo-American novels modeled on the narratives of ex-slaves, also deploy the passing plot.[21] The recurrence of the passing plot in both black and white fiction in the United States would suggest the importance of passing as a social issue from the late nineteenth well into the twentieth century. Indeed, two years following the publication of Larsen's novel, one Caleb Johnson wrote in the *Outlook and Independent* that "crossing the color line is so common an occurrence that the Negroes have their own well-understood word for it. They call it 'passing.'"[22] Writing in *The Saturday Review of Literature* in 1947, Walter White, himself a "voluntary Negro," observed, "Every year approximately 12,000 white-skinned Negroes disappear—people whose absence cannot be explained by death or emigration...men and women who have decided that they will be happier and more successful if they flee from the proscription and humiliation which the American color line imposes on them."[23] Clearly, White's statistics regarding the occurrence and extent of race passing in the United States must be viewed as highly speculative, since evidence supporting such claims, by its very nature, remains scant and anecdotal due to the conditions of secrecy upon which the success of the racial passer is predicated.

Commenting on the theme of passing in the literature of black and white American authors, Swedish sociologist Gunnar Myrdal notes the conditions of secrecy and silence that alone guarantee the success of the racial passer, whom he identifies, broadly speaking, as "a Negro [who] becomes a white man... [who] moves from the lower to the higher caste." Passing can be secured, explains Myrdal, "only by the deception of the white people with whom the passer comes to associate and by a conspiracy of silence on the part of other Negroes who might know about it." Continuing, Myrdal describes the typical passing plot and its reception:

> As a social phenomenon, passing is so deeply connected with the psychological complexes—built around caste and sex—of both groups that it has come to be a central theme of fiction and of popular imagination and story telling. The adventures of the lonesome passer, who extinguishes his entire earlier life, breaks all personal and social anchorings, and starts a new life where he has to fear his own shadow, are alluring to all and have an especially frightening import to whites. There is a general sentimentality for the unhappy mulatto—the "marginal man" with split allegiances and frustrations in both directions which is especially applied to the mulatto who passes.[24]

Although like Myrdal, African-American critic and poet Sterling Brown emphasizes the "unhappiness" or "wretchedness" of the passer, Brown further distinguishes between black- and white-authored treatments of the passing subject during the Harlem Renaissance:

> We have seen that the mulatto who "passes" has been a victim of opposing interpretations. Negro novelists urge his unhappiness, until he is summoned back to his people by the spirituals, or their full-throated laughter, or their simple ways.... White novelists insist upon the mulatto's unhappiness for other reasons. To them he is the anguished victim of a divided inheritance. Mathematically they work it out that his intellectual strivings and self-control come from his white blood, and his emotional urgings, indolence and potential savagery come from his Negro blood. Their favorite character, the octoroon, wretched because of the "single drop of midnight in her veins," desires a white lover above all else, and must therefore go down to a tragic end.[25]

Both Myrdal and Brown emphasize the psychic alienation and social dislocation inhabited by the literary passing subject who is compelled to maintain a position of "disidentification" relative to both the dominant oppressive culture and the dominated oppressed culture.[26] And despite arguments to the contrary, Brown's distinction between popular black- and white-authored representations of the mixed-race subject would seem to be not entirely without justification, especially as it informs the conventional physical, moral, and intellectual ascriptions attached to race in nineteenth-century American literature.

Notably, the popularity of the passing genre before and after the 1920s is attested not only in African-American fiction such as Charles W. Chesnutt's *The House Behind the Cedars* (1900) and his recently recovered *Paul Marchand, F.M.C.* (c. 1920), James Weldon Johnson's *Autobiography of an Ex-Colored Man* (1912; 1927), Walter White's *Flight* (1926), Jessie Fauset's *Plum Bun* (1928), George Schuyler's *Black No More* (1931), and Nella Larsen's *Passing*, but also in Anglo-American fiction such as Rebecca Harding Davis's *Waiting for the Verdict* (1867), William Dean Howells's *An Imperative Duty* (1892), and Mark Twain's *Pudd'nhead Wilson* (1894). Elements of the passing plot also appear in William Faulkner's *Light in August* (1932) and *Absalom, Absalom!* (1936). Later treatments of passing range from Fannie Hurst's popular *Imitation of Life* (1933; made into a movie in 1959) to Danzy Senna's more recent *Caucasia* (1998), along with Philip Roth's *The Human Stain* (2000; made into a movie in 2003).

Contemporary critics not only note the popularity of the passing novel, especially during the Harlem Renaissance, but have examined its social and political function as a genre. Commenting on the irony of passing as a "major theme of the 1920s when race pride was supposedly at a peak," feminist critic Barbara Christian argues that this form, in fact, "heightened the white audience's awareness of the restrictions imposed upon talented blacks who then found it necessary to become white in order to fulfill themselves." Christian also observes that in the African-American version of the passing novel, "the passer is often a woman who believes that through marriage to a wealthy white man, she might gain economic security and more freedom of mobility."[27] Christian's particular focus on the role of the "mulatta," and the significance of gender, sex, and marriage in a domestic plot enframed by a larger social narrative of patriarchy, as we shall see, would constitute key elements of feminist analysis by contemporary critics of Nella Larsen's *Passing*.

Locating the "passing" novel within his cultural and political narrative of nationalism and assimilation, Robert Bone defines the "attack upon passing" by the "Rear Guard" of the Harlem Renaissance as an "affirmation of race loyalty," and thus a "manifestation of...nationalism." Arguing that "if the act of passing is an expression of assimilation carried to its logical conclusion, then surely a novel which condemns passing must have nationalist implications," Bone concludes that the passing novel represents, "in psychological terms, a symbolic rejection of the author's unconscious

desire to be white"—a fictional projection whose repudiation "fortifies...racial loyalty against the threat from within."[28]

On the other hand, Amritjit Singh maintains that the appearance of so many
passing novels during the twenties is "evidence of [the] predominantly middle-class
orientation" of the Harlem Renaissance novelists. In support of this narrative typol-
ogy based on class, Singh cites Claude McKay's claim in *Banjo* (1929) that "passing
white" was a "common [topic] of colored intelligentsia" but had little meaning or
relevance for lower-class blacks. Explaining the attraction of the modernist passing novel for Harlem Renaissance writers, Singh observes the double move of this
genre: "[A]t one level there is an attempt to delineate a dimension of culture and
values which the middle class shared with the white American. At the same time,
these novels inform white readers that middle-class blacks have no intention or
desire to relinquish the joy and abandon of black life for the dullness of the white
bourgeoisie."[29] What Singh identifies here is a contradictory and competing narrative impulse that negotiates between an ideology of universalism at the level of
national culture and an ethos of particularism at the level of lived racial experience.

Not only do Bone and Singh affirm the logic of racial difference implicit in passing, but both emphasize the passing novel's narrative trajectory as one of return,
or "homecoming," deriving from a sense of the subject's racial allegiance/affinity.
What is less clear in their analyses, but more evident in the novels, is that it is precisely the social construction of identity, often due to advantages of class and culture, that allows the passing subject to cross into the "white" world, while a more
essentialist notion of identity, based on atavistic "yearnings" or racial fealty, inevitably returns this character to the racial fold. Thus, while the logic of passing, on
the one hand, subverts the logic of racial difference, on the other, it paradoxically
affirms a racial or cultural essence that has the effect of naturalizing difference. Not
unlike other passing narratives, Larsen's novel expresses the tension between social
constructionism and the competing narrative of essentialism that has engaged postmodern discourse.

And although the passing novel, as suggested, enables some writers to emphasize the uniqueness and particularity of black culture, most black writers also represent passing as a strategy that interrogates the color line and the entitlements
attached to whiteness as a marker of social status and economic privilege. While
Anglo-American writers who treat these issues (e.g., Stowe, Twain, Faulkner)
both critique and at times narratively reproduce the racial (and sometimes racist)
arrangements and practices inscribed in the legal fiction and social custom of racial
classification codified in court decisions such as *Plessy v. Ferguson* (1896), African
American writers have historically deployed passing and the passing subject as narrative devices by which to critique racist and hierarchal social structures and practices while, at the same time, promoting the value of blackness.

Scholars, by now, have amply demonstrated that the modern African-American
novel as a genre owes a great debt, formally and thematically, to the slave narrative.

What is not so well understood is that the African-American novel is similarly indebted to the passing genre, arguably the successor to the slave narrative as the most identifiable black literary form of the early twentieth century. And while never as popular as the slave narrative, the passing novel inscribes several of the same thematics and motifs as its more illustrious predecessor. The passing novels contest and constitute part of the critique of race and racial difference that is first formally articulated in the slave narratives. Further, like the slave narrative, the passing novel is both political and moral in its appeal to the reader. If the slave narrative functions as a critique of slavery (and to some extent Northern racism), the passing novel functions as a critique of postbellum social structures based on racial segregation, white privilege, and black subordination. And if the slave narrative articulates the fundamental humanity of blacks, the passing novel advances its claim to the civil equality of African-Americans. Finally, the passing novel, like the slave narrative, is a form that both explicitly and implicitly challenges hierarchical and discriminatory social, political, and economic practices.

Further, the narrative of slavery and the novel of passing replicate certain formal patterns. Structured by border crossings—social, personal, and sometimes literal— both can be classified as "border" narratives. If the slave narrator crosses the geographical border from South to North, the passing narrator transgresses the racial boundary from "black" to "white." If the slave crosses the Mason-Dixon line, the passer crosses the color line, the one in an attempt to secure physical freedom, the other to secure social freedom. More frequently, however, the passing protagonist rewrites the slave's narrative of geographical "leave-taking" as one of racial "home-coming"—psychically if not always physically.

Historically, the slave narrative and the passing novel have appealed to both black and white writers, but these forms have also attracted both black and white readers. And if it is true, as some critics maintain, that the slave narrative "educate[d] white America about its 'exotic' and unknown 'other,'" the passing novel not only educated whites ethnographically about black life, but also constructed and critiqued "whiteness" for both black and white readers.[30] While its exoticism offered whites a lens into an aspect of black life rarely witnessed by outsiders, its social critique locates the passing novel within the tradition of protest and exposé that characterizes much of nineteenth- and early twentieth-century black literary discourse.

Moreover, just as the slave narrative emerged as a counter-genre to the Southern "plantation tradition," so the novel of passing arose in dialectical response to a body of postbellum literature seeking to reinscribe the color line in the popular literature of the period. Southern novelists like Thomas Dixon, Robert Lee Durham, and Thomas Nelson Page typically portrayed blacks, especially mulattoes, as "dangerous" and "threatening" to civilization and the Southern way of life.[31] The passing novel, on the other hand, often reveals the violence, brutality, and inhumanity of whites toward blacks, as well as the pathos of the mulatto's plight. And like the slave narrative, the passing novel emerges from a precise historical period and, as such, compels both readers and critics alike to take into account the social and cultural history that is formally inscribed in the genre. The motivation and investment in passing was a direct consequence of slavery and its aftermath, which legally defined race as a category by which to ensure the social privilege and material property attached to "whiteness." As David Roediger demonstrates, to be white in the early and mid-nineteenth century meant to be "not black," and to be "not black" meant, as Ruth Frankenberg explains, to be "not slave."[32] (Thus, the idea of the "white slave" in the United States, as Werner Sollors notes, constituted a "cultural oxymoron."[33]) And finally, the alignment of race with social and legal status, as critical race theorist Cheryl Harris explains, marked the distinction between "who was subject to enslavement" and "who was free." Whiteness thus became a "valuable" and "valued" property, the "quintessential property for personhood," and "inherent in the concept of 'being white' was the right to own or hold whiteness to the exclusion and subordination of Blacks."[34] Thus, according to Harris, the social construction of race turns on the "ideological and rhetorical move from 'slave' to 'free' [and] '[b]lack' and 'white' as polar constructs—moves, I might add, to which the slave narrative and passing novel implicitly respond."[35] Since stories of "passing" are, however, also stories of racial intermixing, these narratives threaten the ideology of (white) racial purity and privilege. In fact, it is the offspring of racial fusion, as Eva Saks notes, that "produced the phenomenon of 'passing' ... for white" that is inscribed in the passing novel.[36]

Fundamentally transgressive in ideology, the passing novels not only explore the social, psychological, and economic motivations for passing, but also perform acts of literary trespass in exposing the cultural and legal fiction of race. *Plessy v. Ferguson,* whose consequences can be ignored neither in the social institution of passing nor in the narrativization of that experience in the novel of passing, not only legally codified the color line, relegating blacks for the next half century to a status of "separate but equal," but it also secured the "one drop" rule by which "blackness" was defined. In fact, it was this conception that race was biologically determined, and expressed through what Saks calls "the metaphor of blood," that not only instituted segregation in the form of Jim Crow laws, but also essentialized the notion of race in American jurisprudence. And it was this notion that the infusion of "one drop" of "black blood" was racially determinative that rendered what Joel Williamson describes as "invisible blackness."[37] In literature, it is the function of the passing subject, through whose veins supposedly flow the "contamination" of "black blood," to expose the fiction of race and racial classification as well as to represent the desire of all African-Americans for full access to the rights and privileges of citizenship. As a form, then, the passing novel destabilizes social and personal identities, creating a fluidity and mobility that transgress the boundaries of race inscribed by law and custom; at the same time, this genre denounces a social system based on racial hierarchy and exclusion.

Under the guise of genteel bourgeois domestic fiction, Larsen's passing plot enables the writer to interrogate notions frequently associated with the social sciences, or what subsequently became known as "scientific racism." And although *Passing* did not appear until the end of the third decade of the twentieth century, the novel engages an ongoing historical discourse of race and race difference that continued to inform the emergent "scientific" disciplines of sociology, anthropology, and ethnology, discourses advancing ideas of fundamental racial difference, often couched in notions of social Darwinism and evolutionism designed to provide a rationale for policies aimed at justifying an expanding U.S. imperialism as well as "resolving" what was popularly regarded on the home front as the "race problem."

And just as modern cultural anthropologists like Franz Boas and Melville Herskovits countered the racialist theories of nineteenth- and early twentieth-century social science discourse, so Larsen's passing plot calls into question popular theories contrived to reify notions of race and race difference. Larsen's ironic appropriations and allusions to the discourses of miscegenation, genetics, heredity, eugenics, and genealogy engage popular Victorian pseudoscientific, legal, and religious theories of race and racial difference. Repeated references in Larsen's text to such notions as "Ham," "blood," "fingernails," and so forth, as well as narrative anxieties around issues of the body, color, and reproduction, reflect Larsen's interrogation of popular scriptural justifications of slavery as well as theories of scientific racialism popularized by Louis Agassiz, Josiah C. Nott, Sir Francis Galton,[38] and their successors, who sought—through arcane mathematical calculation, theories of mono- and polygenesis, phrenology, amalgamation, atavism, and so forth—to discover outward racial signs or markers designed to classify race and essentialize racial differences.

The passing plot itself turns centrally on notions of personal and racial identity—and whether it is produced by biology and genetics (nature) or environment and training (culture). Larsen addresses issues of gender, sexuality, and class as they intersect with race to produce the race-marked, middle-class female subject. Further, as Cheryl Wall, Thadious Davis, Judith Butler, and others have argued, Larsen's treatment of the passing female subject and her social location draws on notions of performative identity.[39] By rewriting modernist notions of a constative, immutable, unified notion of selfhood with a conception of identity that is fundamentally performative, the novel of passing interrogates the idea of a transcendent or essentialized identity. Many contemporary theorists reject essentializing notions of identity that have been enlisted historically to justify and rationalize racial, gender, sexual, and national hierarchies whereby women, blacks, gays, and colonials have been subjugated. Nevertheless, in postmodernist literary and theoretical discourse, the relation between essentialism and constructionism remains a site of critique and debate. In her second novel, Larsen, in effect, narratively theorizes the current postmodernist debate around essentialism versus constructionism. And like several other novels of passing, Larsen's plot betrays a certain duplicity in that it challenges the idea of innate racial difference while, at the same time, making a case for racial uniqueness.

Critics have interpreted Larsen's title, and the trope of "passing" itself, in several different registers. For Mary Helen Washington, passing becomes "a metaphor for the risk-taking experience," as well as "a symbol or metaphor of deliverance," albeit it "an obscene form of deliverance," since it requires denial of roots and genealogy.[40] For Cheryl Wall, passing becomes "a metaphor of death and desperation," referring not only to "the sociological phenomenon of blacks' crossing the color line," but also to "the racial identity and the denial of self that is required of women who conform to restrictive gender roles."[41] Deborah McDowell suggests that passing is a metaphor that implies "false, forged, and mistaken" racial, sexual, and narrative identities.[42] As these and other critics suggest, Larsen's title, functioning as the novel's central trope, would seem to refer ambiguously to both Irene Redfield and Clare Kendry, both of whom play the passing game—although for the former, the decision to pass is merely "occasional."

Despite the painstaking and illuminating work of Thadious Davis and Charles Larson, Nella Larsen remains, in many respects, what Mary Helen Washington once described as the "mystery woman of the Harlem Renaissance."[43] The gaps and ambiguities in her biography are similarly reflected in her novel *Passing*, which remains, in some respects, the "mystery text" of the Harlem Renaissance. Critical efforts to unmask Larsen's text have yielded multiple readings, ranging from a focus on race, to psychology, class, gender, (lesbian) sexuality, to an approach based on the intersectionality of multiple categories of analysis. Many critics, including Claudia Tate, Cheryl Wall, Mary Dearborn, Charles Larson, and Deborah McDowell, argue that Larsen deploys a cover story based on race to conceal a deeper, more complex narrative. For Tate, Larsen's narrative draws its power not "from its surface content [race], but from its vivid imagery, subtle metaphors, and carefully balanced psychological ambiguity." Viewing passing as "more a device to sustain suspense than merely a compelling social issue," Tate contends that "racial issues . . . are, at best, peripheral to the story."[44] Cheryl Wall argues that Larsen's text was subject to popular misreadings, concluding that "[r]eaders were so sure they knew the story Larsen was telling they misread the story she actually told." Larsen, in effect, deployed the convention of the tragic mulatta, argues Wall, to "mask her . . . subversive concerns . . . about gender questions."[45] Similarly, for Mary Dearborn, race functions only on the symbolic level, since "the problems Larsen's heroines suffer derive from their identities as women."[46] Each of the foregoing interpretations valorizes Larsen's text not for its engagement with issues of race and identity, but for its modernist aesthetics on the one hand, and its construction and critique of gender and gender ideology on the other.

Similar to critics before her, Deborah McDowell seeks to reveal a "dangerous subplot" underpinning a safer, more conventional surface story of race. In her influential reading, McDowell interprets Larsen's novel as a story of lesbian sexuality that "passes" itself off as a story of race: "Though superficially, Irene's is an account of Clare's passing for white and related to issues of racial identity and loyalty," maintains McDowell, "underneath the safety of that surface is the more dangerous story...of Irene's awakening sexual desire for Clare."[47] Similarly, Charles Larson maintains that "the racial theme" is not "the most important"; rather "the racial question...is the framework for Larsen's...novel, the context she used to develop her major theme of marital instability."[48] In thus overwriting the story of racial passing with a modernist aesthetics of form or an ideological reading of gender, sexuality, and domesticity, contemporary critics seek to revise and expand earlier, more traditional race readings. By relegating the story of race passing to the status of "cover" story, however, these critical accounts risk eclipsing race or segregating it from other important elements of the narrative.

Contrary to many of the writers above, my own analysis will strategically re-center race in order to demonstrate precisely how Larsen's novel critiques and embraces the notion of race as an essentialist construction. From a critical perspective, what seems clear, as Jennifer Brody and Ann duCille suggest, is that Larsen's simultaneous engagement with the interarticulations of race, class, gender, and sexuality ultimately produces a text whose horizon of meaning must inevitably exceed any univocal reading.[49]

Larsen takes as her subject middle-class black women who, like the author herself, often discover themselves marginalized by their mulatta, or biracial, status. And although most critics now agree that Larsen's novel reflects Irene Redfield's rather than Clare Kendry's story, Clare, like her creator, has remained something of an enigma for the reader. Yet Clare Kendry has little in common with earlier nineteenth-century portraits of the tragic mulatta. And while Clare as mulatta may indeed function as a "narrative device of mediation" (Hazel Carby) or "rhetorical device" (Ann duCille), Larsen refuses her character the sentimental incarnation of the tragic mulatta whose plight necessarily enlists the sympathy of the reader.[50] Further, unlike the mulatta characters of earlier abolitionist and black protest fiction, Clare appears devoid of race consciousness, expressing neither commitment nor solidarity to race. (Rather, it is Irene who, perhaps with some irony, is identified as the "race woman" by virtue of her discourse on "race uplift.") Although humorously fashioning herself as "deserter," Clare manifests neither signs of racial self-hatred nor a deep-seated desire to be white.[51] And while it is true that Clare ultimately expresses boredom and disillusionment with her "pale existence," her story nevertheless fails to conform to the conventions of the tragic mulatta who typically experiences guilt and remorse resulting from race betrayal or abandonment. As Irene later describes her,

> [I]t wasn't...that Clare cared at all about the race or what was to become
> of it. She didn't. Or that she had for any of its members great, or even real,

affection.... Nor could it be said that she had even the slightest artistic or sociological interest in the race that some members of other races displayed. She hadn't. No, Clare Kendry cared nothing for the race. She only belonged to it. (75–76)

Thus, unlike the more conventional black portrayal of the tragic mulatta who anguishes over her desertion of the black "race," Larsen's Clare, "determined...to be a person and not a charity or a problem, or even a daughter of the indiscreet Ham," chooses to cross the color line in order to "get all the things [she] wanted and never had had" (33–34). Having gained entry into a white world of wealth and privilege through marriage to an affluent international banker, Clare comes back to Harlem to escape, in its excitement and gaiety, the sterility of a staid and sterile white world. Her "return," so to speak, seems motivated no less by her "having" nature ("Clare always had a...having way with her") than her earlier leave-taking (22). In short, while implicitly calling into question a system of race and gender privilege, Larsen's passing subject would seem to represent what Barbara Christian calls "the not so tragic mulatta"—who is neither racial repentant nor racial rebel.

Larsen's novel refuses easily to surrender its meaning to the questing reader or probing critic. And read as a (post)modernist text, it makes certain demands on the critic and reader, demands that are signaled symbolically in Larsen's revision of the conventional tragic mulatta as modern passing subject, as well as formally in its critical self-reflexivity, narrative ellipses, and dramatic equivocations. The opening of the text, a personal retrospective occurring long after the events rehearsed have transpired, is signified by the opening of a letter. At the outset of Part One ("Encounter"), Irene receives a missive from Clare, a childhood friend whom she has accidently encountered while they were both socially passing in the rooftop tearoom of the fashionable, whites-only Drayton Hotel in Chicago. Here, the reader is introduced to Irene, who muses over a letter addressed in a handwriting she recognizes to be that of her mysterious friend. This "scene of reading," as it were, establishes a structural equivalence between Irene and the reader, on the one hand, and Clare's letter and Larsen's text, on the other.

Unlike Deborah McDowell, who reads the envelope as a "metaphoric vagina," I am more inclined to agree with Claudia Tate that it functions as a kind of foreshadowing device, an Eliotian "objective correlative" of Clare's "daring defiance of unwritten codes of social propriety."[52] Beyond the letter's metonymic significance, however, I would suggest that the *unopened* envelope—while broadly signifying the dangers of writing—functions, paradoxically, as a metaphor of concealment and safe enclosure. Thus, on one level, the enclosed content of the envelope figures as *the textual unconscious*—that which is risky, unsafe, or menacing. As addressee, Irene faces the challenge of opening the letter and confronting the potential dangers of the *psychic unconscious*.

The structural parallels between Irene/the reader and Clare's letter/Larsen's text provide an early narrative clue on how to read Larsen's novel. What the reader/critic subsequently recognizes is that, for Irene, Clare embodies a "performative" text, and more precisely, the performativity of what legal historian Eva Saks elsewhere describes as "the miscegenous body."[53] Clare (whose name means "light") performs "whiteness" and suppresses "blackness" in the "miscegenous body"—a body in which the "races" (*genus*) are mixed (*miscere*). The contents of Clare's letters articulate the "black" text concealed within the "white" body, expressing her despair with "this pale life" and her "longing...for that other." (7). At the heart of Larsen's novel is Irene's readerly performance juxtaposed to Clare's textual performance. Clare as text—as performative text—becomes a work of art and artifice ("one got...[an] aesthetic pleasure from watching her" [122]), and, as such, an object of desire and knowing for Irene and the spectatorial reader. And it is here, in the realm of desire for knowledge (of Self and Other), rather than in latent lesbian desire, that I would locate Clare's true seductiveness for Irene—as well as the seductiveness of the text for the reader.[54] Like Balzac's Zambinella, Clare functions as an illusion, an actress, a sign, a performer who epitomizes not only difference, but the unrepresentability of difference when it is coded as the miscegenous body. Clare's body, figured in the body of the letter, remains an indecipherable text, an illegible sign, an object of knowledge to be "read," repressed, and, finally, repudiated by Irene. Fundamentally coded as surface and artifice, Clare is produced primarily as "affect." When, for example, Irene visits Clare at the exclusive Morgan, she discovers herself

> in a sitting-room, large and high, at whose windows hung startlingly blue draperies which triumphantly dragged attention from the gloomy chocolate-colored furniture. And Clare was wearing a thin floating dress of the same shade of blue, which suited her and the rather difficult room to perfection. (44)

Elsewhere, Clare "[sits] with an air of indifferent assurance, as if arranged for, desired" (37). In these passages, the combination of posture, costume, set, and props, as it were, contrives to achieve a spectacularly dramatic effect in which Clare gets featured stage center.

The opening scene also alerts the reader not only to the art and artifice of *belles lettres*, but to the materiality of the letter as well. Significantly, here it is not so much the signified (content) as the materiality of the signifier that Irene "reads." Yet even when the contents of the letter are revealed, Irene finds herself "puzzling out, as best she could, the carelessly formed words or making instinctive guesses at them" (7). Thus, the illegibility of the letter simultaneously underscores Clare's inscrutability, the elusiveness of the text, and Irene's readerly incompetence. Later, that same inscrutability is written into "the look on Clare's...face," which Irene finds "unfathomable, utterly beyond any experience or comprehension of hers" (65). Importantly, the reader's introduction to Irene and Clare is framed by the act of reading and being read. Just as Clare becomes the text that Irene must learn to decipher, so Irene, in turn, becomes the text to be deciphered by the reader. What defines this moment, then, is a scene of reading in which the miscegenous text, a stand-in for the miscegenous body, results in "a crisis of representation."[55] At stake in this crisis of representation is the incongruity between the visible sign and the social and legal meaning attached to that sign (the body). While legally defined as black, both Irene and Clare possess "unmarked bodies" that signify hidden meaning but lack visible markers of blackness.

This crisis of representation, moreover, is textually embodied in the form and structure of *Passing*. Through its narrative gaps and repressions, as well as its open-ended resistance to closure and resolution, Larsen's novel performs as an early exemplar of black (post)modernist indeterminacy. Thus, in spite of its modernist affinities, Larsen's narrative would seem to be best understood in terms of a contemporary (post)modernist perspective, both in the performance of its narrative strategies and structure as well as in the philosophical assumptions grounding its notions of personal and textual identity. As we shall see, the narrative retrospective is punctuated by gaps and ambiguities that ultimately function to expose the contingency of knowledge, interrogate both racial essentialism and constructionism, and decenter the autonomous and desiring subject.[56] The repressions of this "writerly" text leave it to the reader, finally, to "fill in" the gaps and lacunae, thereby reconstituting the miscegenous text/body.[57] What is at stake here is the readerly reconstitution of a fragmented and/or suppressed social (and textual) identity.

Narratively, the message of the letter (text) is only partially revealed, thus signifying that its full meaning is, in effect, repressed. Not only do the textual ellipses and narrative gaps represent the textual unconscious, but Irene's own repressions as central consciousness leave it to the reader to fill in the textual occlusions. Mindful that the challenge in reading the text is prefigured by Irene's encounter with Clare's letter, the reader/critic, like Irene, must attempt to elicit the mystery of its meaning—to uncover the secret of the text (figured in some respects by the secrecy of Clare's passing). It is indeed only by filling in the gaps of Larsen's elusive, elliptical, and equivocal narrative—a mode of reading that is demanded by the strategies of (post)modernism—that the critic/reader is potentially able to reconstitute the hidden meaning of the miscegenous text/body.

Again, the reader must bear in mind that Clare is represented only through Irene, a narrative strategy that allows Clare only secondary characterization. Metaphorically, Clare's interiority is a gap within the text; her inner life (including her hidden identity) remains sealed in the envelope, whose contents (like Clare herself) are later to be destroyed by Irene. And like the envelope, which bears no return address, its sender is associated with no precise place or origins (although she travels and resides in New York, Chicago, and Europe). Clare, as we shall see, functions as a kind of textualized network of surfaces on which Irene reads (writes) her own psychic projection of otherness. Significantly, upon their first encounter, Irene is figured as a reader who "[fills] in the gap of her history," while Clare—constructed as a surface that lacks depth and interiority—is rendered "silent." But it is her aversive glance ("she had only to turn away her eyes, to refuse [Clare] recognition") that restricts Irene's knowledge of the Otherness that is Clare. For the reader, then, the meaning of Clare's character remains buried in both Irene's unconscious and the textual unconscious that it signifies.

Presented in three parts (or "acts"), "Encounter," "Re-encounter," and "Finale," Larsen's novel structurally mimes and formally thematizes a theatrical perfor- mance. The second "act," as it were, opens with Irene's ruminating over the let- ter she had received from Clare some two years earlier—"a letter that was, to her taste, a bit too lavish in its wordiness, a shade too unreserved in the manner of its expression" (74–75). Not only is Clare further textualized in this passage, but she is associated in Irene's imagery with an aesthetics of theatricality or performa- tivity (her face is an "ivory mask" [30]) whose affect is excess: "It roused again that old suspicion that Clare was acting, not consciously, perhaps—that is, not too consciously—but, nonetheless, acting" (75). Clare's excess is expressed not only in what is described as her "theatrical heroics" (5), but in her dress, which "deliberate[ly] court[ed] ... attention" (113); in her language, characterized by "all those superlatives" (114); in her smile, which is "a shade too provocative" (14); and in her appearance, which renders her "just a shade too good-looking" (105). But if Clare is a duplicitously performative text, associated with *excess*, Irene is arguably an unreliable narrator, associated with *lack*: indeed, it is Irene's psychic anxiety and repression that are reflected in the narrative's gaps and anxieties. Put somewhat differently, if Clare signals a kind of psychic exhibitionism, Irene fig- ures a psychic repression manifest both at the level of the body (sexual repres- sion) as well as narrative (textual repression). But although the reader may indeed share Irene's fear and fascination with the text (Clare) as an aestheticized object of knowledge (and desire), Irene's repressive reading need not be the reader/critic's. Significantly, it is Irene who, at the outset of the novel, fears "being ejected"—or "outed," as it were—from the racially exclusive Drayton Hotel tearoom.[58] What soon becomes evident, however, is that Irene's true "outing" is a consequence of her re-encounter with Clare Kendry, whose "daring" and "having" ways expose Irene to her own alterity or "otherness."

Arguing that Clare, in fact, exists in terms of Irene's own projections of "other- ness" ("the unconscious, the unknowable, the erotic, and the passive"), Cheryl Wall figures Irene and Clare as psychological "doubles."[59] Similarly, for Thadious Davis, Clare embodies "the personal and psychological characteristics that Irene needs to become a complete person."[60] Further, Ann duCille figures Clare as "something more than...another doubling or dividing"; for duCille, Clare functions less as Irene's "alter ego than her alter libido, the buried, long-denied sexual self."[61] Like these readings, my own assumes a relation of complementarity between Irene and Clare, in which the latter functions to disrupt Irene's sense of identity by exposing her long-repressed self-difference. In her portrayal of these two women as mirror-like images, Larsen frequently subverts the opposition claimed by Irene: "Actually they were strangers. Strangers in their ways and means of living. Strangers in their desires and ambitions. Strangers even in their racial consciousness" (92–93). Yet Larsen's character development would suggest that although Irene poses as a proponent of race uplift who professes to be repelled by Clare's passing, she remains intrigued, and "[wishes] to find out about this hazardous business [passing]," and upon meeting Clare's husband, the racist Bellew, Irene "*conceal[s] her own origins*" (30, 75, emphasis added). In thus denying her race, Irene, in effect, "passes" and in so doing, reinforces her identity with Clare. Further, searching for "some clue to [Clare's] identity," Irene feels that "about the woman was some quality, *an intangible something, too vague to define, too remote to seize,* but which was, to Irene Redfield, *very familiar*" (18, 19, emphasis added). Narratively, the notion of otherness indeed evokes "the presence of *something strange… even repugnant*" yet somehow "*compelling,*" and it is this quality of repulsion and attraction that Clare seems to hold for Irene (116, emphasis added). Later, Irene perceives that Clare has the ability to "put into words that which, not so definitely defined, was so often in her own heart" (101–102). At other times, Irene remarks that it was "as if she [Irene] had been in the secret of the other's [Clare's] thoughts" (28), and that it was "uncanny, the way Clare could divine what one was thinking" (48). Such a complex relation of psychic projection and introjection defines a relation of deep intersubjectivity between these characters, one in which Clare functions, on multiple levels, as a kind of doppelgänger for Irene. Significantly, Clare addresses Irene as "'Rene," thereby erasing the "I" in "Irene." In doing so, Clare, in effect, exposes (I)Rene to her long-buried other self, one that threatens to disrupt the placid surface of her safe and orderly life. The clear affinity between these characters is signaled metaphorically at the outset of the novel in the scene of encounter at the downtown Chicago hotel when Irene notes that "the woman sitting on the other side of the table [holds] for [her] a fascination, strange and compelling" (36–37). In effect, this mirroring of the self ("on the other side of the table") sets the stage for Irene's ambivalent negotiation of the difference and identity between herself and a figure toward whom she feels both aversion and attraction.

Irene's ambivalence invokes the logic of a contemporary psychoanalytic discourse of identity and difference. Essential to Irene's sense of "permanence, safety, and security" is the repression of her own otherness—the alterity and *self-difference* that is embodied in the character of Clare. This complex relation of difference and identity—and *difference in identity*—suggests that, for Larsen, the mulatta/passing subject becomes a trope not only for difference or *otherness*, but more precisely for self-difference, or the *otherness of the self*.

Larsen, in effect, externalizes the internal drama of difference and identity staged in her first novel, *Quicksand*. If, in the earlier narrative, the protagonist Helga Crane seeks to reduce her multiplicity and self-difference to sameness (which leads to her certain death), in *Passing,* the central characters are figured as fractured and self-divided, such that each represents not only the *other of the self,* but *the otherness of the self.* In other words, in her second novel, Larsen fractures and externalizes the equivocal drama of identity that is internalized by the protagonist in her earlier novel.

As argued above, the passing plot would seem fundamentally to destabilize the color line; nevertheless, like other Harlem Renaissance black writers, Larsen seems, at times, to support an essentialist view of blackness, thereby affirming Samira Kawash's proposition that the novel of passing is "necessarily constructed around the presumption of the existence of fixed and irrevocable racial identities because it is only in relation to such a conception of race that passing is possible in the first place."[62] At the outset of the novel, Irene seems to challenge a biologically constructed notion of race:

> Absurd! Impossible! White people were so stupid about such things for all that they usually asserted that they were able to tell; and by the most ridiculous means, finger-nails, palms of hands, shapes of ears, teeth, and other equally silly rot. (16)

Yet her dismissal of the physical markers by which some purport to read racial difference seems contradicted by her later conviction that Clare possesses "Negro eyes": "Ah! Surely! They were Negro eyes! mysterious and concealing. And set in that ivory face under that bright hair, there was about them something exotic" (38).[63] Irene's husband, Brian, also suggests that there is something peculiar and unique (and therefore essentializing) about race. Reflecting on the phenomenon of racial passing, Brian concludes that "they [passers] always come back. I've seen it happen time and time again." Answering Irene's query, "But why?," Brian replies, "If I knew that, I'd know what race is" (80). It is for this reason that in response to Hugh Wentworth, the white novelist and friend who ponders over "the trick" of how to "pick some of 'em [the passers]," Irene explains that "[n]obody can [detect who is passing]. Not by looking." Her explanation here is revealing because it suggests that racial difference lies neither in physical "appearance," nor from anything "[done] or said," but rather in "ways [that are not] definite or tangible" (118). Clearly, for Irene, "race" or "racial difference," while discernible by the freemasonry of the race, is something that is neither palpable nor definable. If Larsen's passing plot, then, destabilizes the notion of race, her characters essentialize race, and if Clare deconstructs race through racial performativity, Irene would seem first biologically and later metaphysically to essentialize race by abstracting notions of race and race difference from history and culture. Like Clare's letter (and Larsen's novel), "race" proves to be a subtle and elusive text, not easily read.

As suggested above, the passing novel also enables the reader to examine the construction of whiteness from a location that is racialized as black. If it is true, as Ruth Frankenberg argues, that one of the prerogatives of whiteness is to make "itself invisible precisely by asserting its normalcy, its transparency," then it is the

African-American passing novel that "marks" and "names" whiteness and white privilege.[64] The passing novels inevitably pose the question asked by turn-of-the-century novelist Charles Chesnutt, "What Is a White Man?"—or, in white novelist George Washington Cable's subsequent elaboration, "What is a white woman?"[65] In *de-scribing* the markers of whiteness as appropriated by the passing subject as racial Other, novelists such as Larsen *in-scribe* whiteness as a system or configuration of signs to be manipulated in the assertion and performance of whiteness.

In Larsen's narrative, whiteness is attached not only to social privilege but to a materialist ethic: John Bellew, Clare's white husband, an international banker, "turn[s] up from South America with untold gold" (34). Thus, the flagrantly racist Bellew is attached not only to filthy lucre, but metaphorically to the imperialistic exploitation of a land and its natural resources in the pursuit of money and wealth. And, furthermore, although associated with "latent physical power," Bellew is constructed as something of a male hysteric, manifested in his blatant and unrestrained racist vituperation, as well as in his enervated and effeminate demeanor (he possesses "a soft mouth, somewhat womanish, set in an unhealthy-looking dough-colored face" [54]). Bellew's effeminacy and hysteria must also be read in terms of the racist, albeit affectionate, epithet that he confers on his wife, Clare, who is, unbeknownst to her husband, of African-American descent. Humorously, Bellew explains why he calls his wife "Nig": "When we were first married, she [Clare] was as white as . . . a lily. But I declare she's gettin' darker and darker. I tell her if she don't look out, she'll wake up one of these days and find she's turned into a nigger" (55). In response to Clare's question, "My goodness, Jack! What difference would it make if, after all these years, you were to find out that I was one or two percent colored?," he answers, "Oh, no, Nig . . . nothing like that with me. I know you're no nigger, so it's all right. You can get as black as you please as far as I'm concerned, since I know you're no nigger. I *draw the line* at that. No niggers in my family. Never have been and never will be" (56, emphasis added). In order to secure his own white masculinity, potentially destabilized by his desire for the "exotic other" figured by Clare, Bellew *must draw the (color) line* while, at the same time, fetishizing the object of his fear and desire—the "blackness" of "Nig's" body.[66]

Buried in Larsen's text is an obscure but notable reference to the Rhinelander case, a controversial and highly publicized court trial that can be classified as a part of American miscegenation jurisprudence. While Irene's seemingly offhand reference concerning the Rhinelander case dramatizes the potential legal consequences of Clare's "transgression," it also demonstrates the power of legal discourse to define, construct, and even to criminalize the miscegenous body. Further, it is a case that emphasizes the discrepancy between the visible marker and the legal definition of race that leads to a crisis of representation in the social construction of the miscegenous body. Linking Bellew's comments to Irene's reference to the notorious Rhinelander case highlights the function of the "line" that Bellew "draws" and its demarcation in the courts by means of miscegenation laws designed to protect white property rights as well as the rights of whiteness. Unknowingly, however, Bellew has formed a conjugal alliance that consequently reproduces the miscegenous body within his own family, an action that unwittingly gives the lie to his own claims of racial purity.

Thus, it is the "dangerous mixing" of "white blood" and "black blood" that constitutes a threat not only to white property inheritance, but to the "purity" of the white body politic. The passing body, in particular, is a site of danger since, by betraying no racialized markers, it renders blackness invisible. Not only does Bellew's racist invective express the fears and anxieties of white masculinity around issues of race, race difference, and miscegenation, but Irene's reference to the Rhinelander case calls attention to collective white race anxieties and fears as reflected in American jurisprudence. Basically this case represents for white society an expression of the anxiety over race-mixing, both in its potential to change distribution of property (which is precisely what happened in the Rhinelander case),[67] as well as in its threat to pollute the putative racial purity of the white family, race, and nation.

The issues of race and nation are also raised, albeit obliquely, in the affinity between Brian and Clare. Irene apparently (mis)reads the relationship between her husband and her friend as one of betrayal and infidelity and, characteristically, the text refuses to affirm or undermine Irene's perceptions, leaving it to the reader/critic to reach his or her own conclusions. However, I would propose a reading that would both affirm and challenge Irene's suspicions. Like Clare, Brian is a figure animated by a desire for a life outside the racist proscriptions of American society. His brooding discontent and innate dissatisfaction stem from his "dislike and disgust for his profession and his country" (84). And curiously, like John Bellew, Brian is attracted to South America. Irene has "[made] ... strenuous efforts to repress ... that old, queer, unhappy restlessness ... that craving for someplace strange and different" that often leads to Brian's moodiness (68–69). Arguably, what Irene suspects to be a sexual attraction between Clare and Brian reflects an affinity of desire for social and personal freedom from the confines of race in the United States. Brian's response to American racial arrangements, like Clare's, constitutes an option (escape) that, like passing, is available only to individuals. What links these characters symbolically, then, is that both seek to cross the line, Brian geographically and Clare racially. Brian's desire to cross geographical borders ("rush off to that remote place of his heart's desire" [90]) functions, in effect, as the symbolic equivalent of Clare's desire to cross racial boundaries in pursuit of wealth and status. The symbolic equivalence between expatriation and passing suggests here what Samira Kawash calls "geographies of the color line," that is to say, the metaphorical relation between race and geography in which, as David Goldberg explains, "spatial distinctions ... are racialized [and] racial categories [are] spatialized."[68] In addition, Larsen's symbolic equivalence of race and geography fractures the choices that James Weldon Johnson's narrator collapses in his rationale for passing in *The Autobiography of an Ex-Colored Man*: "I argued to forsake one's race to better one's condition was no less worthy an action than to forsake one's country for the same purpose."[69] Thus, Larsen's intertextual response to Johnson figures Clare and potentially Brian (like the ex-colored man) as "racial expatriates" who transgress the geography of the color line. In fact, Irene's description of passing—"the breaking away from all that was familiar and friendly to take one's chance in another environment"—implicates race and place in a definition that could serve equally well for "expatriation" (30). But, of course, as a racially marked body, Brian "couldn't exactly pass." (Unlike Clare, whose blackness is invisible, Brian's complexion is "of an exquisitely fine texture and deep copper color" [78].)

If, on the one hand, both Brian and Clare repudiate boundaries of race and nationality, Irene, on the other hand, seeks to repress Brian's expatriate impulse and deny Clare's passing preference. For Irene, expatriation, like passing, represents "a dangerous business," that is to say, a threat to her desire for "safety," "security," and "permanence" in her own life. Not only does Irene avow her ties to race, but also her ties to nation: "she would not go to Brazil. She belonged in this land of rising towers. She was an American. She grew from this soil, and she would not be uprooted" (169–170). Here Larsen endows her protagonist with a complex sense of self-definition predicated not only upon racial identity, but an affirmation of national identity as well.

Although Larsen revises the conventional treatment of the tragic mulatta, the death of Clare in the "Finale" would seem to replicate the formulaic conclusion of the nineteenth-century passing novel. Typically, the earlier novel of passing ended with the death of the passer who is caught, unhappily, betwixt and between the black and white worlds. Insofar as Clare has no place in the social order and, therefore, must exit the text, Larsen would seem to conform to prior conventions governing the representation of the tragic mulatta. In the more traditional treatment of the passing novel, the existing racial order is restored and the essentialist assumptions underpinning that order are affirmed. Clare's successful performance of whiteness, however, effectively disrupts the social order and reduces essentialism to a virtual absurdity. Nevertheless, Clare's performance comes at a high price indeed—her death.

Most critics and readers agree that the reasons for Clare's death remain inconclusive. Either she falls, jumps, or is pushed from a sixth-story window, thus rendering her death either an accident, suicide, or homicide. And there is, as Claudia Tate warns, "no tangible proof to support one interpretation over another."[70] Nonetheless, the inevitability of Clare's death is signaled throughout the text by images that foreshadow her fate: the "offending letter," which Irene "[tears] into tiny ragged squares" and scatters over the train's railing, and, later, Irene's "boiling rage" resulting in a "slight crash" and a "shattered cup," leaving "dark stains [which] dotted the bright rug" (68, 144). Indeed, her death is unwittingly anticipated by Brian as he, Clare, and Irene climb up to the sixth-story apartment of the Freelands to attend a Christmas party; Brian jokingly tells Clare, "Mind... you don't fall by the wayside" (173). Moments later, Clare's death is again prefigured by Irene who, opening the "long casement-windows of which the Freelands were so proud," then "finished her cigarette and threw it out, watching the tiny spark drop slowly down to the white ground below" (174).

In the final moments of the novel, Irene hears "a strange man" attributing the event to "death by misadventure," and while it seems likely that Clare's death, on the surface of it, could be the consequence of an accident or mishap, it is equally true that both Bellew and Irene must be regarded as co-implicated in her demise. Earlier Irene desperately desires Clare's death, becoming "faint and sick" while trying vainly to "drive away" the thought that "[i]f Clare should die," she could rid herself of the "menace of impermanence" that Clare represents (158, 159). And, arguably, it is Irene's aphasia, or "[failure] to speak," about her inadvertent encounter with Bellew that leads ultimately to Clare's death (158). On the verge of telling Clare about the meeting with Bellew, Irene fears that Clare "wouldn't avert the results of the encounter [exposure of her racial identity]" (157), and represses "the flood of speech on her lips" (165). In some respects, then, Clare's death can surely be construed as the indirect consequence of Irene's silence (her "keeping back…information" [165]). However, if Irene's aphasia leads indirectly to Clare's discovery, it is Bellew's verbal accusation—"So you're a nigger, a damned dirty nigger!"—that, as we have seen, redraws the color line (175). In so doing, Bellew verbally "pushes" Clare across that line—over which she stumbles. Bellew's speech is, in its affect, performative: the moment of its utterance leads ineluctably to the moment of Clare's fatal fall, symbolically through the blackness of night into the whiteness of the snow below.

Yet, however one interprets Clare's death, the reader must inevitably return to Irene who, through an act of memory ("Such were Irene Redfield's memories" [73]), produces a narrative that is fundamentally, albeit fragmentarily, reconstituted through the various scenes of reading that structure her narrative. At the novel's conclusion, Irene is rendered incapable of reliably reading or remedying her own situation; her story achieves neither resolution nor closure. Rather than invoke her narrative as a modernist stay against chaos, Irene sinks into virtual unconsciousness:

> [Irene's] quaking knees gave way under her. She moaned and sank down, moaned again. Through the great heaviness that submerged and drowned her she was dimly conscious.... *Then everything was dark.* (181–182, emphasis added)

Significantly, Irene's subsequent memory lapse replicates the textual equivocations and ellipses that are typical of (post)modernist narrative. It is in aposiopetic moments such those below in which the thought or sentence suddenly breaks off that the author expresses Irene's repression and denial:

> What happened next, Irene Redfield never afterwards allowed herself to remember. Never clearly....

What would the others think? That Clare had fallen? That she had deliberately leaned backward? Certainly one or the other. Not—....
    She stammered: "Is she—is she—?"....
    "....She just fell, before anybody could stop her. I—" (176–181 *passim*)

Desiring to maintain the modernist ideals of order and harmony in her
world, Irene has attempted to discipline and regulate her life, as well as that of
her husband and sons, for "Irene didn't like change, particularly changes that
affected the smooth routine of her household" (86). Just as Irene represses her
husband's desire for Brazil, so she represses, much to Brian's dismay and protest,
the discussion of certain subjects in her household in an attempt to protect her
sons from the knowledge of ideas such as "sex" and the "race problem." Irene
thus tries to repress not only self-knowledge, but the knowledge of others that
she construes to be threatening or dangerous (and significantly that subjugated
knowledge is characteristically racial and sexual). Yet Irene cannot escape "that
fear which crouched, always deep down within her, stealing away that sense
of security, the feeling of permanence, from the life which she so admirably
arranged for them all, and desired so ardently to remain as it was" (83–84).
But as Irene's final physical collapse suggests, it is she herself who embodies
internally the disorder and instability that would seem to menace the surface
order and organization of her world. In a moment of epiphany, Irene recognizes that although "life went on precisely as before...she...had changed." It
is "knowing" that "had changed her": invoking the image of the Platonic cave,
Irene reflects, "It was as if in a house long dim, a match had been struck, show-
ing ghastly shapes where had been only blurred shadows" (139). Irene's illuminations, however, are submerged in the conclusion by a memory lapse and a
final fall into unconsciousness. Irene must "black out" her epiphany, as well as
its catalyst and agent, Clare.

    Metaphorically, then, it is the opening of the envelope, the door into a repressed
or buried consciousness, that exposes Irene to the repressed knowledge of
self-difference and that results ironically in tragedy for Clare. For, finally, the death
of Clare represents Irene's successful repression, or murder, of self-difference.
Symbolically, Irene's "hand on Clare's arm" links them corporeally in that final
equivocal moment. If Clare indeed represents aspects of the self that Irene seeks to
deny, then Clare's death—whether accident, homicide, or suicide—represents the
death of Irene's alterity or "otherness." In other words, Clare's physical death functions as the equivalent of Irene's psychic suicide.

    Although the cause of Clare's death remains indeterminate, what is of greater
importance is the fact of her death, and its necessity, given the conventions of modernist narrative. Clare's transgressive performance of whiteness is "punished" by
the elaborate essentialist conceptions of her husband and Irene. Narratively, Irene's
nationalist essentialism combines with Bellew's racialist essentialism to, in effect,

reinscribe and reinforce the color line by "killing off" Clare. As author, Larsen's dilemma is that she creates a character who, through the successful performance of whiteness, demonstrates the falsity of black nationalist essentialism, on the one hand, and white racial essentialism, on the other. However, Larsen's refutation is not without a cost for both author and character, a cost prefigured in terms of a kind of discourse of the debt that threads through the novel. Importantly, at the outset, Clare informs her friend, "In fact, all things considered, I think, 'Rene, that [passing is] even worth the price" (36). Later, quoting her father, Clare echoes a similar sentiment: "As my inestimable dad used to say, 'Everything must be paid for,'" a remark later reiterated by Irene (107).

The author, in other words, incurs a debt that her character must "pay" with the sacrifice of her life. (Surely it is ironically significant that Clare's death, which occurs on Christmas, is meant to suggest something of a sacrifice to the dominant notions of essentialized racial identity.) Clare has, in effect, *lived out* the complex identity that Larsen's narrative has *theorized*. At the level of character and narrative, the essentialist divide is finally revealed to be illusory. And Clare's exposure, in full view of Irene and Bellew, ensures her own disappearance in a world of modernity saturated by essentialist conceptions of race. Clearly, at this point Clare is left with no place to occupy in the racially essentialized world of modernity: Irene will not allow her to assume an identity in the black world; Bellew will not allow her to assume an identity in the white world. Yet Clare goes on to claim a postmodernist identity that is predicated on self-difference and an identity that challenges Irene's modernist self-sameness. Clare performs, lives out, and dies in the assertion of an identity that is foreign to Irene's modernist conception of integrated identity. In fact, Clare's complexly reconstructed identity is fundamentally inconsistent and incompatible with the essentializing assumptions of her culture. Larsen has created a character, a mulatta, who affirms a complex, contingent, and multiplicitous postmodernist notion of identity in a modernist world that would nullify her very existence. Her continued existence would menace both Bellew's and Irene's world, so she must cease to exist.

Clare's successful passing from one "essence" ("blackness") to another diametrically opposed "essence" ("whiteness") demonstrates, finally, that these so-called essences are not biological but socially constructed. Larsen's artistic achievement lies in the narrative performance of her refutation of essentialism. She does not challenge the presuppositions of essentialism, either morally, philosophically, or scientifically; rather, through the performativity of her narrative, she presents a *reductio ad absurdum* refutation of the essentialist position. As author, Larsen imagines a position that her narrative demonstrates to entail an absurdity. In other words, the presumption of essentialism would make it impossible for one to switch "essences." It is precisely the successful performance of passing that would render such a presumption absurd.

Just as Irene, in the final scene, sinks into unconsciousness and later, a memory gap, Clare falls into a kind of metaphysical gap. Clare's fall into a metaphysical hole has its counterpart in both the textual "holes" as well as the "holes" in Irene's memory. Such a conclusion can only confirm that there exists no place in the realm of essentialist being for Clare's continued existence; she possesses no ontological claim in the world of essentialized modernity.

Josephine Baker and *La Revue Nègre*

From Ethnography to Performance

I. Dance, the Black Female Body, and the French Colonial Imaginary

Popular culture historian Richard Dyer argues that "performers get to be stars when what they act matters to enough people."[1] It is this relatively simple formulation of a complex thesis that informs my project—which poses the question of how Josephine Baker—rejected by the New York artistic and critical establishment as the not-so-talented, bulging-eyed, buck-toothed daughter of a "St. Louis wash[er] woman"[2]—became the toast of Paris in the 1920s. In other words, what were the circumstances that allowed Baker to "matter" in the French imaginary? My aim is to explore the "matter," as it were, through considering the black body as it circulated in transatlantic culture, particularly during the cultural period that was named by contemporaries as "Le Tumulte Noir"—a moment that we currently identify from a postcolonial and postmodernist perspective as "colonialist" and "modernist."

The hold of this visceral and visual narrative—one which salvages the notion of the "vanishing primitive" and, simultaneously, produces the pleasure of spectatorship in the dancing body—is dramatized in Josephine Baker's performances in Paris in the 1920s and 1930s. Reinscribing a specularized colonial narrative—one that was necessarily heavily racialized, sexualized, and genderized—this drama staged the encounter of colonizer and colonized, spectator and spectacle, the white gaze (coded as male) and the black body (coded as female).

In the theater, music halls, and cabarets of Paris, the encounter of tourist and native was restaged in a setting that was at once more domesticated and more fantastical than its original enactment. And it was the Baker body that became the site of the uncharted terrain to be explored, tamed, and conquered each evening in the French colonial imagination. Baker's performances enacted events in which both the audience and performer participated, the former compelled by a powerful voyeurism coupled by the latter's equally powerful exhibitionism—a dialectical performance re-enacting the obsessive need of the colonizer to "look" and the obsessive desire of the colonized to be "looked at."

The principal query informing this chapter is, quite simply, what are the social and historical preconditions and/or predispositions fueling a demonstratively powerful, collective French fantasy of the black female body? The answer lies, broadly, in the era's expansive colonialism, coupled with an expansive modernity, and the impact of these formations on the visual arts and popular culture in late-nineteenth- and early twentieth-century France. The phenomenon of Josephine Baker's emergence in 1920s Paris can be productively staged in the context of a series of World's Fairs, ethnographic exhibitions, and colonial expositions occurring in France, mainly Paris, roughly between the years 1867 and 1937.

II. The Colonial Exposition and the Tradition of "Ethnographic Display"

European colonialism contrived an image of the black body that appealed to a continental appetite for romanticized notions of the primitive, a construction that functioned to alleviate colonial anxieties. It was the body that became the index of racial difference for the continental Africans as well as their New World descendants. In the wake of its colonial expansion into Africa, France, in particular, located the peoples and cultures of its overseas possessions within what art historian Richard Powell calls "an exotic frame of reference."[3] More specifically, in the European imaginary, it was the black *female* body that not only was associated with the feminizing of Africa, but was often figured as an object of colonial desire. As colonized subject, France's "Ebony Venus" had her counterpart in Britain's "Sable Venus," and European nations rivaled each other to lay claim to the land, wealth, and sexuality signified by these figures.[4] Moreover, the specifically French fascination is historically evident in the ethnographic production of the (often fully or partially unclothed) black female body in mid- to late-nineteenth-century French photography (the counterpart of ethnographic film).[5] Affiliated with state and privately sponsored expeditions (e.g., the 1925 Citroën Croisière Noire expedition, organized by Georges-Marie Haardt, and the 1931 Mission Dakar-Djibouti expedition recorded in Michel Leiris's *Afrique fantôme*),[6] ethnographic photography provided not merely "documentation," but represented notions of the "primitive savage" as constructed in the European imaginary.[7]

Although the Paris *Jardin d'Acclimatation* (zoological gardens) staged at public parks and fair grounds ethnographic expositions in which African peoples were exhibited in an environment designed to reproduce their "natural habitat" as early as the late 1870s, French colonial exhibitions and expositions, since 1867, had featured dioramas, or living displays, of so-called primitive peoples.[8] The narrative of the African "primitive" functioned to secure the "modernity" of the European subject, and the narrative of scientific and social progress was underwritten by the narrative of African primitivism and technological stasis. Thus, in contrast to the modern industrial and technological achievements of the West, African "indigenes" were installed in reconstructed "native villages" at the spectacular 1889 Paris *Exposition Universelle* in order to demonstrate the progress and industrial superiority of the West. Linked historically with the early French anthropological project of hierarchically classifying the races according to the theory of evolution, such installations also functioned as sites for popular ethnological display, public entertainment, and imperial propaganda.[9] By far, the most magnificent of these colonial expositions was the *Exposition coloniale internationale* staged at the Bois de Vincennes. Celebrating the centenary of French colonial rule in Algeria, this dramatic "théâtre of the colonies,"[10] as Sylviane Leprun describes it, running from May 1931 to January 1932, attracted eight million spectators, and yielded a profit to its official sponsor, the French government.[11]

As colonial performances, these extravaganzas would generate popular identification with *La Plus Grande France*, or *La France d'Outre Mer*, as well as what historian Raoul Giradet calls *L'Idée coloniale*.[12] Institutionalized in the colonial exhibits, and later at the colonial expositions, native displays were meant to incite popular support for the official policy of the French *mission civilisatrice*, or "civilizing mission" (the counterpart to the British "White Man's Burden" and the German "Kultermission").[13] Further, the impact of the colonial exposition, a monument to the moral, artistic, and material progress of the *métropole*, was to erect the project of French colonialism upon the oppositional dichotomy between "savagery" and "civilization." Notably, the architectural planning of these expositions was key to hierarchically classifying the colonized according to their evolutionary stage of development, as measured against the material and technological progress of the West. Yet, as we shall see, it was precisely the architectural imaginary of these expositions that threatened to undermine this neatly schematic ideological antithesis, and thus reinscribe the cultural map of the exposition.

According to the *Guide officiel*, the 1931 Colonial Exhibition sought to distinguish itself from the exoticism of previous exhibitions by calling attention to its specifically ethnographic intent. Addressing the visitor as "a person of good taste," André Demaison writes, "You will see no blacks tastelessly throwing themselves about on stage, no belly dancers, no seamy sideshows, those vulgar displays that have brought discredit upon many another exhibition of the colonial sphere; but rather reconstructions of tropical life with all its color and truly picturesque qualities."[14] The *Guide officiel* was designed to offer the visitor a virtual tour of the cities and native villages of the colonies, reconstituted in wood and papier mâché.[15] In this spectacular colonial drama, the actors themselves consisted of "a contingent of natives," primarily "artisans and dancers," who were "recruited in the various colonies [of] French West Africa" in order to "animate these representations of native life."[16] Visitors were advised to "[l]ook closely at their work. Watch what they do. Listen to their chants and their music, and taste the national dishes that they offer you."[17] The fixity of the roles assigned in these dioramas marked the native actors as reified spectacles in a kind of grand colonial theater. In effect, the 1931 Colonial Exhibition constituted "a space of 'illusion and imagination' "[18] in which the specta-tor/traveler embarked on " 'the illusion of a voyage in[to] the colonial world.' "[19] It was a voyage structured as an ethnographic production of the colonized which, simultaneously, promoted a kind of ethnographic consumption of "otherness" by the French. Not least among the "products" of consumption, of course, were the women, who became, as it were, objects of "voyeuristic appropriation."[20]

It is instructive that these carefully fashioned simulacra, putatively faith-ful reproductions of the villages and native reconstructions, were often based on French interpretations and revisions of the originals. This modernization, or "Frenchification," of so-called primitive culture and architecture is evident in the 1931 Colonial Exhibition.[21] The French architects who designed the African pavil-ions for the exhibition erected structures that physically adapted and modified African art and architecture to accommodate French taste and aesthetic sensibility. In fact, the architects and sculptors were officially commissioned to beautify the original African huts, thereby—as they must have conceived it—"improving" on the originals, constructed as *nature*, and architecturally demonstrating the possibili-ties of *culture*, signified by the French "civilizing mission."[22]

Typically, the pavilion interiors displayed the contributions of the *métropole* to the colonies. As art historian Patricia Morton points out, the result appeared as a cultural division represented architecturally by the exterior and interior—the for-mer signifying "savagery" and the latter, "progress" (Figure 12.1). Yet, despite the desire to construct these edifices "à la manière indigène... [d'où] se dégage une savagerie" ("in the indigenous manner [so as to] throw off a savagerie"), even the exteriors were meant to adapt *l'art nègre* (African art) "aux exigences de l'Exposition et de l'esthétique" ("to the demands of the Exposition and the canons of aesthetic taste"). The interior decor (Figure 12.2) characteristically blended the primitive and the modern (art deco) in a design motif extracting formal and structural ele-ments from traditional African artifacts and architecture. Even the ritual masks (Figure 12.3) are artistically arranged in an "appropriate" manner ("figurant dans un ensemble décoratif dû"). The curator, in effect, creates a kind of "decorative ensemble" designed to fit into the aesthetic canons of the Exposition.[23] This *métis-sage*, as it were, represented the architectural equivalent of the French colonial policy of assimilation—although, as Morton astutely observes, this "mingling of representational vocabularies brought architecture at the exposition into the dan-gerous territory of cross-breeding," a move ultimately subversive to the project of maintaining, categorizing, and fixing racial and cultural difference.[24] Of particular interest in the reconstituted French West African villages were the performances of dance troupes from the Ivory Coast, Sudan, Dahomey, and the Upper Niger. And despite the avowed intentions of the organizers to exorcise the exoticism character-izing earlier expositions, the 1931 Colonial Exhibition returned, once more, to the

Figure 12.1 "Un des pavillons de la section du Cameroun et du Togo." *L'Illustration*, August 22, 1931, No. 4616-89.

Figure 12.2 "L'Afrique." *L'Illustration*, August 22, 1931, No. 4616-89.

Figure 12.3 "Masques de la Côte d'Ivoire figurant dans un ensemble décoratif dû,"
L'Illustration, August 22, 1931, No. 4616-89.

motif of the *danse sauvage,* which remained an essential element in the discourse
and iconography of French primitivism. Within the tradition of late-nineteenth- and
early-twentieth-century ethnographic photography, the *kinesthetically staged*—or
dancing—black body, in particular, was linked to notions of the primitive—mapped
onto a deepening interest and identification with the idea of the modern.

Aligned to this embodiment of primitive modernism, the popular obsession with
the dancing ethnic body was complicated by contemporary ethnographic and anthropological associations linking dance, "race," and primitivism.[25] Further, contemporary anthropology and ethnology—"sciences" that developed in the context of the
European colonization of Africa—advanced the link between dance and primitivism
by claiming that "direct observation of the 'natives'" yielded "insight into the nature
of dance."[26] Indeed, some anthropologists and ethnologists regarded dance as a virtual
genetic imprint for "primitive" peoples. Since dance constitutes an art form in which
the dancer's own body is the primary medium of creativity, so they reasoned, dance
preceded all other forms of creative expression. The presumption that dance "play[ed]
[its] biggest role among 'primitive' people," in effect, defined indigenous peoples in
terms of dance culture. Inevitably, such indigenous dance performances, described as
"wild," "exotic," "uninhibited," and "indecent," functioned as indices of lesser developed

Figure 12.4 Charles Beauvais, *Danse Africaine*, 1900. Forney Library, Paris.

cultures.[27] The motif of the dancing black body, then, was to become associated with popular notions of savagery and exotic otherness. The colorfully grotesque black whirling dervishes of Charles Beauvais's 1900 *Danse Africaine* (Figure 12.4) demonstrate how the *tam-tam*, or African group dance, also popularly described as *la danse sauvage*, associated itself in the French artistic imaginary with delirium and erotic frenzy.

The performance of a troupe of Ivory Coast dancers (Figure 12.5) emphasizes the iconographic significance of the *danse du sauvage*, performed to the *tams-tams*, or the *musique du sauvage*. Compared to the Asian performances, the African dances are described as more explicit, simpler, nearer to primitive instinct ("plus direct, plus simple, plus pres des instincts primitifs"). Further, the *tams-tams*, the sorcerers, and the cortèges seduced and swept up the crowds ("Ses tams tams, ses sorciers, ses cortèges…ont séduit et entraîné les foules"). The colonial staging of such dance performances had the effect of demonstrating to the spectator the social location of these "primitive" cultures on the evolutionary scale of Western cultural development. Similarly, a Senegalese troupe performing in the streets of a reconstructed village in an African Pavilion (Figure 12.6) features barely clad natives dancing ecstatically under the fetishizing gaze of fully dressed, formally attired, rather stolid-looking Europeans. While the motif of the dancing black body here epitomizes "exotic otherness," the contrast in vestibulary codes—nudity and clothing—signifies the contrast between "barbarity" and "civilization."

The figure of Josephine Baker, frequently staged in a variety of jungle *mise-en-scènes* in her stage and cinematic performances, derives, then, from this tradition of the

Figure 12.5 "Danseurs de la Côte d'Ivoire." *L'Illustration*, August 22, 1931, No. 4616-89.

Figure 12.6 "La fête sénégalaise des fanaux, dans les rues du village indigène de l'Exposition," *L'Illustration*, August 22, 1931, No. 4616-89.

Figure 12.7 "Josephine Baker Chosen Queen of the Colonies," *Pittsburgh Courier*
February 21, 1931.

ethnographic exhibition of the black body, markedly intersecting an equally powerful tradition of female specularization.[28] It is not without some irony that five
years after her debut performance in *La Revue Nègre*, officials of the 1931 Colonial
Exhibition named Baker as "Queen of the Colonies" (Figure 12.7).[29] While such a
designation signifies Baker's "reign" in the arena of popular culture, it collapses any
difference between Baker as an African-American and the colonized African, once
more affirming essentialized racial difference in the French imaginary. Significantly,
the strategy to install Baker as a surrogate colonial failed because, as her detractors
protested, Baker was not an "authentic" French colonial, suggesting the ambivalent
triumph of French nationalism over racial difference. Nevertheless, the gesture
remains an equivocal affirmation of Baker's iconographic association with the colonies in the French imaginary.

III. Modernist Gender Display: From Exposition to Music Hall

During the first two decades of the twentieth century, Paris music halls featured and
fashionable French society abandoned itself to what was popularly described as *la*

mentalité primitive, prescribed by the Surrealists and other avant-gardist groups as a kind of antidote for an "over-intellectualized" and spiritually bankrupt Old World culture. Unlike the proponents of colonialism, who affirmed reason, technology, and material progress, demonstrating the necessity of the civilizing mission, André Breton, Jean Cocteau, Paul Eluard, and other avant-gardists were attracted to the notion of the primitive as an escape from what they perceived to be the excessive rationality of the West.

It was this group of artists and intellectuals who staged a counter-exposition in protest of the 1931 Colonial Exposition. Significantly, however, this self-constituted counter-cultural group were themselves sometimes collectors of colonial souvenirs and trophies, and aficionados of *l'art nègre.*[30] Thus it is not without some irony that while the function of the counter-exposition was to expose the violence of the colonial practices underlying the Colonial Exposition, its staging of Africa and the black body through music, photography, and cuisine was arguably no less ideological than that of the official exposition.[31] And while the Surrealists condemned the politics of colonization and its staging of the black body in the colonial expositions, many among this group were associated with an emerging French institution of popular culture that featured a somewhat different form of body exhibition.

The French music hall, long an object of fascination for Paris artists and intellectuals, had provided inspiration for Toulouse Lautrec even before the war. For Jean Cocteau, Roland Barthes, Colette, and others, the music hall aesthetic (or "anti-aesthetic")—with its lavish costumes and extravagant settings, lack of rigid structure, and musical association with jazz—continued to constitute a modern and popular alternative to the more traditional theater. Music halls such as the Folies-Bergères, the Casino de Paris, and the Moulin Rouge featured a variety of entertainment acts, including the popular jazz music, dancing, comedy routines, acrobatics, and other forms of entertainment. Commenting on the Paris music halls, Fréjaville wrote of their appeal to a war-torn Paris populace who sought to escape "from the street bathed in gloom [and who] passed with delight into this bedazzling hell [where] one got drunk on the jazz-band, on raised legs, on coarse jokes, on crude pranks."[32] And it was also in the music halls that Parisians, in a light-hearted and carefree setting, typically confronted the Other in performance: the Oriental, American, and Indian typically singing and dancing in stereotypical ethnic scenarios. Moreover, like that of the colonial exposition, the music hall aesthetic was associated with the display of the unclothed female body. Thus, as public and popular institutions of ethnic and gender display, colonial exposition and music hall body culture functioned dialogically, each to expose the other's difference and identity. Nudity—and in the tradition of the music hall, "nude" translates as bare-breasted (female performers wore some form of *cache-sexe*)—first appeared on the Paris stage in 1894. And although a precise connection remains undocumented, the correspondence between the photographs of bare-breasted African women from the 1889 Paris *Exposition universelle* and the emergence, five years later, of upper body female nudity in the Paris music halls suggests an equivocal historical link between ethnic female body display at the colonial exhibitions and the emergence of white female body display in the Paris music hall. Such a conjunction would seem, at the level of popular culture, to mark an intersection of the ethnographic display of black women and the entertainment display of white women. In some respects, then, the institution of music hall nudity functioned to encode the repressed sexuality and sublimated desire associated with the ethnographic female body as it gets relocated into a scopic European economy. (Notably, in traditional African societies, it is not the body's nakedness, but its accessorization, that gives it erotic value.) It is in *La Revue Nègre*, as we shall see, that the tradition/aesthetic of the music hall fuses with that of the ethnographic exposition.

IV. Josephine Baker and *La Revue Nègre*

At age nineteen, Josephine Baker made her dramatic debut onto the Paris stage. And for nearly a half-century, until her death at age sixty-nine in 1970, *La Bakaire,* or the "Ebony Venus," as she was called, animated Parisian fantasies of the black female body. Drawing on well-known cultural codes and conventions in her stage and film performances, as well as photographic, lithographic, and other visual representations, Baker functioned for her colonial audience as a site of identification and desire. By exploiting and manipulating the trope of the primitive, Baker enacted a kind of generic, exoticized, racialized, and sexualized Other. Baker's principal role, however, was in the performance arts; it was the dancing body that brought to Baker the status of *vedette,* or stardom. And although Baker expanded her repertoire to include vocals (indeed the more she matured, the more accomplished her voice became) as well as stage and screen acting (she starred in a revival of Offenbach's *La Créole* and in four French films between 1927 to 1940), her principal role during the 1920s and early 1930s was as *danseuse.*[33] Projecting an image that combined sophistication and naiveté, Baker's performance of a complex ethnic and cultural femininity fused the primitivism associated with Africa and the modernism associated with 1920s American jazz.

In America, Baker had proven her comic genius by performing the blackface pickaninny who had made audiences howl with laughter at her cavorting antics on stage. The European response to black Americans was demonstrably different from that of white Americans, however, and Baker's reception in France was in marked contrast to that in her native America. New World slavery and its aftermath had bequeathed a legacy of minstrelsy, a form that largely centered on the black *male* body enacted by white men. In these performances, the black body was rendered an object of "pathos and humor," a construction of blackness that served to alleviate white racial anxieties.[34] However, the production of the Baker body, in effect, reinscribed the black body—the black *female* body—at the intersection of ethnographic, music hall, and modernist cultures. And rather than drawing on a predominantly continental African tradition of performance, Baker introduced onto the world stage a New World black cultural aesthetic, recoded in the context of the French colonial imaginary and transatlantic modernist performance.

While her emergence remains phenomenal, Baker's Paris debut was not, however, without precedent. Even during the prewar years, the French were introduced by travelers and visitors to a diasporic tradition of black performance, one associated in the French colonial imaginary with Africa, but which paradoxically entered Europe by way of America. African-American cultural performance, in the forms of social dances such as the cakewalk (*la danse de gâteau*), the black bottom, and Charleston, as well as jazz (*le jazz hot*) all represented African-American cultural exports popularized in the French capital during the early twentieth century.[35] African-American entertainers and performers were featured, for instance, in *Le Nouveau Cirque* as early as 1902–1903, when Les Petits Walkers, an African-American brother-sister team, introduced to France the cakewalk, performed to the syncopated rhythms of ragtime. The later introduction of jazz and the Charleston during *les années folles* continued the French fascination with the African-American *bamboula*, the counterpart to the African *tam-tam*.

It was *La Revue Nègre*, an event occurring significantly the same year as the opening of the *Exposition international des arts décoratifs et industriels modernes*, that catapulted Josephine Baker into stardom. And her performance, merging traditional African and black American social dance with her own freestyle movement, was enacted before audiences conditioned by ethnographic theater and the music hall aesthetic. The half-hour show had a six-week run from early October to November 1925. White American impresario, Caroline Dudley Reagan, organized the venture with the express intent of bringing a black spectacle to Paris, one that was meant to capitalize on the currently fashionable exotic primitivism. Baker had been on tour in the United States with Noble Sissle and Eubie Blake's *The Chocolate Dandies*, before joining a revue at New York's Plantation Club, where Dudley, impressed with young Josephine's performance in the chorus line, persuaded her to join a group of dancers and musicians to set sail for Paris to stage an all-black musical revue at the Théâtre des Champs-Elysées. (André Daven, manager of the ailing theater, had been advised by his friend Fernand Léger, "Give them Negroes... Only Negroes can excite Paris."[36]) The cast of the show, consisting primarily of black American performers, highlighted Baker herself as the featured dancer, along with New Orleans saxophonist and clarinetist, Sidney Bechet. The seven-piece jazz band was directed by Claude Hopkins, the music composed by Spencer Williams, the choreography by Louis Douglass, and set designs by Mexican modernist muralist, Miguel Covarrubias, and French caricaturist, Paul Colin (Figure 12.8).

Featuring seven sketches that might be described as a "performance of blackness," the revue included a Mississippi steamboat race, a New York skyscraper scene, a Louisiana camp meeting, and a Charleston cabaret. The

Figure 12.8 Program credits, *La Revue Nègre*, Théâtre des Champs-Elysées, Paris, 1925. Collection Rondel, Bibliothèque de L'Arsenal, Department des Arts du Spectacle, Bibliothèque Nationale, Paris.

opening tableau, "Mississippi Steam Boat Race," features Baker in a role typical of her earlier minstrel performances in the United States. Performing one of the mainstays of her earlier repertoire, Baker appears as a comic ragamuffin who capers along the docks in an antebellum Southern setting. Other tableaux featured Sidney Bechet as a blues-playing street vendor, Maude de Forest singing a "shout," and Baker dancing the Charleston in a cabaret scenario. The stage designs, along with the costumes, choreography, and lighting, all contributed to a kind of "theatrical modernism," characteristic of the dominant music hall aesthetic, that presented itself in stark contrast to the architectural tone of the Théâtre des Champs-Elysées, displaying on its elegant neoclassical façade *bas reliefs* of Isadora Duncan and Vaslav Nijinsky.

Notably, both Caroline Dudley and André Daven publicly vouched for the "authenticity" of the performance. In an interview in *Paris-Soir*, Dudley declared that her desire was to have the cast retain "their independence and their savagery, and also that glorious sensual exuberance that certain critics call indecency." In an interview with *Comoedia*, Daven announced that *La Revue Nègre* would present "scenes that are typical and 'raw' without touch ups and without alterations."[37] Such claims were clearly meant to align the performance of *La Revue Nègre* with French notions of the primitive. In her autobiography, however, Baker herself tells a somewhat different story: "We had thought our show was marvelous and [theater owner] Monsieur

Rolf's verdict—'Catastrophic'—struck us like a thunderclap. But he was an able and agreeable taskmaster and we did what he wanted although it meant working night and day."[38] Thus, when Baker and her company arrived, it is likely that they were prepared to perform the vaudeville routines typical of black performance on the contemporary American stage. However, like the native villages at the colonial exhibitions, Baker's performances were choreographed so as to reinforce European, and specifically French, notions of racial difference, as well as to ensure an "exotic" experience for its audience.

In short, *La Revue Nègre*—like the African native villages and reconstructions, along with the ceremonial artifacts—was re-styled and re-packaged by its producer, director, and designer to conform to a French aesthetics of Africanity. What was perceived by critics to be the savagery and primitivism of the performance was, in fact, fashioned largely according to French notions of what constituted "authentic" blackness, synonymous with French notions of primitivism. Baker and her troupe were, in effect, "primitivized" and the Baker body recoded according to a French colonial aesthetic.[39] Significantly, however, Daven's description suggests not so much a "performance" as it does a glimpse into "real" life ("scenes that are typical and 'raw'"). Daven's staging of "authenticity," in effect, recodes and relocates *La Revue Nègre* within an ethnographic frame of reference, evoking once more the notion of "natives on display."

V. *La Danse Sauvage*

The finale—the scene for which the show became famous (or rather infamous)— was a *pas de deux* entitled, not surprisingly, the *Danse du Sauvage*, in which Baker and her partner, Joe Alex, a Martiniquan, performed to the drum rolls of the *musique du sauvage*. In the *Danse du Sauvage* (Figure 12.9), regarded as the most shocking and sensational vignette in the revue, Alex and Baker wore bracelets around the ankles and wrists, and feathered loin cloths.[40] In the audience on opening night was *le tout Paris*, including Colette, Cocteau, Léger, Janet Flanner, Darius Milhaud, and dance critic André Levinson. And despite the obvious ethnocentrism reflected in his comments, Levinson's description of Baker as "an extraordinary creature of simian suppleness—a sinuous idol that enslaves and incites mankind"—nevertheless communicates the sheer elegance and energy of her performance:

> [T]here seemed to emanate from her violently shuddering body, her bold dislocations, her springing movement, a gushing stream of rhythm. . . . In the short *pas de deux* of the savages, which came as the finale of the *Revue Nègre*, there was a wild splendor and magnificent animality. Certain of

Miss Baker's poses, back arched, haunches protruding, arms entrained
and uplifted in a phallic symbol, had the compelling potency of the finest
examples of Negro sculpture.[41]

The implicit reference to *l'art nègre* in Levinson's description would surely align
African ceremonial art with African-American popular culture in the French cultural
and racial imaginary, while the atavistic signifiers of animality, savagery, and phallic
sexuality all locate Baker within an Africanist frame of reference. And while some in
the audience felt that Baker's performance went beyond the boundaries of decency
and propriety, even by Paris music hall standards, others hailed Baker's performance
as an artistic triumph. Few, however, doubted what history confirmed: Josephine
Baker had produced what the French call a *succès de scandale*.

Undoubtedly Baker's *danse sauvage* would have referenced the native ethnographic dancers (as Daven's remarks suggest), yet it would have been impossible—even for spectators like Levinson, who insisted on the atavism of Baker's
dancing—to confound her stage performance with ethnographic spectacle. Like
the "modernized" and "improved" African villages, Baker's dance and its modernist
mise-en-scène represented a "mixed marriage," or *métissage*, in which the originary
ethnological difference defined by primitive dance remained genealogically present, but with such irrefutable admixtures in artistry, setting, and design that her execution, in the famous dictum of Ezra Pound, "made it new." Further, what Morton
describes architecturally as "a mingling of representational vocabularies" brought
performance into "the dangerous territory of cross-breeding"—in a recoding that
radically called into question the originary and essentialist assumptions underlying
the construction of the primitive.[42]

Baker's performances were also characterized by another kind of modernist
métissage, in which she combined a performance of the *erotic* with elements of the
parodic. As a seasoned comedienne, with impeccable timing, Baker's self-miming
antics (she was known for her "mugging") was a mainstay, and functioned disrup-
tively to carnivalize her performances. Her well-known stage antics, which included
sinking on elastic legs, crossing her eyes, and fanning her famous *derrière*, all had
the effect of mocking her own erotic performances. In fact, contemporary critics
often comment on the comedic idiom typical of even Baker's most erotic performance. Reviewing *La Revue Nègre*, Ivan Goll describes the *Danse du Sauvage* as "a
parody" in which Baker and Alex mock and "make fun of themselves." Following
Baker's lead, even "the musicians play *with*," writes Goll, "they do not merely play
along." Describing the interplay between Baker and the musicians, Goll continues,
"[The musicians] are located left of the stage, then soon enough they are following a
dancer or tossing off their remarks in a song. They are genuine actors. They also help
emphasize the parody. They laugh continuously."[43]

What these observations suggest is that Baker's parodic performances enabled
her to reproduce, manipulate, mime, ridicule, resist, and even derive empowerment

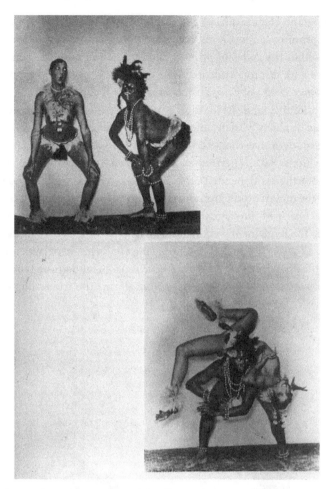

Figure 12.9 Josephine Baker and Joe Alex in *"La Danse Sauvage,"* Paris, 1925. Published in André Levinson, *La Danse d'aujourd'hui*, Paris, 1929.

from her roles. It was her mimicry and ironization that both secured and unsettled the colonial relations her performance re-enacted. And it was precisely Baker's ability to *perform the primitive*—and to do so parodically—that marked the Baker body as a site on which was interrogated and negotiated the iconography of modernist primitivism.

VI. Paul Colin and Modernist *Métissage*

It is Paul Colin's lithographs of Josephine Baker, later collected and published in a volume entitled *Le Tumulte Noir* (1929), that perhaps best demonstrates the iconic duplicity of the Baker body. Advertising *La Revue Nègre*, Colin's most famous lithograph (Figure 12.10) graphically translates Baker's *métissage* of modernism and primitivism. In Colin's representation, an abstractly caricatured Baker is defined, within the codes of primitivism, by lips and hips, but flanked by two jazzmen, one with disproportionately oversized teeth signifying keyboard ivories. In the mass-produced publicity posters created by Colin, the Baker body is typically coded primitive, while its location is modernity. His lithographs, performative in their iconic duplicity, visually and thematically enact the *métissage* of the primitive and the modern that characteristically marked Baker's performance. Like the re-styled pavilions, Baker's performances, which enacted European notions of the primitive, nevertheless depended on modernist references and technologies, evident both in the mass reproduction and circulation of her image as well as in a vocabulary of dance shaped fundamentally by contemporary black American jazz and social dance. The fundamental equivocality of the Baker image is recoded, but well captured, by a Parisian journal, *Eve*, announcing the "invasion of Jazz and American dance" into the French capital. Evoking the *métissage* of modernism (coded Europe) and primitivism (coded Africa), the reporter affirms the iconic duplicity of the

Figure 12.10 Paul Colin, Poster advertising *La Revue Nègre*, 1925.

"great *vedette*": "In truth, when one looks [at Baker] one sees a mulatto [*sic*] with
the sleek figure of the Anglo-Saxon, yet the face, the gestures, the dances, even the
voice, retain all the rhythm and all the strangeness of her original race."[44] Baker thus
became the signifier of a provocative, but potentially threatening, crossbreeding of
the "whitened" body and "black" performance—a somewhat ironic transformation
of the black-faced minstrelsy popular on the American stage.

   In some respects, the iconography of the Baker body functioned as the metaphorical equivalent of the colonial project, which provided the contrast against
which Western modernity was measured. Scripted in Baker's performances—
and encoded in Colin's representations—was a colonialist vision of primitivism
enacted within and enhanced by a modernist setting. At the same time, Baker's
"mixed-blood," or mulatta, status served as a marker of hybridity, or *métissage*—
which transgressed the Manichaean logic of French colonialism. Indeed, the *Eve*
reporter's remarks reveal his specular and somatic identification ("one sees a
mulatto [*sic*] with the sleek figure of the Anglo-Saxon") with an-other who has
been transformed in the French imaginary into a fashionable icon of essentialized
race difference. In other words, as cultural signifier, Baker is transfigured into both
the image and mirror image of the Anglo-Saxon (Gallic) Self. But, importantly, it
is Baker's performative *métissage* that functioned to combine, unmask, and ironize
the contradictory articulations of "black" and "white," colonized and colonizer,
primitive and modern.

VII. Looking Back to the Future: From the "Ebony Venus" to the "Hottentot Venus"

It is tempting from a postmodern and postcolonial moment to misread Baker's performances in the 1920s and 1930s. The contemporary reader of history is likely to
locate Baker within familiar and currently fashionable cultural, political, and discursive structures of resistance and complicity. To some readers, Baker's historical role
will appear capitulatory; to others, it will seem resistant. But to return to Richard
Dyer's paradigm for "stardom," what is apparent is that Baker met the requirements
of what it took to become a star—a transatlantic star—at a time when such roles
were not readily available to African-American women. The present inquiry only
begins to explore the conditions that launched Baker's career onto this trajectory.
The degree to which Baker controlled her own self-production, within the constraints of her historical and social circumstances, is the subject of the larger project
toward which this one only gestures. What is more evident, however, is that Baker
is clearly not an ethnographic spectacle/specimen, colonized by science, medicine, or an expansive political and economic nationalism. The arena of her liberation and confinement is discursive and cultural, rather than personal and material.

And although it is arguable whether or not Baker's precursor, Saartjie (or Sarah) Baartman, had exercised any control over the display of her body, it remains abundantly clear that Baker exercised agency over the representation of her body, both on- and offstage.

Rather than judging Baker's performance according to contemporary standards and expectations, I propose that a somewhat different perspective is achieved by looking backward from 1925, and invoking the proto-colonial figure of Saartjie Baartman as a measure for reading Baker's performances in the 1920s and 1930s. Viewed retrospectively, Baker's performance can be understood in terms of its distance from her most famous female predecessor, popularly known as the "Hottentot Venus," who (although not, strictly speaking, a part of the ethnographic spectacle of the colonial exposition) epitomizes the ethnographic display of the black female body. An indentured South African Khoikhoi woman, Baartman was exhibited as a curiosity, albeit also under the alibi of ethnographic specimen, first in England, from 1810 to 1814 and then in Paris, from 1814 until her death in 1815 (Figure 12.11). Her remains were stored in the Musée de l'Homme in Paris until her posthumous repatriation to her native South Africa.[45]

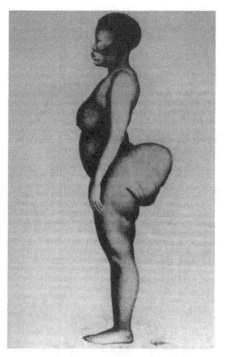

Figure 12.11 "The Hottentot Venus." Georges Cuvier, "Extraits d'observations faites sur le cadaver d'une femme connue à Paris et à Londres sous le nom de Vénus Hottentote," 1817.

Like her nineteenth-century South African precursor, whose steatopygia (pro-truding buttocks) was publicly displayed in Paris during her lifetime, and whose labia minora, the so-called "Hottentot apron," were preserved and displayed after her death, Baker became a cultural signifier of difference commodified through the medium of the body. The cultural codes which these two black women transmitted, however, were vastly different. If the Hottentot body functioned as pure display, it was also intended to be not only an icon of black sexuality, and the (black) female sexual grotesque—excessive and perverse sensuality—but a representation of irre-ducible racial difference. As Rosemary Wiss argues, "Prevailing scientific discourse characterized [Baartman's] 'race' as a missing link in the 'great chain of being....' [Her] categorization was ambiguous due to her position on the dividing edge of nature and culture."[46]

The Baker body, on the other hand, functioned as a desirably erotic and aesthetic commodity. Baker's sexualized femininity and elite sophistication as the Black Venus thus modified—reversed even—the century-old, proto-colonial image of the Venus Hottentot in the French imaginary, infusing the public, sexualized, and commodified black body with a seductive aura of the modern. Further, her iconic significance as a shimmering signifier of elegance and beauty, passion and eroticism, primitivism and modernism, Europe and Africa locates Baker not at the intersec-tion of culture and nature, but in that permeable space of *métissage* that threatens constantly to unsettle the Manichaean logic of racial difference. Finally, however, Baker's distance from Baartman is perhaps measured most profoundly in the rigor

Figure 12.12 Josephine Baker, May 1926. Boris Lipnitzki in the Roger-Viollet collection.

and sophistication of performance. If Baartman's "ethnographic spectacle" represented an essentialist notion of primitivism, Baker's performance symbolized the *savoir-faire* of the actor playing the role of the primitivized (Figure 12.12).

Thus, the ultimate paradox of Baker's performance is in its interrogation and renegotiation of racial difference, since her role-playing of the primitive not only affirmed her modernism, but demonstrated her art in mimicking what had been construed as nature in the ethnographic spectacle. Such performative elegance makes it difficult, if not impossible, to sustain an argument of racial difference when the "performance" of primitivism threatens constantly to deconstruct the "essence" of the primitive. In conclusion, it seems evident that Baker had learned to master the "art of primitivism" in her performances. It is equally evident that, from the outset, she must have recognized the function of what we in the academy have now learned to call the "myth of primitivism." Baker's challenge—whether failed or successful— was to deconstruct that myth while, at the same time, staging its re-enactment in a medium—dance—that has been historically identified as "the most primitive of artforms."[47]

13

Dancing Diaspora

Colonial, Postcolonial, and Diasporic Readings of Josephine Baker as Dancer and Performance Artist

[P]opular culture, commodified and stereotyped as it often is, is not at all, as we sometimes think of it, the arena where we find who we really are, the truth of our experience. It is an experience that is *profoundly* mythic. It is a theater of popular desires, a theater of popular fantasies. It is where we discover and play with the identifications of ourselves, where we are imagined, where we are represented, not only to the audiences out there who do not get the message, but to ourselves for the first time.
—Stuart Hall, "What Is This 'Black' in Popular Culture?"

[I]dentities are about questions of using the resources of history, language, and culture in the process of becoming rather than being: not "who we are" or "where we came from," so much as what we might become, how we have been represented and how that bears on how we might represent ourselves. Identities are therefore constituted within, not outside representation. Above all...identities are constructed through, not outside, difference.
—Stuart Hall, "Introduction: Who Needs 'Identity'?"

Culture is an embodied phenomenon. This implies that one's cultural location is not fixed to any one geographical space. Cultures, in other words, are not inherently provincial by nature. They move and evolve with the bodies that create and live them.
—Jennifer Rahim, "(Not) Know the Difference: Calypso Overseas and the Sound of Belonging in Selected Narratives of Migration"

The previous chapter positions Josephine Baker's performances within the historical and cultural context of early twentieth-century French modernist primitivism. There, I argue that although Baker's early representation is cast in the dye of ethnographic primitivism, her performances are manifestly modernist in their conceptualization and staging.[1] In this chapter, I seek to "flip the script," as it were, and examine Baker's eroticized and parodized dance performances as a set of mediating, self-constituting, and potentially oppositional practices shaped within the context of black vernacular and diasporic culture.

It is important, however, to recognize at the outset that Baker was not only a *product* of the French colonial imaginary, but also the *producer* of an image that contributed toward shaping that imaginary. And although my work has been largely predicated on the assumption that the image of Baker is shaped across the intersecting and sometimes antagonistic discourses of French colonialist and modernist aesthetics, I also seek to establish Baker's agency as a self-authorizing text and self-constituting subject who is herself liable to diverse and sometimes contradictory and paradoxical readings.

Staged as popular entertainment and produced for profit and pleasure, Baker's public dance performances conform to popular culture critic Richard Dyer's definition of entertainment as "a type of performance produced for profit, performed before a generalized audience (the 'public') by a trained, paid [individual] who [does] nothing else, but produce performances which have the sole (conscious) aim of providing pleasure." Arguing that this form of production embodies the "usual struggle between capital (the backers) and labor (the performers)," Dyer insists that it is nevertheless the performers themselves who exercise the "dominant agency" for defining the form because, in entertainment, the workers—or the entertainers themselves—are "in a better position [than many others in the workforce] to determine the form of [their] product [and notably here the product is a 'form' and not a 'thing']."[2]

Such a definition underscores how the performer, in this instance Josephine Baker, is able to exercise a degree of agency even when the conditions of performance and production are governed by the dynamics of the entertainment marketplace. The relationship between this mode of cultural production, especially as it marks and markets ethnic and gender difference, and the demands (consumption and regulation) of the dominant and hegemonic order in the "circuit of culture" remains complex and often problematic.[3] Notably, Dyer's larger argument turns on the escapist and wish-fulfilling, or utopic, functions of popular entertainment that "[offer] the image of 'something better' to escape into, or something we want deeply that our day-to-day lives don't provide."[4] Baker's early stage performances—epitomized in the iconic *danse sauvage*, the finale of *La Revue Nègre*, and in the persona of the native girl Fatou in *La Folie du Jour*, whose sexualized banana dance represents the fulfillment of the sleeping explorer's dream fantasies—mirror and arguably constitute colonial desire as a longing for otherness imagined in terms of sexual and colonial conquest. It was the manipulation of such "utopian" imagery that allowed Baker to exercise control and agency in the marketing of her image in an entertainment economy and cultural circuit based on the production and consumption of otherness.

What Paul Gilroy describes as the "pleasure and danger" offered by black performers to the white spectator often found fulfillment in what anthropologist James

Clifford calls "escapist exoticism." And demonstrably, Baker's artistic and commercial successes were not always incompatible with racist, patriarchal, or colonial assumptions. On the contrary, the dominant order would expect of such performances the ritual re-enactment of what Gilroy calls the "grand narrative of racial [and I would add sexual] domination."[5] In fact, Baker's early performances were deliberately packaged to meet such demands and expectations. Further, important to understanding the impact of Baker's performances is the recognition that like any other signifying system and practice—language or music, for instance—dance plays a special role in the production of social and cultural identity. And arguably, it is the fluidity of dance as movement and modality that serves as a metaphor for articulating the migratory and transformative nature of culture, as well as the instability and contingency of corporate and social identities as they get produced in cultural and artistic performance.

For some critics and theorists, including Jacques Derrida, dance as a cultural and artistic form of expression functions to challenge static notions of identity by disrupting conventional binary constructions of the self. In his interview with Christie McDonald, Derrida speaks theoretically of the liberating and revolutionary potential of dance by invoking Emma Goldman's famous remark, "If I cannot dance, I will not be part of your revolution"[6]—an observation that, as I read it, provides a metaphorical link between political transformation and the circular turns of dance movement. And although Derrida, in his interview, focuses on the deconstruction of sexual binaries, the function of dance as form and metaphor would seem to apply equally to other binary constructions of identity. Thus, Baker's dance performances—the form for which she was best known—position her as a kind of iconic signifier of identity "in the process of becoming rather than being."[7]

In order to situate Josephine Baker in the French cultural and racial imaginary at the moment of her legendary emergence in Paris in the year 1925, I begin with two paradigmatic readings of Baker, one by noted French dance critic, André Levinson, and the other by renowned American poet, e. e. cummings. In his fittingly entitled "The Negro Dance under European Eyes," a review of Baker's performance in *La Revue Nègre*—which no doubt contributed to making this remarkable and historical event the *succès de scandale* that it became—Levinson captures the extraordinarily seductive vitality of Baker's dance aesthetics while at the same time exposing the ethnocentrism of the colonial male gaze. Describing Baker as "an extraordinary creature of simian suppleness—a sinuous idol that enslaves and incites mankind," Levinson writes:

> There seems to emanate from her violently shuddering body, her bold dislocations, her springing movement, a gushing stream of rhythm.... In the short *pas de deux* of the savages, which came as the finale of the *Revue Nègre*, there was a wild splendor and magnificent animality. Certain of

Miss Baker's poses, back arched, haunches protruding, arms entwined and uplifted in a phallic symbol, had the compelling potency of the finest examples of Negro sculpture. The plastic sense of a race of sculptors came to life and the frenzy of African Eros swept over the audience. It was no longer a grotesque dancing girl that stood before them, but the black Venus that haunted Baudelaire. The dancer's personality had transcended the character of her dance.[8]

As noted in the previous chapter, Levinson's allusion to *l'art nègre* in his description of *la danse sauvage* aligns African ceremonial art with African-American popular and vernacular dance culture. And by positioning himself as observer of an *object d'art*, Levinson effectively both domesticates the dance and, simultaneously, executes a defensive maneuver designed to shield himself (but apparently only himself and not the rest of "mankind") from the "frenzy of African Eros [that] swept the audience." Clearly, his narrative strains to contain the threat of difference represented by the powerful phallicism and feral animality encoding his reading of Baker's performance.

Further, bearing out Dyer's thesis, Levinson's reading would seem to construct Baker as surrogate for the colonies and their conquest (or seduction through the French *mission civilisatrice*). Reflecting the historical moment of France's interwar period, the representation of Baker functions here as the utopic object of what critic Elizabeth Ezra designates, in another context, as the "colonial unconscious." Ezra points out that "the apotheosis of *la plus grand France* was also its swan song"—the beginning of the end of the vast overseas empire comprising the Third Republic's expansive colonialism, which extended from the colonies and protectorates in Indochina to central and North Africa, and the South Pacific.[9] In Levinson's reading, however, the dangers of Baker's hypersexualization as a surrogate object of colonial desire are offset, as we shall see, by the safety afforded in her imaginary disembodiment, staged proleptically at the moment of France's future loss of empire.

Comparing Baker's seductiveness to that of Jeanne Duval, the mulatta woman with whom the French poet Charles Baudelaire was obsessed, the French critic's appropriative gaze transforms what he construes as "grotesque" into a kind of *spectral presence* ("the black Venus that haunted Baudelaire"). In his reading, the French critic grounds Baker's performance in the material body, but he then proceeds to *disembody* or *dematerialize* the performing subject ("the dancer's personality had transcended the character of the dance"). Levinson's construction thus separates the dancer from action and movement (the "dance") in a critical turn that amputates the subject, deprives her of identity integration, and, in effect, renders her *phantasmatic*.

By thus consigning Baker's performance to the illusory or "unreal" domain of the *phantasm* or *phantasmagoria*, Levinson is able to safeguard what he regards as "real" or "authentic" dance, presumably represented by the more traditional European concert or balletic dance, as the standard by which this category of performance must finally be adjudged. Further, Levinson's imperial account encodes Baker as a representation of savagery or exotic-erotic otherness within a dominant discourse representing the black woman as *an object to be looked at* rather than as *a self-constituting subject.*

Thus, while Baker's raucous, sensual, polyrhythmic Africanist[10] performances may disrupt and transgress the balletic codes of performance on the one hand, they are also made to serve and reinforce the dominant standards and paradigms that define the signifier Dance in the French colonial imaginary, demonstrating Toni Morrison's observation that "definitions [belong] to the definers—not the defined."[11] In other words, the ability to produce and exercise control over the dominant codes of signification is precisely what defines power and hegemony. From the perspective of dominance that Stuart Hall calls "compulsive Eurocentrism," Baker's dance performance can only be adjudged as deviant, bizarre, unreal, or fantastic.[12] Thus, Baker's performance and Levinson's reading together construct a scenario in which an ostensibly transgressive and potentially liberating performance can be re-signified to recuperate the signs and serve the meanings determined by the dominant order.

From a somewhat different perspective, the American poet, e. e. cummings, in his *Vanity Fair* review (*"Vive la Folie!"*) of Baker's performance in the 1926 production of *La Folie du Jour* in which she debuted her famous banana girdle, recalls Baker's 1924 performance in Eubie Blake and Noble Sissle's New York production of *The Chocolate Dandies*:

> As a member of the *Dandies* chorus, she [Baker] resembled some tall, vital, incomparably fluid nightmare which crossed its eyes and warped its limbs in a purely unearthly manner—some vision which opened new avenues of fear, which suggested nothing but itself and which, consequently, was strictly aesthetic.[13]

As many readers will recognize, cummings's description of Baker here resembles nothing so much as Topsy, Harriet Beecher Stowe's "wild child" in *Uncle Tom's Cabin*—described by the American author (in tones eerily invoking Levinson's French colonialist reading) as "odd," "goblin-like," and "unearthly." Presenting Topsy to his cousin Ophelia as "a funny specimen in the Jim Crow line," her amused master, Augustine St. Clare, instructs the little slave urchin to "give us a song, now, and show us some of your dancing," an invitation to which Topsy responds with a "performance of blackness" that is unmistakably evoked in cummings's description of Baker's performance in *Chocolate Dandies*. Stowe describes her character thusly:

The black, glassy eyes glittered with a kind of wicked drollery, and the thing [Topsy] struck up, in a clear shrill voice, an odd negro [sic] melody, to which she kept time with her hands and feet, spinning round, clapping her hands, knocking her knees together, in a wild, fantastic sort of time, and producing in her throat all those odd guttural sounds which distinguish the native music of her race.[14]

In cummings's rendering, Baker's "crossed eyes" and warbling limbs surely re-enact Topsy's "black, glassy eyes glittering with a kind of wicked drollery," while Topsy's "clapping hands" and "knocking knees" give proleptic embodiment to the "incomparably fluid nightmare" of Baker's minstrel-like performance in *Dandies*. And it is the transformation of this seemingly "terrifying nightmare" into the "most beautiful…star of the Parisian stage" that brings shock and delight to the American poet, who is captivated by the "perfectly fused [and] entirely beautiful body and a beautiful command of its entirety."[15] Describing her performance on the stage of the *Folies Bergère*, the poet further muses:

[Baker] enters through a dense electric twilight, walking backwards on hands and feet, legs and arms stiff, down a huge jungle tree—as a creature neither infrahuman nor superhuman but somehow both: a mysterious unkillable something, equally nonprimitive and uncivilized, or beyond time in the sense that emotion is beyond arithmetic.… By the laws of its own structure, which are the irrevocable laws of juxtaposition and contrast, the revue is a use of everything trivial or plural to intensify what is singular and fundamental…Mlle. Josephine Baker.[16]

Like Levinson's, cummings's review encodes an atavistic and phallic image of "a creature walking backwards…legs and arms stiff," ironically descending from the plinth of nature into the white male colonial dream world, an image that conflates the world of nature and that of human desire. Juxtaposing the effects of modern technology with that of the savage jungle staging ("Baker enters through a dense electric twilight"), cummings's description of her arboreal descent metaphorically fragments her body into "hands and feet [and] legs and arms," enacting a linguistic dismemberment that re-inscribes the discourse of American slavery, but is framed within the discourse of the European primitivist colonial imaginary. Thus, while cummings's reading of Baker's 1926 performance necessarily reflects a postcolonial, that is to say American, perspective not entirely dissimilar from his reading of Baker's earlier performance, his earlier refiguration of Baker also bears the distinct imprint of the colonial gaze exemplified in Levinson's reading.

Again, like Levinson's, cummings's reading of Baker registers the *affect* of her performance more than it does her *presence*; in fact, her presence in both readings is defined paradoxically by her spectacular *absence*. Cummings, in fact, locates Baker

in a space of radical negation—that is to say, in terms of what she is *not*: "as a creature *neither* infrahuman *nor* superhuman but somehow both ... equally *non*primitive
and *un*civilized" (emphasis added). The multiple negations here, in effect, beg the
question of her actual "humanity," culminating in the incantation of "a mysterious
unkillable some*thing*" (emphasis added), an image that not only confounds Baker's
location between the civilized and primitive, but significantly betrays the poet's
inability to position the subject between the *less than* human ("infrahuman") and
more than human ("superhuman"). Finally, unable to successfully de-colonize the
(post)colonial gaze, cummings's construction of Baker morphs from the embodied
and fragmented representation in the "colonial unconscious" into something transcendent, indestructible, and irreducible, suggesting her release—whether from the
captivity of her earlier minstrel masquerade ("the *Folies Bergère* permits Josephine
Baker to appear—for the first time on any stage—as herself") or from her entrap-
ment in the hunter's colonial dreamscape remains equivocal. Unknowable, indefin-
able, unnamable, unclassifiable, the performing subject can only be conjured by the
poet as "a mysterious unkillable some*thing*"—an eerie, but unmistakable, evocation
of Stowe's above description of Topsy as "the thing."

Notably, cummings's readings of Baker's performance in the *Folies Bergère* fixate
on qualities that he describes as "singular and fundamental." And speaking of her
earlier performance in *Chocolate Dandies*, he observes that it "suggests nothing but
itself and ... consequently, was strictly aesthetic."[17] Similar to Levinson, then, who
compares Baker "to the finest examples of Negro sculpture," cummings aligns her
performance with the elitist and modernist notion of "aesthetics" that is defined
by its singularity and self-referentiality. Ultimately, whether grotesque or beautiful,
immanent or transcendent, nightmarish or sublime, in the poet's imagination Baker
is constructed in terms of oxymorons: "uncouth" and "exquisite," "personal" and
"racial," "rigid" and "liquid," contradictions specific to the then prevailing a-cultural
and de-historicized modernist notion of aesthetics. Finally, while revealing himself
transformed by the power and force of Baker's performance, as a spectator, cummings actually fails to apprehend, or "see," the subject who represents, for him, an
abstractly ambiguous and allusive figuration of modernist aesthetics. Words fail
the poet: the image before him remains "beyond time in the sense that emotion is
beyond arithmetic"—or, as I read this rather extraordinary passage, in the sense that
passion exceeds reason, and sensation exceeds the sensible.

These readings are meant not only to expose the workings of the French colonial
and the American postcolonial cultural imaginary—along with the workings of
the dominant (critical and poetic) codes of aesthetic signification in which Baker's
performances are constructed—but, more important to my purposes, they are
intended to make a case for shifting the frame of reference within which to most
productively read Baker's performances. Just as Baker's dance performances disrupt an ethnocentric colonial discourse of dance, on the one hand, and a postcolonial, modernist, aestheticized notion of performance, on the other, so this project

seeks to disrupt the discursive frames of reading and reference represented para-digmatically by Levinson's and cummings's reviews of Baker's performances.

The erasure of Baker's embodied subjectivity encoded in the above readings and representations effectively obliterates dance itself as both an identity-constituting performance and as a signifying system capable of a politics of resistance. The counter-reading proposed here is thus based on a twofold assumption: first, that Baker's dancing—which I reread in the context of Africa and the African diaspora—enacts the potential for resistance (though not in ways that are unproblematic), and second, that her performances are fundamentally personally and culturally identity-constituting. Thus, Baker's dance performances, I argue, manifest the potential to unsettle the (post)colonial gaze, and thereby disrupt the dominant and hegemonic discourse.

Notably, Baker is rarely, if ever, acknowledged as a figure in the history of dance. Although lionized as an entertainer, she has not traditionally been regarded as a serious dancer by scholars in the field—which is to say that she was not, strictly speaking, a concert or ballet dancer (it is noteworthy, however, that Baker performed *en pointe* in pieces choreographed by George Balanchine in the 1936 *Ziegfield Follies*). Moreover, in spite of her likely classification as an ethnic (some would say *primitive*) dancer, Baker is finally associated neither with the "social-protest" dance tradition of a Pearl Primus nor with the anthropologi-cal folk tradition of a Katherine Dunham, both traditions of modern dance that would not take root in the United States until the 1930s and 1940s. And unlike Primus and Dunham, influential figures associated with the history of modern black dance, Baker is regarded not as a choreographer, but as a performer. She is thus not only marginalized, but often neglected, in the histories of American dance, modern dance, and even black dance.

My aim here is not only to claim a chapter for Baker in the history of African-American dance, but to extend that narrative by positioning Baker as a "cul-tural mediator" through her contribution to the transatlantic dispersion of black modern dance. My proposed reading thus situates Baker's dance repertoire as the site of cultural mediation, where her performances negotiate between different cul-tures, translating and transforming the dance codes and practices of one complexly syncretic culture into those of other cultures and traditions.

As such, Baker joins a migratory tribe that art critic Wanda Corn identifies as *le type transatlantic* (the transatlantic type), a cohort defined by its status as "biconti-nental."[18] As evident in the lyrics of her signature song, "*J'ai Deux Amours*" ("I Have Two Loves"), Baker indeed became a "migrant artist," fashioning herself as both an American and a Parisian. But if her lyrics re-inscribe her artistic status as "biconti-nental," her performances associate her with the expansive colonialism of France's Third Republic, the modernity of American jazz, and the primitivism of the tribal rhythms of Africa, thus rendering Baker, in some respects, as "tricontinental"—in a kind of triangulated, transatlantic cultural dance economy.

The history of African-American dance has its roots in an African and African diasporic culture dating back to the arrival of enslaved Africans who brought with them to the shores of North America, South America, and the Caribbean the religious and ceremonial dances that were integral to the indigenous cultures and communities of the African homeland. Plantation dances such as the ring dance and juba were exported from the plantation to the minstrel stage and later to the Broadway musical revue in the late nineteenth and early twentieth centuries. From the introduction of the cakewalk in the 1890s to such popular dances as the Charleston, the black bottom, and the jitterbug in the 1920s and 1930s, black dance in its myriad forms traveled an international circuit from Harlem to Paris and beyond. Black musicals, including the popular *Shuffle Along, Runnin' Wild*, and *Chocolate Dandies*, provided showcases for black dance talent during this period.

Dance critic and historian James Haskins notes that during the early twentieth century, there were no recognized black choreographers or dance "stars" in the United States, though he contends that "the best black dancers were well known among blacks and among white dancers, but not to the general public. The dances themselves were the stars."[19] Haskins further maintains that many whites were disposed to believe that blacks could not perform classical European dances. Typical of this attitude was the comment made in 1933 by *New York Times* dance critic John Martin, who wrote, "Negroes cannot be expected to do dances designed for another race."[20] The conventional (white) wisdom, then, was that blacks were natural-born dancers who required no training and that any attempt to train them would lead to inauthentic dancing—or a loss of originality and spontaneity.[21] Arguably, however, it is the politics and practices of exclusion that would seem both to limit and free the creativity of the black dancer. Nevertheless, such racist and essentialist assumptions not only erase the practice and apprenticeship that inevitably underpin the achievement of black dancers (and this notwithstanding Baker's own naturalizing of her dance performance), but they also fail to consider the ways in which dance as a form of cultural expression works materially to produce social identity; in other words, such racial logic ignores how dance becomes *constitutive* rather than merely *reflective* of identity.

In the common parlance of the 1920s, Baker might also have been described as an *eccentric* dancer, which is to say that her movements were more improvised than formalized. In other words, her performances were "off-center" (that is, *ec-centric*) in the sense that they were fundamentally *non-reiterative*. Today, her performance would most likely be labeled "freestyle" or "ad-lib." Central to Baker's dance performances are the principles of mimicry, syncretism, and improvisation, all compositional strategies marked by the interpolation of *non*-scripted improvisation into the *pre*-scripted vocabulary of black social and vernacular dance. The grammar and syntax of Baker's dance performances are thus governed by her soloist improvisations on black American social and vernacular dance, not infrequently combined with elements of contemporary French music hall performance, in addition to traditional

African and African-derived social dance (Baker learned to dance the popular 1930s beguine in the Martiniquan Pavilion at the 1931 Colonial Exposition). It is precisely for this reason that Baker can be understood as a diasporic dancer whose stage performances represent a creolization or hybridization of cultural performance in the context of a triangulated, transatlantic economy of cultural exchange. (And, importantly, I use the term "creolization" advisedly to refer to dance forms external to the West that became naturalized or acculturated through their importation into a new environment.)

In Europe, Baker instituted a form and style of dancing based on the "performance of quotation"[22] in which she appropriated and recombined diverse social dance grammars and vocabularies. In this way, aesthetic pleasure as well as cultural and economic capital were generated by juxtaposing and intermingling diverse dance articulations in circumstances that were novel and far removed from their original geographical and cultural locations, thus reinforcing the idea that culture is always migratory and subject to transformation. As a diasporic dancer, Baker's performances combine popular, ritual, and social dance with individual improvisation—in a polyglot and creolized style that I term "idiosyncretic," my neologism for designating Baker's *idiosyncratic syncretism* combining multiple and diverse popular dance forms.

As an *idiosyncretic* Africanist dancer, Baker created a diasporic and cross-cultural medley of dance performance that was fundamentally constitutive and mediatory. Baker's most identifiable strategy was her polyrhythmic and improvisatory response to diverse forms and traditions—improvisatory in the sense that her moves are often based on freestyle and fundamentally non-reiterative patterns of repetition with a difference. Notably, most of the vernacular routines quoted in Baker's performances were choreographed for stage musicals, although the dancers were not "trained" in the current sense of the term. After all, black dancers learned their moves not only from the stage, but also in the rural Southern juke joints and their Northern urban counterparts, the local dance halls. Baker's repertoire added to the moves and routines associated with these venues through her appropriation of the Parisian music halls and colonial expositions as sites of training and learning.

However, in contrast to the smoother balletic moves of the French chorines who characteristically performed in French variety shows, Baker's dance performances were based typically on black social and vernacular dances like the acrobatic "flash acts," the shimmy sha wabble, the black bottom, the itch, the heebie jeebies, the eagle rock, the quiver, the bump and grind, the mess around, the funky chicken, and the ever-popular Charleston. Significantly, these dances featured "improvised torso and limb movements" that, according to Gottschild, "rhythmically articulate the breasts, belly, and buttocks."[23]

Like other forms of black expressive culture, social and vernacular dance functions potentially as a marker of collective, or corporate, social identity, a vehicle of social consciousness, and a form of transgression and cultural critique.[24] At the same time, however, Baker's diasporizing and creolizing of black social and vernacular dance notably both confirm and (implicitly) challenge some of Stuart Hall's notions regarding identity and performance—insofar as her performances rework black diasporic dances not necessarily "by imposing an imaginary coherence on the experience of dispersal and fragmentation," nor by "[restoring] an imaginary fullness or plenitude to the collective experience [of diaspora]," but by exporting, disseminating, and creolizing black diasporic dance.[25]

I would argue, then, that Baker's social and cultural identities, insofar as these get constituted in black vernacular and African-derived dance, are grounded in a diasporic culture shaped by migrating and creolized dance forms and conventions that began, in fact, as early as the sixteenth century with the forced transit of African slaves to the Americas—forms and conventions that continue in the current migrations of Afro-Caribbean, Afro-Latino, Afro-Brazilian, and African-American dance culture. It is then, arguably, in large part due to Baker's performances in the 1920s and 1930s that black vernacular and social dance has continued its transatlantic migration, this time extending and reversing the journey back across the Atlantic from the Americas to Europe, Asia, and Africa. As such, it would seem appropriate to fashion black diasporic dance—and its triangulated, transatlantic migrations—as both an embodiment and trope for the global migration of a black cultural identity that continues to impact contemporary world culture.

Emerging from a tradition of minstrelsy and burlesque, Baker brought to her performances a comedic and often carnivalesque turn. And, as I argue elsewhere, Baker's signature mugging (her funny faces and crossed eyes) not only afforded comic relief during her provocative performances, but also had the effect of ironizing her highly sexualized and frequently acrobatic antics. It is evident that the diasporic medley, or pastiche, that characterizes Baker's performances was grounded in the American vaudevillian and burlesque traditions that had provided the early training ground for her comedic improvisation. The compositional strategies driving her performances are thus based on the tactics and techniques of exaggeration, caricature, pantomime, mimicry, pastiche, and parody. However, what sometimes renders Baker's performances controversial—subjecting them to recuperative readings that arguably reinforce dominant race and gender stereotypes—is precisely her appropriation of the strategies by which parody does its work.

Parody is constituted by an alternate system of signification by which codes designated as "parodic" enter into, engage, and interrogate the dominant and hegemonic systems of signification. However, it is precisely the dominant discursive order that controls and produces the available primary codes or signs of signification. The parodic performer must therefore appropriate the dominant codes of signification, even when the aim is to re-signify meaning. Thus, when mocking, satirizing, parodying, or otherwise subverting and calling into question the dominant and hegemonic signifying system, the employment (or re-deployment) of these available signs and codes unavoidably risks validating, if not indeed valorizing, the original system of signification. Thus, in translating black vernacular and diasporic performance into a rhetoric of parodized pastiche, Baker's performances inevitably risk reproducing gender and race clichés, caricatures, and stereotypes as they are produced by the dominant and hegemonic discourse. In a performance vocabulary based on repetition with a difference—that is, repeating the dominant structures of signification, but with an articulation of transgressive difference—the repetition runs the risk (depending on the reader, the reading position, and the scene of reading) of reinforcing dominant codes, while the difference often gets diminished or overshadowed. It is therefore possible for the reader—Levinson or cummings, for example—to decode/recode the grammar and vocabulary of performance according to the dominant (aesthetic, critical, or political) codes of signification. Consequently, such readings often resist or overlook the intended performative re-signification, resulting in the perpetuation and circulation of signs and codes that essentialize, naturalize, and fix difference.[26]

In summary, the conflicting and sometimes controversial readings of Baker's performances—past and present, (post)colonial and diasporic—demonstrate the complex interplay between popular culture, representation, and social identity. Such responses also facilitate an understanding of the politics of reception to the parodic performances of blackness typified in contemporary black popular culture—particularly hip-hop culture—in its risky subversion/recuperation of dominant racial, gender, and sexual stereotypes and clichés.[27] In an attempt to subvert popular and demeaning historical stereotypes of black masculinities and femininities, hip-hop performances often risk the (re)production of stereotypes that become susceptible to re-appropriation by the dominant order to serve its own racist, sexist, and ethnocentric structure of meaning and signification.

This chapter, originally composed as an essay in commemoration of the 100th birthday of Josephine Baker, thus concludes on a celebratory but cautionary note that is meant to call attention to the ways in which performance—the arena in which we are *other-identified and self-imagined*—contains the power and potential to be simultaneously transgressive and recuperative, repressive and liberating, constraining and enabling—a source of danger and pleasure.[28]

About Face, or, What Is This "Back" in B(l)ack Popular Culture?

From Venus Hottentot to Video Hottie

Butt, what a term…The collection of terms that have accrued around
this body part…run the gamut from science, modesty, and euphemism
to nitty-gritty description: butt, buttocks, rump, posterior, hindquarters,
haunches, loins, fundament, seat, bottom, *derrière*, fanny, rear, rear end,
bum, backside, behind, can, duff, tail, ass, buns, heinie, hindpots, hams,
tush, tushie, booty, popo, glutes (for gluteus maximus and minimus, the
principal sets of buttock muscles)—and there are more.
—Brenda Dixon Gottschild, *The Black Dancing Body*

I like big butts and I cannot lie
You other brothers can't deny
That when a girl walks in with an itty bitty waist
And a round thing in your face
You get sprung, wanna pull out your tough
'Cause you notice that butt was stuffed
Deep in the jeans she's wearing
I'm hooked and I can't stop staring
Oh baby, I wanna get with you
And take your picture
My homeboys tried to warn me
But that butt you got makes me so horny…
She's sweat, wet,
Got it goin' like a turbo 'Vette
I'm tired of magazines
Sayin' flat butts are the thing
Take the average black man and ask him that
She gotta pack much back
So, fellas! (Yeah!) Fellas! (Yeah!)
Has your girlfriend got the butt? (Hell yeah!)
Tell 'em to shake it! (Shake it!) Shake it! (Shake it!)
Shake that healthy butt!
Baby got back
—Sir Mix-a-Lot, "Baby Got Back"

Runnin' hot, runnin' cold
I was runnin' into overload
It was, ex-treme
I took it so high, so low

So low, there was nowhere to go
It was like a ba-a-a-a-a-a-d dream
Somehow the wires uncrossed, the tables were turned
Never knew I had such a lesson to learn
I'm feelin' good from my head to my shoes
Know where I'm goin' and I know what to do
I tidied up my point of view
I got a new attitude

—Patti Labelle, "New Attitude"

I. "Economies of the Flesh"

Meditating on the cultural meaning of the "butt," African-American dance critic Brenda Dixon Gottschild's catalogue of more than thirty signifiers for this physical feature suggests that the rear end is as important in the anatomical imaginary of the West as is snow (and the proverbial proliferation of terms for its designation) in the Inuit ecological imaginary.[1] Gottschild's emphasis on the prominence of the butt is underscored by increasing evidence—from the rise of buttock augmentations to workout routines marketing the "Brazilian butt lift" to padded panties promising the "booty pop"—that the notion of the rear end has begun to figure broadly in the cultural, medical, aesthetic, and sexual imaginary of the West. This emerging "ass-obsession,"[2] with its focus on the more "curvaceous" body and the "bigger" butt, has given rise to what has been hailed as the "booty revolution" in the first decade of the new millennium—and to what scholar Moira O'Neal coins as the "assthetics" of the "big butt."[3]

As suggested in the above lyrics, rap artists like Sir Mix-a-Lot ("Baby Got Back"), along with rappers like Juvenile ("Back that Ass Up"), Mystikal ("Shake Ya Ass"), and numerous others promulgating what has come to be known as "booty rap,"[4] have effectively redefined female body aesthetics, marking a transition from a Western aesthetic of the female body emphasizing the breasts as the principal signifier of femininity to one fashioned by the "bootification" of the female body. And, indeed, the black female *body*, with its accentuation on the *booty*, has become a stock feature of contemporary hip-hop culture and, most especially, rap music video. As Fatimah Muhammad observes,

> The video girls represent hip-hop's female beauty codes: if a 40-ounce beer bottle is an identifying marker for hip-hop's male, then a big butt rep-resents the identifying marker for hip-hop's female. The layered cultural

media industrial forces have combined to reduce young Black female hip-hop identity to a body part.[5]

As Muhammad's remarks suggest, the social construction of black femininity in contemporary hip-hop culture and rap music video is centered on the fragmentation and fetishization of the female body.

Significantly, however, the aesthetics of the butt is neither new nor revolutionary within black culture. As hip-hop critic Tricia Rose argues, the valorization of the butt is part of a longstanding tradition in black popular culture, and as a recurring signifier in rap lyrics and music videos, it represents "a contemporary nod to the substantial black folk history of performers and dances and songs that involve [the] celebration of big behinds for men and women." Yet, as Rose contends, it is equally evident that

> the black behind has an especially charged place in the history of both black sexual expression and [the] white classification of it as a sign of sexual perversity and inferiority. It conjures up a complex history of white scrutiny of black female bodies.[6]

And as Rose's observations suggest, the signifier of the black butt has been both celebrated in black culture as a marker of sexual desirability and derogated in the dominant and hegemonic Western culture as a sign of the sexually perverse and grotesque. Thus, the apparent revolution in female body aesthetics in the Western imaginary is somewhat surprising since it is precisely the rear end that has been the glorified and vilified feature of a sometimes oppositional black female body aesthetic.[7] In either instance, however, the emphasis on this particular anatomical feature has been central to the social construction of black femininity, and often associated with what Patricia Hill Collins has defined as the "controlling" images of the black female.[8]

Notably, traditional ("old school") black feminists (like myself) and contemporary "hip-hop" feminists do not always agree on the meanings attached to the contemporary video model and her performance of the black body/booty.[9] Debates, discussion, and dialogues between second- and third-wave black feminists turn, in part, on the following questions: Do contemporary female video models subversively parody a hegemonic Euro-American white male stereotype of the black female body, or do such performances embrace an ambiguously non-hegemonic African-American male aesthetic of the female body? Do these performances simply re-inscribe the historical stereotypes of black women as sexually available, perverse, or excessive—or do they function to deconstruct dominant and hegemonic notions of femininity represented by the thin (anorexic) and esthete images still predominant among supermodels (black, white, and other) on the world's leading runways? Do these performances represent the empowerment of a liberatory self-eroticism, or the vulnerability and powerlessness linked to the pornographic exploitation of black women's bodies shaped by the economies of the marketplace and the desires/fantasies of the Other?

Exploring the "economies of the flesh," defined as the "various markets for [b]lack female bodies," Lisa Collins examines the representation of the black female body in Western museum and popular art, noting that the "avoidance of the black female nude is striking" in an aesthetic tradition that has privileged nudity since ancient Greece and female nudity as an aesthetic subject at least since the seventeenth century. Arguing that the absence or marginalization of the black female body from classical art and popular representation is explained by its evocation of "a racialized, sexualized, and exploitative history," Collins explains that the "entanglement of market and visual economies has consistently linked the [b]lack female with slave, sexual, and service economies" in nineteenth-century European and American visual culture.[10] And, tellingly, even contemporary black women artists like Emma Amos have expressed discomfort with the notion of representing black female nudity—principally because the unclothed black female figure reminds her "too painfully of the slave market."[11]

Commenting on rapper Nelly's by now infamous music video, "Tip Drill," cultural critic Michael Eric Dyson elaborates on the analogy between slavery's auction block and the contemporary music video:

> I'm hard pressed to tell the difference between Nelly's video and the time two hundred years ago when black women and men were looked at for their gluteus maximus, for their latissimus dorsi, for their pectoralis major, for their testicles, to see if they were durable enough to procreate in order to expand slavery. Isolating body parts like that represents a sexualized fetish tied to the racial subjugation of black bodies by white supremacists. Such a state of affairs reinforces the vulgar status of black humanity, even when it has comic overtones like the troubling image struck in the Nelly video.[12]

Dyson's comments here suggest that hip-hop culture stages both black male and female bodies as fungible commodities in a racist economy. And while black male bodies are indeed staged in ways that re-enact stereotypes and myths of black male identities (gangsta, thug, hustler, pimp, "playa"), Levita D. Mondie-Sapp's "The Highest Bidder" correctly suggests that in contemporary rap music video, it is the black female body that is staged on the auction block, with the black male (rather than "the white supremacist") positioned as the auctioneer:

> A white slaveholder announces/'Next on the auction block/we have a nigger wench/naked/strong/who can work as long as the day is long/ look at her back/and those thighs/along with her hips/sturdy and wide/

she is bound to be fertile…'/a commercial rapper raps a rap about his "skank/ho/bitch/who can make it clap"/now ain't that a switch?/instead of the man/an enslaved AfriCAN/make millions/off his lost queen's ass and tits/then justify it/in the name of profits/just business/Even define it as progress…the auction block is now the concert stage and videos/ with rhythmic images of black pimps and voluntary black hos/she's still naked/while he's dressed in furs and drenched in gold/going once going twice sold….[13]

As highlighted in Nelly's "Tip Drill," the camera eye in these video productions is precisely inclined so as to fetishize black female video models ("eye candy") whose staging is designed to secure (black) male performing artists as the centered subjects in productions aimed at promoting and selling their music. And, notably, Nelly's final scenario—with great economy and visual potency—links the *sexual fetishization* of black women's bodies/bootys to their function as *commodity fetishes*, objects meant for private use and public exchange among black males, as well as commodities available in capitalist-consumer culture to anyone possessing the money–or its equivalency in credit or capital.[14] Not only do women's bodies/bootys serve to procure social and economic capital, but as Muhammad notes, in "hip-hop culture's adaptation of the marketplace logic…[black women's] booty [becomes] capital, literally."[15] Thus, "Tip Drill's" final scenario, in which a credit card is swiped down the rear end of a video model, comes to represent a kind of *mise-en-abîme* recapitulating the commodification and exchange of women within an industry dominated by black and white men who control black women's bodies from recruitment to audition, casting, performance, and marketing. And if contemporary hip-hop culture functions to assert a mythical or stereotypical black hypermasculinity through the fetishization and commodification of black women's bodies/bootys, it is also notable that the performance of black hypermasculinity is most often attached to *dark-skinned blackness*, while the corollary performance of black hyperfemininity is attached to *light-skinned blackness*, thereby associating *sexual* and *commodity fetishism* to *skin fetishism*.

II. "Back to the Future": Staging the Black Female Body from Saartjie Baartman to Josephine Baker

It is by now something of a commonplace to compare the performance of the contemporary video model (also popularly known as the "video vixen," "video ho," "video hottie," or "video honey") to that of her forebears, Saartjie Baartman (the "Venus Hottentot") and Josephine Baker (the "Ebony Venus").[16] Yet the comparison is almost unavoidable. And if, as suggested above, the denuded, or unclothed, black female body is associated historically with the fetishization of the black female in the antebellum slave markets and with sexual, commodity, and skin fetishism in the historical and contemporary U.S. cultural imaginary, it is surely the "ethnographic spectacle" of Saartjie Baartman—whose image is textualized in the "scientific" journals and proceedings visualized in the popular iconography of nineteenth-century Europe—that represents the black female body in the European colonial imaginary.[17] Historically, the proverbial "black bottom" is a feature that has been associated with an embodied black femininity and racialized sexuality, at least since Baartman, the South African Khoikhoi woman who was displayed for entertainment and profit as a circus "freak" and ethnographic spectacle—and later, scientific specimen—in early nineteenth-century England and France. And although subject to historical dispute, court records suggest that Baartman entered willingly—or perhaps was cajoled—into a legal contract with her sponsor in which she agreed to share the revenue generated by exhibiting her body to an audience anxious to secure its own sense of superiority in relation to a figure constructed by anthropologists and ethnographers "as the missing link between humans and apes."[18]

Baartman's fascination lay in her small stature, protruding buttocks—a condition known as steatopygia—and, after her death, in the size and shape of her elongated genitalia ("the Hottentot Apron"). Presented as something of a static "artifact," Baartman was inevitably read under the "sign of the primitive."[19] In life, the display of Baartman's body was reduced literally and figuratively to the "rear end" (one spectator was noted to have remarked that "she could be said to carry her fortune behind her, for London may never before have seen such a 'heavy-arsed heathen'").[20] In death, however, Baartman was literally dissected into a collection of parts that signified racially deviant sexuality in the European colonial imaginary. Sadly, her fate as ethnographic spectacle, along with her subsequent display as museum specimen signifies the European colonial fetishization of the black female body in life as well as death.[21] As predecessor of the contemporary video model, the colonized and "mined" body of Saartjie Baartman emblematizes the entanglement of the black female body in a visual and market economy.

The specularization and commodification of the black female body/booty as an object of consumption in the marketplace of exchange and desire represents a concept and image of embodied sexuality that also figures prominently in the dance aesthetics of legendary performing artist, Josephine Baker. Achieving what Jeanne Scheper describes as "diva iconicity" in 1920s and 1930s Europe, Baker arguably represents the bridge between the nineteenth-century ethnographic spectacle of black women in Europe, their display on the auction block, and the post-millennial emergence of the hip-hop video model. And if the discourse of ethnography has confined (and defined) the image of Baartman, the contemporary scholarship on Baker has effectively contained her image, even while rescuing it from the discourse of primitivism. Notably, however, Scheper argues—and convincingly—that Baker learned to recycle "the cultural fantasies attached to her person and mythology" by manipulating her "own uncanny position [and] cannibalizing the tropes of stardom and negrophilia...incorporat[ing] them, digest[ing] them, and recycl[ing] them *to her own ends.*"[22]

Baker's ability to manipulate the fantasies attached to black femininity would seem evident at the outset of her career, as demonstrated by French dance critic André Levinson's 1925 review of Baker's Parisian debut in *La Revue Nègre*: "Certain of Miss Baker's poses, back arched, haunches protruding, arms entwined and uplifted in a phallic symbol, had the compelling potency of the finest of examples of Negro sculpture."[23] Emphasizing Baker's strategic staging of the body, Levinson's description suggests that Baker's buttocks ("protruding haunches") endowed her with phallic potency and aesthetic power.[24] Later, a Swedish critic concludes his rather mixed review of her performance in Stockholm by referencing Baker's comic invocation of animal imagery and calling attention to the artist's accentuation of her protuberant backside while she moved on all fours across the stage: "In all circumstances, here is the fitting and beautiful Swedish homage: The backside crowns the Glory!"[25] And writing in the French newspaper *Le Merle Rose*, author Georges Simenon notes that Baker's *croupe* (or "rump") manifests "a sense of humor" while inspiring "collective fantasies that send a deep incense of desire wafting toward her in steamy waves."[26] As these reflections make evident, Baker's *derrière* became a signal feature of her performance and a mark of her own self-branding. And like her reviewers, Baker herself emphasized the deliberate and strategic accentuation of the buttocks in her performance aesthetics. According to biographer, Phyllis Rose, "Baker herself declared that people had been hiding their *asses* too long": "The rear end exists...I see no reason to be ashamed of it. It's true there are rear ends so stupid, so pretentious, so insignificant that they're good only for sitting on."[27] For Baker, however, the *rear end* was clearly meant to serve *greater ends.*

And in the Western racial imaginary, it is precisely the signifier of the rear end that historically links Baker's embodied performances as the "Ebony Venus" both to her predecessor, "the Venus Hottentot," and to her successors, the so-called "video hotties." If Baartman's representation of the black female body became an index of racial difference and sexual deviance in the European imaginary, rendering her as ethnographic spectacle in the "discourse of the primitive," Baker's *"performance* of the primitive" had the effect of redefining the image of the black woman as exoticized and eroticized Other in the European colonial imaginary.[28] Of course, the Baker image and body cannot be limited or reduced to the rear end. Her stage performances feature the body in its entirety—legs, pelvis, breasts, arms, hair, skin, voice, and face—and does so both erotically and parodically. Remarking that "[a] violinist had his violin, a painter his palette. All I had was myself. I was the instrument that I must care for,"[29] Baker's ownership of the body—her manipulation of its instrumentality—rendered it a medium of pleasure and profit in the cultural and economic marketplace. And, arguably, while her performance of black hyperfemininity links Baker to the contemporary video models, what distinguishes Baker from her successors as well as her precursor are the agency and control of her image, manifest in the staging, promoting, packaging, and marketing of her body for popular consumption.[30] Fashioning her body as social, cultural, and economic capital—creating what Pierre Bourdieu might describe as *body capital*[31]—Baker's self-commodification enables the production (and consumption) of an identity that defined itself on the world stage and in an international marketplace.

III. Theorizing and Historicizing Black Female Fetishization

For Baker, performance became a means of creating a subject position that re-coded the black female body.[32] As performance studies scholar Daphne Brooks suggests, it was the staging of the Baker "bottom" that "re-oriented the spectacular attention directed at black female bodies in public spaces [and] potentially disabled the kind of exploitative spectatorship that circumscribed Sara[h] Baartman."[33] In her stage performances, Baker's control of her image derived from her ability to appropriate and redirect the fetishistic gaze of the Other. Thus, by way of an act of *self-fetishization*— captured metaphorically in the phallic signification of her famous banana belt and encoded in the phallic symbolism of her dance (as noted above in André Levinson's review of her premiere Paris performance), Baker simultaneously renders herself both *fetishized object of desire* and *subject/agent of desire*. Jean-Claude Baker comments that "[m]any will claim to have invented it [the banana costume], but only Josephine would dare to strategically fashion herself as a substitute phallus."[34] And because possession of the phallus is a position theoretically unavailable to the female in Freudian clinical theory (since the notion of fetishism is predicated on the threat of male castration), Baker would seem not only to occupy the culturally defined *female* position, but also to usurp the *male* position (the phallus, of course, signifying *not* the possession of a penis, but the privilege and power attached to the symbolic phallus). Thus, in contrast to Baartman who, as sexualized racial fetish, functioned as phallic substitute, Baker's simultaneous positionalities define her both as *substitute for the phallus* and *possessor of the power symbolized by the phallus*.[35] Symbolically, the bisexuality of Baker's positionality is also expressed in her cross-dressing, most notably in the 1932 production of *La Joie de Paris* in which Baker—playing the role of a bandleader donned in tuxedo and top hat—reprises a classic Duke Ellington pose as well as Marlene Dietrich's 1928 appearance at the Berlin foreign press ball. And beyond what Bennetta Jules-Rosetta describes as the "shock value" of her cross-dressing (and nudity), Baker's transvestism would seem to reinforce her control and manipulation of her performance identities, while also demonstrating the fluidity of gender and sexual identity.[36] Thus, Baker's performance (unlike those of her predecessor, Baartman, and her successors, the video models) can be construed not only as outrageous, as Jules-Rosetta suggests, but also subversive and transgressive in its challenge to binary constructions of gender.

And, importantly, although she performed in multiple venues, by most accounts Baker remained most captivating in live performances that allowed her to interactively "work" the gaze. Recognizing, as she famously put it, that "when it comes to blacks, the imagination of white folks is something else,"[37] Baker's parodic and comedic mugging (clowning and crossing her eyes) during her live performances— antics for which she became famous—allowed her to manipulate the spectatorial gaze by *receiving* and *returning* "the look."[38] Theoretically, then, it was Baker's control of the voyeuristically consuming gaze that guaranteed and became the condition of the performer's racialized and sexualized subjectivity, thereby empowering and promoting her as performing subject. Her live performances, in effect, secured for her a *recognition from the Other* derived both from the "power of seeing" and the "power in being seen."[39]

For Baker, then, the audience's *visual address* served to affirm her material presence and visibility, locating her center stage. And although the lighting, setting, scenery, and stage blocking would have functioned to focus and direct the gaze in Baker's live performances, the audience's perception was neither manipulated nor mediated by the camera eye. In contrast, however, the image of the video model is produced by camera angles, zoom lenses, close-ups, cuts, and other media technologies. Thus, while Baker's live venues often feature the butt, the complete body composition—including the face and often the voice—remains available to the spectator. Such is not the case with the video model, whose image is mediated and controlled by camera angles focusing almost exclusively on the back side. And unlike Baker, who *always* occupied center stage, the contemporary video model— *faceless, voiceless,* and frequently *nameless*—is staged to highlight the role of black male rappers who arguably function in the videos as surrogates, or substitutes, for the predominantly white male spectator.[40]

It is instructive to note that early hip-hop feminist critique often focused on the misogyny in the lyrics and performances of solo male artists and groups, while the defense of women in hip-hop most often addressed the singers and performers who responded by "talking back" to the black male artists and rap groups. Yet, despite the success of black women message rappers like Queen Latifa, MC Lyte, Salt-N-Peppa, Lauryn Hill, and Missy "Misdemeanor" Elliott, and even performers like Lil' Kim, Foxy Brown, and Trina (rappers whose sexualized performances brought them both recognition and control over their images), it is the more recent emergence of the so-called video vixen that undoubtedly serves to (re)define black female bodies in public spaces and in the contemporary cultural imaginary. Like their predecessors, black video models are staged (and sometimes self-staged) in ways that continue the fetishization (and self-fetishization) of black female bodies. And although a few have managed to exercise some control over the marketing of their public images, successful video models like Melyssa Ford, Karrine Steffans, Buffie Carruth, and Angel "Lola" Love remain exceptions to the rule. For the most part, the video model remains an absent presence in the industry, rendered simultaneously invisible and hypervisible by a camera eye focusing fetishistically on the buttocks.[41]

Commenting in an interview on her role as a video model, Karrine "Superhead" Steffans maintains that

> [as a video model,] you are performing a service to help this man sell records.... They give you the clothes to wear, tell you where to stand and how to move. If a man tells you to shake it like a salt shaker and you do it, [people reprimand you] and call you a ho.[42]

Continuing, in her autobiographical *Confessions of a Video Vixen* (2005), Steffans writes, "Having lived that life, I can say it's not everything it's cracked up to be."[43] In contrast, Melyssa Ford, whose original ambition was to become a forensic psychologist, provides a counter-narrative:

> I am the highest-paid video girl to date.... But I'm not the promiscuous twit I'm often mistaken for. I am a businesswoman who has used videos to launch a multimedia career. My product is me.... My job is to sell fantasy and perfection. When the cameras go on, I detach myself and play the sexy vixen who will turn a nigga out."[44]

While such contrasting identity/performance narratives suggest that the experiences of video models can be diverse and subject to varying (self-)constructions and interpretations, they further suggest that the contemporary video model's performance would seem, at best, to reprise the success of Baker, and, at worst, the tragedy of Saartjie Baartman.[45]

Like much Baker scholarship and criticism, the critical discourse of black femininity generated by the video model emphasizes sexual subjectivity and empowerment, on the one hand, and sexual availability and exploitation, on the other. Thus, while some critics take the position that the explicit performance of sexuality represents a strategy of self-empowerment by which black women take control and ownership of their bodies and sexualities, others argue that hip-hop music videos perpetuate stereotypically hypersexualized images of black women, rendering them fungible commodities in black and white masculinist sexual and market economies. Still others, advancing a more Foucauldian perspective, argue that although the relationship between women and hip-hop has long been a vexed one, the genre has become, for black women, a site of oppression as well as a space of liberation. In her ethnographic study on sexual subjectivity and consumer culture, Debra Curtis explores how (self-)commodification and consumerism can signal both sexual freedom and sexual domination.[46] Similarly, Rana Emerson, in her content and textual analysis of select 1997 videos featuring black women, finds "evidence of contestation, resistance, and the assertion of [b]lack women's agency" in spite of "the continuing objectification and exploitation of black women in music video."[47]

Complicating the construction of the image of black women in contemporary culture has been the rise of mega music conglomerates. Media critics argue that it is the mega music corporations, along with producers, record company moguls, directors, and featured (male) artists, who create and control the image of the female music video performer. Hip-hop scholar Meredith Levande argues that the passage of the 1996 Telecommunications Act (and its 2003 revision) had the consequence not only of decreasing the African-American share in the media industry, but of redefining the ideology of black femininity and feminism. Rehearsing a contemporary version of the Frankfurt critique of the culture industry, namely that programming, controlled by a decreasing number of media conglomerates, now has the power "to dictate culture, not reflect it," Levande contends that the power of the industry is such that ideologies, like products, can be assigned to pop stars, and that "the rhetoric of feminism has been hijacked and its hijackers use female pop stars to sell behaviors and attitudes about sexuality itself."[48] Levande's comments suggest that not only are the bodies and images of black women pop stars (and, by extension, video models) corporately defined and controlled, but also that the popularity of these images is predicated on the reconstruction of ideologies of black femininity and feminism in the propagation of a cultural myth equating nudity, sexuality, and pornography with (black) women's power and pleasure.

Considering the increasingly influential role of corporate media, rapper-actor Ice-T (*Law and Order: Special Victims Unit*) invokes a "street" or "hood" analogy to formulate his take on the relations of production:

> There's only two roles in life: the worker or the workee. The person that works for you or the person that has you work.... So you got to understand either you're a pimp or a ho.... Like I'm a ho for NBC.... In business, you're being judged on what you bring in.... I think really I'm more like a ho and like, yo, just don't get yourself confused and think that you're a pimp.[49]

Using the pimp/ho analogy, Ice-T highlights his own role (as male subject) within the corporate hustle, reframing production relations (the "workee" and the "worker") in terms of the street dynamics of the pimp and the prostitute. Similarly, hip-hop scholar Aya de Leon draws on and expands the pimp/ho metaphor to question the authenticity of commodified sexual expression in which "women are paid to enact the sexual fantasy of the disempowered [read: black] male," a dynamic that ultimately enacts capitalist/corporate desire driven by the economy of the marketplace: "This is prostitution. The industry is the pimp, the female emcees [and by extension female video performers] are the hos, and the [paying] audience is the trick." Further, de Leon, like Ice-T, broadens the analogy to reposition the male performer:

> Women aren't the only hos anymore.... [M]ost mainstream male rap artists are hos as well. They may call themselves pimps, but the industry is the only real pimp. If the rappers make a million, the industry makes mega millions.[50]

And shifting the metaphor slightly, hip-hop scholar Mirelle Miller-Young observes that

> the tremendous wealth produced for all these "players" [read: corporate television media, music video directors, producers, artists, agents, and filmmakers] in the hip-hop "game" rests largely on the pornographic performance of the "video model," sometimes known as the "video ho." She is the "eye candy" that sells the rapper, the products of his supposed "lifestyle," and finally, the song, with every wiggle of her body, sway of her hips, and glisten of her skin.[51]

Not only does Miller-Young underscore the "video ho" role of women in the "hip-hop 'game,'" but she also establishes a troublesome growing connection between culture and pornography.[52]

If de Leon and Miller-Young's elaborations on Ice-T's "pimp/ho" metaphor serve to illuminate black women's roles in hip-hop culture, media critic Richard Dyer's configuration of labor/capital relations in the economy of popular culture would seem, in some respects, to flip the script of the above paradigm. Dyer argues that, while entertainment as a form of production embodies the "usual struggle between capital (the backers) and labor (the performers)," it is nevertheless the performers themselves who exercise the "dominant agency" for defining the form because, in entertainment, the workers—or the entertainers themselves—are "in a better position [than many others in the workforce] to determine the form of [their] product."[53] And, importantly, in the instance of hip-hop, the performers comprise not only the rappers, but the video models as well, while the product would include the performances of both rappers and video model. Thus, unlike the paradigms advanced by Ice-T, de Leon, and Miller-Young, Dyer's would ultimately hold the performer accountable for the production of his or her product (in this instance, the product, of course, would be the performance itself). And while it seems undeniable that major record labels, radio conglomerates, and mega music corporations exercise control both in the production and distribution of rap and music videos as well as in the marketing of images/stereotypes that appeal to a mass audience, it is also evident, as Johnnetta B. Cole and Beverly Guy-Sheftall assert, that "young, business-savvy [male] artists maintain a great deal more control over the content and direction of their products... than African American artists did in the past."[54]

Yet, as suggested above, it is notable that many—perhaps most—contemporary hip-hop artists, performers, and video models, along with their critics and promoters, deny responsibility for the perpetuation of abusive and exploitative images of black women by either assigning responsibility to the role of corporate media which, through its production choices and promotion policies, determine what songs get produced and which enter into heavy rotation, or arguing that, as a genre, hip-hop and rap merely *reflect or mirror the values, attitudes, and practices of society*—or the world as it is, including the sexism and misogyny of the dominant culture. Hip-hop mogul Russell Simmons argues that "the hip-hop community is a mirror, a *reflection* of the dirt we overlook—the violence, the misogyny, the sexism,"[55] while cultural critic Michael Eric Dyson claims that "hip hop captures the bigotry toward women... found in the larger society—but on steroids so speak."[56] Testifying in congressional hearings, Radio One CEO Alfred C. Liggins contends that "hip hop *reflects* the realities that many in the [radio] audiences face and observe in their everyday lives," while rapper David Banner (Levell Crump) underscores the cultural logic of such a position in his own testimony, "I can admit that there are some problems in hip-hop, but it is only a *reflection* of what is taking place in our society. Hip-hop is sick because America is sick."[57] Clearly, such comments function to evade, or at best, alleviate, hip-hop's responsibility for the reproduction and perpetuation of the sexism and misogyny that has historically pervaded ideology and social practices.

Such a position, aesthetically, locates the genre of hip-hop within the orthodox Marxist theory of representation that is commonly described as *reflectionism*, associated with Georg Lukács. According to Lukács, literature (and here, by extension, popular culture) reflects ideology and consciousness (superstructure) as determined by economic relations (base). And while the relationship between base and superstructure has become more complexly mediated in contemporary Marxist criticism, the notion of reflectionism, based on an aesthetics of realism, continues to inform popular Marxist understandings of literature, culture, and society.[58] Oddly (or not), hip-hop artists, critics, promoters, and corporate executives lay claim to this notion of reflectionism by espousing the "authenticity" theory of hip-hop ("keeping it real"). The idea advanced here is that hip-hop as a genre reflects the "down and dirty," "raw and real," "unvarnished and uncut" material and social conditions of black urban life. From this perspective, argue the "keeping-it-real" school, the (hetero)sexism and misogyny so prevalent in contemporary hip-hop culture, rap lyrics, and music video merely "reflect" or "mirror" the dominant and hegemonic culture's sexist attitudes and practices toward (black) women.

Responding to such critics, Tricia Rose, in *The Hip Hop Wars* (2008), explains that while "hip hop didn't create sexism... far too much of it glorifies and encourages its growth and maintenance." Further, her comments point to the poignant danger of hip-hop's impact as a subcultural influence and determinant of black self-image and identity formation:

> Unlike the sexism that we find in Hollywood or on television or in politics, the sexism in hip hop resonates with even greater influence on this black youth constituency since it serves as a part of its homegrown identity. It is to hip hop that so many young black men look for models of black manhood that connect with their generation and their experiences. It is to hip hop that many young black women look to find a place in which to belong in their peer group, to figure out how to get attention from men.[59]

Rose's observations make evident that the uncritical representation of sexist and misogynist practices, in effect, reproduces and perpetuates them.

Disturbingly, in addition to the promoters and corporate backers, many hip-hop and cultural critics (Tricia Rose is a notable exception)—who have the responsibility for illuminating the complex dynamics between popular culture and society—would seem to abdicate that responsibility in the instance of hip-hop culture and rap music. What is seemingly inconsistent and contradictory with the reflectionist position is that hip-hop as a music and performance genre is associated with—and indeed is rooted in—an urban, black, working-class and immigrant youth culture driven by a fundamentally counter-hegemonic impulse that (at least in its originary form) functioned to critique dominant practices, ideologies, and structures of oppression. In its social critique of class and race oppression, hip-hop has presented a powerful social critique; yet, when it comes to gender and sexual oppression, hip-hop culture and rap artists often reproduce—and its critics and promoters too often claim—a position that replicates the (hetero)sexism and misogyny of the dominant culture, demonstrating that popular culture can function as a site of both resistance and recuperation.

Notably, cultural theorist Stuart Hall addresses this contradiction with regard to the representation of black masculinities:

> [C]ertain ways in which black men continue to live out their counter-identities as black masculinities and replay those fantasies of black masculinities in the theaters of popular culture are, when viewed from along other axes of difference, the very masculine identities that are oppressive to women, that claim visibility for their hardness only at the expense of the vulnerability of black women....[60]

Thus, Hall's observations suggest that in hip-hop's performance of "black masculinities," black women's bodies get packaged and marketed to sell products, while the women themselves become products in a sexualized exchange economy. What its artists, critics, promoters, and aficionados fail to recognize is that hip-hop itself fails as a genuinely radical genre—and will continue to fall short of its transformative potential—so long as it continues to perpetuate and reproduce the devaluation and derogation of black women, and so long as its practitioners and supporters refuse to recognize that hip-hop is not only *reflective* of dominant and hegemonic social practices, but that it is also *constitutive* of social practices and identities.[61] It is, thus, consequential that not only do many "tweens," teens, and adult black women identify with the "stripper chic" produced in hip-hop culture but, equally importantly, they are all too often regarded and treated like the "bitches" and "skanks" promulgated in hip-hop culture and rap music video.[62] From an Althusserian perspective, these young women (and men) are subjected (and thus become subjects) to a cultural ideology in which females get interpellated as "hos" and males as "pimps."

Remarking on the "relation between the sexual abuse of black women and the visual culture that objectifies black women as sexually available," T. Denean Sharpley-Whiting suggests that popular culture constructs black women's sexuality and justifies black women's subjugation.[63] Similarly, hip-hop scholar James Petersen notes that "the real-life narratives [of young black women]" are "in dialogue with, or influenced by, the misogynistic discourses in the broader culture and in rap music."[64] It is because of the formative and constitutive influence of popular culture on social practices and identities that a sustained critique of the representation of black women in hip-hop becomes critical to the formulation of a theory and practice of creative and transformative *becoming* that does not reproduce and perpetuate gender abuse, exploitation, and inequality, but actively resists the devaluation of women and moves progressively toward the production of more just and equitable race and gender scripts and relations. Thus, rather than position rap and hip-hop as a "mirror" of contemporary culture, I would propose a theory that not only acknowledges the reflective and, importantly, constitutive, role of popular culture, but also draws on the insights of classic and contemporary trauma theory.

IV. Theorizing (Mis)Performance, Mimesis, Witnessing

If it is indeed the case, as suggested above, that the contemporary music video model's performance reprises the historical performances of black female precursors in ways that are demeaning and self-destructive, this chapter invites an intervention on the part of the black feminist scholar and, in so doing, raises the following questions: How does contemporary scholarly work figure into the liberatory reclamation of black female sexuality without re-inscribing or recuperating the all-too-familiar controlling historical stereotype of a lewd and licentious black femininity? And, ethically, how does the work of the scholar function to ensure a future for young black women different from the troubled present and traumatic past? Finally, how can the contemporary scholar position performance—and, indeed, *misperformance*— as a theory and practice of mimetic *becoming* rather than simply an exercise in the non-abreactive re-enactment of the past?[65]

Contemporary psychoanalytic scholarship examines the impact of post-traumatic stress disorder (PTSD) not only on combat veterans, but also on battered women, abused children, concentration camp survivors, political prisoners and, most recently, the survivors of slavery.[66] Typically characterized by a delayed response to a catastrophic or traumatogenic event—an occurrence that cannot be integrated into narrative memory—trauma, so contemporary theorists argue, can be transmitted not only to the survivors, but to their descendants as well. Thus, not only are horrific historical events inscribed on the body and mind of victims, but these effects are potentially transmitted to future generations that, as a consequence, compulsively and involuntarily re-enact the originary trauma. Drawing on the notion of what one scholar has described as post-traumatic slave syndrome (PTSS) and others, post-traumatic slavery disorder (PTSlaveryD), the wounding at the "primal scene" of slavery becomes imprinted on black bodies, internalized in the black psyche, and passed down to subsequent generations.[67] Whether transmitted through "narrative memory, family stories, [or] through certain bodily responses and behaviors," theorists argue that trauma is expressed through the repetition or re-enactment of primal scenes of personal, cultural, and historical wounding.[68] Thus, the historical wounding of slavery, along with its (post)traumatic aftershocks, continue to imprint the bodies and minds of contemporary African-American men and women, rendering the intergenerational transmission of individual, group, or cultural trauma constitutive in the formation of a specifically African-American social identity.

Further, the notion of the intergenerational transmission of trauma provides theoretical scaffolding for an analysis of the critical juxtaposition of black women in contemporary hip-hop music video productions and the originary display of black women on the auction block—an analogue that would position video models as victims of the intergenerational trauma haunting black women from the antebellum slave markets until the present. Scholar Shalanda Faulk Coleman analyzes the contemporary video model's performance as it re-enacts the historical subjection of black women to the wounding "gaze" of the white male at the site of the antebellum slave market.[69] Addressing the "willing participation" of the contemporary video vixen in acts of "(s)exploitation" and self-objectification, Coleman notes the complicity of the video model in performances (re)enacted in response to the white male spectatorial gaze. Here, I would emphasize that the involuntary and unwitting character of these public ritual performances provides dramatic bodily testimony to the historical subjugation and exploitation of black women. And while it is necessary to acknowledge the imprint of American slavery, one must also recognize the imprint of the marginalizing and oppressive social conditions impacting black women subsequent to the experience of slavery. Thus, according to the (psycho)logic of trauma theory, the performance of the video model functions on some level as the public re-inscription of an originary psychic wounding, as well as subsequent social injury. The performance of the video model, then, bears witness to the historical misuse and abuse of the black female body, and the traumatogenic experiences that have been "passed on" or "passed down." And while one may concede that male hip-hop performers, no less than female performers, re-enact the historical violence of slavery through the (self) fetishization of black bodies (arguably a marker of black male castration anxiety due to the trauma of slavery), this chapter engages the performance of the black female video model. And here it is instructive to remember that early Freudian psychoanalysis associated trauma, and specifically *female* trauma (described by Freud as "hysteria"), with *sexual abuse and exploitation.*[70]

In 1980, the American Psychiatric Association officially identified and defined PTSD, emphasizing the *repetition* or *recurrence* of certain thoughts and behaviors associated with past traumatic events and experiences.[71] What makes this definition particularly appropriate to a consideration of the video model's performance is the emphasis on *involuntary re-enactment,* or "repetition compulsion"—what trauma scholar Ruth Leys describes as *mimesis.* Mimesis, as Leys defines it, dates back to the early years of psychoanalytical praxis, and is not only symptomatic of trauma, but fundamental to the psychoanalytic method of recovery.[72] My reading favors Leys's term, mimesis, *not* because it suggests the Marxist notion of mirroring (nor because it references the early Greek notion of art as imitation), but because it connotes the recitation and reiteration of identity performance and performativity—and, further, because it designates a concept conveying the potential of *repetition with a difference,* thereby allowing the subject, through (mis)performance, not simply to *re-enact,* but to *re-imagine or revise,* personal and collective history. Thus, from the perspective of mimesis, the public performances enacted by black female bodies offer performative testimony to historical wounding, thereby rendering the video vixen a site of trauma as well as a potential site of healing. And, at the same time, the notion of mimesis allows the theorist to call into question the "authenticity" (returning to the "keeping-it-real-school") of (mis)performances that lead not to self-recognition, but *mis-recognition.*[73]

Returning to the role of the contemporary black feminist scholar, what I propose is that she must *bear witness* to the *(mis)performance* of the video vixen and to the history imprinted on black female bodily performance. If the video vixen's misperformance can be genealogically recast as a *performance of testimony* re-enacting past abuses, then hip-hop may yet prove itself to be transformative by providing a discursive site at which the scholar can bear cultural and critical witness to the performance of a traumatic history and, in so doing, fulfill what self-identified hip-hop feminist Joan Morgan suggests is "hip hop's ability to articulate the pain our community is in and use that knowledge to create a redemptive space."[74] Further, in acting as *recipient* of the performer's *address*, the scholar may position herself to render shareable the re-enactment of painful historical events. And in providing cultural and critical witnessing to the historical and collective wounding of the black female body, the black feminist scholar may offer a critical/theoretical corpus (or *body* of work) in "response" and "response-ability" to the wounded *body* of the subject.[75] In other words, the process of critical and theoretical witnessing proposed here takes place in the public sphere between the performance of the black female *body* and the scholarly and critical performance of a *body* of work that gives testimony to the traumatic history embodied in that performance. In response and "response-abilty" to the testimonial performance enacted by black women's bodies, the task of the black feminist scholar, I propose, is to provide critical witnessing and "address-ability"—in the form of theoretical testimony, fostering the *(re)making* of the *marked* subject, and allowing for the re-integration of a traumatic historical past into a transcendent narrative of *becoming*.

My proposal, then, is that we black feminist ("old" and "new" school) scholars bear critical witness and provide theoretical testimony to the historical trauma that is (re)enacted in the public (mis)performances of the video models, and that we theorize a genealogy that will enable their transformation from voiceless objects of exchange and desire into speaking subjects who can claim agency—a transformation that can only occur as scholars and performers work *in tandem* toward repossessing (to use an old school phrase) "our bodies and ourselves." To make this happen, we must embark on the difficult journey toward self-recognition, healing, and *becoming*—tasks that can be achieved, in part, through the transformation of hip-hop culture/rap music video into a more truly "counter-hegemonic" genre. The first step toward the accomplishment of such a goal would be the recognition of the necessity to de-fetishize the black female body in its entirety—and that includes the reclamation of black women's "faces" and "voices"—in both the private and public spheres.

I conclude by referencing another kind of performance, one that is described in military formation as an "about face"—namely, a reversal of *attitude* (mental and physical) in which the subject pivots, or turns, so as to face the opposing/oppositional direction.[76] What Ralph Ellison defines as the task of the African-American in his signature 1952 novel, *Invisible Man,* applies even more so to contemporary African-American *women*. To invoke Ellison, as black women, our task (like that of James Joyce's Stephen Dedalus) is not actually one of "creating the uncreated conscience of [our] race [and/or gender]," but of "creating the uncreated features of [our] *face*."[77] And in so doing, we can continue to *face* the challenges of *becoming*— *and re-making ourselves as individuals, as women, and, importantly, as valued members of a community.* Thus, what I submit here is that as black women we become not just the proverbial "sisters with 'attitude' "—but to invoke the inimitable Patti Labelle— sisters with a *"new* attitude." What I envision is a change in black women's self-*imaging* and self-*imagining* in both the public and private spheres—a shift in "attitude" from the *"rear"* to the *face*. Indeed, we must *about face* because *it's all about the face.*[78]

IN RETROSPECT

15

Sherley Anne Williams (1944–1999)

"Someone Sweet Angel Chile"

This ain't the beginnin; maybe it's the end
I'm not gon tell you my story; I know what
you'll say: Sister, that's where we all been.
　　　　　　—Sherley Anne Williams, "The Peacock Poems: 2"

No, I don't know all
the hearts I live in. But I do know the
people who live in mine. And I want to
be on very good terms with all those
who live in my home.

　　　　　　　　　　—Sherley Anne Williams, "Home"

Like poets, critics may have muses. And it is fair to say that Sherley Anne Williams was my muse—my critical muse. Her immense creativity gave inspiration to my critical musings. Yet, at this moment, I can only ask, in the memorable words of Ralph Ellison, "when confronted by such an unexpected situation as this, what does one say?"[1] Ellison's line resonates for me on the occasion of these reflections on the life and death of a muse, poet, novelist, critic, playwright, teacher, mother, and sister-woman whose life and death touch me personally and deeply. I've spent much of my intellectual and professional life teaching and writing about Sherley Anne Williams's superb work. I also knew her, although not so well, I imagine, as I might have. But on the rare occasions when we met, I found her to be observant, demure, somewhat mysterious, even enigmatic, yet always endowed with amazing grace ("My back never was bent, just the self I held in"[2]). As the passages above are meant to suggest, she spoke loudest—and most eloquently—through her song, her literary song:

　　　Life put a hurt on you
　　　　　only one thing you can do.

> When life put a hurt on you
>   not but one thing a po chile can do.
> I just stand on my hind legs and holla
>   just let the sound carry me through.[3]

Sherley Anne Williams, the daughter of a migrant farm worker, was born in Bakersfield, California, and grew up in a place she wrote about in her poetry, "the heart of the farm-rich San Joaquin Valley."[4] When her father succumbed to tuberculosis, the family went on welfare to survive. After her bachelor's degree in English at Fresno State, Sherley studied at Fisk with Robert Hayden. As a protégé of Sterling Brown, she continued her graduate studies at Howard University, later completing her master's degree in American literature at Brown University. Writing of the author of *The Peacock Poems*, Brown professor and poet Michael Harper reflected, "She is a musician whose blues, comedy and heartbreak are a testimony to autobiography/history where both oral and literary Afro-American traditions touch and fuse…in the 'I' is always 'we'; she's met life's terms but never accepted them, for the blues is exercise, not exhibition."[5] Yes, Sherley was a bluesy kinda woman, and like her own muse, Bessie Smith, she was "Someone Sweet Angel Chile." Her fiction and poetry became sacramental expressions of a secular blues ethic and aesthetic. By her own account, Sherley had attempted to escape her birthplace, the San Joaquin Valley, and the insularity it represented:

> *I had hated this,*
> *hated all the squat Valley towns; had left, returned,*
> *left: The memory of the sun on the dirt and grass*
> *graves, on the shiny black skins of my family and*
> *friends draws me back.*

Nevertheless, she was drawn to a "city of light":

> Oh, I see myself as I was
> then skinny little
> piece a woman dying to
> get to Frisco and change.[6]

We must await her biographer to research the details of her life story—to fill in the narrative gap between the San Joaquin Valley, Frisco, and San Diego, where she died in the summer of 1999. But what we do know is that the publication of her novel *Dessa Rose* (1986) became a landmark in contemporary American fiction, arguably representing the inaugural moment of a genre that has since come to be known as the "neo-slave narrative."[7] It is a novel that I have written about again and again, and may yet write about again. But surely future generations will continue to write about the extraordinary work of an equally extraordinary woman—whose work is significant to me because it emphasizes the very ordinariness of that extraordinariness. Sherley wrote about ordinary women ("Tell Martha Not to Moan") who become extraordinary in their ability to live through and transcend experience. She wrote about her mother and her sisters and her girlfriends—and her work spoke to me about my mother and my sisters and my girlfriends (Oh, why did I not tell her that we had more in common than she would ever know?). I suspect, however, that I am a better reader of her writing than I could ever be of her life; yet and still, hers was a life that shared notable parallels and intersections with my own (we were about the same age, both lost a parent early in our lives, and grew up "on welfare").

I recall the occasion of our first meeting: a closing reception for the now historic Reconstruction of Instruction NEH Seminar held at Yale in the late 1970s. The reception marked the finale of what had been an exhilarating experience for the twenty or thirty or so young scholars and artists participating—many of whom, along with Sherley herself, would become literary illuminaries. We had spent weeks together—reading, arguing, partying, and sharing other intimacies ("*And shared love lives, even when the people move on*"[8]).

I was a graduate student and Sherley had just published her collection of critical essays *Give Birth to Brightness* (1972) and would shortly publish her first book of poetry *The Peacock Poems* (1975), a volume nominated for both the National Book Award and the Pulitzer Prize. It was a memorable evening, marked on the calendar of my memory by a historic but (to my knowledge) heretofore unrecorded moment—one that Ellison might have described as part of the "underground of our unwritten history."[9]

The formal reception that evening was the culmination of what had been, for many of us, a rite of passage, marking endings and beginnings. And while the reception was not exactly a love feast, it was most certainly a communal celebration, and a celebration of community. The spirit of community being with us and upon us, Sherley was moved to speak—in a spirit of adoration and anguish, of veneration and rebuke. I recall this moment as the one rather remarkable exception to what I always perceived to be her rather remarkable equanimity. Passionately, the younger woman poet gave both tribute and censure to her self-acknowledged model and precursor, Amiri Baraka (*aka* LeRoi Jones). While I cannot recall the exchange—time enough, I always thought, for us to reminisce about that moment—my recollection is that Sherley took him to task on the woman's issue, importuning him to attend to the needs of the "sister" as well as the "brother." Afterward, if memory serves (I cannot always be sure that it does), they embraced—perhaps not an uncommon exchange between the brother and sister writers and activists during the 1970s, but, for me, a luminous and unforgettable moment!

That event became the inspiration for a brainstorm among an enthusiastic young group of black and white women graduate students at Yale, a group that included Hazel Carby, Susan Willis, Shelley Fisher [Fishkin], Carolyn Jackson, and myself. African-American Studies invited Sherley, along with a host of young black women writers—including Paule Marshall, Alice Walker, Buchi Emecheta, as well as Joanne Braxton and Gloria Naylor (both of whom were then Yale graduate students)—to participate in what was most likely the first hemispheric conference on black women in the diaspora (it was entitled Black Women in Their Own Write). The next time I saw Sherley was in February 1992 in Paris. We were both attending a conference on African Americans and Europe, and ended up at the same hotel in the Latin Quarter (I think it was Hôtel Résidence de Lutèce). The evening following the closing sessions, we hung out, drank, and discussed Dessa Rose. Sherley told me she had heard through the grapevine about a controversial piece I had recently given at Harvard University comparing Dessa Rose to Pauline Réage's Story of O. Neither confirming nor denying my imputed literary connection between Réage and herself, she nonetheless seemed pleased with reports on an interpretation of her novel that acknowledged its sexual and political transgressive power.

My next meeting with Sherley was in Chicago, shortly after our Paris encounter. Her full-length, one-woman drama, "Letters from a New England Negro," was presented at the Chicago International Theatre Festival in 1992, and I attended with students from the Black Women Writers class that I was then teaching at the University of Illinois in Chicago.[10] I had a surprise for her. By chance, I had discovered some of her personal belongings that she had inadvertently left behind at the hotel (our rooms were adjacent) where we had both stayed in Paris. (As I recollect, she was dashing to make her return flight to the U.S.!) After the performance, I presented her with the several items of clothing that had been left behind in Paris, explaining that I'd been intending to send them to her. Indeed, she had missed them, and rejoiced that that which was lost was now found. I rejoiced in another meeting and another encounter with her extraordinary talent.

The last time I saw Sherley was at a conference held in her honor at the University of California at San Diego in May 1998, a conference organized by Ann duCille to mark the twelfth anniversary of the publication of Sherley's novel Dessa Rose. As honoree at the conference on Black Women Writers and the "High Art" of Afro-American Letters, Sherley graciously shared her presence with the critics and scholars there to celebrate her work. She expressed her thanks to the conferees with a simple, "Thank you for giving me my book back." Once again, we reminisced about earlier years, but especially Paris. For the first time, we spoke conspiratorially and spiritedly (we were both inspirited) about the people we knew and the quirky things that had happened to us. She was carefree and so was I, and we both were gay at dinner that evening, thinking about what it must mean to be a BAP in Paris![11]

Having taught and written about Sherley Anne Williams's work, I think it now perhaps fitting to meditate, as it were, not so much on her history, as on those small moments, seemingly so insignificant at the time, but which are now etched in memory. Our lives touched only tangentially, perhaps less than a half dozen times; yet her work and those few random encounters bear much meaning for me. She was of my generation, and her untimely death, in some ways, harbingers its passing. But more important, her achievements betoken the legacy this generation will pass on to its survivors. Our community is a poorer place without Sherley Anne Williams; our inheritance, a richer one because of her song: "These is old blues / and I sing em like any woman do. / These the old blues / and I sing em, sing em, sing em. Just like any woman do. / My life ain't done yet. / Naw. My song ain't through."[12]

16

Bebe Moore Campbell (1950–2006)

"Literature as Equipment for Living"

[Jane Campbell]: How do you want to be remembered? How do
you want people to think about your work? What impressions
would you like people to have of your work as a whole?
[Bebe Moore Campbell]: That it helped us, and America,
become a better place, [that] we healed some race wounds. [That]
my work led to people talking with each other, and we
began a dialogue about race. [That] we began to focus on the
love between us.

—Jane Campbell, "An Interview with Bebe Moore Campbell"

Even though we had both attended Girls High in the 1960s, I did not know Bebe
Moore Campbell then. In age, we were five years apart: I brought up the rear of the
Baby Boomers while she brought in the Cold War generation. We both, however,
came of age during the post–*Brown v. Board of Education* era in Philadelphia, a site
historically marked as the city of "brotherly love," but for us, as Girls' High gradu-
ates, a site geographically and forever sentimentally marked by "sisterly love"—and
"contest" (the annual intramural athletic competition symbolizing a rite of passage
in our journey toward achieving that sublime state proclaimed in our high school
motto, *vincit qui se vincit*[1]). But Bebe Moore Campbell and I had much more in
common—indeed, more than I could have imagined. My first real introduction to
Campbell was through reading her coming-of-age memoir, *Sweet Summer: Growing
Up with and without My Dad* (1989), a tribute to George Moore, her disabled father,
from an only daughter of divorced parents.

What to my surprise—and delight—was the discovery that not only had we
both graduated from the same high school, but that we had even earlier shared the
Carolina-Philly connection, although her journey was an immersion narrative (from
North to South) while mine was an ascent narrative (from South to North). Raised
in black matriarchal households, both Campbell and I had commuter and migratory
childhoods. If Campbell spent the "sweet summers" of her girlhood with a beloved

234

paraplegic father in North Carolina, I spent my winters with an overburdened, alcoholic mother in Philadelphia. Even as Bebe, during the summer months, left the "Bosoms" in Philadelphia, I was returning to the starched and fanning "gray-haired old ladies" and tobacco-chewing old men in my native North Carolina. Yet, somewhere between the tracks of our genealogical and geographical lines and lineages, I met Bebe, in my imagination, two-stepping on a North Philly sidewalk between the ropes of double dutch, chanting "Miss Mary Mack, Mack, Mack...all dressed in black, black, black...with silver buttons, buttons, buttons...all down her back, back, back...." It was Campbell's autobiographical memoir that brought me into an imaginary intimacy with a sister-girl who conjured up the Motown music idols (Sam Cook who "sent me" and Diana, Flo, and Mary with whom I, too, "baby-babied"), the social dancing (the "slop" and the "new cha-cha"), the slang ("daaag"), the guilty pleasures (*True Confessions*), the sweet addictions (Raisinets and Jordan Almonds), the cultural envy (American Bandstand), and the underground way stations ("Susquehanna and Dauphin") of my Philly girlhood. Not only, however, did Bebe and I become homegirls in my cultural imaginary, we also met as admirers of Toni Morrison's *Sula* and *Beloved*, novels teaching us that we were "neither white nor male," but that we must learn, finally, to be our own "best thing."

Bebe Moore Campbell's reception in the press and media attests to her success as a popular writer. Her memoir and novels have been reviewed in the *New York Times,* the *Los Angeles Times,* and the *Washington Post;* her voice was frequently heard on the "Morning Edition" of National Public Radio and her prose appeared in the pages of popular and influential magazines such as *Essence, Ebony, Ms.,* and *Black Enterprise.* But Campbell was more than a popular writer; she was also a writer of enormous clarity, wit, grace, eloquence, commitment, and, perhaps, a writer whose real literary legacy has yet to be determined.

If such iconic black writers as Toni Morrison and Alice Walker acknowledge their artistic debts to ancestors and foremothers like Nella Larsen, Zora Neale Hurston, Dorothy West, Ann Petry, Gwendolyn Brooks, and other pre–Civil Rights black women writers, Campbell's generation of authors continues the tradition of black women writing in ways that pay tribute to the past while, at the same time, addressing the imperatives of the present. Campbell was, I believe, unique from this perspective. And unlike Terry McMillan, who became, in some respects, the priestess of black women's popular romance fiction, Campbell's *forte* resides in the range and breadth of her fiction and nonfiction. Much of her draw was that she achieved what one critic described as "crossover appeal," due in large part to her complex literary explorations not only of social and familial relations between men and women, (grand)mothers and daughters, fathers and daughters, and sons and fathers, but also cross-cultural relations between blacks, whites, and other ethnic groups, most often within the landscape and against the background of a modern and diverse urban America.

Like her self-proclaimed mentors, Toni Morrison and James Baldwin, Campbell writes about love—and the failure of love—and its consequences for the self, the family, the community, and the larger society. In examining these themes, Campbell addresses issues of race, racism, and race relations; marriage, divorce, and single motherhood; friendship, loyalty, and betrayal; age, death, and mental illness. Her subject, broadly speaking, is the modern condition and the human condition—not universalized and flattened out, but read through the complex lens of race, gender, and class, as these categories intersect to shape our lives in a society dominated by corporate, mass, and popular culture, as well as ethnic diversity and continuing social and class inequities.

What Campbell provides is what the great cultural critic Kenneth Burke describes in his landmark essay of the same name, and that is "literature as equipment for living."[2] Burke argues that literature equips us—presumably both author and reader— with the knowledge, values, and strategies that enable us to confront lived lives. To this end, Campbell's novels address both the social and psychic challenges and conflicts facing those of us who seek to live principled and accountable lives, informed by a sense of social justice and an ethic of care. Like Baldwin, Campbell chooses to address in her fiction and nonfiction the challenges of contemporary life, especially as these confront black, middle-class, professional women. As she put it in the above cited interview with Jane Campbell (no relation), her intent was "to write stories present tense...stories that take place now."[3] Her characters are people we know: they speak our language, and they wrestle with the personal, social, racial, and political issues confronting the contemporary reader.

What distinguishes Campbell's fiction and, in large part, her nonfiction, is her emphasis on the "utility," or instructional value, of literature. Yet it is a major achievement of her literary aesthetic that she is able to do justice to the Horatian dictum that literature should be both *dolce et utile*—"sweet and useful." Linking her novelistic mission to "teach" with her early career as a primary and secondary grade school teacher, Campbell speaks directly to this mission: "I consider my books a continuation of that profession in that I try to impart a message."[4] While acknowledging that, as a novelist, her job is to entertain so that she can instruct, Campbell—the daughter of a social worker, growing up against the backdrop of the Civil Rights movement—insists that, for her, "there's no point in writing merely to entertain.... If I'm not out to enlighten, or change your mind about something, or change your behavior, then I really don't want to take the journey."[5] As an engaged writer, then, Campbell's novels are meant heuristically to instruct the reader about life, a task requiring not only genuine talent, but a serious ethical sensibility, as well as a breadth and depth of knowledge. As her novels demonstrate, Campbell possesses these qualities and requirements in abundance.

What is distinctive about Campbell's narrative strategy is her adroit use of dialogue (external and internal) and multiple perspectives to represent the complex dimensions of contemporary social realities. Campbell's first novel, *Your Blues Ain't Like Mine* (1992), returns South, to Money, Mississippi, in a fictional exploration of the impact of the murder of Emmett Till on the families of the black victim and the white perpetrator. As Campbell herself revealed in a *New York Times Book Review* interview, her intent was to "give racism a face."[6] Remarkably, two of the most compelling characters are Lily and Floyd Cox, modeled on the figures of Carolyn Bryant, the white woman with whom Till allegedly flirted, and her husband, Floyd Cox. Recreating family and community histories, Campbell is intrigued by the ways in which dysfunctional family life contributes to racist violence. And although it is clear that Campbell researched her novel, she does not attempt, strictly speaking, to produce a historical novel. Rather, she reconfigures the drama of Emmett Till in a narrative that is fundamentally psychological, and aims to provide the hope of redemption for a town and community that have been historically wounded.

In her second novel, *Singing in the Comeback Choir* (1998), Campbell shifts the landscape from rural Mississippi and southside Chicago to Los Angeles and Philadelphia. An executive producer of a successful West Coast talk show, Maxine McCoy, pregnant and dealing with the infidelity of her remorseful husband, is summoned back to Philadelphia, the home of her geriatric grandmother, former blues diva Lindy Walker, who—like her house and neighborhood—is depressed and in a state of decline. Telling the story from multiple perspectives and in multiple voices, Campbell creates in her second novel a narrative inspired by her own grandmother and the legendary Alberta Hunter. A tale of redemption for the individual and for the community—though not without spiritual struggle—the lesson of this narrative, as Campbell puts it, is that "anyone who is willing to work hard deserves a second chance....A neighborhood can come back, a marriage can come back, an old lady who smokes and drinks, whose voice is worn out and rusty, can come back."[7]

If Campbell's first novel focuses on both the inter-racial and intra-racial relations confronting the communities and generations impacted by the tragic events in Money, Mississippi, her second novel foregrounds the black family and black community, although it engages somewhat marginally events affecting homeless Puerto Rican children, as well as the professional and personal anxieties animating the glitzy, but flawed and hypocritical, world of Hollywood talk show hosts, producers, and sponsors. Campbell's third novel, *Brothers and Sisters* (1994), takes place against the backdrop of the post–Los Angeles riots following the brutal police beating of Rodney King, and is perhaps, in some respects, her most ambitious work.

In this novel, Campbell examines the cross-cultural friendship between two women—Esther Jackson, a successful, but still aspiring, mid-level, Los Angeles bank manager, and her white friend and bank lender, Mallory Post. Representing the changing demographics of Los Angeles, the corporate world—and surrounding communities—expand to include blacks, whites, Latinos, and Asians as they vie for a piece of the pie and an ascendant rung on the corporate ladder, all the while negotiating issues of personal and racial (or ethnic) loyalty, class difference, racism, affirmative action, failed relationships, glass ceilings, and sexual harassment. Again, the author allows her characters to speak from their own perspectives and in their own voices, while at the same time creating complex, diverse, and multifaceted social realities. Campbell's characters struggle with personal, social, and political issues that challenge their principles, professional positions, and personal relationships. Nevertheless, through soulful self-examination and with the help of friends, Campbell's characters emerge as survivors, and not always worse for the wear.

Campbell's fourth novel, *What You Owe Me* (2001), set in post–World War II Los Angeles, focuses on the friendship and partnership between Hosanna Clarke, a black migrant from Texas and survivor of family violation and racial dispossession, and Gilda Rosenstein, a Polish Jewish immigrant and Holocaust survivor. These women meet as hotel cleaning women in the 1940s, and become friends and partners in building a fledging but promising business in women's cosmetics. When Gilda betrays the trust of her friend and partner, absconding with their asset funds, Hosanna struggles to achieve her dream of establishing a small cosmetics company, while her erstwhile partner and confidante founds a major conglomerate, becoming a mogul in the world of women's cosmetics. Hosanna's betrayal and failed dream motivates her daughter Matriece's mission. Talented and motivated by a dead mother's injunction, from the other side, to "make things right," Matriece makes a name for herself in the cosmetics industry, becoming president of Brown Sugar, a black women's makeup line, in a deliberate and calculated scheme to exact maternal retributive justice. In this complex and kaleidoscopic novel, narrated from multiple and varied perspectives, Campbell takes up the issues of cross-racial and inter-generational dues, debts, reparations, dispossessions, legacies, and inheritances, symbolized by the spectral presences that haunt the text and the lives of characters who often possess material wealth and class privilege, but nevertheless experience spiritual desuetude, moral bankruptcy, and emotional despondency. In reaching across racial, geographical, and generational divides, these characters seek revenge, justice, reconciliation, healing, and forgiveness from mothers, fathers, children, friends, and lovers. In the end, they must learn that while debts are owed to the past, these claims cannot be allowed to foreclose the future. Healing the wounds of the past requires that debts be collected and dues paid, but sometimes that they be simply forgiven. As Hosanna, the spectral mother, finally acknowledges, "past due never lasts forever."[8]

Campbell's last published novel is *72-Hour Hold* (2005), the title referring to what the author describes as "the amount of time that a psychiatric facility can hold a mentally ill person against his or her will if he or she meets the criteria of a danger to self or danger to others or [is] gravely disabled."[9] In this remarkable novel, the author, inspired by her own experiences with a family loved one, breaks the silence regarding mental illness in the black community, launching the reader on a terrifying journey into the world of schizophrenia and bipolar disorder that the narrator compares to slavery in the sense that the individual loses independence, free will, and self-control. Like slavery, mental illness gives rise to a regime of physical and emotional violence—including alcoholism, (illegal) drug addiction, and oftentimes encounters with the penal system. In this novel of family suffering and redemption, a successful, divorced, educated, entrepreneurial, middle-class mother, Keri Whitmore, struggles to cope with the overwhelming and seemingly insurmountable difficulties facing her mentally ill daughter, Trina, along with the threat posed to her own mental sanity by the obstructions inherent in a seemingly impenetrable and resistant psychiatric system. Tellingly, this is a novel about the need for healing in a world that promises neither a rose garden, nor an "impenetrable fortress." The victory after what the narrator calls "the devastation" is temporary at best and, like Harriet Tubman, the traveler must always be prepared for the contingencies of the journey. Perhaps it is in her final work—and in its final moment—that Campbell reaches back to the nineteenth century in order to provide the contemporary traveler with something of a map and metaphor for modern life in twenty-first century America:

> There was always another swamp to cross. Passengers are both lost and found. Ol' Harriet learned that the hard way, the first time, she retraced her path, erased her scent, outwitted the dogs, and followed the only star that lit the way, only to discover that when she got where she was going, new hounds were waiting. But there was that cool space on the bank of the murky water where she lay on fragrant moss, undisturbed for hours, and there was no barking, no sound of twigs snapping. A breather.[10]

And so, finally, what Bebe More Campbell leaves us with is neither a safe place nor a perilous place in this world, but rather a space of liminality, betwixt and between, in which we can learn to take "a breather"—and perhaps a moment in which to read a novel that can provide us with "equipment for living."

Coda

Where Toni Morrison Meets Josephine Baker

How sad, I thought... that these two women never met.
—Sherley Anne Williams, "Author's Note" to *Dessa Rose*

It has been my intention in the foregoing pages to stage an imaginary introduction—across time and geography—between two rather extraordinary black women, Toni Morrison and Josephine Baker. What, one might ask, would these two women have in common, beyond the fact that both became successful in their own mediums and milieus? It seems to me that in perhaps her most remarkable character, Sula, Morrison created a figure who could well have been modeled on the equally remarkable, but real-life, figure of Josephine Baker. And Morrison's Sula certainly could be claimed by Baker as sister, a twin even. For when each discovers that she is "neither white nor male, and that all freedom and triumph was forbidden to [her]," both "set about creating something else to be."[1] Both choose experimental lives outside of their communities. Each in her way was regarded as a kind of outlaw figure, and, as Morrison puts it, "disallowed in the community because of her imagination or activity or status... [each became] a kind of anarchic figure."[2] And if Sula was "an artist without form," Baker became an artist whose own body became her medium of expression.[3] Now what links these two women, one fictional and the other a historical figure, is not only that the latter lives out the fictive possibilities of the former, but that both are self-invented women—*sui generis*, unique and original. Both function in their environments as free-floating signifiers—embodying the projections, fantasies, and fears of others. And even when they are cast as pariahs—Sula in the Bottom and Baker in a more global arena—such figures possess, as Morrison reflects, something in their presence against which others measure themselves, something that allows others to reimagine themselves. And so it is, here in these pages, between these covers, in my critical imaginary, I seek to create a fictive space in which to stage a fanciful encounter between writer and performer, the one who speaks in tongues and the other who dances diaspora.

NOTES

Introduction

1. Jacques Derrida, for instance, challenges what he regards as the prevailing Western tradition of "logocentrism" privileging speech, offering in its stead what he proposes as a "grammatology" privileging writing and textuality. See Jacques Derrida, *Of Grammatology*, trans. Gayatri Chakravorty Spivak (Baltimore, MD: John Hopkins University Press, 1998).

2. Mary Helen Washington, "I Love the Way Janie Crawford Left Her Husbands: Zora Neale Hurston's Emergent Hero," in *Invented Lives: Narratives of Black Women, 1860–1960* (New York: Doubleday, 1987), 237–254; and Carla Kaplan, "The Erotics of Talk: 'That Oldest Human Longing' in *Their Eyes Were Watching God*," *American Literature* 67, no. 1 (1995): 115–142 (later reprinted as "'That Oldest Human Longing': The Erotics of Talk in *Their Eyes Were Watching God*," in *The Erotics of Talk: Women's Writing and Feminist Paradigms* [New York: Oxford University Press, 1996], 93–122).

3. On the trope of the "talking book," see Olaudah Equiano, *The Interesting Narrative of the Life of Olaudah Equiano, or Gustavus Vassa, the African, Written by Himself* (London, 1789); on the tropes of the "speakerly text," the "talking text," and "signifyin'," see Henry Louis Gates, Jr., *The Signifying Monkey: A Theory of African-American Literary Criticism* (New York: Oxford University Press, 1988). On other tropes, see Robert B. Stepto, *From Behind the Veil: A Study of Afro-American Narrative* (Urbana: University of Illinois Press, 1979); Houston A. Baker, Jr., *Blues, Ideology, and Afro-American Literature: A Vernacular Theory* (Chicago: University of Chicago Press, 1984); Geneva Smitherman, *Talkin and Testifyin: The Language of Black America* (Detroit, MI: Wayne State University Press, 1986); bell hooks, *Talking Back: Thinking Feminist, Thinking Black* (Boston: South End Press, 1989); Cheryl A. Wall, *Worrying the Line: Black Women Writers, Lineage, and Literary Tradition* (Chapel Hill: University of North Carolina Press, 2005); and my own essay, "Speaking in Tongues: Dialectics, Dialogics, and the Black Woman Writer's Literary Tradition" (Chapter 3 in the present volume).

4. See 1 Corinthians 14:34 ("Let your women keep silence in the churches: for it is not permitted unto them to speak; but they are commanded to be under obedience, as also saith the law") and 1 Corinthians 13:1 ("Though I speak with the tongues of men and of angels, and have not charity, I am become as sounding brass, or a tinkling cymbal"). Notably, however, Deborah was a judge and a prophetess (Judges 4:4: "And Deborah, a prophetess, the wife of Lapidoth, she judged Israel at that time") and the prophet, Joel, predicted that "the sons and 'daughters' should prophesy" (Joel 2:28: "And it shall come to pass afterward, that I will pour out my spirit upon all flesh; and your sons and your daughters shall prophesy"). Further, the daughters of Philip prophesied (Acts 21:9: "And the same man had four daughters, virgins, which did prophesy"). And even the Apostle Paul gives instructions and warnings to women

who prophesy (1Corinthians 11:5: "But every woman that prayeth or prophesieth with her head uncovered dishonoureth her head: for that is even all one as if she were shaven").

5. David Martin writes, "Pentecostalism arose as a religion mainly of the poor in the USA, and at least some of its roots lie among those who were not only poor but black." Martin further maintains that "it is clear that women are among the 'voiceless' given a new tongue in the circle of Pentecostal communication." Notably, for Martin, Pentecostalism is "a system of signs fostering spiritual communication." David Martin and Peter Mullen, eds., *Strange Gifts?: A Guide to Charismatic Renewal* (New York and Oxford: Blackwell, 1984), 234, 181.

6. See Katherine Clay Bassard, *Spiritual Interrogations: Culture, Gender, and Community in Early African American Women's Writing* (Princeton, NJ: Princeton University Press, 1999), 3–4.

7. Sue E. Houchins, "Introduction," in *Spiritual Narratives*, The Schomburg Library of Black Women Writers Series, gen. ed. Henry Louis Gates, Jr. (New York: Oxford University Press, 1988), xxx.

8. Stepto, *From Behind the Veil*.

9. Carla L. Peterson, *"Doers of the Word": African-American Women Speakers and Writers in the North (1830–1880)* (New York: Oxford University Press, 1995. Paperback, New Brunswick, NJ: Rutgers University Press, 1998).

10. See David Martin and Peter Mullen, eds., *Strange Gifts?: A Guide to Charismatic Renewal*.

11. See William J. Samarin, *Tongues of Men and Angels: The Religious Language of Pentecostalism* (New York: The Macmillan Company, 1972). Also see John P. Kildahl, who writes, in *The Psychology of Speaking in Tongues* (New York: Harper & Row, 1972), 18–19: "The Pentecostal church in the United States may be said to have begun with Charles Parham a Methodist minister who in 1900 started a Bible school in Topeka, Kansas.…Five years later he opened a second school in Houston, Texas. One of his students at this institution was W. J. Seymour, a Negro minister.…Seymour began preaching on the Holy Spirit, particularly the gift of tongues.…In 1906 he moved to an old…building at 312 Azusa Street…which became the center of Pentecostalism. The revival meeting on Azusa Street in Los Angeles lasted for three years and was attended by persons from all over the world. When they returned home they found similar Pentecostal groups there.… The background of the Pentecostal churches was the Holiness movement which began in the United States after the Civil War.… The Pentecostal doctrine is fundamentalist with the added belief that 'the *full* New Testament baptism in the Spirit was made manifest by the *glossolalia*, and that it was the will of God to pour out His Spirit in this manner upon all flesh.'" (Kildhal quotes Carl Brumback, *What Meaneth This?* [Springfield, MO: Gospel Publishing House, 1947], 92.)

12. Notably Mother Tate's followers initially regarded her tongue-speaking as an act of insanity, but "her Pentecostalism prevailed." See Jesse Carney Smith, *Notable Black American Women, Book II* (Detroit, MI: Gale Research, 1996).

13. Cheryl Townsend Gilkes, "'Together and in Harness': Women's Traditions in the Sanctified Church," in *Black Women in America: Social Science Perspectives*, ed. Elizabeth Mudimbe, Micheline Malson, and Jean O'Barr (Chicago: University of Chicago Press, 1990), 226.

14. 1 Corinthians 14:22 ("Wherefore tongues are for a sign, not to them that believe, but to them that believe not").

15. John S. Pobee, "Oral Theology and Christian Oral Tradition: Challenge to Our Traditional Archival Concept," *Mission Studies* 6 (1989): 89.

16. Furthermore, in noting the energy of theological activity among African women, John Parratt observes, "It is also true that the theology of the majority of African women is not written down but oral.…It is communal theology and not individual. Professional theologians feel frustrated with this kind of theology because they cannot engage with it as done in the Western theologies. However, it is theology all the same, and Africa, which is basically an oral society, has to take oral theology seriously." See John Parratt, *Introduction to Third World Theologies* (Cambridge, MA: Harvard University Press, 2004), 153. Also see Michael A. Rynkiewich, *Cultures and Languages of Papua New Guinea: The Story of the Origins, Migrations and Settlement of Melanesian Peoples, Languages, and Cultures* (Goroka, Eastern Highlands Province, Papua New Guinea: Melanesian Institute, 2004), 21.

17. Toni Morrison, "Rootedness: The Ancestor as Foundation," in *Black Women Writers (1950–1980): A Critical Evaluation,* ed. Mari Evans (Garden City, NY: Anchor Press, 1984), 340.

18. Charles W. Conn, "Glossolalia and the Scriptures," in *The Glossolalia Phenomenon,* ed. Wade H. Horton (Cleveland, TN: Pathway Press, 1966), 23.

19. Watson E. Mills, *A Theological/Exegetical Approach to Glossolalia* (Lanham, MD: University Press of America, 1985), 19–23, as well as his *Understanding Speaking in Tongues* (Grand Rapids, MI: Williams B. Eerdmans Publishing, 1972), in which he writes that "the earliest recorded instance of glossolalia in this century [in the United States] was in Topeka, Kansas, in 1901 when the 'baptism of the Spirit' fell upon Miss Agnes N. Ozman, a student at [Charles Parham's] Bethel Bible College" (14). See also C. G. Williams, "Speaking in Tongues," in David Martin and Peter Mullen, eds., *Strange Gifts?: A Guide to Charismatic Renewal,* 72–83.

20. Harryette Romell Mullen, "African Signs and Spirit Writing," *Callaloo* 19, no. 3 (1996): 672. Also see Robert Farris Thompson, *Flash of the Spirit: African and Afro-American Art and Philosophy* (New York: Random House, 1984), xvii *passim.*

21. Morrison, "Rootedness," 341.

22. Jacques Derrida, *The Ear of the Other: Otobiography, Transference, Translation,* trans. Peggy Kamuf, ed. Christine Macdonald (Lincoln: University of Nebraska Press, 1985), 49–50. Notably, for Derrida, the smaller the ear, the keener its powers of perception.

23. Derrida, *The Ear of the Other,* 51, emphasis added.

24. Roland Barthes, *The Responsibility of Forms: Critical Essays on Music, Art, and Representation,* trans. Richard Howard (New York: Hill and Wang, 1985), 245–256 *passim.*

25. I quote from Elzbieta Sklodowska, "Spanish American Testimonial Novel: Some Afterthoughts," in *The Real Thing: Testimonial Discourse and Latin America,* ed. George M. Gugelberger (Durham, NC: Duke University Press, 1996), 87. Sklodowska is summarizing concepts explored by Jean-François Lyotard, *The Differend: Phrases in Dispute* (Minneapolis: University of Minnesota Press, 1988), 9–13.

26. Arguably, Hurston seeks here to reclaim the feminine, a name attached to Phoebus Apollo's twin sister Artemis as well as to his grandmother.

27. Romans 16:1 ("I commend unto you Phebe our sister, which is a servant of the church which is at Cenchrea"). Biblical scholars speculate that Phebe, most likely a deacon, received a commendation from St. Paul, and became the bearer of his epistle to the church of Cenchrea. See John Gill's discussion of Romans 16 in his *Exposition of the Old and New Testament* (1746–1763), available online: http://www.sacred-texts.com/bib/cmt/gill/rom016.htm.

28. Zora Neale Hurston, *Their Eyes Were Watching God* (1937; Urbana: University of Illinois Press, 1978), 9–10, emphasis added. Subsequent references will appear within parentheses in the text. Significantly, Pheoby appears only in the opening and closing chapters framing Hurston's novel, thus providing an important perspective from which to read the text.

29. Nelle Morton, *The Journey Is Home* (Boston: Beacon Press, 1985), 205.

30. Henry Louis Gates, Jr., *The Signifying Monkey,* 208–209.

31. Doubtlessly, some, perhaps many, will take issue with this reading of Pheoby's position, but I advance a hypothetical reading here to make a critical point, namely that the roles of listener and speaker are singularly intertwined and never mutually exclusive. On "horizon of expectation," see Hans Robert Jauss's pioneering work on reception theory, *Toward an Aesthetic of Reception,* ed. Timothy Bahti (Minneapolis: University of Minnesota Press, 1982).

32. Mills, *Understanding Speaking in Tongues,* 30–32; George Barton Cutten, *Speaking with Tongues* (New Haven, CT: Yale University Press, 1927), *passim.*

33. There exists not only a historical debate among sixteenth-century theologian and Protestant Reformer John Calvin, eighteenth-century cleric and theologian John Wesley, and others on the interpretation of Pentecost as a miracle of *speaking* versus a miracle of *hearing,* but also a contemporary debate among scholars on the correct interpretation of Pentecost.

34. Notably, the term *hermeneia,* found in 1 Corinthians 12:10 and 14:26, is a "word meaning to explain or interpret and is used for explaining words of different languages... the word includes the name Hermes who in Greek mythology was the son of Jupiter and Maia. Hermes is the Greek name of the pagan god, Mercury, who was regarded as the messenger and interpreter

of the gods. Thus, the translator was God's Hermes, who interpreted the message supernaturally given through the gift of tongues." See Ronald E. Baxter, *The Charismatic Gift of Tongues* (Grand Rapids, MI: Kregel Publications, 1981), 106.

35. See H. Newton Malony and A. Adams Lovekin, *Glossolalia: Behavioral Science Perspectives on Speaking in Tongues* (New York and Oxford: Oxford University Press, 1985), 24–25.

36. The reader will certainly make a connection here between *ermeneglossia* and reception theory.

37. Acts 1:8, emphasis added.

38. Kelly Oliver, *Witnessing: Beyond Recognition* (Minneapolis and London: University of Minnesota Press, 2001), 86.

39. Here, I refer to Sethe's trial and Eulalia Bon's affidavits to her attorney in Morrison's and Faulkner's respective novels.

40. Marianne Hirsch, "The Generation of Postmemory," *Poetics Today* 29, no. 1 (2008): 103–128. Hirsh writes, "The 'post' in 'postmemory' signals more than a temporal delay and more than a location in an aftermath.... I see it, rather, as a structure of inter- and trans-generational transmission of traumatic knowledge and experience. It is a consequence of traumatic recall but (unlike posttraumatic stress disorder) at a generational remove" (106). And although Hirsch specifies postmemory as a condition that pertains specifically to second-generation writers and visual artists of survivors of massive traumatic events, I use this term more broadly to apply to trans-generational descendants.

41. See Peter Brooks, *Reading for the Plot: Design and Intention in Narrative* (Cambridge, MA: Harvard University Press, 1984), 25.

42. See Sigmund Freud, "Remembering, Repeating and Working-Through," in *The Standard Edition of the Works of Sigmund Freud*, ed. James Strachey, vol. 12 (London: Hogarth Press, 1975), 146–157.

43. The reader will note here that I employ terms introduced by Robert Stepto in his *From Behind the Veil*.

44. Oliver, 71; Oliver further maintains, "If...'I' can say 'I' only in *response* to an address from another, or as an addressee, it is also true that 'I' can say 'I' only by *supposing* an addressee, the one to whom I address myself. Without an addressee, without a witness, I cannot exist" (88).

45. Oliver, 15

46. Dori Laub, "An Event Without a Witness: Truth, Testimony and Survival," in *Testimony: Crises of Witnessing in Literature, Psychoanalysis, and History*, by Shoshana Felman and Dori Laub (New York: Routledge, 1992), 75–76.

47. Laub, "Bearing Witness or the Vicissitudes of Listening," in Felman and Laub, 63.

48. Laub, "Bearing Witness," 69.

49. Laub, "An Event Without a Witness," 85, emphasis in the original.

50. Laub, "An Event Without a Witness," 85.

51. Laub, "Bearing Witness," 58.

52. Brooks, 218, 221.

53. Thomas F. DeFrantz, "The Black Beat Made Visible: Hip Hop Dance and Body Power," in *Of the Presence of the Body: Essays on Dance and Performance Theory*, ed. André Lepecki (Middletown, CT: Wesleyan University Press, 2004), 66. Notably, DeFrantz draws on Eve Kosofsky Sedgwick's notion that performative utterances "do not merely describe, but actually perform the actions they name: 'J'accuse'; 'Be it resolved...'; ...'I apologize'; 'I dare you.'" See Eve Kosofsky Sedgwick, *Tendencies* (Durham, NC: Duke University Press, 1993).

54. DeFrantz, 66–67, emphasis in original.

55. DeFrantz, 66.

56. Zora Neale Hurston, "Characteristics of Negro Expression," in *Negro: An Anthology*, collected and ed. Nancy Cunard (1934), ed. and abridged Hugh Ford (New York: Continuum/F. Ungar, 1970), 26.

57. Oliver, 18; Hurston, "Characteristics of Negro Expression," 24–31.

58. Readers will recognize this statement as an invocation of "Perfect Thunder, Perfect Mind" from the *Nag Hammadi*, as quoted by Toni Morrison in the epigraph to her sixth novel, *Jazz*.

59. See Conn, 21-65; see also Wesley L. Duewel, *The Holy Spirit and Tongues* (Winona Lake, IN: Light and Life Press, 1974; revised 1983).
60. 1 Corinthians 12:10. Also see Kildahl.
61. Conn, 58–59.

Chapter 1

1. I refer specifically to the English tradition, since eighteenth-century French women writers such as Marie-Jeanne Riccoboni (1714–1792) and Françoise de Graffigny (1695–1758) also utilized the epistolary form.
2. Ray Anello and Pamela Abramson, "Characters in Search of a Book," *Newsweek* (June 21, 1982): 67.
3. Janet Todd, *Women's Friendship in Literature* (New York: Columbia University Press, 1980), 1.
4. Cherríe Moraga and Gloria Anzaldúa, eds., *This Bridge Called My Back: Writings by Radical Women of Color* (Watertown, MA: Persephone Press, 1981).
5. Of the ninety letters that constitute the novel, well over half are from Celie to God, fourteen from Celie to Nettie, and twenty-one from Nettie to Celie.
6. In the United States, the sentimental novels, published from the 1820s to the 1870s, became national bestsellers. Drawing on the eighteenth-century novel of sensibility, these works prescribe the conventional social roles and responsibilities of women, emphasizing the virtues of purity, piety, and submission to father, husband, and God as prerequisites for spiritual salvation and secular success. Marriage, motherhood, wealth, social status, and control over the domestic sphere became the rewards for obedience and chastity; rebellion or submission to seduction, on the other hand, frequently led to the expiration of the unfortunate heroine, or at best, penitent acquiescence to the scheme of patriarchy. See Nina Baym's *Women's Fiction: A Guide to Novels by and about Women in America, 1820–1870* (Ithaca, NY: Cornell University Press, 1978). See also Barbara Welter, *Dimity Convictions: The American Woman in the Nineteenth Century* (Athens: Ohio University Press, 1976).
7. Alice Walker, *The Color Purple* (New York: Harcourt Brace Jovanovich, 1982), 3. Subsequent references will appear within parentheses in the text.
8. Walker, *The Third Life of Grange Copeland* (New York: Harcourt Brace Jovanovich, 1970).
9. Walker, "In the Closet of the Soul: A Letter to an African-American Friend," *Ms. Magazine* (November 1986): 32–35.
10. See Zora Neale Hurston, *Mules and Men*, rev. ed. (Bloomington: Indiana University Press, 1978), 205.
11. As Walker indicates, men, too, are subjected to scarification in some African societies, although Walker problematizes the issue as it affects the women. See Alice Walker, *Possessing the Secret of Joy* (New York: Harcourt Brace Jovanovich, 1992) for a later novelistic treatment of this subject. Clitoridectomy, however, is perhaps a more appropriate example of female mutilation here, since according to *The Hosken Report* (Lexington, MA: Women's International Network News, 1982), the genital and sexual mutilation of females "violates the human right to health of the victims [and] represents a violation of the very essence and spirit of femaleness by drastically altering and curtailing the natural female potential, thus ensuring submission to male exploitation and demands."

Some years ago, I delivered an earlier version of this paper before a gathering at the University of Michigan, which included a group of black social scientists who attacked Walker's perspective (and presumably my own) as culturally relativistic. According to their position, clitoridectomy and scarification are practices that can only be understood within the context of values and beliefs of a specific culture. My own position is that while these practices often constitute rites in female initiation ceremonies, and may be important in the preservation of local customs and values, they are nevertheless medically unsafe and oppressive to women. Although charges of ethnocentrism have been leveled against those who challenge the humanness of such practice, such critics fail to acknowledge objections raised by African women themselves who speak out against the mutilation of women.

Awa Thiam, in *La Parole aux Négresses* (Paris: Gonthier, Éditions Donoe, 1978, quoted in *The Hoskens Report*) condemns "the universal exploitation and degradation of women, who are...mutilated...for no other reason than they are female." Speaking at a seminar sponsored by the World Health Organization in 1979, Raqiya Haji Dualeh also censured the practice: "Women are victims of outdated customs...female circumcision may be considered as another form of female sexual oppression" (quoted in *The Hoskens Report*). The former Director of Public Health in Egypt, Nawal El Saadawi, contends that "girls are...exposed to a whole series of misfortunes as a result of outdated notions and values related to virginity, which still remains the fundamental criterion of a girl's honour" in a number of countries. Describing her experiences as a rural physician who was frequently called upon to treat complications resulting from female circumcision, Saadawi cites not only the severe hemorrhaging that was a common occurrence, sometimes leading to loss of life, but also "the lifelong psychological shock of this cruel procedure [which leaves] its imprint on the personality of the child and [accompanies] her into adolescence, youth, and maturity" (*The Hidden Face of Eve* [Boston: Beacon Press, 1982]). While tradition and customs are important in the preservation of culture (and, indeed, this seems to be Walker's point), they are not sacrosanct. And although we acknowledge that Western civilization has institutionalized traditions of class, racial, and gender oppression, as feminist scholars we must recognize that such cultural practices, whether in the West or the Third World, must give way to change in order to preserve those values that ensure human dignity.

12. As Carol Gilligan suggests in her pioneering work, *In Another Voice* (Cambridge, MA: Harvard University Press, 1982), current social science theory frequently confirms the literary perception of women writers who write about women's experiences. Walker's triadic paradigm is also supported, for example, in the object-relations theory of Nancy Chodorow, who contends in *The Reproduction of Mothering: Psychoanalysis and the Sociology of Gender* (Berkeley: University of California Press, 1978) that the pre-Oedipal maternal attachment is primary for women and extends to include a secondary connection with the father during the Oedipal phase. What results, according to Chodorow, is a pre-latent Oedipal triangle, which is ultimately reproduced in women's desire to become mothers—that is, to bear and rear children. In her essay "[E]merging Identities: The Dynamics of Female Friendship in Contemporary Fiction by Women" (*Signs: Journal of Women in Culture and Society* 6, no. 3 [Spring 1981]: 413–435), Elizabeth Abel extends Chodorow's thesis to account for the images of women's friendships in the literature of women writers. Women's friendships, like mothering, argues Abel, reconstitute the mother-daughter pre-Oedipal attachments.

13. Ephesians 5:22 ("Wives, submit yourselves unto your own husbands, as unto the Lord").

Chapter 2

1. Sherley Anne Williams's subsequent novel, *Dessa Rose* (New York: William Morrow, 1986), an elaboration of "Meditations on History" (in *Midnight Birds: Stories by Contemporary Black Women Writers*, ed. Mary Helen Washington [Garden City, NY: Anchor Books/ Doubleday, 1980]: 200–248), was published after this essay was substantially completed. I treat the novel in two other essays in this volume, Chapter 3 ("Speaking in Tongues") and Chapter 5 ("The Stories of [O] Dessa"). References to "Meditations on History" are to the edition published in Washington's *Midnight Birds* and will appear within parentheses in the text.

2. Clearly, I have drawn on modern critical revisionist strategies. But revisionism, like metaphor, is a term that subsumes much—in this instance, a variety of literary critical practices. While acknowledging my debt to Harold Bloom's (*The Anxiety of Influence: A Theory of Poetry* [New York: Oxford University Press, 1973]) notions of *misprision* and intertextuality, I prefer to describe my own methods more in terms of *re*reading than *mis*reading and *contra*textuality rather *inter*textuality. His definition of revisionism notwithstanding, Bloom's strategies appear to emphasize the generative or, perhaps more accurately, engendering aspects of the

text, as opposed to the corrective purposes of writing (and reading). My contratextual reading of Williams's novella is designed to demonstrate her deconstruction of the racist and sexist misreadings of an anterior text (regardless of intentionality) in order to reassert a prior (oral and biographical) text. As a corrective gesture, it cuts back through the detritus concealing the contours of the original in order to reclaim the primal experience from the deformation of race and gender-inflected historical-fictional misrepresentation—or reconstruction—of the original experience. If the relationship between Styron and Turner can be described as creative misreading (*misprision*), I would describe that between Williams and Styron as one of corrective rereading. I am indebted to a conversation with my colleague Keneth Kinnamon for a clearer formulation of this strategy.

3. William Styron, "Author's Note," in *The Confessions of Nat Turner* (New York: Random House, 1967), ix, emphasis added.
4. Henry Louis Gates, Jr., *Black Literature and Literary Theory* (New York and London: Methuen, 1984), 294–296.
5. Styron, "Author's Note," ix, emphasis added.
6. See John Henrik Clarke, ed., *William Styron's Nat Turner: Ten Writers Respond* (Boston: Beacon Press, 1968).
7. In "Back with the Wind: Mr. Styron and the Reverend Turner" (in Clarke), Mike Thelwell writes:

    Is it possible...for a white southern gentleman to tune in on the impulses, belief, emotions, and thought-patterns of a black slave? This miracle of empathy entails an imaginative leap not only into history, but across cultures. It necessitates that writer [*sic*] divorcing himself from that vast mythic tradition about slavery, black people, and history which is so integral a part of his background. Then he has to devise a literary idiom through which to record, since the gentleman and the slave lack common language or experience. (80)

8. In her novel *Dessa Rose*, treated in Chapter 5 of this volume, Williams assigns a name, Nehemiah Adams, to this unnamed fictional character.
9. Angela Davis, "Reflections on the Black Woman's Role in the Community of Slaves," *The Black Scholar* (December 1971): 10, 13–15.
10. See Stanley Elkins, *Slavery: A Problem in American Institutional and Intellectual Life* (Chicago: University of Chicago Press, 1959). In "This Quiet Dust," an essay included in John B. Duff and Peter M. Mitchell's *The Nat Turner Rebellion: The Historical Event and the Modern Controversy* (New York: Harper and Row, 1971), Styron writes:

    One of the most striking aspects of the institution [of slavery] is the fact that in 250 years of its existence in America, it was singularly free of organized uprising, plots, and rebellions. (It is curious that as recently as the late 1940's, scholarly insights were lagging, and I could only have suspected then what has since been made convincing by such historians as...Stanley Elkins: that American Negro slavery, unique in its psychological oppressiveness—the worst the world has ever known—was simply so despotic and emasculating as to render organized revolt next to impossible. (125–127)

11. See Herbert Aptheker, *American Negro Slave Revolts*, 1943 (New York: International Publishers, 1969), 11. Notably, Aptheker contends that Styron's work contains substantial historical distortions: see Aptheker, "A Note on the History," in Duff and Mitchell, 191–195.
12. See note 2 above.
13. If Styron assumes the voice of a black slave speaking as Nat Turner himself in the first person, Williams's narrator presumes to speak for Dessa. (What is implicit in Styron—his appropriation of Turner's voice—is explicit in Williams's characterization.) Moreover, while Styron's character speaks standard, formal English in a style that critic Richard Gilman ("Nat Turner Revisited," in Duff and Mitchell, 228–237) describes as "novelistic," Williams's heroine preserves the idiom of the black vernacular. See Gates, 286–296.
14. See, for example, John Blassingame, *The Slave Community* (New York: Oxford University Press, 1972), and Lawrence W. Levine, *Black Culture and Black Consciousness: Afro-American Thought from Slavery to Freedom* (New York: Oxford University Press, 1977).

15. Commenting on the relationship between literary and historical discourse in his review of Styron's *Confessions*, Thelwell writes: "Because the book is both 'history' and a novel the public mind seems to have invested it with qualities it does not necessarily possess. The events and situations are assumed to be accurate because by being 'historical' they must of necessity be 'true.' And as the 'facts' of history are true, so, in a different sense, are the insights (read 'symbolic truths') of the novel" (79).

16. Barbara Johnson, *The Critical Difference: Essays in the Contemporary Rhetoric of Reading* (Baltimore, MD: Johns Hopkins University Press, 1980), 126.

17. Styron, "This Quiet Dust," 126–127.

18. Thomas R. Gray, "To the Public," in *The Confessions of Nat Turner* [Baltimore, MD: Lucas & Deaver, 1831], reprinted in the Appendix to Clarke, 96.

19. Gray, 97.

20. Styron, "This Quiet Dust," 126.

21. Aptheker and Styron, "Truth and Nat Turner: An Exchange," in Duff and Mitchell, 198 (originally published in *The Nation* 22 [April 1968]: 543–547).

22. Styron, "Truth and Nat Turner," 198–199.

23. Eugene D. Genovese, "The Nat Turner Case," in Duff and Mitchell, 205 (originally published in *The New York Review of Books* [September 12, 1968]: 34–37).

24. Genovese, 205.

25. Quoted in Styron, "Truth and Nat Turner," in Duff and Mitchell, 199.

26. Thelwell, 91.

27. See Ralph Ellison, William Styron, Robert Penn Warren, and C. Vann Woodward, "The Uses of History in Fiction," *Southern Literary Journal* 1, no. 2 (Spring 1969): 57–90. Ellison's position on the relation of history and literature points to some of the problems confronting the novelists:

    I'm all for the autonomy of fiction; that's why I say that novelists should leave history alone. But I would also remind us that the work of fiction finally comes alive through a collaboration between the reader and the writer.... If you move far enough into the historical past, you don't have that problem.... [When writing historical fiction] one, without hedging his bets, has to be aware that he does operate within an area dense with prior assumptions. (74, 73)

28. Quoted from Angela Davis, "Reflections on the Black Woman's Role in the Community of Slaves," in Williams, "Meditations on History," 200 (emphasis in original).

29. Davis, 3.

30. Davis, 11. Davis bases her account on an event originally cited in Aptheker, *American Negro Slave Revolts*, 287–288.

31. Since the original publication of this essay, Mary Kemp Davis has identified the "historical prototype" of the unnamed female slave rebel to whom Williams refers in her epigraph to "Meditations on History." Davis speculates that Williams was unfamiliar with the historical figure who remained unnamed in her identified source (Angela Davis), and based on a reference (John Winston Coleman, Jr., *Slavery Times in Kentucky* [Chapel Hill: University of North Carolina Press, 1940]) in Herbert Aptheker's *American Negro Slave Revolts* (Angela Davis's source), Mary Kemp Davis identifies this figure as "Dinah." See Mary Kemp Davis, "Everybody Knows Her Name: The Recovery of the Past in Sherley Anne Williams's *Dessa Rose*," *Callaloo* 40, no. 1 (1989): 544–558.

32. See Robert B. Stepto, *From Behind The Veil: A Study of Afro-American Narrative* (Urbana: University of Illinois Press, 1979), for a treatment of the significance of prefatory texts in black narrative writing.

33. Sherley Anne Williams, *Give Birth to Brightness: A Thematic Study in Neo-Black Literature* (New York: Dial Press, 1972), 35–36.

34. Critics Robert Stepto and Henry Louis Gates, Jr., demonstrate the significance of literacy and formal discourse in gaining freedom and recognition for the slave. For a different perspective,

somewhat closer to my own in its emphasis on "the voice of the unwritten self," see Houston
A. Baker's "Autobiographical Acts: The Voice of the Southern Slave," in *The Journey Back*
(Chicago: University of Chicago Press, 1980), 27–52.
35. Alex Haley, *Roots* (Garden City, NY: Doubleday, 1976).
36. This bit of riffing by Williams on the practice of conjuring (colloquially described as "root
work" in black vernacular discourse) was suggested as a result of my correspondence with
Houston Baker.
37. Gabriel Prosser, along with Jack Bowler, planned a slave revolt in Henrico County, Virginia.
On August 30, 1800, over 1,000 slaves met "armed with clubs, homemade bayonets, and a few
guns." Their attack on the city was thwarted, however, by a severe storm. Moreover, two slaves
informed their master of the plot and Governor Monroe quickly mobilized the state militia. As
a consequence, 35 blacks were hanged, 4 escaped, and 1 committed suicide. Prosser himself was
executed on October 7, 1800. Denmark Vesey was a free black carpenter (having purchased
his own freedom in 1800) who lived in Charleston, South Carolina. Along with Peter Poyas,
Mingo Harth, and others, Vesey made extensive preparations to revolt. Over a period of many
months, slaves were recruited by appointed leaders and arms were stored, including "two hundred and fifty pike heads and bayonets and over three hundred daggers." Vesey had even written
to Santo Domingo for assistance. The revolt was planned to take place on the second Sunday in
July 1822, but was moved forward one month because of betrayal. Because many of his followers
were miles outside Charleston, however, Vesey was unable to communicate his change of plans.
Ultimately, 139 blacks were arrested, and 49 sentenced to die. Thirty-seven of those condemned
were hanged and the others were pardoned. Reportedly, estimates of numbers involved range as
high as 9,000. Cited in Aptheker, *American Negro Slave Revolts*, 219–226, 267–273.
38. Friedrich Wilhelm Nietzsche, *Thus Spoke Zarathustra: A Book for All and None*, trans. Walter
Kaufmann (New York: Penguin, 1978); Claude Lévi-Strauss, *Conversations with Claude
Lévi-Strauss*, ed. Georges Charbonnier (London: Cape, 1969), 30.
39. Erik H. Erikson, *Life History and the Historical Moment* (New York: W. W. Norton, 1975), 20. In
the contest of power relations, Michel Foucault defines "the other" as "the one over whom power
is exercised." See Hubert L. Dreyfus and Paul Rabinow, *Michel Foucault Beyond Structuralism
and Hermeneutics* (Chicago: University of Chicago Press, 1982; 2nd ed., 1983), 220.
40. Erikson, 20–21.
41. Williams, *Give Birth to Brightness*, 35.
42. Baker, *The Journey Back*, 43.
43. See Sandra M. Gilbert and Susan Gubar's discussion of this concept, based on Wolfgang
Lederer's notion of woman's tendency to "kill herself into art," in Gilbert and Gubar, *The
Madwoman in the Attic: The Woman Writer and the Nineteenth-Century Literary Imagination*,
(New Haven, CT, and London: Yale University Press, 1979), 14–15.
44. If Styron relates his protagonist's sexual ambiguities to the white slave mistress, Williams
defines Dessa's sexuality in relation to Kaine, her slave husband.
45. Mary Helen Washington, ed., "In Pursuit of Our Own History," in *Midnight Birds: Stories by
Contemporary Black Women Writers*, xiii.
46. Geneva Smitherman, *Talkin and Testifyin: The Language of Black America* (Detroit, MI: Wayne
State University Press, 1986), 73.
47. Smitherman, 108.
48. Smitherman, 109.
49. Stanley E. Fish, *Self-Consuming Artifacts* (Berkeley and Los Angeles: University of California
Press, 1974).
50. Ellison, Styron, Warren and Woodward, 68–69, emphasis in the final two sentences added.
51. Adrienne Rich, "When We Dead Awaken: Writing as Re-vision," in *On Lies, Secrets, and
Silence: Selected Prose 1966–1978* (New York: W. W. Norton, 1979), 35.
52. I am grateful to Kathleen Diffley, William Caine, Peter Thornton, and Keneth Kinnamon for their
helpful readings of earlier versions of this essay, and to Houston Baker for his detailed comments.

Chapter 3

1. Gloria Hull, Patricia Bell Scott, and Barbara Smith, eds., *All the Women Are White, All the Blacks Are Men, But Some of Us Are Brave* (Old Westbury, NY: Feminist Press, 1982). The original publication has more recently been succeeded by another volume: Stanlie Myrise James, Frances Smith Foster, and Beverly Guy-Sheftall, eds., *Still Brave: The Evolution of Black Women's Studies* (New York: The Feminist Press at CUNY, 2009).

2. Fredric Jameson, *The Political Unconscious: Narrative as a Socially Symbolic Act* (Ithaca, NY: Cornell University Press, 1981), 53.

3. The phrase "gender subtext" is used by Nancy Fraser (and attributed to Dorothy Smith) in Fraser's critique of Habermas in Nancy Fraser, "What's Critical about Critical Theory?: The Case of Habermas and Gender," in *Feminism as Critique*, ed. Seyla Benehabib and Drucilla Cornell (Minneapolis: University of Minnesota Press, 1987), 42.

4. See Barbara Smith, ed., *Home Girls: A Black Feminist Anthology* (New York: Kitchen Table: Women of Color Press, 1983), xxxii.

5. John Carlos Rowe, "To Live Outside the Law, You Must Be Honest: The Authority of the Margin in Contemporary Theory," *Cultural Critique: International Journal of Cultural Studies* 1, no. 2 (1985/1986): 67–68.

6. Mikhail Bakhtin, "Discourse in the Novel," reprinted in *The Dialogic Imagination: Four Essays by M. M. Bakhtin*, ed. Michael Holquist (Austin: University of Texas Press, 1981), 292. Bakhtin's social groups are designated according to class, religion, generation, region, and profession. The interpretative model that I propose extends and rereads Bakhtin's theory from the standpoint of race and gender, categories absent in Bakhtin's original system of social and linguistic stratification.

7. V. N. Volosinov [Mikhail Bakhtin], *Marxism and the Philosophy of Language* (New York: Seminar Press, 1973), 11, 29, 38. Originally published in Russian as *Marksizm I Filosofija Jazyka* (Leningrad, 1930). Notably, this concept of the "subjective psyche," constituted primarily as a "social entity," distinguishes the Bakhtinian notion of self from the Freudian notion of identity. See note 9 below.

8. Bakhtin, "Discourse in the Novel," 292.

9. According to Bakhtin [Volosinov], "The processes that basically define the content of the psyche occur not inside but outside the individual organism.... Moreover, the psyche "enjoys extraterritorial status ... [as] a social entity that penetrates inside the organism of the individual personal" (*Marxism and Philosophy of Language*, 25, 39). Explicating Caryl Emerson's position on Bakhtin, Gary Saul Morson argues that selfhood "derives from an internalization of the voices a person has heard, and each of these voices is saturated with social and ideological values." "Thought itself," he writes, "is but 'inner speech,' and inner speech is outer speech that we have learned to 'speak' in our heads while retaining the full register of conflicting social values." See Gary Saul Morson, "Dialogue, Monologue, and the Social: A Reply to Ken Hirshkop," in *Bakhtin: Essays and Dialogues on His Work*, ed. Morson (Chicago: University of Chicago Press, 1986), 85.

10. Teresa de Lauretis, *Technologies of Gender: Essays on Theory, Film, and Fiction* (Bloomington: Indiana University Press, 1987), 2.

11. Audre Lorde, "Eye to Eye," included in *Sister Outsider* (Freedom, CA: Crossing Press, 1984), 147.

12. Barbara Christian, "The Dynamics of Difference: Book Review of Audre Lorde's *Sister Outsider*," in *Black Feminist Criticism: Perspectives in Black Women Writers* (New York: Pergamon Press, 1985), 209.

13. While acknowledging the importance of historicism, I can only agree with Frank Lentricchia's conclusion that in some respects Gadamer's "historicist argument begs more questions than it answers. If we can applaud the generous intention, virtually unknown in structuralist quarters, of recapturing history for textual interpretation, then we can only be stunned by the implication of what he has uncritically to say about authority, the power of tradition, knowledge, our institutions, and our attitudes." See Frank Lentricchia, *After the New Criticism*

(Chicago: University of Chicago Press, 1980), 153. Certainly, Gadamer's model privileges the individual's relation to history and tradition in a way that might seem problematic in formulating a discursive model for the "non-canonical" or marginalized writer. However, just as the above model of dialogics is meant to extend Bakhtin's notion of class difference to encompass gender and race, so the present model revises and limits Gadamer's notion of tradition. See Hans-Georg Gadamer, *Truth and Method* (New York: Seabury Press, 1975), 321–325. My introduction to the significance of Gadamer's work for my own reading of black women writers was first suggested by Don Bialostosky's excellent paper entitled "Dialectic and Anti-Dialectic: A Bakhtinian Critique of Gadamer's Dialectical Model of Conversation," delivered at the International Association of Philosophy and Literature in May 1989 at Emory University in Atlanta, Georgia.

14. I extend Rachel Blau DuPlessis's term designating white women as a group privileged by race and oppressed by gender to black men as a group privileged by gender and oppressed by race. In this instance, I use "ambiguously (non)hegemonic" to signify the discursive status of both these groups.

15. Black women enter into dialogue with other black women in a discourse that I would characterize as primarily testimonial, resulting from a similar discursive and social positionality. It is this commonality of history, culture, and language that, finally, constitutes the basis of a tradition of black women's expressive culture. In terms of actual literary dialogue among black women, I would suggest a relatively modern provenance of such a tradition, but again, one based primarily on a dialogue of affirmation rather than contestation. As I see it, this dialogue begins with Alice Walker's response to Zora Neale Hurston. Although the present chapter is devoted primarily to the contestorial function of black women's writing, my forthcoming work will deal more extensively with relationships among black women writers. In the present volume, I explore the notion of witnessing in Chapter 14 to suggest the testimonial relationship between black feminist critics/theorists and black women performers.

16. Zora Neale Hurston, *Their Eyes Were Watching God* (1937; rpt., Urbana: University of Illinois Press, 1978). All subsequent references appear within parentheses in the text.

17. Geneva Smitherman, *Talkin and Testifyin: The Language of Black America* (Detroit, MI: Wayne State University Press, 1986), 58.

18. Alice Walker, "In Search of Our Mothers' Gardens," in *In Search of Our Mothers' Gardens: Womanist Prose* (New York: Harcourt Brace Jovanovich, 1984), 232.

19. See Julia Kristeva, *Revolution in Poetic Language* (1974), trans. Margaret Waller (New York: Columbia University Press, 1984) and *Desire in Language: A Semiotic Approach to Literature and Art*, trans. Thomas Gora, Alice Jardine, and Leon Roudiez (New York: Columbia University Press, 1980). For Kristeva, semiotics, or the "mother tongue," is associated with childhood and the mother–child relationship. Expressed in music, art, poetry, and rhythm, the mother tongue disrupts the symbolic, recognizes and speaks across difference, listens to the spoken and unspoken in discourse, and embraces the notion of ethical dialogue between Self and Other. For greater detail on Kristiva's use of the semiotic, see note 36 below.

20. Not only does such an approach problematize conventional categories and boundaries of discourse, but, more important, it signals the collapse of the unifying consensus posited by the discourse of universalism and reconstructs the concept of unity in diversity implicit in the discourse of difference.

21. The arrogant and misogynistic Paul tells us, "I thank God that I speak in tongues more than all of you. But in church I would rather speak five intelligible words to instruct others [i.e., to prophesy] than ten thousand words in a tongue" (1 Corinthians 14:18–19). Even though we are perhaps most familiar with Paul's injunction to women in the church to keep silent, the prophet Joel, in the Old Testament, speaks to a diversity of voices that includes women: "In the last days, God says, I will pour out my Spirit on all people. Your sons and *daughters* will prophesy.... Even on my servants, both men and *women*, I will pour out my Spirit in those days, and they will prophesy" (Joel 2:28–29, emphasis added). See also Acts 2:18: "And on

my servants and on my handmaidens I will pour out in those days of my Spirit; and they shall prophesy." I am grateful to the Rev. Joseph Stephens, whose vast scriptural knowledge helped guide me through these and other revelations.

22. Sherley Anne Williams, *Dessa Rose* (New York: William Morrow, 1986), and Toni Morrison, *Sula* (New York: Alfred A. Knopf, 1973; rpt., Bantam, 1975). Page references for these two works appear within parentheses in the text.

23. I draw on the distinction between the political connotation of *suppression* and the psychological connotation of *repression*. Suppression results from external pressures and censorship imposed by the dominant culture, while repression refers to the internal self-censorship and silencing emanating from the sub-dominative community.

24. Nehemiah, a minor prophet in the Old Testament, is best remembered for rebuilding the walls around Jerusalem in order to fortify the city against invasion by hostile neighbors of Israel. Under his governorship, Ezra and the Levites instructed the people in the law of Moses "which the Lord had commanded for Israel." He is represented as a reformer who restored the ancient ordinances regarding proper observance of the Sabbath and the collection of the tithes; he also enforced bans against intermarriage with the Gentiles. He is perhaps most noted for the reply he sent, while rebuilding the walls, to a request from his enemies, Sanaballat and Gesham, to meet with him: "I am doing a great *work* and cannot go down" (see Nehemiah 6:1–3, emphasis added). Williams's Nehemiah, like his prototype, is devoted to the completion of a project he calls *The Work*—in this instance a book entitled *The Roots of Rebellion in the Slave Population and Some Means of Eradicating Them*. Significantly, the name of Williams's character, Adam Nehemiah, reverses the name of Nehemiah Adams, author of *A South-side View of Slavery* (1854), and a Boston minister who wrote an account of his experience in the South from a point of view apostate to the northern antislavery cause.

25. The mark of the whip inscribes Dessa as a slave while she remains within the discursive domain of slavery—a domain architecturally figured by the prison from which she escapes, but also a domain legally and more discursively defined by the Fugitive Slave Act, the runaway ads, and the courts and depositions of the nation. Note, however, that within the Northern lecture halls and the slave narratives—the spatial and discursive domains of abolitionism—the marks do not identify an individual, but signify upon the character and nature of the institution of slavery.

26. Monique Wittig, "The Straight Mind," *Feminist Issues* 1, no. 1 (Summer 1980): 105–106, emphasis added.

27. Although the status of slave is not a "misreading" within the discursive domain of slavery, it is clearly a misreading according to Dessa's self-identification.

28. One might describe Sula's birthmark as an iconicized representation rather than, strictly speaking, an inscription. For our purposes, however, it has the force of a sign marking her birth or entry into black discourse.

29. Morrison's epigram to the novel highlights the cultural significance of the birthmark by quoting from Tennessee Williams's *The Rose Tattoo*: "Nobody knew my rose of the world but me....I had too much glory. They don't want glory like that in nobody's heart." In "The Mission of the Flowers," Frances Ellen Watkins Harper describes the rose as "a thing of joy and beauty" whose mission is to "lay her fairest buds and flowers upon the altars of love." Walker's protagonist Celie compares her own sex to the "inside of a wet rose." See Frances E. W. Harper, *Idylls of the Bible* (Philadelphia: George S. Ferguson, 1901), quoted in Erlene Stetson, ed., *Black Sister* (Bloomington: Indiana University Press, 1981), 34–36, and Alice Walker, *The Color Purple* (New York: Harcourt Brace Jovanovich, 1982), 69. In naming her own character Dessa Rose, Williams not only plays on the above connotations, but links them, at the same time, to the transcendence implicit in "arising" and the insurgence suggested in "uprising."

30. Signifying perhaps on Hawthorne's short story "The Birthmark," Sula's mark can be reread as a sign of human imperfection and mortality, a consequence of Eve's seduction by the serpent in the Garden.

31. The fire and water image, associated with the tadpole and ashes, respectively complement and contrast with that of the snake—a symbol of death and renewal—and that of the stemmed rose, an image suggesting not only love and sexuality, but the beauty and brevity of life as a temporal experience.

32. I do not develop here the interviewer's misreadings of Dessa in the early part of the novel, nor the specific insurgent strategies with which Dessa continually outwits him. These details are treated extensively, however, in my essay on Williams's "Meditations on History," the novella on which the novel is based. See Chapter 2 of this volume.

33. See Ralph Ellison, "The Art of Fiction: An Interview," in *Shadow and Act* (New York: New American Library, 1955), 169–183.

34. Williams also uses onomastics to signify upon a less rebellious female heroine, somewhat more complicitous with female ascription by the Other. For a more extensive treatment of the subject, see Chapter 5 of this volume.

35. Williams, in her earlier version of this story, "Meditations on History," privileges orality (rather than writing)—as I attempt to demonstrate in my essay "(W)Riting *The Work* and Working the Rites." See Chapter 2 of this volume.

36. As discussed above (note 19), for Julia Kristeva, the "mother tongue" is associated with child-hood and the mother–child relationship. Kristeva further argues that "language as symbolic function constitutes itself at the cost of repressing the instinctual drive and continuous relation to the mother" (*Desire in Language*, 136). This order of expression, contends Kristeva, is pre-symbolic and linked with the mother tongue. According to Nelly Furman's interpretation, the existence of this order "does not refute the symbolic but is anterior to it, and associated with the maternal aspects of language. This order, which [Kristeva] calls 'semiotic,' is not a separate entity from the symbolic, on the contrary, it is the system which supports symbolic coherence." Continuing, Furman quotes Josette Feral in establishing a dialogical relationship between the semiotic and symbolic orders "which places the semiotic *inside* the symbolic as a condition of the symbolic, while positing the symbolic as a condition of the semiotic and founded on its repression. Now it happens that the Name-of-the-Father, in order to establish itself, needs the repression of the mother. It needs the otherness in order to reassure itself about its unity and identity, but is unwittingly affected by the otherness that is working within it." Nelly Furman, "The Politics of Language: Beyond the Gender Principle?," in *Making A Difference: Feminist Literary Criticism*, ed. Gayle Greene and Coppélia Kahn (London and New York: Methuen, 1985), 72–73.

37. In contrast to Dessa, who disrupts the dominant discourse, Sula would seem to disrupt not only discourse but, indeed, language itself.

38. Adrienne Munich, "Feminist Criticism and Literary Tradition," in Greene and Khan, 245–254.

39. Rachel Blau DuPlessis uses these terms to describe the "tactics of revisionary mythopoesis" created by women poets whose purpose is to "attack cultural hegemony." "Narrative displacement is like breaking the sentence," writes DuPlessis, "because it offers the possibility of speech to the female in this case, giving voice to the muted. Narrative delegitimation 'breaks the sequence'; a realignment that puts the last first and first last has always ruptured conventional morality, politics, and narrative." Rachel Blau DuPlessis, *Writing beyond the Ending: Narrative Strategies of Twentieth-Century Women Writers* (Bloomington: Indiana University Press, 1985), 108.

40. Bakhtin, "Discourse in the Novel," 271–272.

41. Gadamer, 321.

42. Myra Jehlen, "Archimedes and the Paradox of Feminist Criticism," in *The Signs Reader: Women, Gender and Scholarship*, ed. Elizabeth Abel and Emily K. Abel (Chicago: University of Chicago Press, 1983), 575–601.

43. See Harold Bloom, *The Anxiety of Influence: A Theory of Poetry* (New York: Oxford University Press, 1973); Sandra M. Gilbert and Susan Gubar, *The Madwoman in the Attic: The Woman Writer and the Nineteenth-Century Literary Imagination* (New Haven, CT: Yale University Press,

1979); and Joseph T. Skerrett, "The Wright Interpretation: Ralph Ellison and the Anxiety of Influence," *Massachusetts Review* 21 (Spring 1980): 196–212.

44. Andrea Stuart in an interview with Toni Morrison, "Telling Our Story," *Spare Rib* (April 1988): 12–15.

Chapter 4

1. Toni Morrison, "The Site of Memory," in *Inventing the Truth: The Art and Craft of Memoir*, ed. William Zinsser (Boston: Houghton-Mifflin, 1987), 109–110.
2. Morrison, "The Site of Memory," 110, emphasis added.
3. Morrison, "The Site of Memory," 110, 113.
4. See W. E. B. Du Bois, "The Forethought," in *The Souls of Black Folk* (Chicago: A. C. McClurg, 1903), viii.
5. See Toni Morrison's "Unspeakable Things Unspoken," *Michigan Quarterly Review* 28, no. 1 (Winter 1989): 1–34.
6. According to Morrison, this figure "is the best educated guess of the number of black Africans who never even made it into slavery—those who died either as captives in Africa or on slave ships" (Walter Clemons, "The Ghosts of 'Sixty Million and More,'" *Newsweek* [September 28, 1987]: 75). My colleague William A. Darity, Jr., however, observes,

   > My reason for being skeptical about Morrison's number is the fact that the upward...estimates for Africans landed in the Americas and sold into slavery is Joseph Inikori's 15 million. If 60 million Africans were killed in the process of procurement or delivery for sale (or 45 million if Morrison is counting those landed among the ghosts), this was a business—and it *was* a business—that was extraordinarily inefficient and, presumably, less profitable than it appears to have been. We do know now, as horrific as the Middle Passage had to have been, mortality during the Atlantic crossing of enslaved Africans was lower than it was during the "seasoning" period in the Americas.... Slavers had strong incentives to keep as many of their captives alive as long as possible prior to landing in the Americas.

   Additionally, Darity notes that Walter Rodney, in *How Europe Underdeveloped Africa*, "estimates that in 1650 the continent's entire population was 100 million people. Unlike [in] other parts of the world he indicates that Africa's population remained fairly stable, growing only to 120 million people by 1900. He attributes the stagnant size of the continent's population to the impact of the slave trade" (see Walter Rodney, *How Europe Underdeveloped Africa* [Washington, DC: Howard University Press, 1982]). Darity thus concludes that, "for 60 million Africans to have died across the various stages of the slave trade, we should have observed an absolute decline in Africa's population. Now admittedly these estimates are fraught with uncertainty, and one scholar, Diop-Maes, actually claimed that Africa's population dropped from 650 million to 150 million over the course of the slave trade—but his estimates are vastly different from all others." See Reiko Hayasi, "Long Term Population Dynamics in Africa: A Perspective from the Urban Structure," available online: http://uaps2007.princeton. edu/papers/70296. See also Herbert S. Klein, *The Middle Passage: Comparative Studies in the Atlantic Slave Trade* (Princeton, NJ: Princeton University Press, 1978).
7. Romans 3:28: "Therefore we conclude that a man is justified by faith without the deeds of the law"; cf. Galatians 3:11: "But that no man is justified by the law in the sight of God, *it is* evident: for, The just shall live by faith."
8. Contemporary black writers whose work fictionalizes history include, among others, Margaret Walker (*Jubilee*), Ernest Gaines (*The Autobiography of Miss Jane Pittman*), David Bradley (*The Chaneysville Incident*), Alice Walker (*The Color Purple*), Sherley Anne Williams (*Dessa Rose*), and Barbara Chase-Riboud (*Sally Hemings* and *Echo of Lions*).
9. Gloria Naylor and Toni Morrison, "A Conversation," *The Southern Review* 21, no. 3 (Summer 1985): 583–584.

10. Naylor and Morrison, "A Conversation," 584.
11. Naylor and Morrison, "A Conversation," 584.
12. Morrison, "The Site of Memory," 111–112.
13. Morrison, "The Site of Memory," 113–114.
14. Collingwood argues that, like the novelist, the historian constructs an imaginary picture consistent with the historical data, testimony, memory, documentation. In an attempt to explain a fragmentary or incomplete record of the historical past, Collingwood further argues that the historian must employ what he calls "the constructive imagination" to create a "coherent and continuous picture" consistent with the available historical data. R. G. Collingwood, *The Idea of History* (London: Oxford University Press, 1946), 245–246.
15. Henry Louis Gates, Jr., "Frederick Douglass and the Language of Self," *The Yale Review* 70, no. 4 (July 1981): 592–610.
16. See Jacques Derrida, *Memories for Paul de Man* (New York: Columbia University Press, 1986), 102–150 *passim*.
17. Toni Morrison, *Beloved* (New York: Alfred Knopf, 1987). Page references for this work appear within parentheses in the text.
18. Hayden White, *Tropics of Discourse: Essays in Cultural Criticism* (Baltimore, MD: Johns Hopkins University Press, 1979), 33–34.
19. Paul Ricoeur, *The Reality of Historical Past* (Milwaukee: Marquette University Press, 1984), 11.
20. See Elsie B. Washington, "Talk with Toni Morrison," in *Conversations with Toni Morrison*, ed. Danille Taylor-Guthrie (Jackson: University Press of Mississippi, 1994), 235.
21. See Waldo E. Martin, Jr., *The Mind of Frederick Douglass* (Chapel Hill: University of North Carolina Press, 1984) for a discussion of the relation between the ethnologist and the cultural historian in the context of nineteenth-century practice: "Practitioners of a broad and allegedly scientific discipline, ethnologists...attempted to uncover stages and meanings of human developments primarily in cultural and related physical terms and secondarily in historical terms" (225).
22. Nathaniel Hawthorne, *The Scarlet Letter* (New York: E. P. Dutton, 1938), 42, 51.
23. See White, *Tropics of Discourse*, 151. Unlike the notion of historical reconstruction, which seeks to account for otherness by questioning the normative model, this method seeks to identify *difference* with *deviance* and/or *diminishment*.
24. Williams and Morrison share a commentary on disciplines and disciplinary behaviors insofar as their works constitute a critique of certain aspects of both practitioners and their praxis. Like Williams's Adam Nehemiah, Morrison's schoolteacher (who might as appropriately be designated ethnographer as historian), represents the author's indictment of the kind of "scholarly" and "scientific" discourse in which the preconceptions of the inquirer lead to gross distortions. For critical treatments of Williams's work from this perspective, see my "(W)Riting *The Work* and Working the Rites" (Chapter 2 of this volume) and "Speaking in Tongues: Dialogics, Dialectics, and the Black Woman Writer's Literary Tradition" (Chapter 3 of this volume).
25. See Hélène Cixous, "The Laugh of the Medusa," in *New French Feminisms: An Anthology*, ed. Elaine Marks and Isabelle de Courtivron (Amherst: University of Massachusetts Press, 1980), 251.
26. See Sandra Gilbert and Susan Gubar, *Madwoman in the Attic: The Woman Writer and the Nineteenth-Century Literary Imagination* (New Haven: Yale University Press, 1970).
27. These are alternative translations of Galatians 3:24.
28. See Paul Ricoeur, *Time and Narrative*, 3 vols. (Chicago: University of Chicago Press, 1988).
29. See White on Collingwood, *Tropics of Discourse*, 83.
30. According to Ricoeur, emplotment "brings together diverse and heterogeneous story elements...agents, goals, means, interactions, [and] circumstances...[A]n event must be more than just a singular occurrence. It gets its definition from its contribution to the development

of the plot. A story, too, must be more than just an enumeration of events in serial order; it must organize them into an intelligible whole, of a sort such that we can always ask what is the "thought" of this story. In short, emplotment is the operation that draws a configuration out of a simple succession." See Ricoeur, *Time and Narrative*, Vol. 1, 65.

31. Gates, "Frederick Douglass and the Language of Self," 593.

32. See White, *Tropics of Discourse*, 87.

33. Gates, "Frederick Douglass and the Language of Self," 599.

34. Naylor and Morrison, "A Conversation," 585.

35. Teresa de Lauretis, *Alice Doesn't: Feminism, Semiotics, Cinema* (Bloomington: Indiana University Press, 1984).

36. Freud, according to Norman Brown's reading, extends this notion to recapitulation theory (ontogeny recapitulates phylogeny) in which "each individual recapitulates the history of the race.... From this it follows that the theory of neurosis must embrace a theory of history; and conversely a theory of history must embrace a theory of neurosis." See Norman O. Brown, *Life against Death: The Psychoanalytical Meaning of History* (Middletown, CT: Wesleyan University Press, 1959), 19, 12–13. Robert Guthrie elaborates further: "The recapitulation theory held that an individual organism, in the process of growth and development, passes through a series of stages representing those in the evolutionary development of the species. G. Stanley Hall, for example, believed 'that in its play activity the child exhibits a series of phases corresponding to the cultural phase of human society, a hunting period, a building period, and so on.' Hall's attempt to mold individual development (ontogeny) with racial characteristics (phylogeny) was supported by many leading behavioral scientists of this time [early twentieth century]. (John Mark Baldwin's *Mental Development in the Child in the Race,* for example, was a frequently quoted source.)" Robert V. Guthrie, *Even the Rat Was White: A Historical View of Psychology* (New York: Harper & Row, 1976), 82.

37. Sigmund Freud, "Remembering, Repeating and Working-Through," in Vol. 12 of *The Standard Edition of the Works of Sigmund Freud*, ed. James Strachey (London: Hogarth Press, 1914), 146–157.

38. Michel de Certeau, *Heterologies: Discourse on the Other*. Theory and History of Literature Vol. 17 (Minneapolis: University of Minnesota Press, 1986), 3.

39. Alfred Schutz as quoted in Ricoeur, *Time and Narrative*, Vol. 3, 109.

40. Although White's work speaks eloquently to a "classification of discourses based on tropology" (*Tropics of Discourse*, 22), Philip Stambovsky's work on metaphor and historical writing addresses my concerns more specifically in this instance. Using Maurice Mandelbaum's "three historical forms—explanatory, sequential, and interpretive" as a "context for determining the functioning...of...metaphor in historical discourse," Stambovsky identifies three functions of metaphor: heuristic, depictive, and cognitive. See Philip Stambovsky, "Metaphor and Historical Understanding," *History and Theory* 27, no. 2 (1988): 125–134.

41. See Kaja Silverman, *The Acoustic Mirror: The Female Voice in Psychoanalysis and Cinema* (Bloomington: Indiana University Press, 1988) for an interesting discussion of the notions of interiority and exteriority.

42. Genesis 5:25. Seth was also the name of the Egyptian god of confusion, described as a trickster-like marginal figure located "beyond or between the boundaries of social definition...[who] gleefully breaks taboos and violates the limits that preserve order." See Anna K. Nardo "'Sung and Proverb'd for a Fool': Samson as Fool and Trickster," *Mosaic* 22 (Winter 1989): 2.

43. Continuing, Collingwood writes, "The history of myself is thus not memory as such, but a peculiar case of memory. Certainly a mind which could not remember could not have historical knowledge. But memory as such is only the present thought of past experience as such, be that experience what it may; historical knowledge is that special case of memory where the

object of present thought is past thought, the gap between present and past being bridged not only by the power of past thought to think of the past, but also by the power to reawaken itself in the present." R. G. Collingwood, *The Idea of History*, 293–294.

44. I use Collingwood's term advisedly, heeding the admonitions of Ricoeur that although the "re-enactment" of the past in the present operates under the sign of the same, "to re-enact does not consist in reliving what happened," primarily because it involves the notion of "rethinking." And according to Ricoeur, "rethinking already contains the critical moment that requires us to detour by way of the historical imagination." See Ricoeur, *Time and Narrative*, Vol. 3, 144–145. Rather than locate this process under the sign of the same, which implies repetition, I would rather locate it under both the same and the other—repetition with a difference.

45. Ricoeur designates these modes alternatively as mimesis 1, mimesis 2, and mimesis 3. (His formulation of mimesis includes what we normally [after Aristotle] call diegesis—thus expanding the notion of the imitation of an action to include description.) Ricoeur makes it clear that refiguration (or mimesis 3) is a stage that "marks the intersection of the world of the text and the world of the hearer or reader," thereby relating the world configured by the text to the world of "real action." I have modified and extended his model by using the term to describe both the intersection of the inner world of the character and the outer world of her actions, as well as the intersection of the world of the text and the world of the reader. See Ricoeur, *Time and Narrative*, Vol. 1, 54–76.

46. "The basic thesis [of refiguration] from which all the others are derived holds that the meaning of a literary work rests upon the dialogical relation established between the work and its public in each age. This thesis, similar to Collingwood's notion that history is but a re-enactment of the past in the mind of the historian, amounts to including the effect produced by the work—in other words, the meaning the public attributes to it—within the boundaries of work itself." Ricoeur, *Time and Narrative*, Vol. 3, 171.

47. Romans 4:15: "Because the law worketh wrath: for where no law is, there is no transgression."

48. Naylor and Morrison, "A Conversation," 585.

49. Toni Morrison, "The Pain of Being Black," *Time Magazine* (May 22, 1989): 120.

50. Richard Hofstader, *The Progressive Historians* (New York: Alfred A. Knopf, 1968), 3.

Chapter 5

1. See, in this volume, Chapter 2, "(W)Riting *The Work* and Working the Rites," and Chapter 3, "Speaking in Tongues," for examples of Williams's intertextual strategies as novelist.

2. Ross Chambers, *Story and Situation: Narrative Seduction and the Power of Fiction* (Minneapolis: University of Minnesota Press, 1984).

3. For information on the slave rebel known as "Dinah," Dessa's "historical prototype," see Mary Kemp Davis, "Everybody Knows Her Name: The Recovery of the Past in Sherley Anne Williams's *Dessa Rose*." *Callaloo* 40, no. 1 (1989): 544–558. Also see note 31 in Chapter 2 of this volume.

4. See Elizabeth Fox-Genovese, *Within the Plantation Household* (Chapel Hill: University of North Carolina Press, 1988). Fox-Genovese writes, "Within the slave community tendencies to differentiate between men and women resulted in a view of violent organized revolt as a specialized political and insurrectionary male responsibility. None of the most visible revolts took a woman's name. None of these were attributed to a woman's leadership. Nor did slave women organize any of those 'women's' revolts which were common in Europe or Africa" (307–308).

5. Angela Davis, "Reflections on the Black Woman's Role in the Community of Slaves," *The Black Scholar* (December 1971): 1–15.

6. See Chapter 2 of this volume. This chapter draws heavily on my earlier work on Williams and Styron, but extends the implications of that reading into a new direction.

7. William Styron, "Author's Note," in *The Confessions of Nat Turner* (New York: Random House, 1967), ix, emphasis added.

8. These retrenchments included a reconstituted conservative Supreme Court and the polarized presidential politics of Reaganomics in the 1980s. Also, Melissa Walker, *Down From the Mountaintop* (New Haven, CT: Yale University Press, 1991), discusses the political climate surrounding the setting and production of Williams's novella and novel, although her work does not situate these texts in the context of nineteenth- and twentieth-century women's rights politics. See Walker, however, for another treatment of racial politics somewhat different from my own.

9. Sherley Anne Williams, *Dessa Rose* (New York: William Morrow, 1986), 5. Subsequent page references for this work appear within parentheses in the text.

10. See Leo Bersani, "Representations and Its Discontents," in *Allegory and Representation*, ed. Stephen J. Greenblatt (Baltimore, MD: Johns Hopkins University Press, 1981); Susan Sontag, "The Pornographic Imagination," in *Styles of Radical Will* (New York: Farrar, Straus, Giroux, 1969, 35–73); and Jessica Benjamin, *The Bonds of Love: Psychoanalysis, Feminism, and the Problem of Domination* (New York: Pantheon Books, 1988).

11. This is Angus Fletcher's definition of allegory, paraphrased by Lynda Zwinger in "What She Gets for Saying Yes: O," in *Daughters, Fathers and the Novel: The Sentimental Romance of Heterosexuality* (Madison: University of Wisconsin Press, 1991), 97–98.

12. Susan Gubar, "Representing Pornography: Feminism, Criticism, and Depictions of Female Violation," *Critical Inquiry* 13, no. 4 (Summer 1987), 713.

13. I am indebted to Susan Gubar for these terms. See Gubar, 730.

14. In "Replacing Feminist Criticism," Kamuf rejects the reduction of a "literary work to its signature" as well as what she regards as the tautological assumption that "women's writing is writing signed by women." Her project is to "take an anonymous work which (in the absence of a signature) must be read blind" as an opportunity to interrogate what she describes as "the masks of truth with which phallocentrism hides its fictions." See Peggy Kamuf, "Writing Like a Woman," in *Women and Language in Literature and Society*, ed. Sally McConnell-Ginet, Ruth Borker, and Nelly Furman (New York: Praeger, 1980), 284–299, and "Replacing Feminist Criticism," *Diacritics* 12 (1982): 42–47. See also Nancy K. Miller, "The Text's Heroine: A Feminist Critic and Her Fictions," *Diacritics* 12 (1982): 48–53.

15. From the date of its publication in France in 1954, and in the United States in 1965, the *Story of O* has been steeped in controversy over its content and authorship. A *New Yorker* article (August 1, 1994) establishes conclusively that the author was French writer and journalist, Anne Desclos, who wrote under the *nom de plume*, Pauline Réage (and sometimes under the pseudonym of Dominique Aury). As lover of the writer, critic, and publisher Jean Paulhan (who provided the introduction to the novel), Réage/Aury/Desclos explained in an interview that she wrote the novel to rekindle Paulhan's romantic interest. The politics of this authorial collaboration corroborate Hélène Cixous's caveat about equating the sex of the author with that of the text:

> Most women are like this: they do someone else's—man's—writing, and in their innocence sustain it and give it voice, and end up producing writing that's in effect masculine. Great care must be taken working on feminine writing not to get trapped by names: to be signed with a woman's name doesn't necessarily make a piece of writing feminine. It could quite well be masculine writing, and conversely, the fact that a piece of writing is signed with a man's name does not, in itself, exclude femininity. It's rare, but you can sometimes find femininity in writings signed by men: it does happen. ("Castration," quoted in Toril Moi, *Sexual/Textual Politics: Feminist Literary Theory* [London and New York: Methuen, 1985], 108)

16. Simone de Beauvoir, *The Second Sex*, 1949 trans. and ed. Howard M. Parshley (New York: Vintage, 1989), 143.

17. Jean Paulhan, "Preface" to Pauline Réage, *Story of O*, tr. Sabine d'Estree (New York: Grove Press, 1965), xxi–xxxvi. Subsequent references to Paulhan's "Preface" and to the narrative proper of *Story of O* will appear within parentheses in the text.

18. To this end, I read the *Story of O*, perhaps oxymoronically, as a "pornographic classic" rather than an "erotic classic." I would suggest that a distinction between pornography and female eroticism might well be based on where or with whom the *power* resides. In my working definition, I would further suggest that in pornography, as conventionally represented, the power resides with the male, while in what some would claim as "female eroticism," the power resides with the female.

19. Frederick Douglass, *Narrative of the Life of Frederick Douglass*, 1845 (New York: New American Library, 1968), 24–25.

20. See George Cunningham, "Called into Existence: Desire, Gender, and Voice in Frederick Douglass's *Narrative* of 1845," *Differences* 1, no. 3 (Fall 1989): 108–136. See also Deborah McDowell, "In the First Place: Making Frederick Douglass and the Afro-American Narrative Tradition," in *Critical Essays on Frederick Douglass*, ed. William Andrews (Boston: G. K. Hall, 1991; rpt. in *African American Autobiography: A Collection of Critical Essays*, ed. William L. Andrews [Englewood Cliffs, NJ: Prentice Hall, 1993], 36–58) and Jenny Franchot, "The Punishment of Esther: Frederick Douglass and the Construction of the Feminine," *Frederick Douglass: New Literary and Historical Essays*, ed. Eric J. Sundquist (Cambridge: Cambridge University Press, 1990), 141–165.

21. See, for example, Gerda Lerner, *The Creation of Patriarchy* (New York: Oxford University Press, 1986), and Orlando Patterson, *Slavery and Social Death: A Comparative Study* (Cambridge, MA: Harvard University Press, 1982).

22. Dorothy Wertz, "Women and Slavery: A Cross-Cultural Perspective," unpublished paper.

23. The name of Williams's character, Adam Nehemiah, reverses the name of Nehemiah Adams, a Boston minister who wrote a pro-slavery account of his experiences in the South, *A South-side View of Slavery* (1854). Writing for the Associated Clergymen of Massachusetts, this same Nehemiah Adams warned women in 1837 against "the dangerous perversion" of "speaking out in public ... on such incendiary issues as slavery"—a statement positioning him in opposition to women's rights and in support of slavery. Quoted from Mary P. Ryan, *Womanhood in America: From Colonial Times to the Present* (New York: New Viewpoints, 1975).

24. See Catherine A. MacKinnon, "Feminism, Marxism, Method, and the State: An Agenda for Theory," *Signs: Journal of Women in Culture and Society* 7, no. 3 (Spring 1982): 515–544.

25. I am indebted to Kaja Silverman's fine reading of Pauline Réage's "*Histoire D'O*: The Story of a Disciplined and Punished Body," *Enclitic* 7, no. 2 (Fall 1983): 63–81.

26. See Gerard Genette, *Introduction à l'architexte* (Paris: Ed. du Seuil, 1979).

27. Williams, "Meditations on History," in *Midnight Birds: Stories by Contemporary Black Women Writers*, ed. Mary Helen Washington (Garden City, NY: Anchor Books/Doubleday, 1980), 248.

28. Gubar, 726.

29. See Michel Foucault, *Discipline and Punish: The Birth of the Prison*, trans. Alan Sheridan (New York: Pantheon, 1977).

30. Chambers, 158.

31. Readers will recognize that Silverman references here Freud's first postulation of the existence of the "death drive" as an impulse "beyond the pleasure principle." In his essay Freud provides as evidence his grandson's *fort-da* game, which symbolically enacts (through the repetition-compulsion) the pain of the mother's departure and the pleasure of her anticipated return. See Sigmund Freud, "*Beyond the Pleasure Principle*" (1922), in Vol. 18 of *The Standard Edition of the Works of Sigmund Freud*, ed. James Strachey (London: Hogarth Press, 1956–1974), 7–23.

32. Silverman, "Masochism and Subjectivity," in *Male Subjectivities at the Margins* (New York and London: Routledge, 1992), 185–213.

33. Chambers elaborates here, "and that is the role that can be performed by a reading of the situational self reflexivity—the devices of readability—of so-called 'readerly' texts" (27).

Chapter 6

1. Houston A. Baker, Jr., "There Is No More Beautiful Way: Theory and the Poetics of Afro-American Women's Writing," in *Afro-American Literary Study in the 1990s*, ed. Houston A. Baker, Jr., and Patricia Redmond (Chicago: University of Chicago Press, 1989), 136.
2. Baker, "There Is No More Beautiful Way," 137.
3. Mae G. Henderson, "Speaking in Tongues: Dialectics, Dialogics, and the Black Woman Writer's Literary Tradition," in *Changing Our Own Words: Essays on Criticism, Theory, and Writing by Black Women*, ed. Cheryl A. Wall (New Brunswick: Rutgers University Press, 1989), 16–37. See Chapter 3 of this volume.
4. See Alice Walker, "In Search of Our Mothers' Gardens," in *In Search of Our Mothers' Gardens: Womanist Prose* (New York: Harcourt Brace Jovanovich, 1983), 231–243.
5. Houston A. Baker, Jr., and Patricia Redmond, "Introduction," in *Afro-American Literary Study in the 1990s*, 10.
6. Michael S. Harper and Robert B. Stepto, eds., *Chant of Saints: A Gathering of Afro-American Literature, Art, and Scholarship* (Urbana: University of Illinois Press, 1978), 213.
7. Julia Kristeva, "Women's Time," *Signs: Journal of Women in Culture and Society* 7, no. 1 (1981): 15.
8. Plato, *Timeus*, as quoted and translated by Kristeva, 16 note 4.
9. Gaston Bachelard, *The Poetics of Space*, trans. Maria Jolas (New York: Orion Press, 1964).
10. Kristeva, 16-17 *passim*.
11. Quoted in Baker, "There Is No More Beautiful Way," 146. For original citations, see Mathew Arnold, "The Function of Criticism at the Present Time," *The National Review* 2, no. 1 (November 1864): 280, and Walter Pater, *The Renaissance: Studies in Art and Poetry*, 1893 (New York: Boni and Liveright, 1919). Also see Mary Russo, *The Female Grotesque: Risk, Excess, and Modernity* (New York: Routledge, 1995).
12. Baker, "There Is No More Beautiful Way," 154.
13. Luce Irigaray, "This Sex Which Is Not One," in *New French Feminisms*, ed. Elaine Marks and Isabelle de Courtivron (New York: Schocken, 1981), 101.
14. Jacques Lacan, *The Four Fundamental Concepts of Psycho-Analysis* (New York: W. W. Norton, 1981), 106.
15. Baker's original formulation reads: "The answer is a painful No. Painful because the incumbency for the non-Afro-American critic is to finger the jagged grains of a brutal experience in which—if he or she is white—he or she is brutally implicated" ("There Is No More Beautiful Way," 144).
16. See Baker, "There Is No More Beautiful Way," 147–150.
17. Juliet F. MacCannell, *Figuring Lacan: Criticism and the Cultural Unconscious* (Lincoln: University of Nebraska Press, 1986), 135. See also Laura Mulvey, "Visual Pleasure and Narrative Cinema," *Screen* 16.3 (1975): 6–18.
18. Fredric Jameson, cited in William C. Dowling, *Jameson, Althusser, Marx: An Introduction to "The Political Unconscious"* (Ithaca, NY: Cornell University Press, 1984), 11.
19. Houston A. Baker, Jr., *Blues, Ideology, and Afro-American Literature: A Vernacular Theory* (Chicago: University of Chicago Press, 1984).
20. Roland Barthes, "What Is Criticism?," in *Critical Essays*, trans. Richard Howard (Evanston, IL: Northwestern University Press, 1972), 260.
21. See Fredric Jameson, *The Political Unconscious: Narrative as a Socially Symbolic Act* (Ithaca, NY: Cornell University Press, 1981); also see Baker, *Blues, Ideology, and Afro-American Literature: A Vernacular Theory*.

Chapter 7

1. Quoted by Mary Helen Washington in "I Sign My Mother's Name," in *Mothering the Mind: Twelve Studies of Writers and Their Silent Partners*, ed. Ruth Perry and Martine Watson

Brownley (New York: Holmes & Meier, 1984), 148, 149. This quotation, attributed to Barbara Christian by Mary Helen Washington, in fact represents Washington's useful reformulation of Christian.

2. Charles H. Rowell, "Gayl Jones: An Interview," *Callaloo* no. 16 (Oct. 1982): 53.

3. Rowell, 53.

4. Although the author concedes that "there might be more thematic patterns [connecting the stories]," Jones denies "an intentional thematic pattern": "They were a collection of stories I'd written. There are some similarities. Most are written in first person and most deal with tensions in relationships, dynamics of psychology—psychic landscape—and what you called the 'inward'" (Rowell, 49). Jones's remarks are suggestive here, especially as the title, *White Rat*, itself invokes behaviorist John B. Watson and Rosalie Rayner's famous 1920 Little Albert experiment on classical conditioning. Given Jones's reference above to the "dynamics of psychology," one must unavoidably link these stories of inward psychic landscapes to Jones's demonstrated preoccupation with obsessions, neuroses, and what she describes as "abnormal psychology." For further discussion of the significance of the "white rat" in the Little Albert experiment, see John B. Watson and Rosalie Rayner, "Conditioned Emotional Reactions," *Journal of Experimental Psychology* 3, no. 1 (1920): 1–14.

5. Michael S. Harper, "Gayl Jones: An Interview," in *Chant of Saints: A Gathering of Afro-American Literature, Art, and Scholarship*, ed. Michael S. Harper and Robert B. Stepto (Urbana: University of Illinois Press, 1979), 375.

6. Rowell, 49.

7. Rowell, 49.

8. Gayl Jones, *White Rat: Short Stories* (Boston: Northeastern University Press, 1991), 18. Subsequent references will appear within parentheses in the text.

9. Claudia C. Tate, "Gayl Jones," in *Black Women Writers at Work*, ed. Claudia C. Tate (New York: Continuum, 1983), 99.

10. In the uncorrected page proofs to Gayl Jones's *The Healing* (Boston: Beacon Press, 1998), Helen Atwan, then Director of Beacon Press, wrote the following:

> Some of you will remember when Random House editor Toni Morrison published Gayl Jones's first two novels, in the early 1970s. The reviews were spectacular (everyone from Baldwin to Updike), and she followed them with a powerful story collection, while working on plays and poetry. In the late seventies, Gayl left the U.S. after what she describes to me as "an incident of racial injustice of a perennial mode," walked away from a tenured position at Ann Arbor as well as from her growing readership, and lived in self-imposed exile in France for several years. She has published fiction only in Germany and with Lotus Press, African-American publishers based in Detroit, since 1977.

The works that remain unnamed in the above open letter include *Die Vogelfängerin* (*The Birdwatcher*), published in 1986 in Germany, as well as the collection of poetry entitled *Xarque and Other Poems* (Detroit, MI: Lotus Press, 1985).

11. See Peter Manso, "Chronicle of a Tragedy Foretold," *New York Times Magazine* (July 19, 1998): 32–37.

12. Rowell, 49, emphasis added.

13. Rowell, 49.

14. Harper, 372.

15. Gayl Jones, *Corregidora* (New York: Random House, 1975), 114.

16. Harper, 372.

17. Wolfgang Iser, *The Act of Reading: A Theory of Aesthetic Response* (Baltimore, MD: Johns Hopkins University Press, 1978), 21, 10.

18. Harper, 355.

19. Harper, 352.

20. Harper, 358.

21. Rowell, 33.

22. William Andrews, *To Tell a Free Story: The First Century of Afro-American Autobiography, 1760–1865* (Urbana-Champagne: University of Illinois Press, 1988), 255.

23. The moniker "White Rat" suggests here a kind of Pavlovian conditional reflex to whiteness. Notably, it was John B. Watson (see note 4 above) who introduced to the West the work of the Russian Ivan Pavlov on conditioning and involuntary reflex. See Ivan Petrovich Pavlov, *Conditioned Reflexes: An Investigation of the Physiological Activity of the Cerebral Cortex*, trans. and ed. G. V. Anrep (London: Oxford University Press, 1927).

24. Willa Cather, "The Novel Démeublé," in *Not Under Forty* (New York: Alfred A. Knopf, 1922), 43–51.

25. Colette Guillaumin, "The Practice of Power and Belief in Nature, Part I: The Appropriation of Women," *Feminist Studies* 1, no. 2 (Winter 1981): 87–109.

26. Rowell, 52.

27. Rowell, 37.

28. Tate, 97–98.

29. In her interview with Charles Rowell, Jones remarks on Janheinz Jahn's characterization of the blues as "subjective testimony," adding that it is "of course the 'I' [that] is the witness." Jones thus establishes "a relationship between the 'I' storyteller and the blues singer." See Rowell, 37. Also see Janheinz Jahn, *Neo-African Literature: A History of Black Writing* (New York: Grove Press, 1969), 173.

30. Jones, *Corregidora*, 96.

31. Jones, *Corregidora*, 59.

32. Harper, 359.

33. Jones, *Corregidora*, 185.

34. Jones, *Corregidora*, 185.

35. Harper, 360.

36. Rowell, 42.

37. Tate, 96.

38. Harper, 361; Rowell, 48.

39. Tate, 92.

40. Tate, 96, 97.

41. Tate, 92.

42. Tate, 95.

43. Gloria Anzaldúa, Preface to *Borderlands/La Frontera: The New Mestiza* (San Francisco: Spinsters/Aunt Lute, 1987).

44. Rowell, 54. It should be noted that the present chapter is a substantially revised and expanded version of the original essay, published as the "Foreword" to the 1991 edition of *White Rat* by Gayl Jones (Boston: Northeastern University Press, 1991).

Chapter 8

1. *The Women's Review of Books* explains the literary symposium from which this interview is excerpted as follows: "*The Women's Review* asked several black feminist critics and theorists to comment on the problems, politics and possibilities of their enterprise—which tools are being discarded, which taken up, what houses are being constructed and what others torn down? In the forum that follows, Nellie McKay, Patricia Hill Collins, Mae Henderson and June Jordan respond to our questions" ("The State of the Art," *The Women's Review of Books* 8, no. 5 [February 1991]: 23).

2. Houston A. Baker, Jr., *Workings of the Spirit: The Poetics of Afro-American Women's Writing* (Chicago: University of Chicago Press, 1991), 1.

3. Barbara Christian, "The Race for Theory," *Cultural Critique* 6 (Spring 1987): 52.

4. Cheryl A. Wall, "Introduction: Taking Positions and Changing Words," in *Changing Our Own Words: Essays on Criticism, Theory, and Writing by Black Women*, ed. Cheryl A. Wall (New Brunswick, NJ: Rutgers University Press, 1989), 1–15.

5. Paul A. Baran, "The Commitment of the Intellectual," address delivered to the American Association for the Advancement of Science in New York on December 27, 1960, and published in *Monthly Review* 13, no. 1 (1961).

6. Abdul R. JanMohamed, "The Economy of Manichean Allegory: The Function of Racial Difference in Colonialist Literature," *Critical Inquiry* 12, no. 1 (Autumn 1985): 59–87.

7. Henry Louis Gates, Jr., "Editor's Introduction: Writing, 'Race' and the Difference It Makes," *Critical Inquiry* 12, no. 1 (Autumn 1985), 15.

8. Barbara Smith, "Toward a Black Feminist Criticism," in *All the Women Are White, All the Blacks Are Men, But Some of Us Are Brave: Black Women's Studies*, ed. Gloria T. Hull, Patricia Bell Scott, and Barbara Smith (Old Westbury, NY: The Feminist Press, 1982), 159.

Chapter 9

1. Michel Foucault, "The Order of Discourse," trans. Ian McLeod, in *Untying the Text: A Poststructuralist Reader*, ed. Robert Young (Boston: Routledge and Kegan Paul, 1981), 48–78.

2. Trinh T. Minh-ha, *Woman, Native, Other: Writing Postcoloniality and Feminism* (Bloomington: Indiana University Press, 1989), 76.

3. Houston A. Baker, Jr., "There Is No More Beautiful Way: Theory and the Poetics of Afro-American Women's Writing," in *Afro-American Literary Study in the 1990s*, ed. Houston A. Baker, Jr., and Patricia Redmond (Chicago: University of Chicago Press, 1989), 135–155.

4. For an insightful and neglected early treatment of this issue, see Frederick C. Stern's "Black Lit., White Crit.?," *College English* 35, no. 6 (March 1974): 637–658.

5. Minh-ha, 76; Linda Alcoff, "The Problem of Speaking for Others," *Cultural Critique* 20 (Winter 1991–1992): 17.

6. Valerie Smith, "Black Feminist Theory and the Representation of the 'Other,'" in *Changing Our Own Words: Essays on Criticism, Theory, and Writing by Black Women*, ed. Cheryl A. Wall (New Brunswick, NJ: Rutgers University Press, 1989), 57.

7. Alcoff, 17.

8. Susan Stanford Friedman, "Authority in the Feminist Classroom: A Contradiction in Terms?," *Gendered Subjects: The Dynamics of Feminist Teaching*, ed. Margo Culley and Catherine Portuges (Boston: Routledge and Kegan Paul, 1985), 206.

9. Margo Culley, "Anger and Authority in the Introductory Women's Studies Classroom," in Culley and Portuges, 211.

10. Culley, 213.

11. Culley, 213.

12. See Toni Cade Bambara, Preface, in *Daughters of the Dust: The Making of an African American Woman's Film*, by Julie Dash (New York: The New Press, 1992), xi–xvi. Interestingly, I was introduced to Bambara's concepts in an oral presentation prior to its publication—and consequently misread "eye" for "I." When I subsequently read the published version of her text, my misreading expanded into a revised reading acknowledging the slippage between the "eye" and the "I."

13. We must not forget that African-American students themselves frequently resist the role of authenticating texts, although clearly the class can and should provide a framework for relating personal experience and textual representation.

14. Marian Yee, "Are You the Teacher?," in *Composition and Resistance*, ed. C. Mark Hurlbert and Michael Blitz (Portsmouth, NH: Heinemann-Boynton/Cook, 1991), 25.

15. John Schib, "Pedagogy of the Oppressors?," in Culley and Portuges, 254.

16. I am grateful to several of my graduate students at the University of Illinois at Chicago for responding to a questionnaire soliciting their responses to my own pedagogical practices. I am particularly indebted to Jennifer Cohen for her thoughtful responses, which have provoked and influenced my own thinking on some of the issues involved in black feminist pedagogy.

17. My thanks to Helen Moglen for sharing with me her unpublished manuscript, "Transference and the Erotics of Teaching," which she presented at the Multicultural and Feminist Pedagogies Conference, UCSC, May 1991.

18. Quoted in Moglen.

19. Roland Barthes, *Roland Barthes*, trans. Richard Howard, 1977 (Berkeley: University of California Press, 1994), 171.

20. Michael Holquist, *Dialogism: Bakhtin and His World* (New York: Routledge, 1990), 87.

Chapter 10

1. Jane Tompkins, "Fighting Words: Unlearning to Write the Critical Essay," *Georgia Review* 42 (1988): 589.

2. Tompkins, 590.

3. John Milton, *Areopagitica* (1644), in *John Milton: Complete Poems and Major Prose*, ed. Merritt Y. Hughes (New York: Macmillan, 1957), 720.

4. Quoted by William H. Pritchard, "Nasty Reviews: Easy to Give, Hard to Take," *New York Times Book Review* (May 7, 1989).

5. Virginia Woolf, "Reviewing," in *The Captain's Death Bed and Other Essays* (New York: Harcourt, 1950), 129.

6. Steve Weinberg, "The Unruly World of Book Reviews," *Columbia Journalism Review* 28, no. 6 (March–April 1990): 54.

7. Since the original publication of this piece, R. R. Bowker LLC, an American limited liability company that publishes *Books in Print* and issues ISBNs (International Standard Book Numbers), has reported that more than three million books were published in the U.S. alone in 2010. See "Print isn't dead, says Bowker's Annual Book Production Report," *Bowker*, May 18, 2011: http://www.bowker.com/en-US/aboutus/press_room/2011/pr_05182011.shtml.

8. Women in Publishing, *Reviewing the Reviews: A Woman's Place on the Book Page* (London: Journeyman, 1987), 19.

9. Women in Publishing, 9.

10. Women in Publishing, 13.

11. SallyAnn H. Ferguson, "Passionate Critics," rev. of *Changing Our Own Words: Essays on Criticism, Theory and Writing by Black Women* by Cheryl A. Wall; *Reading Feminist: A Critical Anthology* by Henry Louis Gates, Jr., *The Women's Review of Books* 9, no. 3 (December 1991): 28.

12. Toni Morrison, *Playing in the Dark: Whiteness and the Literary Imagination* (Cambridge, MA: Harvard University Press, 1992), 91.

13. Linda S. Kauffman, "The Long Goodbye: Against Personal Testimony, or An Infant Grifter Grows Up," in *American Feminist Thought at Century's End: A Reader*, ed. Linda S. Kauffman (Cambridge, MA, and Oxford: Blackwell, 1993), 266.

14. Woolf, 128.

15. See Brackette F. Williams, rev. of *The Black Atlantic: Modernity and Double Consciousness* by Paul Gilroy, *Social Identities: Journal for the Study of Race, Nation and Culture* 1, no. 1 (February 1995): 175–192; George Lipsitz, rev. of *The Black Atlantic: Modernity and Double Consciousness* by Paul Gilroy, *Social Identities: Journal for the Study of Race, Nation and Culture* 1, no. 1 (February 1995): 193–200; and Tommy Lee Lott, rev. of *The Black Atlantic: Modernity and Double Consciousness* by Paul Gilroy, *Social Identities: Journal for the Study of Race, Nation and Culture* 1, no. 1 (February 1995): 200–220.

16. Kenneth Warren and Gerald Graff, "Kenneth Warren and Gerald Graff on the Politics of Talking Back: Gerald Graff's *Beyond the Culture Wars: How Teaching the Conflicts Can Revitalize*

American Education," The Journal of the Midwest Modern Language Association 26, no. 1 (Spring 1993): 75–81.

Chapter 11

1. See James de Jongh, *Vicious Modernism* (Cambridge: Cambridge University Press, 1990).
2. Werner Sollors, *Neither Black Nor White Yet Both: Thematic Explorations of Interracial Literature* (New York: Oxford University Press, 1997), 247–248.
3. Rita Felski, *The Gender of Modernity* (Cambridge, MA: Harvard University Press, 1995), 13.
4. Arthur Davis, for instance, speculates that "the present-day reader may wonder at this morbid concern…with the passing theme" (*From The Dark Tower: Afro-American Writers, 1900–1960* [Washington, DC: Howard University Press, 1974], 6). This sentiment is shared by Amritjit Singh, Hoyt Fuller, and other earlier critics of the genre.
5. W. E. B. Du Bois, *The Crisis* (1929); also cited in Hoyt Fuller's Introduction, in *Passing*, by Nella Larsen (New York: Collier Books, 1971), 13.
6. According to Gayle Wald, the "postpassing" narratives "[articulate] collective values of pride in the 'Negro' identity and [challenge] the social and economic pressures that promote passing as an 'alternative' to racial segregation." Wald, *Crossing the Color Line: Racial Passing in Twentieth-Century U.S. Literature and Culture* (Durham, NC: Duke University Press, 2000), 119.
7. See Claudia Tate, "Nella Larsen's *Passing*: A Problem of Interpretation," *Black American Literary Forum* 14, no. 4 (Winter 1980): 146.
8. W. E. B. Du Bois, *The Crisis* (1928); also cited in Hiroko Sato, "Under the Harlem Shadow: A Study of Jessie Fauset and Nella Larsen," in *The Harlem Renaissance Remembered: Essays*, ed. Arna Bontemps (New York: Dodd, Mead, 1972), 63–89.
9. W. E. B. Du Bois, *The Crisis* (July 1929), 234; also cited in Fuller.
10. Robert Bone, *The Negro Novel in America* (New Haven, CT: Yale University Press, 1958; revised 1965), 102.
11. Fuller, 18.
12. Sato, 88, 89.
13. Nathan Irvin Huggins, *Harlem Renaissance* (New York: Oxford University Press, 1971), 157, 159.
14. David Levering Lewis, *When Harlem Was in Vogue* (New York: Knopf, 1981; Oxford University Press, 1989), 231.
15. George Hutchinson, "Subject to Disappearance: Interracial Identity in Nella Larsen's *Quicksand*," in *Temples for Tomorrow: Looking Back at the Harlem Renaissance*, ed. Geneviève Fabre and Michel Feith (New York: Oxford University Press, 2001), 177–192.
16. Cheryl A. Wall, *Women of the Harlem Renaissance* (Bloomington and Indianapolis: Indiana University Press, 1995), 132.
17. See Charles R. Larson, *Invisible Darkness: Jean Toomer and Nella Larsen* (Iowa City: University of Iowa Press, 1993), 86, and Thadious M. Davis, *Nella Larsen, Novelist of the Harlem Renaissance: A Woman's Life Unveiled* (Baton Rouge: Louisiana State University Press, 1994). Arthur Davis describes Larsen's first novel as "a moving story," although "not as good a novel as *Quicksand*" (97). Bernard Bell regards *Quicksand* as "structurally…the better of [Larsen's] two novels" (*The Afro-American Novel and Its Tradition* [Amherst: University of Massachusetts Press, 1987], 110). And although questioning the grounds of earlier evaluations of *Passing*, Mary Mabel Youman does not "quarrel with the overall [critical] judgment" that ranks Larsen's second novel "inferior" to her first ("Nella Larsen's *Passing*: A Study of Irony," *CLA Journal* 18 [1974]: 235–241).
18. Gayle Wald aptly deploys this term.
19. This is the second version of William Wells Brown's *Clotel, or, the President's Daughter* (1853), which is currently regarded as the first novel published by an African-American.

20. See David Kirkpatrick, "On Long-Lost Pages, a Female Slave's Voice" (*New York Times*, Nov. 11, 2001: A1, A6), which provides the account of Henry Louis Gates, Jr.'s remarkable "discovery" of this volume. Other African-American passing novels, recovered since the original publication of this essay, include Pauline Hopkins's *Of One Blood: Or the Hidden Self* (1902–1903) and Charles Chesnutt's *Mandy Oxendine* (c. 1897, published 1997).

21. Werner Sollors speculates that "[t]he first American instances in which the word 'passing' was used to signify 'crossing the color line' would seem to have appeared in notices concerning runaway slaves, and the term 'passing'—first for 'free,' and then for (its later part-synonym) 'white'—may have entered American fiction through the citing of such bills" (255).

22. Caleb Johnson, "Crossing the Color Line," *Outlook and Independent* 158 (Aug. 26, 1931): 526; also cited in Sollors, 245.

23. Walter White, "Why I Remain a Negro," *The Saturday Review of Literature*, Oct. 22, 1947; quoted in Amritjit Singh, *The Novels of the Harlem Renaissance: Twelve Black Writers, 1923–1933* (University Park: The Pennsylvania State University Press), 92.

24. Gunnar Myrdal, *An American Dilemma: The Negro Problem and Modern Democracy* (New York and London: Harper & Brothers, 1944), 683, 688.

25. Sterling Brown, *The Negro in American Fiction*, 1937 (New York: Atheneum, 1969), 142.

26. For another treatment of the concept of "disidentification," see José Esteban Muñoz, *Disidentifications: Queers of Color and the Performance of Politics* (Minneapolis: University of MinnesotaPress, 1999).

27. Barbara Christian, *Black Women Novelists: The Development of a Tradition, 1892–1976* (Westport, CT: Greenwood Press, 1980), 44, 45.

28. Bone, 98.

29. Singh, 93.

30. Donald Goellnicht, "Passing as Autobiography: James Weldon Johnson's *The Autobiography of an Ex-Colored Man*," *African-American Review* 30, no. 1 (1996): 19.

31. Examples of works by such Southern writers include Thomas Dixon's *The Clansman* (1905) and *The Leopard's Spots* (1902), Robert Lee Durham's *The Call of the South* (1908), and Thomas Nelson Page's *Red Rock: A Chronicle of Reconstruction* (1898).

32. David Roediger, *The Wages of Whiteness: Race and the Making of the American Working Class* (New York: Verso, 1991); also cited in Ruth Frankenberg, *Displacing Whiteness: Essays in Social and Cultural Criticism* (Durham, NC: Duke University Press, 1997), 10.

33. Sollors, 260.

34. Cheryl I. Harris, "Whiteness as Property," in *Critical Race Theory: The Key Writings That Formed the Movement*, ed. Kimberlé Crenshaw, Neil Gotanda, Gary Peller, and Kendall Thomas (New York: The New Press, 1996), 278.

35. Harris, 278.

36. Eva Saks, "Representing Miscegenation Law," *Raritan* 8, no. 2 (1988): 57.

37. Joel Williamson, *New People: Miscegenation and Mulattoes in the United States* (New York: Free Press, 1980), 98.

38. Sir Francis Galton, the inventor of fingerprinting techniques, began his project, *Finger Prints* (1892), in an attempt to discover an indicator of "Race and Temperament" in the character and patterns of fingerprints. Josiah C. Nott, in his *Two Lectures on the Natural History of the Caucasian and Negro Races* (1844), moved from the scriptural evocation of the curse of Ham to a biological argument for racial difference that was based on a theory of polygenesis. Harvard professor Louis Agassiz, who developed his racial ideas in 1863, is widely acknowledged as one of the major formulators of "scientistic racism." See Sollors, 157, 109, 131.

39. Drawing out the implications of J. L. Austin's work on performative utterances, contemporary theorists such as Jacques Derrida and Judith Butler postulate the performativity of identities constructed through practices of citationality and iterability. "Performativity," Butler argues, "consists in a reiteration of norms which precede, constrain, and exceed the performer and in that sense cannot be taken as the fabrication of the performer's 'will' or 'choice.'" For Butler, then, "The reduction of performativity to performance would be a mistake" (Judith Butler, *Bodies That Matter* [New York: Routledge, 1993], 234).

40. See Mary Helen Washington, "Nella Larsen: Mystery Woman of the Harlem Renaissance," *Ms. Magazine* (December 1980): 44–50. Arguably, of course, the same indictment could be brought against what might be regarded as "compulsory blackness," in which, by virtue of the one-drop rule, one's "roots and genealogy" are also denied.

41. For Wall, these roles are defined as "the perfect lady" and "the exotic Other." Wall argues, correctly, that Irene is "the perfect lady" and Clare "the exotic Other"—both roles rejected by Larsen's earlier protagonist, Helga Crane, in *Quicksand*. See Wall, 121.

42. Deborah McDowell, Introduction, in *Quicksand and Passing*, by Nella Larsen (New Brunswick, NJ: Rutgers University Press, 1986), xxx.

43. Washington, 41. Also see George Hutchinson's *In Search of Nella Larsen: A Biography of the Color Line* (Cambridge, MA: Belknap Press of Harvard University Press, 2006), which appeared after the original publication of this essay. Hutchinson's research has filled in some of the gaps in what we know about the life and work of Nella Larsen.

44. Tate, 143.

45. Wall, 138.

46. Mary V. Dearborn, *Pocahontas's Daughters: Gender and Ethnicity in American Culture* (New York: Oxford University Press, 1986), 59.

47. McDowell, xxvi, xxx. In *Bodies That Matter*, Judith Butler both extends and revises McDowell's reading of *Passing* by arguing that race and sexuality are "inextricably linked, such that the text offers a way to read the racialization of [sex and] sexual conflict" (272).

48. Larson, 82.

49. See Ann duCille, *The Coupling Convention: Sex, Text, and Tradition in Black Women's Fiction* (New York: Oxford University Press, 1993), and Jennifer DeVere Brody, "Clare Kendry's 'True' Colors: Race and Class Conflict in Nella Larsen's *Passing*," *Callaloo* 15, no. 4 (1992): 1053–1065.

50. Hazel V. Carby suggests that the mulatta "is a narrative device of mediation; it allows for a fictional exploration of the relationship between the races while being at the same time an imaginary expression of the relation between the races." See Carby, *Reconstructing Womanhood: The Emergence of the Afro-American Woman Novelist* (New York: Oxford University Press, 1987), 171. Similarly, Ann duCille describes the mulatta as "both a rhetorical device and a political strategy" (7).

51. Nella Larsen, *Passing* (1929), The Modern Library, intro. Ntozake Shange, critical foreward and notes Mae Henderson (New York: Random House, 2002), 51. Subsequent references will appear within parentheses in the text.

52. McDowell, xxvi; Tate, 144.

53. Saks, 44.

54. See Deborah McDowell's argument, cited above, that Irene's attraction to Clare is based on latent or repressed lesbian desire.

55. Saks argues that because "the deviance of social form from legal form makes social form an unreliable sign of legal form (and vice versa), this deviance causes a crisis of representation" (63).

56. Referencing the black postmodernist subject, W. Lawrence Hogue compares the decentered subject of postmodernism to the modernist subject: "Unlike the alienated, modern subject who seeks temporal unification of the past and the future with the present, the postmodern subject is free from all metaphysical narratives, free to simply desire and want. He or she no longer seeks social change; he or she exists only to satisfy his or her own desires." See W. Lawrence Hogue, *Race, Modernity, Postmodernity: A Look at the Literatures of People of Color since the 1960s* (Albany: State University of New York Press, 1996), 152.

57. In his *S/Z*, Roland Barthes distinguishes between *le scriptible* (the writerly) and *le lisible* (the readerly) text, the latter allowing the reader to collaborate in the production of meaning. See Roland Barthes, *S/Z*, trans. Richard Miller (New York: Hill and Wang, 1974). Also see Wolfgang Iser's reader-response model of reading in which the "act of reading" generates new meanings, and even new identities, on the part of the reader: Wolfgang Iser, *The Implied Reader: Patterns of Communication in Prose Fiction from Bunyan to Beckett* (Baltimore, MD: Johns Hopkins

University Press, 1978) and *The Act of Reading: A Theory of Aesthetic Reception* (Baltimore, MD: Johns Hopkins University Press, 1978). Both models of reading would seem especially useful for understanding the consequences of Irene's "act of reading" Clare.

58. My reading here signifies on Deborah McDowell's reading of Larsen's *Passing*.

59. Wall, 130. Curiously, Wall focuses on Irene's function as Clare's double, rather than vice versa. While acknowledging the mutuality of this relation of doubles, my own analysis emphasizes Clare's role as Irene's double.

60. Davis, *Nella Larsen: Novelist of the Harlem Renaissance*, 315.

61. DuCille, 105. DuCille both challenges and expands Wall's and McDowell's readings of Irene.

62. Samira Kawash, *Dislocating the Color Line: Identity, Hybridity, and Singularity in African American Narrative* (Stanford, CA: Stanford University Press, 1997), 18.

63. Significantly, both William Wells Brown's *Clotel* and Frank Webb's *The Garies and Their Friends* refer to the "mezzotinto" of the iris as a physical marker betraying African ancestry in the passing subject.

64. Frankenberg, 6.

65. In response to Chesnutt's article ("What Is a White Man?," *New York Independent* [May 30, 1889]), Cable wrote the following: "You know that all my earlier stories about quadroons really ask this question, 'What is a white man, What is a white woman?'" George Washington Cable, letter to Charles Chesnutt, June 12, 1889. Charles Waddell Chesnutt Collection, Fisk University, Nashville; also cited in Stephen P. Knadler, "Un-tragic Mulatto: Charles Chesnutt and the Discourse of Whiteness," *American Literary History* 8, no. 3 (Fall 1966): 426–448.

66. In its draft stage, Larsen's *Passing* was entitled "Nig"—perhaps, as Thadious Davis speculates, as a "play" upon Carl Van Vechten's *Nigger Heaven* (1926). What is equally intriguing to me is that its initial title ironically echoed the then "undiscovered" novel by Harriet Wilson, entitled *Our Nig* (1859).

67. See Mark J. Madigan, "Miscegenation and 'The Dicta of Race and Class': The Rhinelander Case and Nella Larsen's *Passing*," *Modern Fiction Studies* 36.4 (Winter 1990): 523–529, and James L. Wacks, "Reading Race, Rhetoric and the Female Body: The Rhinelander Case and 1920s American Culture," senior thesis, Harvard University, 1995.

68. David Theo Goldberg, *Racist Culture: Philosophy and the Politics of Meaning* (Cambridge, MA: Blackwell, 1955), 185; also cited in Kawash, 8–9.

69. James Weldon Johnson, *The Autobiography of an Ex-Colored Man* (New York: Hill and Wang, 1960), 190.

70. Tate, 145.

Chapter 12

1. Quoted in Ramsay Burt, *Alien Bodies: Representations of Modernity, "Race," and Nation in Early Modern Dance* (London and New York: Routledge, 1998), 59.

2. "New Plays in Manhattan," *Time* (February 10, 1936): 59.

3. Richard J. Powell and David A. Bailey, "Re/Birth of a Nation," in *Rhapsodies in Black: Art of the Harlem Renaissance* (Berkeley: University of California Press, 1997), 29.

4. Consider, for example, the iconographic and literary representations of the black woman as "The Sable Venus" in William Grainger's engraving of Thomas Stothard's painting, entitled "The Voyage of the Sable Venus" (1794), which was meant to illustrate Issac Teale's 1765 poem, "The Sable Venus; An Ode." Deborah Willis and Carla Williams correctly point out that this "desired and desirable" image figures the colony [Jamaica] as a "depersonalized object of colonial lust." Willis and Williams, *The Black Female Body: A Photographic History* (Philadelphia: Temple University Press, 2002), 9–10. Saartjie (Sarah) Baartman, the "Ebony" or "Hottentot Venus," is discussed later in this chapter.

5. See Fatimah Tobing Rony's insightful exploration of ethnographic cinema in the production of the primitive: *The Third Eye: Race, Cinema, and Ethnographic Spectacle* (Durham, NC, and London: Duke University Press, 1996).

6. See Michel Leiris's revealing account of this expedition: *L'Afrique fantôme:* [*de Dakar à Djibouti, 1931–1933*] (Paris: Gallimard, 1934).

7. Willis and Williams underscore the significance of the distinction here between "documentation" and "construction" (21). It was, of course, by virtue of such expeditions that *l'art nègre* was first introduced to France, as expeditioners returned with the souvenirs and spoils of travel.

8. Exhibits sponsored by the *Jardin d'Acclimatation* and, later, the French government, provided observation laboratories for the French Anthropological Society, which was developing typologies for human classification according to the current ideas of evolution—ideas clearly enlisted as justification for colonial conquest and expansionism.

9. The tradition of the Industrial Exposition began with the Great Exhibition at the Crystal Palace in London in 1851. Historically, the idea for the Exposition is associated with Prince Albert, the husband and consort of Queen Victoria. Its stated purpose was to promote peace and harmony among the nations in an age of technological advance—the railroad, telegraph, and steamship. Subsequently, other nations, including France and America, staged their own industrial expositions, emphasizing industrial progress and nationalism, in contrast to less developed "primitive" cultures. See Willis and Williams's treatment of the representation of the black body at the World's Fairs and exhibitions in Europe and the United States. For broader treatments of the World's Fairs and Expositions, see Robert Rydell's *All the World's a Fair: Visions of Empire at American International Expositions* (Chicago: University of Chicago Press, 1984); John Allwood, *The Great Exhibitions* (London: Studio Vista, 1977); Catherine Hodier and Michel Pierre, eds., *L'Exposition coloniale* (Paris: Editions Complexe, 1991); William H. Schneider, *An Empire for the Masses: The French Popular Image of Africa, 1870–1900* (Westport, CT: Greenwood Press, 1982); Robert C. Young, *Colonial Desire: Hybridity in Theory, Culture and Race* (London and New York: Routledge, 1995); and Susanne Zantop, *Colonial Fantasies: Conquest, Family, and Nation in Precolonial Germany, 1770–1870* (Durham, NC: Duke University Press, 1997).

10. This term is appropriated from Sylviane Leprun, *Le Théâtre des colonies: Scenographie, acteurs et discourse de l'imaginaire dans les expositions, 1855–1937*. Paris: L'Harmattan, 1986.

11. Citing Catherine Coquery's *Histoire de la France Coloniale* (Paris: A. Colin, 1991), Christopher Miller states that attendants included four million Parisians, four million provincials, and one million foreign visitors. See Miller, "Hallucinations of France and Africa in the Colonial Exhibition of 1931 and Ousmane Socé's *Mirages de Paris*," *Paragraph: A Journal of Modern Critical Theory*, 18, no. 1 (March 1995): 45.

12. See Raoul Giradet, *L'Idée coloniale en France de 1871 à 1962* (Paris: Hachette, 1972).

13. Elizabeth Ezra clarifies the distinction between the policies of *assimilation* and *association*, both goals of the French *mission civilisatrice*: "At the turn of the century, the doctrine of association challenged assimilationist policies, which sought to transform colonial possessions into miniatures of France. Implemented by Hubert Lyautey in the 'pacification' of Morocco shortly after the turn of the century, association emphasized the cultural distinctiveness of each colonial possession, its unassimilability to the *métropole*....Association, as it was promoted, would have amounted to a recognition of the cultural, if not political, autonomy of the countries under colonial rule. The goal of assimilation, in contrast, inspired by the equalitarian rhetoric of the French Revolution, was to make model French citizens of colonial subjects, who were taught the intricacies of French language and culture in a centralized educational system." Elizabeth Ezra, *The Colonial Unconscious: Race and Culture in Interwar France* (Ithaca, NY, and London: Cornell University Press, 2000), 4.

14. Cited in Herman Lebovics, *True France: The Wars over Cultural Identity, 1900–1945* (Ithaca, NY, and London: Cornell University Press, 1992), 52. It is instructive to recall here that "the display of the native" was not limited to France, but incorporated into the colonial exhibitions and world's fairs hosted by other countries. For example, the Congolese pygmy Ota Benga was not only featured in the 1904 St. Louis World's Fair, but later in a cage in the New York Central Park Zoo. See Miller, 54–55.

15. An exception to the temporality of most these structures was the Permanent Museum of the Colonies which survived as the Musée des Africains et Océaniens. Notably, the Museum of Ethnography, located in the Palais du Trocadéro, was originally constructed as the exhibition center for ethnographic displays at the 1878 Exposition (it was later replaced by the Musée de l'Homme which opened in 1937). Similarly, the Eiffel Tower was erected at the 1889 Exhibition.

16. What Miller identifies as this "census of the natives" is published in "La délégation indigène" in the fifth volume of the seven-volume *Rapport Général* (1932). The following "inventory of participants" is cited by Miller: "from Senegal, 'six fishermen, three jewelers, one weaver, one embroiderer'; from Dahomey, 'two copperworkers, four pirogue-rowers, fifteen dancers, two jewelers, two wood-sculptors, one medical aide, one midwife.'" Further, adds Miller, the inventory includes an indefinite "number of 'native women who served as cooks'" (47–48).

17. *Guide officiel*, 20. Cited in Miller.

18. Catherine Hodier and Michel Pierre, *L'Exposition coloniale* (Paris: Editions Complexe, 1991). Cited in Miller, 49.

19. Coquery, *Histoire de la France Coloniale*. Cited in Miller, 49.

20. Lebovics employs these terms in describing André Maurois's response to the women of New Caledonia (74).

21. Two cases in point: Michel Leiris remarks that the "'reproduction' of the Djenne temple was modeled on a building that the French in Africa had already rebuilt according to their own idea of 'Sudanese' architectural style." In the second instance, Demaison, in the *Guide officiel*, confesses that the Algerian building constitutes a "stylized synthesis of Algerian architecture" rather than, strictly speaking, a faithful reproduction of the original. As Lebovics suggests, "Not only are the French rulers able to create native cultural traditions when they must, but they can invent characteristic architecture" (81).

22. The following quote is taken from the Exposition catalogue (*L'Illustration*, August 22, 1931, No. 4616-89, translated by Haun Saussy, emphasis added):

   And, in fact, most of those who peer into the primitive huts of black Africans experience a feeling much more of pity than of satisfied curiosity. That is why we are grateful to the organizers of the [French] Equatorial Africa and Mandated Territories sections [of the Exposition] *for interpreting nature by giving free rein to their fantasy, a fantasy that condenses local art and reflects our sensibility.* Earthen walls, multicolored and sculpted totems, straw roofing and enormous logs of wood: nothing but what makes up, for us, the attractive face of Africa.

   The [French] Equatorial Africa pavilion, designed by the architect Fichet under orders from the commissioner general Mirabel, is inspired by the native dwellings of Logon....

   The Cameroon and Togo section is no less suggestive.... For the architects, Messrs Boileau and Carrière, *have brought a rare taste to adapting Negro art to the demands of the Exposition and of aesthetics.* Built with materials from Cameroon, these huts make up an ensemble that André Bonamy, the general commissioner, must be proud of.

23. "Le sculpteur Camille Garnier, chargé de la décoration intérieure du palais, les mêle avec bonheur aux motifs ornementaux qui composent à l'entrée de la grande tour comme une manière de tente aux plis retombants." ("Camille Garnier, sculptor, who received the commission for the interior decoration of the palace, happily mixes them with the ornamental motifs which form, at the entrance of the great tower, a type of tent with hanging folds/pleats.") (*L'Illustration*, August 22, 1931, No. 4616-89, translated by Régine Latortue). Notably, however, in indigenous culture, these masks were sacred objects defined by their spiritual significance. Used in sacred rituals, they were associated with the gods, and shielded from public display. Their viewing required special preparation; even pre-initiate young people could not look on these masks. Thus, to put them on display—to expose them to a secular and foreign gaze—would be a sacrilege in the context of the indigenous culture.

24. Patricia Morton, *Hybrid Modernities: Architecture and Representation at the 1931 Colonial Exhibition in Paris* (Cambridge, MA: MIT Press, 2000).
25. Notably, in the Third Edition of the *Encyclopedia Britannica* (1788–1797), the editors write under the entries "dance" and "dancing" the following: "As barbarous people are observed to have the strongest passions, so they are observed to be the most easily affected by sound, and the most addicted to dancing" (qtd. in Roderyk Lange, *The Nature of Dance: An Anthropological Perspective* [London: Taylor and Francis, 1976], 11).
26. For instance, late-nineteenth- and early-twentieth-century anthropological works "contained data and formulations" that connected dance to native or indigenous culture. See Edward Burnett Tylor's *Primitive Culture* (1871) and *Anthropology* (1881). Cited in Lange, 18.
27. See G. Buschan, as cited in Lange, 18.
28. See work by Sander L. Gilman, Rita Felski, and others who have considered the female body as object of spectacle in Western culture.
29. "Josephine Baker Chosen Queen of the Colonies," *Pittsburgh Courier* (February 21, 1931): 1.
30. *L'art nègre*, or "Negro Art," refers to the so-called "discovery" of African, or "primitive," art and its influence on artistic circles that drew their inspiration from African sculpture in early-nineteenth-century France. Many of these masks and figurines were first encountered in the Musée d'Ethnographie du Trocadéro in which were displayed art and artifacts acquired from France's colonial possessions in Africa. Best known among the artistic works produced during this period are Picasso's *Demoiselles d'Avignon* (1907) and Matisse's *Blue Nude* (1907). The movement also migrated to other European countries, where its influence was evident in the works of such artists as Klee, Brancusi, Modigliani, and others.
31. The Surrealists, under the auspices of the Anti-imperialist League, organized a counter-exposition entitled La Vérité sur les Colonies (The Truth about the Colonies) in which they denounced the plundering of colonial artifacts. Of course, by incorporating these same artifacts into a Western aesthetics of modernism, the Surrealists exposed themselves to a critique of appropriative violence.
32. Gustave Fréjaville, *Au music-hall* (Paris: Editions du monde nouveau, 1923). Quoted in Jody Blake, *Le Tumult Noire: Modernist Art and Popular Entertainment in Jazz-Age Paris, 1900–1930* (University Park: The Pennsylvania State University Press, 1999), 80.
33. Baker starred in four films, including *La Sirène des Tropiques* (1927), *Zouzou* (1934), *Princess Tam-Tam* (1935), and *The French Way* (1940).
34. See Eric Lott, *Love and Theft: Blackface Minstrelsy and the American Working Class* (New York: Oxford University Press, 1993).
35. For interesting treatments of African-Americans in Paris during the early part of the twentieth century, see Blake; Burt; Tyler Stovall, *Paris Noir: African Americans in the City of Light* (New York: Houghton Mifflin, 1996); and Petrine Archer-Straw, *Negrophilia: Avant-Guarde Paris and Black Culture in the 1920s* (New York: Thames and Hudson, 2000). See also Brent Hayes Edwards, *The Practice of Diaspora: Literature, Translation, and the Rise of Black Internationalism* (Cambridge, MA: Harvard University Press, 2003), a volume that appeared after the original publication of the present essay.
36. Quoted in Lynn Haney, *Naked at the Feast: A Biography of Josephine Baker* (New York: Dodd, Mead & Company, 1981), 44.
37. Interviews quoted in Blake, 93.
38. Josephine Baker and Jo Bouillon, *Josephine*, trans. Mariana Fitzpatrick (New York: Paragon House Publishers, 1988), 50.
39. Identifying primitivism as a "product of the European psyche," Petrine Archer-Straw usefully distinguishes between the terms "primitive" and "primitivized": "[Primitivism] was a label conferred by nineteenth-century Europeans in an act of *self*-definition. The word primitive was created to be oppositional to or to complement the relational 'I.' The primitive represented the process through which Europeans suggest their own superiority by placing inferior status on others.... If primitivism is viewed as a product of the European psyche, then what seems to be

a relationship between two parties—the 'civilized' and the 'savage'—is in fact singular, involving only the self and its actions. If any duality exists it is in the act of one party's 'primitvizing' the other. So this book changes perspective, looking only at the 'primitivized,' rather than the 'primitive.'" (11–12).

40. Notably, Baker's feathered loin cloth was created by the famous Parisian designer, Paul Poiret, whose *haute couture* gowns she would later model.

41. Joan Acocella and Lynn Garafola, eds., *André Levinson on Dance: Writings from Paris in the Twenties* (Middletown, CT: Wesleyan University Press, 1991).

42. Morton, 197.

43. Ivan Goll, "The Negroes are Conquering Europe." Originally published as "Die Neger erobern Europa," *Die literarische Welt* no. 2 (January 15, 1936): 3–4, emphasis added.

44. Cited in *E. E. Cummings: A Miscellany Revised*, ed., with an Introduction and Notes, by George J. Firmage (New York: October House, 1965).

45. On January 30, 2002, the French Senate passed a unanimous resolution to repatriate the remains of Saartjie Baartman to her homeland in South Africa. Baartman's genitalia had been on display in the Musée de l'Homme until 1976. Georges Cuvier, a comparative anatomist, had made an examination of Baartman during her lifetime, and when she died in 1814, he made a plaster cast of her body, which he later dissected, preserving her skeleton, brain, and genitalia. The autopsy results were reported in medical studies, and formed the basis for nineteenth-century European notions of innate, biological racial difference. See Sander L. Gilman, "Black Bodies, White Bodies: Toward an Iconography of Female Sexuality in Late Nineteenth-Century Art, Medicine, and Literature," *Critical Inquiry* 12, no. 1 (Autumn 1985): 204–242, and "The Hottentot and the Prostitute: Toward an Iconography of Female Sexuality," in *Difference and Pathology: Stereotypes of Sexuality, Race and Madness* (Ithaca, NY: Cornell University Press, 1985), 76-108; and Rosemary Wiss, "Lipreading: Remembering Saartjie Baartman," *The Australian Journal of Anthropology* 5, nos. 1–2 (1994): 11–40.

46. Wiss, 13, 15.

47. Roger Copeland, "The Search for Origins," *Dance Theatre Journal* 13 (Summer 1996): 9.
I wish to express sincere appreciation to my ideal readers for this chapter, George Cunningham and Sandra Richards; to my translators, Régine Latortue and Haun Saussy; to Janice Ross for her scholarly generosity; to Stephen Lewis for his assistance with the images; and to the Stanford Humanities Center for its support of this work. And, finally, I would like to thank E. Patrick Johnson for his inspiration to complete this essay.

Chapter 13

1. Mae G. Henderson, "Josephine Baker and *La Revue Nègre*: From Ethnography to Performance," *Text and Performance Quarterly* 23, no. 2 (April 2003): 107–133. See Chapter 12 of this volume.

2. Richard Dyer, "Entertainment and Utopia," in *The Cultural Studies Reader*, 2nd ed., ed. Simon During (London and New York: Routledge, 1993), 372.

3. See Stuart Hall, *Representation: Cultural Representations and Signifying Practices*, ed. Stuart Hall (Thousand Oaks, CA: Sage Publications, 1997).

4. Dyer, 373.

5. Paul Gilroy, "'To Be Real': The Dissident Forms of Black Expressive Culture," in *Let's Get It On: The Politics of Black Performance*, ed. Catherine Ugwu (London and Seattle: Bay Press, 1995), 21.

6. Jacques Derrida and Christie V. McDonald, "*Cherchez la Femme*: Feminist Critique/ Feminine Text," *Diacritics* 12, no. 2 (Summer 1982); quoted in Derrida, *The Ear of the Other: Otobiography, Transference, Translation*, trans. Peggy Kamuf, ed. Christie McDonald (Lincoln: University of Nebraska Press, 1985), 163.

7. Stuart Hall, "Introduction: Who Needs 'Identity'?," in *Questions of Cultural Identity*, ed. Stuart Hall and Paul du Gay (London: Sage Publications, 1996), 4.

8. Originally published in *Theatre Arts Monthly*, April 1927; reprinted in *André Levinson on Dance: Writings from Paris in the Twenties*, ed. Joan Acocella and Lynn Garafola (Middletown, CT: Wesleyan University Press, 1991), 74.

9. Elizabeth Ezra, *The Colonial Unconscious: Race and Culture in Interwar France* (Ithaca, NY, and London: Cornell University Press, 2000), 113.

10. Here, I appropriate dance critic Brenda Dixon Gottschild's useful term denoting "African-derived." See Gottschild, *Digging the Africanist Presence in American Performance: Dance and Other Contexts* (Westport, CT: Praeger Publishers, 1996).

11. Toni Morrison, *Beloved* (New York: Alfred A. Knopf, 1987), 190.

12. Hall, "Introduction: Who Needs 'Identity'?," 16.

13. Originally published in *Vanity Fair*, 1926; reprinted in *E. E. Cummings: A Miscellany Revised*, ed. George J. Firmage (New York: October House, Inc., 1965), 161.

14. Harriet Beecher Stowe, *Uncle Tom's Cabin*, 1852 (New York: Random House/Bantam Books, 1981), 271.

15. Firmage, 161–162.

16. Firmage, 162–163.

17. Firmage, 161.

18. Wanda Corn, *The Great American Thing: Modern Art and National Identity, 1915–1935* (Berkeley: University of California Press, 2000), 91.

19. James Haskins, *Black Dance in America: A History Through Its People* (New York: HarperCollins, 1990), 53.

20. Haskins, 81.

21. Haskins, 82.

22. Simon Firth, "Music and Identity," in *Questions of Cultural Identity*, ed. Stuart Hall and Paul du Gay (London: Sage Publications, 1996), 17.

23. Gottschild, 158–159.

24. See Lawrence Levine, *Black Culture and Black Consciousness: Afro-American Folk Thought from Slavery to Freedom* (New York: Oxford University Press, 1977).

25. Stuart Hall, "Cultural Identity and Diaspora," in *Colonial Discourse and Post-colonial Discourse: A Reader*, ed. Patrick Williams and Laura Chrisman (London: Harvester Wheatsheaf, 1994), 394.

26. Stuart Hall, "The Work of Representation," in *Representation: Cultural Representations and Signifying Practices*, 13–74.

27. See Chapter 14 of this volume.

28. This essay is part of a larger project on Josephine Baker as performing artist and political activist. I would like to express my genuine appreciation to Thomas F. DeFrantz, Peggy Phelan, and David Palumbo-Liu for their generous and thought-provoking responses to this phase of my project. I also wish to thank the staff at Emory University's Manuscript, Archives, and Rare Book Library for granting me access to the Josephine Baker papers.

Chapter 14

1. Brenda Dixon Gottschild, *The Black Dancing Body: A Geography from Coon to Cool* (New York: Palgrave MacMillan. 2003), 145.

2. Hip-hop scholar Chyann L. Oliver notes that black girls are torn between rejecting and embracing their butts in what she terms "this ass-obsessed society." See her "for sepia 'colored girls' who have considered self/when hip-hop is enuf," in *Home Girls Make Some Noise: Hip Hop Feminism Anthology*, ed. Gwendolyn D. Pough, Elaine Richardson, Aisha Durham, and Rachel Raimist (Mira Loma, CA: Parking Publishing, 2007), 259.

3. Moira O'Neil, "'Assthetics': Commodification and Consumption of Black Feminine Bodies in a Popular Women's Magazine," Paper presented at the annual meeting of the American Sociological Association, Hilton San Francisco & Renaissance Parc 55 Hotel, San Francisco, CA, August 14, 2004. Available online: http://www.allacademic.com/meta/p110539_index.html.

4. Notably, 2 Live Crew, who arguably inaugurated the genre of the "booty rap," was the notorious rap group defended by African-American scholar Henry Louis Gates, Jr., against charges of obscenity in 1990.

5. See Fatimah N. Muhammad's "How to NOT be 21st Century Venus Hottentots," in Pough, Richardson, Durham, and Raimist, 124.

6. Tricia Rose, *Black Noise: Rap Music and Black Culture in Contemporary America* (Middletown, CT: Wesleyan University Press, 1994), 167–168.

7. Noting the continuing "fascination with black 'butts'...in the traditional black pornographic imagination," bell hooks argues that in Spike Lee's film, *School Daze*, "the black 'butts' on display are unruly and outrageous," thereby constituting "the most transgressive and provocative moment" in the film. See bell hooks, *Black Looks: Race and Representation* (Boston: South End Press, 1992), 62.

8. Patricia Hill Collins defines "controlling images" as negative stereotypes originating during slavery that have been applied to African-American women, and are "fundamental to [b]lack women's oppression." See Collins, *Black Feminist Thought: Knowledge, Consciousness, and the Politics of Empowerment* (Boston: Unwin Hyman, 1990).

9. See Kimala Price's definitions and distinctions between feminisms: "[Hip hop feminism] is often loosely defined as young feminists born after 1964 who identify with hip hop culture, roughly feminists forty-two years of age and under. In this sense, it works as a generational marker that distinguishes those who identify with hip hop from older feminists (particularly those of the civil rights generation or part of the so-called second wave of feminism). However, this term can serve as a marker *within* younger generations; that is, it is a way to distinguish hip-hop feminists from third-wave feminists, who, some may argue, are too narrowly focused on personal politics and not enough on community-building issues. Sometimes, it is used as a distinction along racial lines; that is, it is a term reserved for women of color." See Price, "Hip-Hop Feminism at the Political Crossroads: Organizing for Reproductive Justice and Beyond," in Pough, Richardson, Durham, and Raimist, 391. Also see Joan Morgan's *When Chickenheads Come Home to Roost: A Hip Hop Feminist Breaks It Down* (New York: Simon & Shuster, 1999), an early manifesto of hip-hop feminism.

For a discussion of the often somewhat vexed relations between these positions, see Whitney A. Peoples's "'Under Construction': Identifying Foundations of Hip-Hop Feminism and Exploring Bridges between Black Second-Wave and Hip-Hop Feminisms," *Meridians: feminism, race, transnationalism* 8, no. 1 (2007): 19–52. For an example of second-wave black feminist criticism of hip-hop culture and rap music, see Johnetta Betsch Cole and Beverly Guy-Sheftall, "No Respect: Gender Politics and Hip-Hop," in *Gender Talk: The Struggle for Women's Equality in African American Communities* (New York: One World Ballantine, 2003), 182–215. And for another perspective on feminism and hip-hop, see Patricia Hill Collins, "Is the Personal Still Political?: The Women's Movement, Feminism, and Black Women in the Hip-Hop Generation," in *From Black Power to Hip Hop: Racism, Nationalism, and Feminism* (Philadelphia: Temple University Press, 2006), 161–196.

10. Lisa Collins, "Economies of the Flesh: Representing the Black Female Body in Art," in *Skin Deep, Spirit Strong: The Black Female Body in American Culture*, ed. Kimberly Wallace-Sanders (Ann Arbor: The University of Michigan Press, 2002) 101, 102.

11. Cited in Lisa Collins, 113.

12. Michael Eric Dyson, *Know What I Mean? Reflections on Hip Hop* (New York: Basic Civitas Books, 2007), 99.

13. Levita D. Mondie-Sapp, "The Highest Bidder," in Pough, Richardson, Durham, and Raimist, 387–388. Notably, Cole and Guy-Sheftall make a similar analogy between women in rap and women on the auction block: "Some rappers have made millions rapping about women [*sic*] giving up sex in exchange for liquor, jewelry, and less. The message that young black women's bodies can be purchased cheaply on the open market is a grim, modern-day reminder of slavery. In some ways, Black women are still on the auction block! What makes this scenario so devastating, however, is that it is our own men…who are frequently doing the bidding and buying in this century" (199).

14. The post-nineties millennial representation of black women in hip-hop corporate culture and industry is dramatically illustrated in the 2004 production of rapper Nelly's highly controversial and provocative "Tip Drill," a music video (song produced by David Banner) that has become a defining moment marking the sexual fetishization and commodification of black women in hip-hop music video culture. At the end of the video, Nelly swipes a credit card down the crack in the rear end of scantily clad video dancer Whyte Chocolate, flashes a bejeweled-tooth smile at the camera, and gives the viewer a "thumps up," after which the dancer begins a series of furious fanny gyrations.

15. Muhammad, 134.

16. See, for instance, Muhammad (cited above) and Kaila Adia Story's "Performing Venus—From Hottentot to Video Vixen: The Historical Legacy of Black Female Body Commodification," in Pough, Richardson, Durham, and Raimist.

17. See Anne Fausto-Sterling, "Gender, Race, and Nation: The Comparative Anatomy of 'Hottentot' Women in Europe, 1815–17," in Wallace-Sanders. Also see the frequently cited early scholarship on Baartman by Sander L. Gilman, *Difference and Pathology: Stereotypes of Sexuality, Race, and Madness* (Ithaca, NY: Cornell University Press, 1985).

18. Fausto-Sterling, 84.

19. Brenda Dixon Gottschild describes Baartman as a kind of "static…artifact" (153).

20. Quoted in Bernth Lindfors, "The Hottentot Venus and Other African Attractions" [unpublished], 2; quoted in Stuart Hall, ed., *Representation: Cultural Representations and Signifying Practices* (London: Sage, 1997), 265.

21. In May 2002 Baartman's remains were repatriated to South Africa. See Mae G. Henderson, "Josephine Baker and *La Revue Nègre*: From Ethnography to Performance," *Text and Performance Quarterly* 23, no. 2 (April 2003): 108–133. See Chapter 12 in this volume.

22. Jeanne Scheper, "'Of la Baker, I Am Disciple': The Diva Politics of Reception," *Camera Obscura* 22 [65, no. 2] (2007): 88, emphasis added. For a meditation on Josephine Baker and the politics of the "bottom," see Suzan-Lori Parks, "The Rear End Exists," *Grand Street* 55 (1986): 10–18.

23. Joan Acocella and Lynn Garafola, eds., *André Levinson on Dance: Writings from Paris in the Twenties* (Middletown, CT: Wesleyan University Press, 1991), 74; originally published in *Theatre Arts Monthly*, April 1927.

24. For further discussion of Levinson on Baker, see Mae G. Henderson, "Colonial, Postcolonial and Diasporic Readings of Josephine Baker as Dancer and Performance Artist," *Josephine Baker: A Century in the Spotlight, Scholar & Feminist Online Double Issue* 6, nos. 1–2 (Fall 2007/ Spring 2008). See Chapter 13 in this volume.

25. Arthur Johnson, "Svartkonst Revyprat med Arthur Johnson," *Filmjournalen*; cited in Ylva Habel, "To Stockholm, with Love: The Critical Reception of Josephine Baker, 1927–35," *Film History* 17, no. 1 (2005): 134.

26. Jean-Claude Baker and Chris Chase, *Josephine: The Hungry Heart* (New York: Random House, 1994), 154.

27. Quoted in Phyllis Rose, *Jazz Cleopatra: Josephine Baker in Her Time* (New York: Doubleday, 1989), 24, emphasis added.

28. See Henderson, "Josephine Baker and *La Revue Nègre*."

29. Baker and Chase, 131.

30. Examples of her self-marketing include the production of Josephine Baker dolls; the hair product Baker-Fix; the opening of her own clubs; the commercialization of her chateau, *Les Milandes*; as well as her ability, despite her lack of formal education, to parley her image and performance into a fortune that made her, at one time, the wealthiest black woman in the world.
31. See Pierre Bourdieu, *Distinction: A Social Critique of the Judgement of Taste* (Cambridge, MA: Harvard University Press, 1984).
32. See Henderson, "Josephine Baker and *La Revue Nègre*."
33. Daphne Brooks, "The End of the Line: Josephine Baker and the Politics of Black Women's Corporeal Comedy," *Josephine Baker: A Century in the Spotlight, Scholar & Feminist Online Double Issue* 6, nos. 1–2 (Fall 2007/Spring 2008), 2.
34. Baker and Chase, 248.
35. See Margo Crawford's *Dilution Anxiety and the Black Phallus* (Columbus: Ohio State University Press, 2008) for a suggestive discussion of fetishism and black literary performance.
36. Bennetta Jules-Rosetta argues that cross-dressing and nudity were "sources of feminine empowerment that created shock value" in *Josephine Baker in Art and Life: The Icon and the Image* (Urbana and Chicago: University of Illinois Press, 2007), 66.
37. Phyllis Rose, 81.
38. My position here expands that of Phyllis Rose, who argues that "[f]rom the later twenties date the striking photographs of [Josephine Baker] in glamorous designer dresses crossing her eyes, and at this stage of her life, the eye-crossing seems…to function like a magical gesture of self-defense in a specifically erotic arena. It wards off the relentlessly erotic gaze of whoever might have been looking at her, as mythically one warded off vampires by making the sign of the cross. Afraid…of evoking undiluted sexual excitement, she thwarts the deeply provocative contact of eye with eye not just by averting her own eyes but by jamming them grotesquely up against one another" (109).
39. For Laura Mulvey, "looking itself is a source of pleasure, just as in the reverse formation, there is pleasure in being looked at." Importantly, the notion advanced above revises Mulvey's thesis in that it attaches not only *pleasure*, but *power*, both to the *subject* (possessor) of the gaze as well as to the *object* (or recipient) of the gaze. See Laura Mulvey, *Visual and Other Pleasures* (Bloomington: Indiana University Press, 1989), 204.
40. Arguably, then, the white male spectator is interpellated into the video by the black male video artist and performer. Notably, Mediamark Research Inc. (MRI), which tracks the racial demographic of rap consumers, has reported that for the years 1995, 1999, and 2001 the percentage of white consumers numbered between 70 and 75 percent. In the fall of 2004, MRI revised its estimate to 60 percent. See Carl Bialik, "Is the Conventional Wisdom Correct in Measuring Hip-Hop Audience?," *The Wall Street Journal* (May 5, 2005).
41. Evelynn M. Hammonds argues that black women are imprinted by a history that has rendered them "simultaneously invisible (exposed), hypervisible, and pathologized in dominant discourses." See "Toward a Genealogy of Black Female Sexuality: The Problematic of Silence," in *Feminist Theory and the Body: A Reader*, ed. Janet Price and Margaret Shildrick (New York: Routledge, 1997), 93.
42. Jenee Osterheldt, "For Some, Misogyny's Spelled R-A-P," *Seattle Times* (August 19, 2005).
43. Karrine Steffans, *Confessions of a Video Vixen* (New York: HarperCollins, 2005), xiv.
44. Quoted in dParker2.0, "Video Vixens: Victims of Exploitation, or Using Feminism to Their Advantage," Blog Post, *Blissfully Clueless* (March 26, 2006): http://blissfullyclueless.blogspot.com/2006/03/video-vixens-victims-of-exploitation.html.
45. Karrine Steffans has since published *The Vixen Diaries* (2007) and *The Vixen Manual* (2009).
46. Debra Curtis, "Commodities and Sexual Subjectivities: Capitalism and Its Desires," *Cultural Anthropology* 19, no. 1 (2004): 95–121.
47. Rana A. Emerson, "'Where My Girls At?': Negotiating Black Womanhood in Music Videos," *Gender and Society* 2, no. 115 (2002). Emerson argues that these videos allow black women viewers "to place themselves as subjects of the text and narrative" and that the black woman

performer "is able to construct a subject position for herself and her women viewers." Her thesis turns on the construction of male bodies as objects of the female gaze. However, while such a reversal does indeed reposition the black female performer, it does so only by way of a kind of defensive reaction formation.

48. See Meredith Levande, "Women, Pop Music, and Pornography," *Meridians: feminism, race, transnationalism* 8, no. 1 (2008): 299–301.

49. See Ice-T, "Ice T Speaks on His Life, Coco and Making It in the Hip Hop Industry," video interview, *DimeWars*: http//dimewars.com/Video/Ice-T-Speaks-on-His-Life--Coco-and-Making-It-In-the-Hip-Hop-Industry.

50. Aya de Leon, "Hip-Hop Ventriloquism: From Sexism to Corporate Control," in Pough, Richardson, Durham, and Raimist, 441.

51. Mireille Miller-Young, "Hip-Hop Honeys and Da Hustlaz: Black Sexualities in the New Hip-Hop Pornography," *Meridians: feminism, race, transnationalism* 8, no. 1 (2008): 261–292. While I regard the connection between hip hop and porn as troublesome, Miller-Young argues that "hip-hop porn provides black women and men . . . a space for work, survival, consumption . . . identity-formation [and] . . . an opportunity to explore the gendering of black (post) modern desires" (262–263). For another perspective, see Meredith Levande, who "as a singer/songwriter on the college circuit [is] . . . unsettled by the increasing presence of pornography in the music industry" (293).

52. The connection between hip-hop culture and hardcore pornography is attested, for instance, by the release of rapper/MC Snoop Dogg's *Doggystyle*, and *Hustlaz: Diary of a Pimp*, both produced by *Hustler* and respective recipients of the 2002 and 2004 Adult Video News Awards.

53. Richard Dyer, "Entertainment and Utopia," in *The Cultural Studies Reader*, 2nd ed., ed. Simon During (London and New York: Routledge, 1993), 372.

54. Cole and Guy-Sheftall, 201.

55. See Russell Simmons's remarks on the April 17, 2007, episode of *The Oprah Winfrey Show:* "After Imus: The Hip-Hop Community Responds," emphasis added.

56. Dyson further argues that "[H]ip hop [is] the ugly exaggeration of viewpoints that are taken for granted in many conservative circles across the nation" (116).

57. "From Imus to Industry: The Business of Stereotypes and Degrading Images," Congressional Hearing before House Energy and Commerce Commission subcommittee, convened by Rep. Bobby Rush and held on September 26, 2007, emphasis added.

58. See Georg Lukács, *Theory of the Novel*, 1920, trans. Anna Bostock (Cambridge, MA: MIT Press, 1971). The Marxian aesthetic of reflectionism associated with Lukács draws on the well-established notion that art reflects material reality, superstructure reflects base, and consciousness reflects being. Notably, it was the Frankfurt School, a neo-Marxist group that arose during the post–World War II period as a response to German Fascism, that launched the classic critique of mass and popular culture (the "culture industry") as agents of socialization promoting the values and ideologies of the dominant society. And while critics like Walter Benjamin take the position that culture can be both progressive and oppositional, later Marxists like Antonio Gramsci maintain the defining relationship between base and superstructure, although he reverses this relationship by arguing that it is the superstructure (or social relations of production, including literature and popular culture) that effectively controls the base (economic relations). In contemporary Marxist theory, the notion of art as reflection of material reality has since evolved into a more complex notion of art as "mediation." Louis Althusser, for instance, formulates a more interdependent relationship between base and superstructure, one in which individual subjectivities get constituted by what he calls ISAs, or ideological state apparatuses, which include family, religion, education, and important to our purposes, media culture—all of which "interpellate" the individual into subjectivity. Interestingly, Althusser returns to Lukács in that his theory posits an identity that is fundamentally shaped by and reflected in ideology. See Louis Althusser, "Ideology and Ideological State Apparatuses (Notes towards an Investigation)," in *Lenin and Philosophy, and Other Essays*, trans. Ben Brewster (New York: Monthly Review Press, 1971), 127–188.

59. After substantively completing this essay, I read Tricia Rose's *The Hip Hop Wars* (New York: Basic Civitas Books, 2008), a valuable contribution to the dialogue that addresses the "keeping it real" argument and its "affirmation and glorification" of what she describes as "street-based ghetto fictions" (142, 146, 158).

60. Stuart Hall continues as follows: "The way in which a transgressive politics in one domain is constantly sutured and stabilized by reactionary or unexamined politics in another is only to be explained by this continuous cross-dislocation of one identity by another, one structure by another." See Stuart Hall, "What Is This 'Black' in Black Popular Culture?," in *Black Popular Culture*, ed. Gina Dent (Seattle: Bay Press, 1992), 31.

61. Stuart Hall, "What Is This 'Black' in Black Popular Culture?," 31.

62. T. Deanean Sharpley-Whiting notes that "black women's bodies are ubiquitous—from strip clubs to porn to hip hop videos; they have been critical to popular culture's promulgation of 'stripper chic,' and indeed hip hop culture in its latest permutation." See *Pimps Up, Ho's Down: Hip Hop's Hold on Young Black Women* (New York and London: New York University Press, 2007), 145.

63. Sharpley-Whiting, 82.

64. Dyson, 142.

65. The concept of "misperformance" (and its uses) was suggested to me by the Performance Studies International Conference #15: Misfiring, Misfitting, Misreading that took place in Zagreb, Croatia, June 24–28, 2009, and at which I presented an earlier version of this project.

66. See Cathy Caruth, ed., *Trauma: Explorations in Memory* (Baltimore, MD: The Johns Hopkins University Press, 1995) and *Unclaimed Experience: Trauma, Narrative, and History* (Baltimore, MD: The Johns Hopkins University Press, 1996); Dominick LaCapra, *Writing History, Writing Trauma* (Baltimore, MD: The Johns Hopkins University Press, 2001); and Judith Herman, *Trauma and Recovery: The Aftermath of Violence* (New York: Basic Books, 1992).

67. For more popular, rather than, strictly speaking, scholarly treatments of this topic, see Joy Degruy Leary, *Post Traumatic Slave Syndrome: America's Legacy of Enduring Injury and Healing* (Portland, OR: Uptone Press, 2005), in which she defines Post Traumatic Slave Syndrome (PTSS) as "a condition that exists when a population has experienced multigenerational trauma resulting from centuries of slavery and continues to experience oppression and institutionalized racism" (125); and Omar G. Reid, Sekou Mims, and Larry Higginbottom, *Post Traumatic Slavery Disorder: Definition, Diagnosis, and Treatment* (Charlotte, NC: Conquering Books, 2005).

68. Quoted in Jennifer Griffiths, "Uncanny Spaces: Trauma, Cultural Memory, and the Female Body in Gayl Jones's *Corregidora* and Maxine Hong Kingston's *The Woman Warrior*," *Studies in the Novel* 38, no. 3 (2006): 354. See Kathleen Olympia Nadar, "Violence: Effects of Parents' Previous Trauma on Currently Traumatized Children," in *International Handbook of Multigenerational Legacies of Trauma*, ed. Yael Danieli (New York: Plenum Press, 1998), 571–584, and Maria P. P. Root, "Reconstructing the Impact of Trauma on Personality," in *Personality and Psychopathology: Feminist Reappraisals*, ed. Laura S. Brown and Mary Balou (New York: Guilford Press, 1992), 229–266. Notably, Besel A. van der Kolk and others have recently argued that traumatic memory is physiologically encoded in the brain, thus advancing a neurobiological, rather than a psychoanalytic, notion of trauma.

69. Shalanda Faulk Coleman, "Look[-ing] Back at It": (Re)Enacting Historical Trauma and White Hegemonic Desire through Black (S)exploitation in Hip Hop" (unpublished essay). See also Saidiya V. Hartman, *Scenes of Subjection: Terror, Slavery, and Self-Making in Nineteenth-Century America* (New York and Oxford: Oxford University Press, 1997) and Walter Johnson, *Soul by Soul: Life Inside the Antebellum Slave Market* (Cambridge, MA: Harvard University Press, 1999).

70. Although, in the late 1890s, Freud abandoned his "seduction theory," tracing the etiology of female neurosis to repressed infantile sexual fantasies, his motives for recantation have not been lost upon revisionist psychoanalysts and psychoanalytic scholars. See Sándor Ferenczi and others.

71. See the *Diagnostic and Statistical Manual of Mental Disorders* (DSM) published by the American Psychiatric Association that defined PTSD in 1980 (*DSM-III*). It was revised in 1994 (*DSM-IV*), and *DSM-V* was published in 2013.
72. Ruth Leys, *Trauma: A Genealogy* (Chicago and London: The University of Chicago Press, 2000).
73. I draw here on Jacques Lacan's notion of *méconnaissance*.
74. Morgan, 76.
75. I draw on Kelly Oliver's useful notions of "response-ability" and "address-ability" here. See Kelly Oliver, *Witnessing: Beyond Recognition* (Minneapolis: University of Minnesota Press, 2001) as well as Shoshana Felman and Dori Laub, *Testimony: Crisis of Witnessing in Literature, Psychoanalysis, and History* (New York: Routledge, 1992).
76. Derived from the French and Italian terms connoting "disposition" and "posture," in its original seventeenth-century usage, "attitude" was a term related to the arts of design. According to the *Oxford English Dictionary*, as a technical term in the fine arts [read: contemporary visual and media culture], "attitude" designates (1) "the 'disposition' of a figure in statuary or painting; hence, the posture given to it" and, merging with its second definition, (2) "a posture of the body proper to, or implying, some action or mental state assumed by human beings." *The Compact Edition of the Oxford English Dictionary*, Complete Text Reproduced Micrographically (Oxford: Oxford University Press, 1971).
77. Ralph Ellison, *Invisible Man*, Second Vintage International Edition (New York: Vintage, 1995), 354; originally published by Random House, 1952.
78. For an introduction to hip-hop and the musical genre of rap, and for an appreciation of its importance in both American and global popular culture, I wish to thank my former undergraduate and graduate students, including Egygirba High, Kinitra Brooks, and Shalanda Faulk Coleman, who sent me more links and leads than I could possibly acknowledge in the present essay. And for their generous readings of drafts of this essay, I am indebted to my colleagues Charlene Regester and Cheryl A. Wall.

Chapter 15

1. Ralph Ellison, "Portrait of Inman Page: A Dedication Speech," in *Going to the Territory* (1986), First Vintage International Edition (New York: Vintage, 1995), 113.
2. Sherley Anne Williams, "The Peacock Poems: 2," in *The Peacock Poems* (Middletown, CT: Wesleyan University Press, 1975), 41.
3. Williams, "A Pavonine Truth," in *The Peacock Poems*, 46.
4. Williams, Autobiographical Preface to "Meditations on History," in *Midnight Birds: Stories of Contemporary Black Women Writers*, ed. Mary Helen Washington (Garden City, NY: Anchor Books/Doubleday,1980), 195.
5. This quotation comes from Michael Harper's blurb on the back cover of the book jacket of Sherley Anne Williams's *The Peacock Poems*.
6. I quote here from "Any Woman's Blues," in Williams's The Peacock Poems (13), as well as from "The House of Desire," in the same volume (51).
7. This term is attributed to Bernard Bell, who defines the "neo-slave narratives" as "residually oral, modern narratives of escape from bondage to freedom." See *The Afro-American Novel and Its Tradition* (Amherst: The University of Massachusetts Press, 1987), 289.
8. Williams, "Home," in *The Peacock Poems*, 28.
9. Ellison, "Going to the Territory," in *Going to the Territory*, 126.
10. The 1992 International Theatre Festival of Chicago featured Williams's "Letters From a New England Negro," presented by Rites & Reason, a theater company associated with Brown University's Afro-American Studies Program.
11. For those who may not recognize it, "BAP" is the acronym in the vernacular for "Black American Princess."
12. Williams, "Any Woman's Blues," in *The Peacock Poems*, 25.

Chapter 16

1. From the Latin, translated as "She conquers who conquers herself."
2. Kenneth Burke, "Literature as Equipment for Living," *Direction* 1 (1938): 10–13.
3. Jane Campbell, "An Interview with Bebe Moore Campbell," *Callaloo* 22, no. 4 (1999): 970.
4. Transcript of Online Chat between Bebe Moore Campbell and *barnesandnoble.com*, posted to the Website for the African American Literature Book Club, *aalbc.com*: http://aalbc.com/authors/bebecampbellchattext.htm.
5. "Between the Lines with Bebe Moore Campbell," *Time Online* (August 6, 2005): http://content.time.com/time/nation/article/0,8599,1090784,00.html.
6. Laurel Graeber, "'It's About Childhood'" (Interview with Bebe Moore Campbell), *New York Times Book Review* (September 20, 1992): 13.
7. Jane Campbell, "An Interview with Bebe Moore Campbell," 963.
8. Bebe Moore Campbell, *What You Owe Me* (New York: G. P. Putnam, 2001), 533.
9. "Bebe Moore Campbell's New Book," Interview on CBS News's *The Early Show*, August 1, 2005: http://www.cbsnews.com/videos/bebe-moore-campbells-new-book/.
10. Bebe Moore Campbell, *72-Hour Hold* (New York: Alfred A. Knopf, 2005), 319.

Coda

1. Toni Morrison, *Sula* (New York: Alfred A. Knopf, 1973; Bantam, 1975), 44.
2. Pam Houston, "The Truest Eye" (Interview with Toni Morrison), *O, The Oprah Magazine* (November 2003); available online: http://www.oprah.com/omagazine/Toni-Morrison-Talks-Love/1.
3. Morrison, 105.

BIBLIOGRAPHY

Abel, Elizabeth. "[E]merging Identities: The Dynamics of Female Friendship in Contemporary Fiction by Women." *Signs: Journal of Women in Culture and Society* 6, no. 3 (Spring 1981): 413–435.

Abel, Elizabeth, and Emily K. Abel, eds. *The Signs Reader: Women, Gender and Scholarship.* Chicago: University of Chicago Press, 1983.

Acocella, Joan, and Lynn Garafola, eds. *André Levinson on Dance: Writings from Paris in the Twenties.* Middletown, CT: Wesleyan University Press, 1991.

Adams, Nehemiah. *A South-side View of Slavery; or, Three Months at the South in 1854.* Boston: T. R. Marvin and B. B. Mussey, 1854.

"After Imus: The Hip-Hop Community Responds." *The Oprah Winfrey Show,* April 17, 2007.

Alcoff, Linda. "The Problem of Speaking for Others." *Cultural Critique* 20 (Winter 1991–1992): 5–32.

Allwood, John. *The Great Exhibitions.* London: Studio Vista, 1977.

Althusser, Louis. "Ideology and Ideological State Apparatuses (Notes towards an Investigation)." *Lenin and Philosophy, and Other Essays.* Trans. Ben Brewster. New York: Monthly Review Press, 1971. 127–188.

Andrews, William. *To Tell a Free Story: The First Century of Afro-American Autobiography, 1760–1865.* Urbana-Champagne: University of Illinois Press, 1988.

Anello, Ray, and Pamela Abramson. "Characters in Search of a Book." *Newsweek* (June 21, 1982): 67.

Angelou, Maya. *I Know Why the Caged Bird Sings.* New York: Random House, 1969.

Anzaldúa, Gloria. *Borderlands/La Frontera: The New Mestiza.* San Francisco: Spinsters/Aunt Lute, 1987.

Aptheker, Herbert. *American Negro Slave Revolts.* 1943. New York: International Publishers, 1969.

——. "A Note on the History." *The Nat Turner Rebellion: The Historical Event and the Modern Controversy.* Ed. John B. Duff and Peter M. Mitchell. New York: Harper and Row, 1971. 191–195.

Aptheker, Herbert, and William Styron. "Truth and Nat Turner: An Exchange." *The Nat Turner Rebellion: The Historical Event and the Modern Controversy.* Ed. John B. Duff and Peter M. Mitchell. New York: Harper and Row, 1971. 195–202.

Archer-Straw, Petrine. *Negrophilia: Avant-Garde Paris and Black Culture in the 1920s.* New York: Thames and Hudson, 2000.

Arnold, Matthew. "The Function of Criticism at the Present Time." *The National Review* 2, no. 1 (November 1864): 280–307.

Austin, J. L. *How to Do Things with Words.* 2nd ed. Ed. J. O. Urmson and Marina Sbisà. Cambridge, MA: Harvard University Press, 1975.

——. *Philosophical Papers.* Oxford: Oxford University Press, 1961.

Bachelard, Gaston. *The Poetics of Space.* Trans. Maria Jolas. New York: Orion Press, 1964.

Baker, Houston A., Jr. *Blues, Ideology, and Afro-American Literature: A Vernacular Theory.* Chicago: University of Chicago Press, 1984.

——. *The Journey Back*. Chicago: University of Chicago Press, 1980.

——. "There Is No More Beautiful Way: Theory and the Poetics of Afro-American Women's Writing." *Afro-American Literary Study in the 1990s*. Ed. Houston A. Baker, Jr., and Patricia Redmond. Chicago: University of Chicago Press, 1989. 135–155.

——. *Workings of the Spirit: The Poetics of Afro-American Women's Writing*. Chicago: University of Chicago Press, 1991.

Baker, Houston A., Jr., and Patricia Redmond. "Introduction." *Afro-American Literary Study in the 1990s*. Ed. Houston A. Baker, Jr., and Patricia Redmond. Chicago: University of Chicago Press, 1989. 1–13.

Baker, Houston A., Jr., and Patricia Redmond, eds. *Afro-American Literary Study in the 1990s*. Chicago: University of Chicago Press, 1989.

Baker, Jean-Claude, and Chris Chase. *Josephine: The Hungry Heart*. New York: Random House, 1994.

Baker, Josephine, and Jo Bouillon. *Josephine*. Trans. Mariana Fitzpatrick. New York: Paragon House Publishers, 1988.

Bakhtin, Mikhail. "Discourse in the Novel." *The Dialogic Imagination: Four Essays by M. M. Bakhtin*. Ed. Michael Holquist. Trans. Caryl Emerson and Michael Holquist. Austin: University of Texas Press, 1981. 259–422.

Baldwin, James. *Go Tell It on the Mountain*. New York: Alfred A. Knopf, 1953.

Balzac, Honoré de. *Sarrasine*. S/Z. By Roland Barthes. Trans. Richard Miller. New York: Hill and Wang, 1974. 221–254.

Bambara, Toni Cade. Preface. *Daughters of the Dust: The Making of an African American Woman's Film*. By Julie Dash. New York: The New Press, 1992. xi–xvi.

Baran, Paul A. "The Commitment of the Intellectual." Address delivered to the American Association for the Advancement of Science in New York on December 27, 1960, and published in *Monthly Review* 13, no. 1 (1961).

Barthes, Roland. *The Responsibility of Forms: Critical Essays on Music, Art, and Representation*. Trans. Richard Howard. New York: Hill and Wang, 1985.

——. *Roland Barthes*. Trans. Richard Howard. 1977. Berkeley: University of California Press, 1994.

——. *S/Z*. Trans. Richard Miller. New York: Hill and Wang, 1974.

——. "What Is Criticism?" *Critical Essays*. Trans. Richard Howard. Evanston, IL: Northwestern University Press, 1972. 255–260.

Bassard, Katherine Clay. *Spiritual Interrogations: Culture, Gender, and Community in Early African American Women's Writing*. Princeton, NJ: Princeton University Press, 1999.

Baxter, Ronald E. *The Charismatic Gift of Tongues*. Grand Rapids, MI: Kregel Publications, 1981.

Baym, Nina. *Women's Fiction: A Guide to Novels by and about Women in America, 1820–1870*. Ithaca, NY: Cornell University Press, 1978.

"Bebe Moore Campbell's New Book." Interview on CBS News's *The Early Show*. August 1, 2005: http://www.cbsnews.com/videos/bebe-moore-campbells-new-book/.

Bell, Bernard. *The Afro-American Novel and Its Tradition*. Amherst: The University of Massachusetts Press, 1987.

Benjamin, Jessica. *The Bonds of Love: Psychoanalysis, Feminism, and the Problem of Domination*. New York: Pantheon Books, 1988.

Benjamin, Walter. *Illuminations*. Trans. Harry Zohn. New York: Schocken Books, 1969.

Bersani, Leo. "Representations and Its Discontents." *Allegory and Representation*. Ed. Stephen J. Greenblatt. Baltimore, MD: Johns Hopkins University Press, 1981.

"Between the Lines with Bebe Moore Campbell." *Time Online* (August 6, 2005): http://content. time.com/time/nation/article/0,8599,1090784,00.html.

Bhabha, Homi K. *The Location of Culture*. New York: Routledge, 1994.

Bialik, Carl. "Is the Conventional Wisdom Correct in Measuring Hip-Hop Audience?" *The Wall Street Journal* (May 5, 2005).

Bialostosky, Don. "Dialectic and Anti-Dialectic: A Bakhtinian Critique of Gadamer's Dialectical Model of Conversation." Paper delivered at the International Association of Philosophy and Literature. Emory University, Atlanta, GA. May 1989.

Blake, Jody. *Le Tumult Noire: Modernist Art and Popular Entertainment in Jazz-Age Paris, 1900–1930*. University Park: The Pennsylvania State University Press, 1999.

Blassingame, John. *The Slave Community*. New York: Oxford University Press, 1972.

Bloom, Harold. *The Anxiety of Influence: A Theory of Poetry*. New York: Oxford University Press, 1973.

Bone, Robert. *The Negro Novel in America*. New Haven, CT: Yale University Press, 1958; revised 1965.

Bontemps, Arna, ed. *The Harlem Renaissance Remembered: Essays*. New York: Dodd, Mead, & Co., 1972.

Bourdieu, Pierre. *Distinction: A Social Critique of the Judgement of Taste*. Cambridge, MA: Harvard University Press, 1984.

Bradley, David. *The Chaneysville Incident*. New York: Harper & Row, 1981.

Brody, Jennifer DeVere. "Clare Kendry's 'True' Colors: Race and Class Conflict in Nella Larsen's *Passing*." *Callaloo* 15, no. 4 (1992): 1053–1065.

Brooks, Daphne. "The End of the Line: Josephine Baker and the Politics of Black Women's Corporeal Comedy." *Josephine Baker: A Century in the Spotlight, Scholar & Feminist Online Double Issue* 6, nos. 1–2 (Fall 2007/Spring 2008).

Brooks, Peter. *Reading for the Plot: Design and Intention in Narrative*. Cambridge, MA: Harvard University Press, 1984.

Brown, Norman O. *Life against Death: The Psychoanalytical Meaning of History*. Middletown, CT: Wesleyan University Press, 1959.

Brown, Sterling. *The Negro in American Fiction*. 1937. New York: Atheneum, 1969.

Brown, William Wells. *Clotel; or, The President's Daughter*. London: Partridge & Oakley, 1853.

——. *Clotel, A Tale of the Southern States*. Boston: J. Redpath, 1864.

Brumback, Carl. *What Meaneth This?* Springfield, MO: Gospel Publishing House, 1947.

Burke, Kenneth. "Literature as Equipment for Living." *Direction* 1 (1938): 10–13.

Burt, Ramsay. *Alien Bodies: Representations of Modernity, "Race," and Nation in Early Modern Dance*. London and New York: Routledge, 1998.

Butler, Judith. *Bodies That Matter*. New York: Routledge, 1993.

Cable, George Washington. Letter to Charles Chesnutt, June 12, 1899. Charles Waddell Chesnutt Collection. Fisk University, Nashville, TN.

Campbell, Bebe Moore. *72-Hour Hold*. New York: Alfred A. Knopf, 2005.

——. *Brothers and Sisters*. New York: G. P. Putnam, 1994.

——. *Singing in the Comeback Choir*. New York: G. P. Putnam, 1998.

——. *Sweet Summer: Growing Up with and without My Dad*. New York: G. P. Putnam, 1989.

——. *What You Owe Me*. New York: G. P. Putnam, 2001.

——. *Your Blues Ain't Like Mine*. New York: G. P. Putnam, 1992.

Campbell, Jane. "An Interview with Bebe Moore Campbell." *Callaloo* 22, no. 4 (1999): 954–972.

Carby, Hazel V. *Reconstructing Womanhood: The Emergence of the Afro-American Woman Novelist*. New York: Oxford University Press, 1987.

Carroll, Rebecca. *I Know What the Red Clay Looks Like: The Voice and Vision of Black Women Writers*. New York: Crown Trade Paperbacks, 1994.

Carson, Josephine. *Silent Voices: The Southern Negro Woman Today*. New York: Delacorte Press, 1969.

Caruth, Cathy. *Unclaimed Experience: Trauma, Narrative, and History*. Baltimore, MD: The Johns Hopkins University Press, 1996.

Caruth, Cathy, ed. *Trauma: Explorations in Memory*. Baltimore, MD: The Johns Hopkins University Press, 1995.

Cather, Willa. "The Novel Démeublé." *Not Under Forty*. New York: Alfred A. Knopf, 1922. 43–51.

Chambers, Ross. *Story and Situation: Narrative Seduction and the Power of Fiction*. Minneapolis: University of Minnesota Press, 1984.

Chase-Riboud, Barbara. *Echo of Lions*. New York: William Morrow, 1989.

——. *Sally Hemings*. New York: Viking, 1979.

Chesnutt, Charles W. *The House Behind the Cedars*. Boston: Houghton Mifflin, 1900.

——. *Mandy Oxendine*. 1897. Ed. Charles Hackenberry. Urbana: University of Illinois Press, 1997.

——. *Paul Marchand, F. M. C.* 1921. Intro. Matthew Wilson. Jackson: University Press of Mississippi, 2005.

——. "What Is a White Man?" *New York Independent* (May 30, 1889).

Chodorow, Nancy. *The Reproduction of Mothering: Psychoanalysis and the Sociology of Gender.* Berkeley: University of California Press, 1978.

Christian, Barbara. *Black Women Novelists: The Development of a Tradition, 1892–1976.* Westport, CT: Greenwood Press, 1980.

——. "The Dynamics of Difference: Book Review of Audre Lorde's *Sister Outsider." Black Feminist Criticism: Perspectives in Black Women Writers.* New York: Pergamon Press, 1985. 205–210.

——. "The Race for Theory." *Cultural Critique* 6 (Spring 1987): 51–63.

Cixous, Hélène. "The Laugh of the Medusa." *New French Feminisms: An Anthology.* Ed. Elaine Marks and Isabelle de Courtivron. Amherst: The University of Massachusetts Press, 1980. 245–264.

Clarke, John Henrik, ed. *William Styron's Nat Turner: Ten Writers Respond.* Boston: Beacon Press, 1968.

Clemons, Walter. "The Ghosts of 'Sixty Million and More.'" *Newsweek* (September 28, 1987): 75.

Cole, Johnetta Betsch, and Beverly Guy-Sheftall. *Gender Talk: The Struggle for Women's Equality in African American Communities.* New York: One World Ballantine, 2003.

Coleman, John Winston, Jr. *Slavery Times in Kentucky.* Chapel Hill: University of North Carolina Press, 1940.

Coleman, Shalanda Faulk. "Look[-ing] Back At It": (Re)Enacting Historical Trauma and White Hegemonic Desire through Black (S)exploitation in Hip Hop." Unpublished essay.

Colin, Paul. *Josephine Baker and* La Revue Nègre: *Paul Colin's Lithographs of* Le Tumulte Noir *in Paris, 1927.* Intro. Henry Louis Gates, Jr., and Karen C. C. Dalton. New York: Harry N. Abrams, 1998.

Collingwood, R. G. *The Idea of History.* London: Oxford University Press, 1946.

Collins, Lisa. "Economies of the Flesh: Representing the Black Female Body in Art." *Skin Deep, Spirit Strong: The Black Female Body in American Culture.* Ed. Kimberly Wallace-Sanders. Ann Arbor: The University of Michigan Press, 2002. 99–127.

Collins, Patricia Hill. *Black Feminist Thought: Knowledge, Consciousness, and the Politics of Empowerment.* Boston: Unwin Hyman, 1990.

——. *From Black Power to Hip Hop: Racism, Nationalism, and Feminism.* Philadelphia: Temple University Press, 2006.

The Compact Edition of the Oxford English Dictionary. Complete Text Reproduced Micrographically. Oxford: Oxford University Press, 1971.

Conn, Charles W. "Glossolalia and the Scriptures." *The Glossolalia Phenomenon.* Ed. Wade H. Horton. Cleveland, TN: Pathway Press, 1966. 21–65.

Copeland, Roger. "The Search for Origins." *Dance Theatre Journal* 13 (Summer 1996): 8–14.

Coquery, Catherine. *Histoire de la France Coloniale.* Paris: A. Colin, 1991.

Corn, Wanda. *The Great American Thing: Modern Art and National Identity, 1915–1935.* Berkeley: University of California Press, 2000.

Craft, William, and Ellen Craft. *Running a Thousand Miles for Freedom; or the Escape of William and Ellen Craft from Slavery.* London: William Tweedie, 1860.

Crafts, Hannah. *The Bondwoman's Narrative.* 1853–1861. Ed. Henry Louis Gates, Jr. New York: Warner Books, 2003.

Crawford, Margo. *Dilution Anxiety and the Black Phallus.* Columbus: Ohio State University Press, 2008.

Croker, John Wilson. Rev. of *Endymion* by John Keats. *Quarterly Review* 29 (April 1818): 204–208.

Culley, Margo. "Anger and Authority in the Introductory Women's Studies Classroom." *Gendered Subjects: The Dynamics of Feminist Teaching.* Ed. Margo Culley and Catherine Portuges. Boston: Routledge and Kegan Paul, 1985. 209–217.

Culley, Margo, and Catherine Portuges, eds. *Gendered Subjects: The Dynamics of Feminist Teaching.* Boston: Routledge and Kegan Paul, 1985.

cummings, e. e. *A Miscellany Revised.* Ed. George J. Firmage. New York: October House, 1965.

Cunningham, George. "Called Into Existence: Desire, Gender, and Voice in Frederick Douglass's *Narrative* of 1845." *Differences* 1, no. 3 (Fall 1989): 108–136.

Curtis, Debra. "Commodities and Sexual Subjectivities: Capitalism and Its Desires." *Cultural Anthropology* 19, no. 1 (2004): 95–121.

Cutten, George Barton. *Speaking with Tongues*. New Haven, CT: Yale University Press, 1927.

Darity, William A., Jr. Email to author. December 28, 2013.

Davis, Angela. "Reflections on the Black Woman's Role in the Community of Slaves." *The Black Scholar* (December 1971): 1–15.

Davis, Arthur. *From the Dark Tower: Afro-American Writers, 1900–1960*. Washington, DC: Howard University Press, 1974.

Davis, Mary Kemp. "Everybody Knows Her Name: The Recovery of the Past in Sherley Anne Williams's *Dessa Rose*." *Callaloo* 40, no. 1 (1989): 544–558.

Davis, Rebecca Harding. *Waiting for the Verdict*. New York: Sheldon, 1867.

Davis, Thadious M. *Nella Larsen, Novelist of the Harlem Renaissance: A Woman's Life Unveiled*. Baton Rouge: Louisiana State University Press, 1994.

Dearborn, Mary V. *Pocahontas's Daughters: Gender and Ethnicity in American Culture*. New York: Oxford University Press, 1986.

de Beauvoir, Simone. *The Second Sex*. 1949. Trans. and ed. H. M. Parshley. New York: Vintage, 1989.

de Certeau, Michel. *Heterologies: Discourse on the Other*. Theory and History of Literature Vol. 17. Minneapolis: University of Minnesota Press, 1986.

DeFrantz, Thomas F. "The Black Beat Made Visible: Hip Hop Dance and Body Power." *Of the Presence of the Body: Essays on Dance and Performance Theory*. Ed. André Lepecki. Middletown, CT: Wesleyan University Press, 2004. 64–81.

de Graffigny, Françoise. *Lettres d'une Péruvienne*. 1747. Ed. Gianni Nicoletti. Bari: Adriatica, 1967.

de Jongh, James. *Vicious Modernism: Black Harlem and the Literary Imagination*. Cambridge: Cambridge University Press, 1990.

de Lauretis, Teresa. *Alice Doesn't: Feminism, Semiotics, Cinema*. Bloomington: Indiana University Press, 1984.

——. *Technologies of Gender: Essays on Theory, Film, and Fiction*. Bloomington: Indiana University Press, 1987.

de Leon, Aya. "Hip-Hop Ventriloquism: From Sexism to Corporate Control." *Home Girls Make Some Noise: Hip Hop Feminism Anthology*. Ed. Gwendolyn D. Pough, Elaine Richardson, Aisha Durham, and Rachel Raimist. Mira Loma, CA: Parking Publishing, 2007. 439–443.

Dent, Gina, ed. *Black Popular Culture*. Seattle: Bay Press, 1992.

Derrida, Jacques. *The Ear of the Other: Otobiography, Transference, Translation*. Trans. Peggy Kamuf. Ed. Christi McDonald. Lincoln: University of Nebraska Press, 1985.

——. *Memories for Paul de Man*. New York: Columbia University Press, 1986.

——. *Of Grammatology*. Trans. Gayatri Chakravorty Spivak. Baltimore, MD: Johns Hopkins University Press, 1998.

Derrida, Jacques, and Christie V. McDonald. "*Cherchez la Femme*: Feminist Critique/Feminine Text." *Diacritics* 12, no. 2 (Summer 1982): 66–76.

Diagnostic and Statistical Manual of Mental Disorders (DSM). The American Psychiatric Association. 1980.

Dixon, Thomas. *The Clansman: An Historical Romance of the Ku Klux Klan*. New York: Grosset and Dunlap, 1905.

——. *The Leopard's Spots*. New York: Doubleday, Page & Co., 1902.

Douglass, Frederick. *Narrative of the Life of Frederick Douglass*. 1845. New York: New American Library, 1968.

Dowling, William C. *Jameson, Althusser, Marx: An Introduction to "The Political Unconscious."* Ithaca, NY: Cornell University Press, 1984.

dParker2.0. "Video Vixens: Victims of Exploitation or Using Feminism to Their Advantage." Blog Post. *Blissfully Clueless* (March 26, 2006). http://blissfullyclueless.blogspot.com/2006/03/video-vixens-victims-of-exploitation.html.

Dreyfus, Hubert L., and Paul Rabinow. *Michel Foucault beyond Structuralism and Hermeneutics*. Chicago: University of Chicago Press, 1982; 2nd ed., 1983.

Du Bois, W. E. B. *The Souls of Black Folk*. Chicago: A. C. McClurg, 1903.

duCille, Ann. *The Coupling Convention: Sex, Text, and Tradition in Black Women's Fiction*. New York: Oxford University Press, 1993.

Duewel, Wesley L. *The Holy Spirit and Tongues*. Winona Lake, IN: Light and Life Press, 1974; revised 1983.

Duff, John B., and Peter M. Mitchell, eds. *The Nat Turner Rebellion: The Historical Event and the Modern Controversy*. New York: Harper and Row, 1971.

DuPlessis, Rachel Blau. *Writing beyond the Ending: Narrative Strategies of Twentieth-Century Women Writers*. Bloomington: Indiana University Press, 1985.

Durham, Robert Lee. *The Call of the South*. Boston: L. C. Page, 1908.

Dyer, Richard. "Entertainment and Utopia." *The Cultural Studies Reader*. 2nd ed. Ed. Simon During. London and New York: Routledge, 1993.

——. *Stars*. London: British Film Institute, 1998.

Dyson, Michael Eric. *Know What I Mean? Reflections on Hip Hop*. New York: Basic Civitas Books, 2007.

Edwards, Brent Hayes. *The Practice of Diaspora: Literature, Translation, and the Rise of Black Internationalism*. Cambridge, MA: Harvard University Press, 2003.

Elaw, Zilpha. *Memoirs of the Life, Religious Experience, Ministerial Travels, and Labours of Mrs. Zilpha Elaw, an American Female of Colour*. London: Charter-House Lane, 1846.

Elkins, Stanley. *Slavery: A Problem in American Institutional and Intellectual Life*. Chicago: University of Chicago Press, 1959.

Ellison, Ralph. "The Art of Fiction: An Interview." *Shadow and Act*. New York: New American Library, 1955. 169–183.

——. *Going to the Territory*. 1986. First Vintage International Edition. New York: Vintage, 1995.

——. *Invisible Man*. 1952. Second Vintage International Edition. New York: Vintage, 1995.

Ellison, Ralph, William Styron, Robert Penn Warren, and C. Vann Woodward. "The Uses of History in Fiction." *Southern Literary Journal* 1, no. 2 (Spring 1969): 57–90.

Emerson, Rana A. "'Where My Girls At?': Negotiating Black Womanhood in Music Videos." *Gender and Society* 2, no. 115 (2002): http://www.sagepub.com/cgi/content/refs/16/1/115.

Equiano, Olaudah. *The Interesting Narrative of the Life of Olaudah Equiano, or Gustavus Vassa, the African, Written by Himself*. London, 1789.

Erikson, Erik H. *Life History and the Historical Moment*. New York: W. W. Norton, 1975.

Ezra, Elizabeth. *The Colonial Unconscious: Race and Culture in Interwar France*. Ithaca, NY, and London: Cornell University Press, 2000.

Faulkner, William. *Absalom, Absalom!* New York: Random House, 1936.

——. *Light in August*. New York: Harrison Smith, 1932.

Fauset, Jessie Redmon. *Plum Bun, a Novel without a Moral*. New York: Frederick A. Stokes, 1929.

Fausto-Sterling, Anne. "Gender, Race, and Nation: The Comparative Anatomy of 'Hottentot' Women in Europe, 1815–17." *Feminism and the Body*. Ed. Londa Schiebinger. New York: Oxford University Press, 2000. 203–233.

——. "Gender, Race, and Nation: The Comparative Anatomy of 'Hottentot' Women in Europe, 1815–17." *Skin Deep, Spirit Strong: The Black Female Body in American Culture*. Ed. Kimberly Wallace-Sanders. Ann Arbor: The University of Michigan Press, 2002. 66–95.

Felman, Shoshana, and Dori Laub. *Testimony: Crises of Witnessing in Literature, Psychoanalysis, and History*. New York: Routledge, 1992.

Felski, Rita. *The Gender of Modernity*. Cambridge, MA: Harvard University Press, 1995.

Ferenczi, Sándor. *Thalassa: A Theory of Genitality*. 1924. Trans. Henry Alden Bunker. New York: W. W. Norton, 1968.

Ferenczi, Sándor, and Otto Rank. *The Development of Psychoanalysis*. Trans. Caroline Newton. New York and Washington, DC: Nervous and Mental Disease Publishing, 1925.

Ferguson, SallyAnn H. "Passionate Critics." Rev. of *Changing Our Own Words: Essays on Criticism, Theory and Writing by Black Women* by Cheryl A. Wall; *Reading Feminist: A Critical Anthology* by Henry Louis Gates, Jr. *The Women's Review of Books* 9, no. 3 (December 1991): 27–28.

Firmage, George J., ed. *E. E. Cummings: A Miscellany Revised*. New York: October House Inc., 1965.

Firth, Simon. "Music and Identity." *Questions of Cultural Identity*. Ed. Stuart Hall and Paul du Gay. London: Sage Publications, 1996. 108–127.

Fish, Stanley E. *Self-Consuming Artifacts*. Berkeley and Los Angeles: University of California Press, 1974.

Fisher, Rudolph. *The City of Refuge: The Collected Stories of Rudolph Fisher*. Ed. John McCluskey, Jr. Columbia: University of Missouri Press, 1987.

——. *The Conjure-Man Dies: A Mystery Tale of Dark Harlem*. 1932. Ann Arbor: University of Michigan Press, 1992.

——. *The Walls of Jericho*. 1928. New York: Arno Press, 1969.

Foote, Julia A. J. *A Brand Plucked from the Fire: An Autobiographical Sketch*. Cleveland, OH: Lauer & Yost, 1879.

Forman, Murray, and Mark Anthony Neal, eds. *That's the Joint: The Hip-Hop Studies Reader*. New York: Routledge, 2004.

Foucault, Michel. *Discipline and Punish: The Birth of the Prison*. Trans. Alan Sheridan. New York: Pantheon, 1977.

——. *History of Sexuality, Volume I: An Introduction*. Trans. Robert Hurley. New York: Random House, 1978.

——. "The Order of Discourse." Trans. Ian McLeod. *Untying the Text: A Poststructuralist Reader*. Ed. Robert Young. Boston: Routledge and Kegan Paul, 1981. 48–78.

——. "The Subject and Power." *Critical Inquiry* 8, no. 4 (1982): 777–795.

Fox-Genovese, Elizabeth. *Within the Plantation Household*. Chapel Hill: University of North Carolina Press, 1988.

Franchot, Jenny. "The Punishment of Esther: Frederick Douglass and the Construction of the Feminine." *Frederick Douglass: New Literary and Historical Essays*. Ed. Eric J. Sundquist. Cambridge: Cambridge University Press, 1990. 141–165.

Frankenberg, Ruth. *Displacing Whiteness: Essays in Social and Cultural Criticism*. Durham, NC: Duke University Press, 1997.

Fraser, Nancy. "What's Critical about Critical Theory?: The Case of Habermas and Gender." *Feminism as Critique*. Ed. Seyla Benehabib and Drucilla Cornell. Minneapolis: University of Minnesota Press, 1987. 31–56.

Fréjaville, Gustave. *Au music-hall*. Paris: Editions du monde nouveau, 1923.

Freud, Sigmund. *The Standard Edition of the Works of Sigmund Freud*. Ed. James Strachey. 24 vols. London: Hogarth Press, 1956–1974.

Freud, Sigmund, and Sándor Ferenczi. *The Correspondence of Sigmund Freud and Sándor Ferenczi*. Ed. Eva Brabant, Ernst Falzeder, and Patrizia Giampieri-Deutsch. Trans. Peter Hoffer. 3 vols. Cambridge, MA: Harvard University Press, 1993-2000.

Friedman, Susan Stanford. "Authority in the Feminist Classroom: A Contradiction in Terms?" *Gendered Subjects: The Dynamics of Feminist Teaching*. Ed. Margo Culley and Catherine Portuges. Boston: Routledge and Kegan Paul, 1985. 203–208.

"From Imus to Industry: The Business of Stereotypes and Degrading Images." Congressional Hearing before U.S. House Energy and Commerce Commission Subcommittee. Convened by Rep. Bobby Rush. Held on September 26, 2007.

Fuller, Hoyt. Introduction. *Passing*. By Nella Larsen. New York: Collier Books, 1971. 11–24.

Furman, Nelly. "The Politics of Language: Beyond the Gender Principle?" *Making a Difference: Feminist Literary Criticism*. Ed. Gayle Greene and Coppélia Kahn. London and New York: Methuen, 1985. 59–79.

Gadamer, Hans-Georg. *Truth and Method*. New York: Seabury Press, 1975.

Gaines, Ernest. *The Autobiography of Miss Jane Pittman*. New York: Dial Press, 1971.

Galton, Francis. *Finger Prints*. London and New York: Macmillan, 1892.

Gates, Henry Louis, Jr. *Black Literature and Literary Theory*. New York and London: Methuen, 1984.

——. "Editor's Introduction: Writing 'Race' and the Difference It Makes." *Critical Inquiry* 12, no. 1 (Autumn 1985): 1–20.

——. "Frederick Douglass and the Language of the Self." *The Yale Review* 70, no. 4 (July 1981): 592–610.

——. *The Signifying Monkey: A Theory of African-American Literary Criticism.* New York: Oxford University Press, 1989.

Genette, Gerard. *Introduction to l'architexte.* Paris: Ed. du Seuil, 1979.

Genovese, Eugene D. "The Nat Turner Case." *The Nat Turner Rebellion: The Historical Event and the Modern Controversy.* Ed. John B. Duff and Peter M. Mitchell. New York: Harper and Row, 1971. 203–216.

Gilbert, Sandra M., and Susan Gubar. *The Madwoman in the Attic: The Woman Writer and the Nineteenth-Century Literary Imagination.* New Haven, CT, and London: Yale University Press, 1979.

Gilkes, Cheryl Townsend. "'Together and in Harness': Women's Traditions in the Sanctified Church." *Black Women in America: Social Science Perspectives.* Ed. Elizabeth Mudimbe, Micheline Malson, and Jean O'Barr. Chicago: University of Chicago Press, 1990. 223–244.

Gill, John. *Exposition of the Old and New Testament.* 1746–1763. Available online: http://www. sacred-texts.com/bib/cmt/gill/index.htm.

Gilligan, Carol. *In Another Voice.* Cambridge, MA: Harvard University Press, 1982.

Gilman, Richard. "Nat Turner Revisited." *The Nat Turner Rebellion: The Historical Event and the Modern Controversy.* Ed. John B. Duff and Peter M. Mitchell. New York: Harper and Row, 1971. 228–237.

Gilman, Sander L. "Black Bodies, White Bodies: Toward an Iconography of Female Sexuality in Late Nineteenth-Century Art, Medicine, and Literature." *Critical Inquiry* 12, no. 1 (Autumn 1985): 204–242.

——. "The Hottentot and the Prostitute: Toward an Iconography of Female Sexuality." *Difference and Pathology: Stereotypes of Sexuality, Race, and Madness.* Ithaca, NY: Cornell University Press, 1985. 76–108.

Gilroy, Paul. *The Black Atlantic: Modernity and Double Consciousness.* Cambridge, MA: Harvard University Press, 1995.

——. "'To Be Real': The Dissident Forms of Black Expressive Culture." *Let's Get It On: The Politics of Black Performance.* Ed. Catherine Ugwu. London and Seattle: Bay Press, 1995. 12–33.

Giradet, Raoul. *L'Idée coloniale en France de 1871 à 1962.* Paris: Hachette, 1972.

Goellnicht, Donald. "Passing as Autobiography: James Weldon Johnson's *The Autobiography of an Ex-Colored Man.*" *African-American Review* 30, no. 1 (1996): 17–33.

Goldberg, David Theo. *Racist Culture: Philosophy and the Politics of Meaning.* Cambridge, MA: Blackwell, 1955.

Goll, Ivan. "Die Neger erobern Europa" [The Negroes are Conquering Europe]. *Die literarische Welt* no. 2 (January 15, 1936): 3–4.

Gordon, George, Lord Byron. "John Keats." *The Poetical Works of Lord Byron: Complete in One Volume.* Ed. Thomas Moore et al. New York: D. Appleton & Co., 1867. 584.

Gottschild, Brenda Dixon. *The Black Dancing Body: A Geography from Coon to Cool.* New York: Palgrave MacMillan, 2003.

——. *Digging the Africanist Presence in American Performance: Dance and Other Contexts.* Westport, CT: Praeger Publishers, 1996.

Graeber, Laurel. "'It's About Childhood.'" Interview with Bebe Moore Campbell. *New York Times Book Review* (September 20, 1992): 13.

Graff, Gerald. *Beyond the Culture Wars: How Teaching the Conflicts Can Revitalize American Education.* New York: W. W. Norton, 1992.

Gramsci, Antonio. *Prison Notebooks.* Trans. Joseph A. Buttigieg. 3 vols. New York: Columbia University Press, 2007.

Gray, Thomas R. "To the Public." *The Confessions of Nat Turner* [Baltimore, MD: Lucas & Deaver, 1831]. Appendix. *William Styron's Nat Turner: Ten Writers Respond.* Ed. John Henrik Clarke. Boston: Beacon Press, 1968. 92–117.

Greene, Gayle, and Coppélia Khan, eds. *Making a Difference: Feminist Literary Criticism.* London and New York: Methuen, 1985.

Griffiths, Jennifer. "Uncanny Spaces: Trauma, Cultural Memory, and the Female Body in Gayl Jones's *Corregidora* and Maxine Hong Kingston's *The Woman Warrior.*" *Studies in the Novel* 38, no. 3 (2006): 353–370.

Gubar, Susan. "Representing Pornography: Feminism, Criticism, and Depictions of Female Violation." *Critical Inquiry* 13, no. 4 (Summer 1987): 712–741.

Gugelberger, George M., ed. *The Real Thing: Testimonial Discourse and Latin America.* Durham, NC: Duke University Press, 1996.

Guillaumin, Colette. "The Practice of Power and Belief in Nature, Part I: The Appropriation of Women." *Feminist Studies* 1, no. 2 (Winter 1981): 87–109.

Guilleragues, Gabriel Joseph de Lavergne, vicomte de. *Lettres Portugaises: Traduites en François.* Paris: Claude Barbin, 1669.

———. *The Portuguese Letters: Love Letters of a Nun to a French Officer.* Trans. Donald E. Ericson. New York: Bennett-Edwards, 1986.

Guthrie, Robert V. *Even the Rat Was White: A Historical View of Psychology.* New York: Harper & Row, 1976.

Habel, Ylva. "To Stockholm, with Love: The Critical Reception of Josephine Baker, 1927–35." *Film History* 17, no. 1 (2005): 125–138.

Habermas, Jürgen. *The Structural Transformation of the Public Sphere: An Inquiry into a Category of Bourgeois Society.* Trans. Thomas Burger and Frederick Lawrence. Cambridge, MA: MIT Press, 1991.

Haley, Alex. *Roots.* Garden City, NY: Doubleday, 1976.

Hall, Stuart. "Cultural Identity and Diaspora." *Colonial Discourse and Post-colonial Discourse: A Reader.* Ed. Patrick Williams and Laura Chrisman. London: Harvester Wheatsheaf, 1994. 392–403.

———. "Encoding/Decoding" in *Culture, Media, Language.* Ed. Stuart Hall, Dorothy Hobson, Andrew Lowe, and Paul Willis. London: Routledge, 1980.

———. "Introduction: Who Needs 'Identity'?" *Questions of Cultural Identity.* Ed. Stuart Hall and Paul du Gay. London: Sage Publications, 1996. 1–17.

———. "What Is This 'Black' in Popular Culture?" *Black Popular Culture.* Ed. Gina Dent. Seattle: Bay Press, 1992. 21–33.

Hall, Stuart, ed. *Representation: Cultural Representations and Signifying Practices.* London: Sage Publications, 1997; reprinted 2003.

Hall, Stuart, and Paul du Gay, eds. *Questions of Cultural Identity.* London: Sage Publications, 1996.

Hammond, Bryan, and Patrick O'Conner, eds. *Josephine Baker.* Boston: Bulfinch, 1988.

Hammonds, Evelynn M. "Toward a Genealogy of Black Female Sexuality: The Problematic of Silence." *Feminist Theory and the Body: A Reader.* Ed. Janet Price and Margaret Shildrick. New York: Routledge, 1997. 93–104.

Haney, Lynn. *Naked at the Feast: A Biography of Josephine Baker.* New York: Dodd, Mead & Company, 1981.

Harper, Frances Ellen Watkins. *Idylls of the Bible.* Philadelphia: George S. Ferguson, 1901.

———. *Iola Leroy or, Shadows Uplifted.* Boston: James H. Earle, 1892.

Harper, Michael S. "Gayl Jones: An Interview." *Chant of Saints: A Gathering of Afro-American Literature, Art, and Scholarship.* Urbana: University of Illinois Press, 1979. 352–375.

Harper, Michael S., and Robert B. Stepto, eds. *Chant of Saints: A Gathering of Afro-American Literature, Art, and Scholarship.* Urbana: University of Illinois Press, 1979.

Harris, Cheryl I. "Whiteness as Property." *Critical Race Theory: The Key Writings That Formed the Movement.* Ed. Kimberlé Crenshaw, Neil Gotanda, Gary Peller, and Kendall Thomas. New York: The New Press, 1996. 276–291.

Hartman, Saidiya V. *Scenes of Subjection: Terror, Slavery, and Self-Making in Nineteenth-Century America.* New York and Oxford: Oxford University Press, 1997.

Haskins, James. *Black Dance in America: A History Through Its People.* New York: HarperCollins, 1990.

Hawthorne, Nathaniel. "The Birthmark." *Mosses from the Old Manse: In Two Volumes.* Vol. 1. Boston and New York: Houghton Mifflin, 1900. 48–77.

——. *The Scarlet Letter.* 1850. New York: E. P. Dutton & Co., 1938.

Hayasi, Reiko. "Long Term Population Dynamics in Africa: A Perspective from the Urban Structure." Available online: http://uaps2007.princeton.edu/papers/70296.

Henderson, Mae G. "Colonial, Postcolonial, and Diasporic Readings of Josephine Baker as Dancer and Performance Artist." *Josephine Baker: A Century in the Spotlight, Scholar & Feminist Online Double Issue* 6, nos. 1–2 (Fall 2007/Spring 2008).

——. "Josephine Baker and *La Revue Nègre*: From Ethnography to Performance." *Text and Performance Quarterly* 3, no. 2 (April 2003): 107–133.

——. "Speaking in Tongues: Dialectics, Dialogics, and the Black Woman Writer's Literary Tradition." *Changing Our Own Words: Essays on Criticism, Theory, and Writing by Black Women.* Ed. Cheryl A. Wall. New Brunswick: Rutgers University Press, 1989. 16–37.

Herman, Judith. *Trauma and Recovery: The Aftermath of Violence.* New York: Basic Books, 1992.

Hildreth, Richard. *The Slave; or, Memoirs of Archy Moore.* Boston: John H. Eastburn, 1836.

Hirsch, Marianne. "The Generation of Postmemory." *Poetics Today* 29, no. 1 (2008): 103–128.

Hodier, Catherine, and Michel Pierre. *L'Exposition coloniale.* Paris: Editions Complexe, 1991.

Hofstader, Richard. *The Progressive Historians.* New York: Alfred A. Knopf, 1968.

Hogue, W. Lawrence. *Race, Modernity, Postmodernity: A Look at the Literatures of People of Color since the 1960s.* Albany: State University of New York Press, 1996.

Holquist, Michael. *Dialogism: Bakhtin and His World.* New York: Routledge, 1990.

Holy Bible. King James Version.

Holy Bible. New International Version.

hooks, bell. *Black Looks: Race and Representation.* Boston: South End Press, 1992.

——. *Talking Back: Thinking Feminist, Thinking Black.* Boston: South End Press, 1989.

Hopkins, Pauline E. *Of One Blood: Or the Hidden Self.* 1902–1903. New York: Washington Square Press, 2004.

Horton, Wade, ed. *The Glossolalia Phenomenon.* Cleveland, TN: Pathway Press, 1966.

The Hosken Report. Lexington, MA: Women's International Network News, 1982.

Houchins, Sue E. "Introduction." *Spiritual Narratives.* The Schomburg Library of Black Women Writers Series. Gen. ed. Henry Louis Gates, Jr. New York: Oxford University Press, 1988. xxix–xliv.

Houston, Pam. "The Truest Eye." Interview with Toni Morrison. *O, The Oprah Magazine* (November 2003); available online: http://www.oprah.com/omagazine/Toni-Morrison-Talks-Love/1.

Howells, William Dean. *An Imperative Duty.* New York: Harper & Brothers, 1892.

Huggins, Nathan Irvin. *Harlem Renaissance.* New York: Oxford University Press, 1971.

Hull, Gloria, Patricia Bell Scott, and Barbara Smith, eds. *All the Women Are White, All the Blacks Are Men, But Some of Us Are Brave.* Old Westbury, NY: Feminist Press, 1982.

"Human Bondage: The Story of a Slave and Her Master." Transcript. *The Geraldo Rivera Show.* 1985.

Hurst, Fannie. *Imitation of Life.* New York: P. F. Collier, 1933.

Hurston, Zora Neale. "Characteristics of Negro Expression." *Negro: An Anthology.* Collected and ed. Nancy Cunard. 1934. Ed. and abridged Hugh Ford. New York: Continuum/F. Ungar, 1970. 24–31.

——. *Mules and Men.* Rev. ed. Bloomington: Indiana University Press, 1978.

——. *The Sanctified Church.* Berkeley, CA: Turtle Island, 1981.

——. *Their Eyes Were Watching God.* 1937. Urbana: University of Illinois Press, 1978.

Hutchinson, George. *In Search of Nella Larsen: A Biography of the Color Line.* Cambridge, MA: Belknap Press of Harvard University Press, 2006.

——. "Subject to Disappearance: Interracial Identity in Nella Larsen's *Quicksand*." *Temples for Tomorrow: Looking Back at the Harlem Renaissance.* Ed. Geneviève Fabre and Michel Feith. New York: Oxford University Press, 2001. 177–192.

Ibsen, Henrik. *Hedda Gabler.* London: William Heinemann, 1891.

Ice-T. "Ice T Speaks On His Life, Coco And Making It In The Hip Hop Industry." Video interview. *DimeWars*: http//dimewars.com/Video/Ice-T-Speaks-on-His-Life--Coco-and-Making-It-In-the-Hip-Hop-Industry.

L'Illustration. August 22, 1931, No. 4616-89.

Irigaray, Luce. "This Sex Which Is Not One." *New French Feminisms.* Ed. Elaine Marks and Isabelle de Courtivron. New York: Schocken, 1981. 99–106.

Iser, Wolfgang. *The Act of Reading: A Theory of Aesthetic Response.* Baltimore, MD: Johns Hopkins University Press, 1978.

——. *The Implied Reader: Patterns of Communication in Prose Fiction from Bunyan to Beckett.* Baltimore, MD: Johns Hopkins University Press, 1978.

Jackson, Rebecca Cox. *Gifts of Power: The Writings of Rebecca Jackson, Black Visionary, Shaker Eldress.* Ed. Jean McMahon Humez. Amherst: University of Massachusetts Press, 1981.

Jahn, Janheinz. *Neo-African Literature: A History of Black Writing.* New York: Grove Press, 1969.

James, Stanlie Myrise, Frances Smith Foster, and Beverly Guy-Sheftall, eds. *Still Brave: The Evolution of Black Women's Studies.* New York: The Feminist Press at CUNY, 2009.

Jameson, Fredric. *The Political Unconscious: Narrative as a Socially Symbolic Act.* Ithaca NY: Cornell University Press, 1981.

JanMohamed, Abdul R. "The Economy of Manichean Allegory: The Function of Racial Difference in Colonialist Literature." *Critical Inquiry* 12, no. 1 (Autumn 1985): 59–87.

Jauss, Hans Robert. *Toward an Aesthetic of Reception.* Ed. Timothy Bahti. Minneapolis: University of Minnesota Press, 1982.

Jehlen, Myra. "Archimedes and the Paradox of Feminist Criticism." *The Signs Reader: Women, Gender and Scholarship.* Ed. Elizabeth Abel and Emily K. Abel. Chicago: University of Chicago Press, 1983. 575–601.

Johnson, Barbara. *The Critical Difference: Essays in the Contemporary Rhetoric of Reading.* Baltimore, MD: Johns Hopkins University Press, 1980.

Johnson, Caleb. "Crossing the Color Line." *Outlook and Independent* 158 (Aug. 26, 1931): 526–528.

Johnson, James Weldon. *The Autobiography of an Ex-Colored Man.* 1912; 1927. New York: Hill and Wang, 1960.

Johnson, Walter. *Soul by Soul: Life Inside the Antebellum Slave Market.* Cambridge, MA: Harvard University Press, 1999.

Jones, Gayl. *Corregidora.* New York: Random House, 1975.

——. *Eva's Man.* New York: Random House, 1976.

——. *The Healing.* Boston: Beacon Press, 1998.

——. *The Hermit-Woman.* Detroit, MI: Lotus Press, 1983.

——. *Liberating Voices: Oral Tradition in African-American Literature.* Cambridge, MA: Harvard University Press, 1991.

——. *Mosquito.* Boston: Beacon Press, 1999.

——. *Song for Anninho.* Detroit, MI: Lotus Press, 1981.

——. *Die Vogelfängerin* [*The Birdwatcher*]. Reinbek, Hamburg, Berlin: Rowohlt, 1986.

——. *White Rat: Short Stories.* Foreword Mae G. Henderson. Boston: Northeastern University Press, 1991.

——. *White Rat: Short Stories.* New York: Random House, 1977.

——. *Xarque and Other Poems.* Detroit, MI: Lotus Press, 1985.

"Josephine Baker Chosen Queen of the Colonies." *Pittsburgh Courier* (February 21, 1931): 1.

The Josephine Baker Papers. Emory University Manuscript, Archives, and Rare Book Library.

The Josephine Baker Papers. The Schomberg Center for Research in Black Culture-New York Public Library.

Joyce, James. *A Portrait of the Artist as a Young Man.* New York: B. W. Huebsch, 1916.

Jules-Rosetta, Bennetta. *Josephine Baker in Art and Life: The Icon and the Image.* Urbana and Chicago: University of Illinois Press, 2007.

Kaes, Anton, Martin Jay, and Edward Dimendberg, eds. *The Weimer Republic Sourcebook.* Berkeley: University of California Press, 1994.

Kamuf, Peggy. "Replacing Feminist Criticism." *Diacritics* 12 (1982): 42–47.

——. "Writing Like a Woman." *Women and Language in Literature and Society.* Ed. Sally McConnell-Ginet, Ruth Borker, and Nelly Furman. New York: Praeger, 1980. 284–299.

Kaplan, Carla. *The Erotics of Talk: Women's Writing and Feminist Paradigms.* New York: Oxford University Press, 1996.

——. "The Erotics of Talk: 'That Oldest Human Longing' in *Their Eyes Were Watching God.*" *American Literature* 67, no. 1 (1995): 115–142.

Kauffman, Linda S. "The Long Goodbye: Against Personal Testimony, or An Infant Grifter Grows Up." *American Feminist Thought at Century's End: A Reader.* Ed. Linda S. Kauffman. Cambridge, MA, and Oxford: Blackwell, 1993. 258–277.

Kawash, Samira. *Dislocating the Color Line: Identity, Hybridity, and Singularity in African American Narrative.* Stanford, CA: Stanford University Press, 1997.

Kay, William K., and Anne E. Dyer. *Pentecostal and Charismatic Studies: A Reader.* London: SCM Press, 2004.

Kildahl, John P. *The Psychology of Speaking in Tongues.* New York: Harper & Row, 1972.

Kirkpatrick, David. "On Long-Lost Pages, a Female Slave's Voice." *New York Times* (November 11, 2001): A1, A6.

Klein, Herbert S. *The Middle Passage: Comparative Studies in the Atlantic Slave Trade.* Princeton, NJ: Princeton University Press, 1978.

Knadler, Stephen P. "Un-tragic Mulatto: Charles Chesnutt and the Discourse of Whiteness." *American Literary History* 8, no. 3 (Fall 1966): 426–448.

Kristeva, Julia. *Desire in Language: A Semiotic Approach to Literature and Art.* Trans. Thomas Gora, Alice Jardine, and Leon Roudiez. New York: Columbia University Press, 1980.

——. *Revolution in Poetic Language.* 1974. Trans. Margaret Waller. New York: Columbia University Press, 1984.

——. "Stabat Mater." *Poetics Today* 6, nos. 1/2 (1985): 133–152.

——. "Women's Time." *Signs: Journal of Women in Culture and Society* 7, no. 1 (1981): 13–35.

Labelle, Patti, performer. "New Attitude." *Beverly Hills Cop.* Written by Sharon Teresa Robinson, Jon Gilutin, and Bunny Hull. MCA, 1985.

Lacan, Jacques. *The Four Fundamental Concepts of Psycho-Analysis.* New York: W. W. Norton, 1981.

LaCapra, Dominick. *Writing History, Writing Trauma.* Baltimore, MD: The Johns Hopkins Press, 2001.

Laing, R. D. *The Politics of Experience.* New York: Ballatine Books, 1967.

Lange, Roderyk. *The Nature of Dance: An Anthropological Perspective.* London: Taylor and Francis, 1976.

Larsen, Nella. *Passing.* New York: Collier Books, 1971.

——. *Passing.* The Modern Library. Intro. Ntozake Shange. Foreword Mae Henderson. New York: Random House, 2002.

——. *Quicksand and Passing.* Intro. Deborah McDowell. New Brunswick, NJ: Rutgers University Press, 1986.

Larson, Charles R. *Invisible Darkness: Jean Toomer and Nella Larsen.* Iowa City: University of Iowa Press, 1993.

Laub, Dori. "Bearing Witness, or the Vicissitudes of Listening." *Testimony: Crises of Witnessing in Literature, Psychology, and History.* By Shosana Felman and Dori Laub. New York: Routledge, 1992. 57–74.

——. "An Event Without a Witness: Truth, Testimony and Survival." *Testimony: Crises of Witnessing in Literature, Psychology, and History.* By Shosana Felman and Dori Laub. New York: Routledge, 1992. 75–92.

Leary, Joy Degruy. *Post Traumatic Slave Syndrome: America's Legacy of Enduring Injury and Healing.* Portland, OR: Uptone Press, 2005.

Lebovics, Herman. *True France: The Wars over Cultural Identity, 1900–1945.* Ithaca, NY, and London: Cornell University Press, 1992.

Lee, Jarena. *Religious Experience and Journal of Mrs. Jarena Lee, Giving an Account of Her Call to Preach the Gospel. Received and Corrected from the Original Manuscript, Written by Herself.* Philadelphia, PA: Printed and Published for the Author, 1849.

Leiris, Michel. *L'Afrique fantôme*: [*de Dakar à Djibouti, 1931–1933*]. Paris: Gaillmard, 1934.

Lentricchia, Frank. *After the New Criticism*. Chicago: University of Chicago Press, 1980.

Lepecki, André, ed. *Of the Presence of the Body: Essays on Dance and Performance Theory*. Middletown, CT: Wesleyan University Press, 2004.

Leprun, Sylviane. *Le Théâtre des colonies: Scenographie, acteurs et discours de l'imaginaire dans les expositions, 1855–1937*. Paris: L'Harmattan, 1986.

Lerner, Gerda. *The Creation of Patriarchy*. New York: Oxford University Press, 1986.

Levande, Meredith. "Women, Pop Music, and Pornography." *Meridians: feminism, race, transnationalism* 8, no. 1 (2008): 293–321.

Lévi-Strauss, Claude. *Conversations with Claude Lévi-Strauss*. Ed. Georges Charbonnier. London: Cape, 1969.

Levine, Lawrence. *Black Culture and Black Consciousness: Afro-American Folk Thought from Slavery to Freedom*. New York: Oxford University Press, 1977.

Lewis, David Levering. *When Harlem Was in Vogue*. New York: Knopf, 1981; New York: Oxford University Press, 1989.

Leys, Ruth. *Trauma: A Genealogy*. Chicago and London: University of Chicago Press, 2000.

Lindfors, Bernth. "The Hottentot Venus and Other African Attractions." *Australasian Drama Studies* 1, no. 2 (1983): 82–104.

Lionnet, Françoise. *Autobiographical Voices: Race, Gender, Self-Portraiture*. Ithaca, NY: Cornell University Press, 1989.

Lipsitz, George. Rev. of *The Black Atlantic: Modernity and Double Consciousness* by Paul Gilroy. *Social Identities: Journal for the Study of Race, Nation and Culture* 1, no. 1 (February 1995): 193–200.

Longinus. "On the Sublime." Trans. W. Rhys Roberts. *Critical Theory Since Plato*. Ed. Hazard Adams. New York: Harcourt Brace Jovanovich, 1971. 76–98.

Lorde, Audre. *Sister Outsider: Essays and Speeches*. Freedom, CA: Crossing Press, 1984.

Lott, Eric. *Love and Theft: Blackface Minstrelsy and the American Working Class*. New York: Oxford University Press, 1993.

Lott, Tommy Lee. Rev. of *The Black Atlantic: Modernity and Double Consciousness* by Paul Gilroy. *Social Identities: Journal for the Study of Race, Nation and Culture* 1, no. 1 (February 1995): 200–220.

Lukács, Georg. *Theory of the Novel*. 1920. Trans. Anna Bostock. Cambridge, MA: MIT Press, 1971.

Lyotard, Jean-François. *The Differend: Phrases in Dispute*. Minneapolis: University of Minnesota Press, 1988.

MacCannell, Juliet F. *Figuring Lacan: Criticism and the Cultural Unconscious*. Lincoln: University of Nebraska Press, 1986.

MacKinnon, Catherine A. "Feminism, Marxism, Method, and the State: An Agenda for Theory." *Signs: Journal of Women in Culture and Society* 7, no. 3 (Spring 1982): 515–544.

Madigan, Mark J. "Miscegenation and 'The Dicta of Race and Class': The Rhinelander Case and Nella Larsen's *Passing*." *Modern Fiction Studies* 36, no. 4 (Winter 1990): 523–529.

Malony, H. Newton, and A. Adams Lovekin. *Glossolalia: Behavioral Science Perspectives on Speaking in Tongues*. New York and Oxford: Oxford University Press, 1985.

Manso, Peter. "Chronicle of a Tragedy Foretold." *New York Times Magazine* (July 19, 1986): 32–37.

Martin, David, and Peter Mullen, eds. *Strange Gifts?: A Guide to Charismatic Renewal*. New York and Oxford: Blackwell, 1984.

Martin, Waldo E., Jr., *The Mind of Frederick Douglass*. Chapel Hill: University of North Carolina Press, 1984.

Martin, Wendy. "'Remembering the Jungle': Josephine Baker and Modernist Parody." *Prehistories of the Future: The Primitivist Project and the Culture of Modernism*. Ed. Elazar Barkan and Ronald Bush. Stanford, CA: Stanford University Press, 1995. 310–325.

McDowell, Deborah. "In the First Place: Making Frederick Douglass and the Afro-American Narrative Tradition." *Critical Essays on Frederick Douglass*. Ed. William Andrews. Boston: G. K. Hall, 1991. Rpt. in *African American Autobiography: A Collection of Critical Essays*. Ed. William L. Andrews. Englewood Cliffs, NJ: Prentice Hall, 1993. 36–58.

———. Introduction. *Quicksand and Passing*. By Nella Larsen. New Brunswick, NJ: Rutgers University Press, 1986. ix–xxxvii.

McKay, Claude. *Banjo: A Story without a Plot.* New York and London: Harper & Brothers, 1929.

Meridians: feminism, race, transnationalism 8, no. 1 (2008).

Miller, Christopher. "Hallucinations of France and Africa in the Colonial Exhibition of 1931 and Ousmane Socé's *Mirages de Paris."* *Paragraph: A Journal of Modern Critical Theory* 18, no. 1 (March 1995): 39–63.

Miller, Nancy K. "The Text's Heroine: A Feminist Critic and Her Fictions." *Diacritics* 12, no. 2 (1982): 48–53.

Miller-Young, Mireille. "Hip-Hop Honeys and Da Hustlaz: Black Sexualities in the New Hip-Hop Pornography." *Meridians: feminism, race, transnationalism* 8, no. 1 (2008): 261–292.

Mills, Watson E. *A Theological/Exegetical Approach to Glossolalia.* Lanham, MD: University Press of America, 1985.

——. *Understanding Speaking in Tongues.* Grand Rapids, MI: Williams B. Eerdmans Publishing, 1972.

Milton, John. *John Milton: Complete Poems and Major Prose.* Ed. Merritt Y. Hughes. New York: Macmillan, 1957.

Minh-ha, Trinh T. *Woman, Native, Other: Writing Postcoloniality and Feminism.* Bloomington: Indiana University Press, 1989.

Moglen, Helen. "Transference and the Erotics of Teaching." Unpublished paper presented at the Multicultural and Feminist Pedagogies Conference. UCSC, May 1991.

Moi, Toril. *Sexual/Textual Politics: Feminist Literary Theory.* London and New York: Methuen, 1985.

Mondie-Sapp, Levita D. "The Highest Bidder." *Home Girls Make Some Noise.* Ed. Gwendolyn Pough, Elaine Richardson, Aisha Durham, Rachel Raimist. Mira Loma, CA: Parking Publishing, 2007. 387–388.

Moraga, Cherríe, and Gloria Anzaldúa, eds. *This Bridge Called My Back: Writings by Radical Women of Color.* Watertown, MA: Persephone Press, 1981.

Morgan, Joan. *When Chickenheads Come Home to Roost: A Hip Hop Feminist Breaks It Down.* New York: Simon & Shuster, 1999.

Morrison, Toni. *Beloved.* New York: Alfred A. Knopf 1987.

——. *The Bluest Eye.* New York: Holt, Rhinehart, and Winston, 1970.

——. *The Dancing Mind: Speech upon Acceptance of the National Book Foundation Medal for Distinguished Contribution to American Letters.* New York: Alfred A. Knopf, 1996.

——. *Jazz.* New York: Alfred A. Knopf, 1992.

——. "The Pain of Being Black." *Time Magazine* (May 22, 1989): 120–123.

——. *Paradise.* New York: Alfred A. Knopf, 1997.

——. *Playing in the Dark: Whiteness and the Literary Imagination.* Cambridge, MA: Harvard University Press, 1992.

——. "Rootedness: The Ancestor as Foundation." *Black Women Writers (1950–1980): A Critical Evaluation.* Ed Mari Evans. Garden City, NY: Anchor Press, 1984. 339–345.

——. "The Site of Memory." *Inventing the Truth: The Art and Craft of Memoir.* Ed. William Zinsser. Boston: Houghton-Mifflin, 1987. 183–200.

——. *Sula.* New York: Alfred A. Knopf, 1973; Bantam, 1975.

——. "Unspeakable Things Unspoken." *Michigan Quarterly Review* 28, no. 1 (Winter 1989): 1–34.

Morson, Gary Saul. "Dialogue, Monologue, and the Social: A Reply to Ken Hirshkop." *Bakhtin: Essays and Dialogues on His Work.* Ed. Gary Saul Morson. Chicago: University of Chicago Press, 1986. 81–88.

Morton, Nelle. *The Journey Is Home.* Boston: Beacon Press, 1985.

Morton, Patricia. *Hybrid Modernities: Architecture and Representation at the 1931 Colonial Exhibition in Paris.* Cambridge, MA: MIT Press, 2000.

Muhammad, Fatimah N. "How to NOT be 21st Century Venus Hottentots." *Home Girls Make Some Noise.* Ed. Gwendolyn Pough, Elaine Richardson, Aisha Durham, Rachel Raimist. Mira Loma, CA: Parking Publishing, 2007. 115–140.

Muhanji, Cherry. "Popsicle Sticks." *Tight Spaces.* By Kesho Scott, Cherry Muhanji, and Egyirba High. San Francisco: Spinsters/Aunt Lute, 1987. 76–78.

Mullen, Harryette Romell. "African Signs and Spirit Writing." *Callaloo* 19, no. 3 (1996): 670–689.

Mulvey, Laura. *Visual and Other Pleasures.* Bloomington: Indiana University Press, 1989.

——. "Visual Pleasure and Narrative Cinema." *Screen* 16.3 (1975): 6–18.

Munich, Adrienne. "Feminist Criticism and Literary Tradition." *Making a Difference: Feminist Literary Criticism.* Ed. Gayle Greene and Coppélia Kahn. London and New York: Methuen, 1985. 245–254. 238–259.

Muñoz, José Esteban. *Disidentifications: Queers of Color and the Performance of Politics.* Minneapolis: University of Minnesota Press, 1999.

Myrdal, Gunnar. *An American Dilemma: The Negro Problem and Modern Democracy.* New York and London: Harper & Brothers, 1944.

Nadar, Kathleen Olympia. "Violence: Effects of Parents' Previous Trauma on Currently Traumatized Children." *International Handbook of Multigenerational Legacies of Trauma.* Ed. Yael Danieli. New York: Plenum Press, 1998. 571–584.

Nardo, Anna K. "'Sung and Proverb'd for a Fool': Samson as Fool and Trickster." *Mosaic* 22 (Winter 1989): 1–16.

Naylor, Gloria. *Linden Hills.* New York: Ticknor & Fields, 1985.

Naylor, Gloria, and Toni Morrison. "A Conversation." *The Southern Review* 21, no. 3 (Summer 1985): 567–593.

Neal, Larry. *The Glorious Monster in the Bell of the Horn. Callaloo* 23 (1985): 87–169.

"New Plays in Manhattan." *Time* (February 10, 1936): 59–60.

Nietzsche, Friedrich Wilhelm. *Thus Spoke Zarathustra: A Book for All and None.* Trans. Walter Kaufmann. New York: Penguin, 1978.

Nora, Pierre. "Between Memory and History: *Les Lieux de Mémoire.*" Trans. Marc Roudebush. *Representations* 26 (Spring 1989): 7–24.

Nott, Josiah C. *Two Lectures on the Natural History of the Caucasian and Negro Races.* Mobile, AL: Dade and Thompson, 1844.

O'Connor, Flannery. *The Complete Stories.* New York: Farrar, Straus and Giroux, 1971.

Oliver, Chyann L. "for sepia 'colored girls' who have considered self/when hip-hop is enuf." *Home Girls Make Some Noise: Hip Hop Feminism Anthology.* Ed. Gwendolyn D. Pough, Elaine Richardson, Aisha Durham, and Rachel Raimist. Mira Loma, CA: Parking Publishing, 2007. 248–270.

Oliver, Kelly. *Witnessing: Beyond Recognition.* Minneapolis and London: University of Minnesota Press, 2001.

O'Neil, Moira. "'Assthetics': Commodification and Consumption of Black Feminine Bodies in a Popular Women's Magazine." Paper presented at the annual meeting of the American Sociological Association. Hilton San Francisco & Renaissance Parc 55 Hotel, San Francisco, CA. August 14, 2004. Available online: http://www.allacademic.com/meta/p110539_index.html.

Osterheldt, Jenee. "For Some, Misogyny's Spelled R-A-P." *Seattle Times,* August 19, 2005: http://seattletimes.com/html/musicnightlife/2002444859_misogyny19.html.

Page, Thomas Nelson. *Red Rock: A Chronicle of Reconstruction.* New York: Charles Scribner's Sons, 1898.

Parker, Gwendolyn M. *These Same Long Bones.* Boston: Houghton Mifflin, 1994.

Parks, Suzan-Lori. "The Rear End Exists." *Grand Street* 55 (1996): 10–18.

Parratt, John. *Introduction to Third World Theologies.* Cambridge: Cambridge University Press, 2004.

Pater, Walter. *The Renaissance: Studies in Art and Poetry.* 1893. New York: Boni and Liveright, 1919.

Patterson, Orlando. *Slavery and Social Death: A Comparative Study.* Cambridge, MA: Harvard University Press, 1982.

Paulhan, Jean. "Preface." *Story of O.* By Pauline Réage. Trans. Sabine d'Estree. New York: Grove Press, 1965. xxi–xxxvi.

Pavlov, Ivan Petrovich. *Conditioned Reflexes: An Investigation of the Physiological Activity of the Cerebral Cortex.* Trans. and ed. G. V. Anrep. London: Oxford University Press, 1927.

Peoples, Whitney A. "'Under Construction': Identifying Foundations of Hip-Hop Feminism and Exploring Bridges between Black Second-Wave and Hip-Hop Feminisms." *Meridians: feminism, race, transnationalism* 8, no. 1 (2008): 19–52.

Perry, Ruth, and Martine Watson, eds. *Mothering the Mind: Twelve Studies of Writers and Their Silent Partners*. New York: Holmes & Meier, 1984.

Peterson, Carla L. *"Doers of the Word": African-American. Women. Speakers and Writers in the North (1830–1880)*. New York: Oxford University Press, 1995.

Plato. *The Dialogues of Plato*. Trans. B. Jowett. 2 vols. New York: Random House, 1937.

Pobee, John S. "Oral Theology and Christian Oral Tradition: Challenge to Our Traditional Archival Concept." *Mission Studies* 6 (1989): 87–93.

———. *Toward an African Theology*. Nashville, TN: Abingdon Press, 1979.

Pough, Gwendolyn D. *Check It While I Wreck It: Black Womanhood, Hip-Hop Culture, and the Public Sphere*. Boston: Northeastern University Press, 2004.

Pough, Gwendolyn D., Elaine Richardson, Aisha Durham, and Rachel Raimist, eds. *Home Girls Make Some Noise: Hip Hop Feminism Anthology*. Mira Loma, CA: Parking Publishing, 2007.

Pound, Ezra. *Make It New*. London: Faber & Faber, 1934.

Powell, Richard J., and David A. Bailey. "Re/Birth of a Nation." *Rhapsodies in Black: Art of the Harlem Renaissance*. Berkeley: University of California Press, 1997.

Price, Kimala. "Hip-Hop Feminism at the Political Crossroads: Organizing for Reproductive Justice and Beyond." *Home Girls Make Some Noise*. Ed. Gwendolyn Pough, Elaine Richardson, Aisha Durham, and Rachel Raimist. Mira Loma, CA: Parking Publishing, 2007. 389–408.

"Print isn't dead, says Bowker's Annual Book Production Report." *Bowker*. May 18, 2011: http://www.bowker.com/en-US/aboutus/press_room/2011/pr_05182011.shtml.

Pritchard, William H. "Nasty Reviews: Easy to Give, Hard to Take." *New York Times Book Review* (May 7, 1989): 1, 36–37.

Rahim, Jennifer. "(Not) Knowing the Difference: Calypso Overseas and the Sound of Belonging in Selected Narratives of Migration." *Anthurium: A Caribbean Studies Journal* 3, no. 2 (Fall 2005).

Réage, Pauline [Anne Desclos *aka* Dominique Aury]. *Story of O*. Trans. Sabine d'Estree. New York: Grove Press, 1965.

Reid, Omar G., Sekou Mims, and Larry Higginbottom. *Post-Traumatic Slavery Disorder: Definition, Diagnosis, and Treatment*. Charlotte, NC: Conquering Books, 2005.

Rennert, Jack. *100 Affiches de Paul Colin*. New York: Images Graphiques, 1977.

Riccoboni, Marie-Jeanne. *Lettres de Milady Juliette Catesby*. Amsterdam: Aux dépens de la Compagnie, 1759.

Rich, Adrienne. "When We Dead Awaken: Writing as Re-vision." *On Lies, Secrets, and Silence: Selected Prose 1966–1978*. New York: W. W. Norton, 1979. 33–49.

Ricoeur, Paul. *The Reality of Historical Past*. Milwaukee, WI: Marquette University Press, 1984.

———. *Time and Narrative*. 3 vols. Chicago: University of Chicago Press, 1988.

Rodney, Walter. *How Europe Underdeveloped Africa*. Washington, DC: Howard University Press, 1982.

Roediger, David. *The Wages of Whiteness: Race and the Making of the American Working Class*. New York: Verso, 1991.

Rony, Fatimah Tobing. *The Third Eye: Race, Cinema, and Ethnographic Spectacle*. Durham, NC, and London: Duke University Press, 1996.

Root, Maria P. P. "Reconstructing the Impact of Trauma on Personality." *Personality and Psychopathology: Feminist Reappraisals*. Ed. Laura S. Brown and Mary Balou. New York: Guilford Press, 1992. 229–266.

Rose, Phyllis. *Jazz Cleopatra: Josephine Baker in Her Time*. New York: Doubleday, 1989.

Rose, Tricia. *Black Noise: Rap Music and Black Culture in Contemporary America*. Middletown, CT: Wesleyan University Press, 1994.

———. *The Hip Hop Wars*. New York: Basic Civitas Books, 2008.

Roth, Philip. *The Human Stain*. Boston and New York: Houghton Mifflin, 2000.

Rowe, John Carlos. "To Live Outside the Law, You Must Be Honest: The Authority of the Margin in Contemporary Theory." *Cultural Critique: International Journal of Cultural Studies* 1, no. 2 (1985/86): 35–68.

Rowell, Charles H. "Gayl Jones: An Interview." *Callaloo* no. 16 (Oct. 1982): 32–53.

Russo, Mary J. *The Female Grotesque: Risk, Excess, and Modernity*. New York: Routledge, 1995.

Ryan, Mary P. *Womanhood in America: From Colonial Times to the Present.* New York: New Viewpoints, 1975.

Rydell, Robert. *All the World's a Fair: Visions of Empire at American International Expositions.* Chicago: University of Chicago Press, 1984.

Rynkiewich, Michael A. *Cultures and Languages of Papua New Guinea: The Story of the Origins, Migrations and Settlement of Melanesian Peoples, Languages, and Cultures.* Goroka, Eastern Highlands Province, Papua New Guinea: Melanesian Institute, 2004.

Saadawi, Nawal El. *The Hidden Face of Eve.* Boston: Beacon Press, 1982.

St. Jorre, John. "The Unmasking of O." *The New Yorker* (August 1, 1994): 42–50.

Saks, Eva. "Representing Miscegenation Law." *Raritan* 8.2 (1988): 39–69.

Samarin, William J. *Tongues of Men and Angels: The Religious Language of Pentecostalism.* New York: The Macmillan Company, 1972.

Sato, Hiroko. "Under the Harlem Shadow: A Study of Jessie Fauset and Nella Larsen." *The Harlem Renaissance Remembered: Essays.* Ed. Arna Bontemps. New York: Dodd, Mead, & Co., 1972. 63–89.

Scheper, Jeanne. "'Of la Baker, I Am Disciple': The Diva Politics of Reception." *Camera Obscura* 22 [65, no. 2] (2007): 72–101.

Schib, John. "Pedagogy of the Oppressors?" *Gendered Subjects: The Dynamics of Feminist Teaching.* Ed. Margo Culley and Catherine Portuges. Boston: Routledge and Kegan Paul, 1985. 253–264.

Schneider, William H. *An Empire for the Masses: The French Popular Image of Africa, 1870–1900.* Westport, CT: Greenwood Press, 1982.

Schuyler, George S. *Black No More.* New York: The Macauley Co., 1931.

Sedgwick, Eve Kosofsky. *Tendencies.* Durham, NC: Duke University Press, 1993.

Senna, Danzy. *Caucasia.* New York: Riverhead, 1998.

Sharpley-Whiting, T. Denean. *Black Venus: Sexualized Savages, Primal Fears, and Primitive Narratives in French.* Durham, NC: Duke University Press, 1999.

——. *Pimps Up, Ho's Down: Hip Hop's Hold on Young Black Women.* New York and London: New York University Press, 2007.

Silverman, Kaja. *The Acoustic Mirror: The Female Voice in Psychoanalysis and Cinema.* Bloomington: Indiana University Press, 1988.

——. "*Histoire D'O*: The Story of a Disciplined and Punished Body." *Enclitic* 7, no. 2 (Fall 1983): 63–81.

——. "Masochism and Male Subjectivity." *Male Subjectivities at the Margins.* New York and London: Routledge, 1992. 185–213.

Simon, Paul, writer and performer, and Art Garfunkel, performer. "The Sound of Silence." *The Sounds of Silence.* Columbia, 1965.

Singh, Amritjit. *The Novels of the Harlem Renaissance: Twelve Black Writers, 1923–1933.* University Park: Pennsylvania State University Press, 1976.

Sir Mix-a-Lot, writer and performer. "Baby Got Back." *Mack Daddy.* Def American, 1992.

Skerrett, Joseph T. "The Wright Interpretation: Ralph Ellison and the Anxiety of Influence." *Massachusetts Review* 21 (Spring 1980): 196–212.

Sklodowska, Elzbieta. "Spanish American Testimonial Novel: Some Afterthoughts." *The Real Thing: Testimonial Discourse and Latin America.* Ed. George M. Gugelberger. Durham, NC: Duke University Press, 1996. 84–100.

Smith, Amanda Berry. *An Autobiography: The Story of the Lord's Dealings with Mrs. Amanda Smith, the Colored Evangelist: Containing an Account of Her Life Work of Faith, and Her Travels in America, England, Ireland, Scotland, India, and Africa as an Independent Missionary.* Chicago: Meyer & Brother Publishers, 1893.

Smith, Barbara. "Toward a Black Feminist Criticism." *All the Women Are White, All the Blacks Are Men, But Some of Us Are Brave: Black Women's Studies.* Ed. Gloria T. Hull, Patricia Bell Scott, and Barbara Smith. Old Westbury, NY: The Feminist Press, 1982. 157–175.

Smith, Barbara, ed. *Home Girls: A Black Feminist Anthology.* New York: Kitchen Table: Women of Color Press, 1983.

Smith, Jesse Carney. *Notable Black American Women, Book II.* Detroit, MI: Gale Research, 1996.

Smith, Valerie. "Black Feminist Theory and the Representation of the 'Other.'" *Changing Our Own Words: Essays on Criticism, Theory, and Writing by Black Women.* Ed. Cheryl A. Wall. New Brunswick: Rutgers University Press, 1989. 38–57.

Smitherman, Geneva. *Talkin and Testifyin: The Language of Black America.* Detroit, MI: Wayne State University Press, 1986.

Sollors, Werner. *Neither Black Nor White Yet Both: Thematic Explorations of Interracial Literature.* New York: Oxford University Press, 1997.

Sontag, Susan. *Styles of Radical Will.* New York: Farrar, Straus and Girous, 1969.

Stambovsky, Philip. "Metaphor and Historical Understanding." *History and Theory* 27, no. 2 (1988): 125–134.

"The State of the Art." *The Women's Review of Books* 8, no. 5 (February 1991): 23–26.

Steffans, Karrine. *Confessions of a Video Vixen.* New York: HarperCollins, 2005.

——. *The Vixen Diaries.* New York: Grand Central Publishing, 2007.

——. *The Vixen Manual: How to Find, Seduce, and Keep the Man You Want.* New York: Grand Central Publishing, 2009.

Stepto, Robert B. *From Behind the Veil: A Study of Afro-American Narrative.* Urbana: University of Illinois Press, 1979.

Stern, Frederick C. "Black Lit., White Crit?" *College English* 35, no. 6 (March 1974): 637–658.

Stetson, Erlene, ed. *Black Sister.* Bloomington: Indiana University Press, 1981.

Stewart, Maria W. *Meditations from the Pen of Mrs. Maria W. Stewart: Presented to the First African Baptist Church and Society, in the City of Boston.* Boston: Printed by Garrison and Knapp, 1835.

——. *Productions of Mrs. Maria W. Stewart Presented to the First African Baptist Church and Society of the City of Boston.* Boston: Friends of Freedom and Virtue, 1879.

Story, Kaila Adia. "Performing Venus—From Hottentot to Video Vixen: The Historical Legacy of Black Female Body Commodification." *Home Girls Make Some Noise.* Ed. Gwendolyn Pough, Elaine Richardson, Aisha Durham, and Rachel Raimist. Mira Loma, CA: Parking Publishing, 2007. 235–247.

Stovall, Tyler. *Paris Noir: African Americans in the City of Light.* New York: Houghton-Mifflin, 1996.

Stowe, Harriet Beecher. *Uncle Tom's Cabin.* 1852. New York: Random House/Bantam Books, 1981.

Stuart, Andrea. "Telling Our Story." Interview with Toni Morrison. *Spare Rib* (April 1988): 12–15.

Styron, William. *The Confessions of Nat Turner.* New York: Random House, 1967.

——. "This Quiet Dust." *The Nat Turner Rebellion: The Historical Event and the Modern Controversy.* Ed. John B. Duff and Peter M. Mitchell. New York: Harper and Row, 1971. 120–140.

Tate, Claudia C. "Gayl Jones." *Black Women Writers at Work.* Ed. Claudia C. Tate. New York: Continuum, 1983. 89–99.

——. "Nella Larsen's *Passing*: A Problem of Interpretation." *Black American Literature Forum* 14, no. 4 (Winter 1980): 142–146.

Thelwell, Mike. "Back with the Wind: Mr. Styron and the Reverend Turner." *William Styron's Nat Turner: Ten Writers Respond.* Ed. John Henrik Clarke. Boston: Beacon Press, 1968. 79–91.

Thompson, Robert Farris. *Flash of the Spirit: African and Afro-American Art and Philosophy.* New York: Random House, 1984.

Thiam, Awa. *La Parole aux Négresses.* Paris: Denoël/Gonthier, 1978.

Thurman, Wallace. *The Blacker the Berry: A Novel of Negro Life.* New York: Macaulay Co., 1929.

——. *Infants of the Spring.* New York: Macaulay Co., 1932.

Todd, Janet. *Women's Friendship in Literature.* New York: Columbia University Press, 1980.

Tompkins, Jane. "Fighting Words: Unlearning to Write the Critical Essay." *Georgia Review* 42 (1988): 585–590.

Toomer, Jean. *Cane.* New York: Boni and Liveright, 1923.

Transcript of Online Chat between Bebe Moore Campbell and *barnesandnoble.com.* Posted to the Website for the African American Literature Book Club. *aalbc.com*: http://aalbc.com/authors/bebecampbellchattext.htm.

Twain, Mark. *The Tragedy of Pudd'nhead Wilson and the Comedy Those Extraordinary Twins.* Hartford, CT: American Publishing Company, 1894.

Tylor, Edward Burnett. *Anthropology: An Introduction to the Study of Man and Civilization.* London: Macmillan and Co., 1881.

——. *Primitive Culture: Researches into the Development of Mythology, Philosophy, Religion, Languages, Art and Customs.* London: John Murray, 1871.

van der Kolk, Besel A., Alexander C. McFarlane, and Lars Weisaeth, eds. *Traumatic Stress: The Effects of Overwhelming Experience on Mind, Body, and Society.* New York: The Gilford Press, 1996.

Van der Zee, James. *The Harlem Book of the Dead.* Dobbs Ferry, NY: Morgan and Morgan, 1978.

Van Vechten, Carl. *Nigger Heaven.* New York: Alfred A. Knopf, 1926.

Volosinov, V. N. [Mikhail Bakhtin]. *Marxism and the Philosophy of Language.* New York: Seminar Press, 1973.

Wacks, James L. "Reading Race, Rhetoric and the Female Body: The Rhinelander Case and 1920s American Culture." Senior thesis. Harvard University, 1995.

Wald, Gayle. *Crossing the Color Line: Racial Passing in Twentieth-Century U.S. Literature and Culture.* Durham, NC: Duke University Press, 2000.

Walker, Alice. *The Color Purple.* New York: Harcourt Brace Jovanovich, 1982.

——. "In the Closet of the Soul: A Letter to an African-American Friend." *Ms. Magazine* (November 1986): 32–35.

——. "In Search of Our Mothers' Gardens." *In Search of Our Mothers' Gardens: Womanist Prose.* New York: Harcourt Brace Jovanovich, 1984. 231–243.

——. *Possessing the Secret of Joy.* New York: Harcourt Brace Jovanovich, 1992.

——. *The Third Life of Grange Copeland.* New York: Harcourt Brace Jovanovich, 1970.

Walker, Margaret. *Jubilee.* Boston: Houghton Mifflin, 1966.

Walker, Melissa. *Down From the Mountaintop.* New Haven, CT: Yale University Press, 1991.

Wall, Cheryl A. "Introduction: Taking Positions and Changing Words." *Changing Our Own Words: Essays on Criticism, Theory, and Writing by Black Women.* Ed. Cheryl A. Wall. New Brunswick, NJ: Rutgers University Press, 1989. 1–15.

——. *Women of the Harlem Renaissance.* Bloomington and Indianapolis: Indiana University Press, 1995.

——. *Worrying the Line: Black Women Writers, Lineage, and Literary Tradition.* Chapel Hill: University of North Carolina Press, 2005).

Wall, Cheryl A., ed. *Changing Our Own Words: Essays on Criticism, Theory, and Writing by Black Women.* New Brunswick, NJ: Rutgers University Press, 1989.

Wallace-Sanders, Kimberly, ed. *Skin Deep, Spirit Strong: The Black Female Body in American Culture.* Ann Arbor: The University of Michigan Press, 2002.

Warren, Kenneth, and Gerald Graff. "Kenneth Warren and Gerald Graff on the Politics of Talking Back: Gerald Graff's *Beyond the Culture Wars: How Teaching the Conflicts Can Revitalize American Education.*" *The Journal of the Midwest Modern Language Association* 26, no. 1 (Spring 1993): 75–81.

Washington, Elsie B. "Talk with Toni Morrison." *Conversations with Toni Morrison.* Ed. Danille Taylor-Guthrie. Jackson: University Press of Mississippi, 1994. 234–238.

Washington, Mary Helen. "I Love the Way Janie Crawford Left Her Husbands: Zora Neale Hurston's Emergent Hero." *Invented Lives: Narratives of Black Women, 1860-1960.* New York: Doubleday, 1987). 237–254.

——. "I Sign My Mother's Name: Alice Walker, Dorothy West, Paule Marshall." *Mothering the Mind: Twelve Studies of Writers and Their Silent Partners.* Ed. Ruth Perry and Martine Watson Brownley. New York: Holmes & Meier, 1984. 142–163.

——. "In Pursuit of Our Own History." *Midnight Birds: Stories of Contemporary Black Women Writers.* Ed. Mary Helen Washington. Garden City, NY: Anchor Books/Doubleday, 1980. xiii–xxv.

——. "Nella Larsen: Mystery Woman of the Harlem Renaissance." *Ms. Magazine* (December 1980): 44–50.

Washington, Mary Helen, ed. *Midnight Birds: Stories of Contemporary Black Women Writers.* Garden City, NY: Anchor Books/Doubleday, 1980.

Watson, John B., and Rosalie Rayner. "Conditioned Emotional Reactions." *Journal of Experimental Psychology* 3, no. 1 (1920): 1–14.

Webb, Frank J. *The Garies and Their Friends.* London: G. Routledge & Co., 1857.

Weinberg, Steve. "The Unruly World of Book Reviews." *Columbia Journalism Review* 28, no. 6 (March–April 1990): 51–54.

Welter, Barbara. *Dimity Convictions: The American Woman in the Nineteenth Century.* Athens: Ohio University Press, 1976.

Wertz, Dorothy. "Women and Slavery: A Cross-Cultural Perspective." Unpublished paper.

Wheatley, Phillis. "To Maecenas." *The Collected Works of Phillis Wheatley.* Ed. John C. Shields. New York and Oxford: Oxford University Press, 9–12.

White, Hayden. *Tropics of Discourse: Essays in Cultural Criticism.* Baltimore, MD: Johns Hopkins University Press, 1979.

White, Walter. *Flight.* New York and London: Alfred A. Knopf, 1926.

——. "Why I Remain a Negro." *The Saturday Review of Literature* (Oct. 22, 1947): 13–14, 49.

Williams, Brackette F. Rev. of *The Black Atlantic: Modernity and Double Consciousness* by Paul Gilroy. *Social Identities: Journal for the Study of Race, Nation and Culture* 1, no. 1 (February 1995): 175–192.

Williams, C. G. "Speaking in Tongues." *Strange Gifts?: A Guide to Charismatic Renewal.* Ed. David Martin and Peter Mullen. New York and Oxford, England: 1984. 72–83.

Williams, Patrick, and Laura Chrisman, eds. *Colonial Discourse and Post-colonial Discourse: A Reader.* London: Harvester Wheatsheaf, 1994.

Williams, Sherley Anne. Autobiographical Preface to "Meditations on History." *Midnight Birds: Stories of Contemporary Black Women Writers.* Ed. Mary Helen Washington. Garden City, NY: Anchor Books/Doubleday, 1980. 195–198.

——. *Dessa Rose.* New York: William Morrow, 1986.

——. *Give Birth to Brightness: A Thematic Study in Neo-Black Literature.* New York: Dial Press, 1972.

——. "Letters from a New England Negro." *Callaloo* 24, no. 3 (2001): 912–922.

——. "Meditations on History." *Midnight Birds: Stories of Contemporary Black Women Writers.* Ed. Mary Helen Washington. Garden City, NY: Anchor Books/Doubleday, 1980. 200–248.

——. *The Peacock Poems.* Middletown, CT: Wesleyan University Press, 1975.

——. *Someone Sweet Angel Chile.* New York: William Morrow, 1982.

——. "Tell Martha Not to Moan." *Massachusetts Review* 9, no. 3 (Summer 1968): 443–458.

Williams, Tennessee. *The Rose Tattoo.* New York: New Directions, 1951.

Williamson, Joel. *New People: Miscegenation and Mulattoes in the United States.* New York: Free Press, 1980.

Willis, Deborah, and Carla Williams. *The Black Female Body: A Photographic History.* Philadelphia: Temple University Press, 2002.

Wilson, Harriet E. *Our Nig; or, Sketches from the Life of a Free Black.* 1859. Intro. and notes Henry Louis Gates, Jr. New York: Vintage/Random House, 1983.

Wiss, Rosemary. "Lipreading: Remembering Saartjie Baartman." *The Australian Journal of Anthropology* 5, nos.1–2 (1994): 11–40.

Wittig, Monique. "The Straight Mind." *Feminist Issues* 1, no. 1 (Summer 1980): 105–106.

Women in Publishing. *Reviewing the Reviews: A Woman's Place on the Book Page.* London: Journeyman, 1987.

Woolf, Virginia. "Reviewing." *The Captain's Death Bed and Other Essays.* New York: Harcourt, 1950. 127–145.

——. *A Room of One's Own.* London: Hogarth Press, 1929.

Yee, Marian. "Are You the Teacher?" *Composition and Resistance.* Ed. C. Mark Hurlbert and Michael Blitz. Portsmouth, NH: Heinemann-Boynton/Cook, 1991. 24–42.

Youman, Mary Mabel. "Nella Larsen's *Passing*: A Study of Irony." *CLA Journal* 18 (1974): 235–241.

Young, Robert C. *Colonial Desire: Hybridity in Theory, Culture and Race.* London and New York: Routledge, 1995.

Zantop, Susanne. *Colonial Fantasies: Conquest, Family, and Nation in Precolonial Germany, 1770–1870.* Durham, NC: Duke University Press, 1997.

Zwinger, Lynda. "What She Gets for Saying Yes: O." *Daughters, Fathers and the Novel: The Sentimental Romance of Heterosexuality.* Madison: The University of Wisconsin Press, 1991. 96–116.

INDEX

abolitionist movement, in Williams's *Dessa Rose*, 101

Absalom, Absalom! (Faulkner), 14–20, 156

academia, black feminist studies in, 138–144; book reviewing and, 145–151; violence in, 145–151; *see also* black feminist pedagogy

accountability, authority and, 138–144

"address-ability" (Oliver), 16, 18, 226, 279n. 75; *see also* "response-ability"

Adams, Nehemiah, 247n. 8, 252n. 24, 259n. 23, 281; *see also* Nehemiah, Adam

"The Aesthetics of Silence" (Sontag), 122, 124

Africa, African American diasporic dance and, 187, 205–208; French colonial expansion into, 177; gender roles in, 245 n. 11; image of black female body and, 117, 177; in Walker's *The Color Purple*, 28, 30, 31; theological activity among women of, 242n. 16, 245n. 11; *see also* Africans

African American cultural performance, 2, 15, 19; African and African diasporic roots of, 205; black popular culture, body imagery in, 209–226; colonial and postcolonial interpretations of, 198–204; French history of, 187; *see also* black women; dancing black body; performance testimony; performativity

African American women, *see* black women

Africanist, dancing and performance, Josephine Baker and, 190, 201, 206; frame of reference, 190

Africanity, French aesthetics of, 189

Africans, in Europe, "ethnographic display" tradition and, 177–184; Middle Passage, mortality among, 254n. 6; nakedness and accessorization of, 186; racial difference and continental, 177; *see also* Africa; primitivism

Afrique fantôme, 177, 268n. 6, 292

Agassiz, Louis, 160, 266n. 38

Alcoff, Linda, 140, 263n.5, 263n. 7, 281

Alex, Joe, 189, 190, 191

All Nations Pentecostal Church, 6

All the Women Are White, All the Blacks Are Men, But Some of Us Are Brave (Hull, Scott, and Smith), 59, 250n. 1, 263n. 8, 290, 297

alterity, in Larsen's *Passing*, 166–173; risks of substituting Black and Woman to status of irreducible, 135; *see also* Other and otherness

Althusser, Louis, 223, 260n. 18, 277n. 58, 281

ambiguously (non)hegemonic (DuPlessis), 62, 63, 69, 70, 74, 75, 116, 211, 251n. 14

Amos, Emma, 212

Andrews, William, 127, 259n. 20, 262n. 22, 281, 293

Angelou, Maya, 120

"Anger and Authority in the Introductory Women's Studies Classroom" (Culley), 138, 263n. 9, 284

anxiety of authorship (Gilbert and Gubar), 75

anxiety of influence (Bloom), 75, 246n. 2, 253n. 43, 283

Anzaldúa, Gloria, 23, 132, 245n. 4, 262n. 43, 281, 294

a priori imagination (Collingwood), 80; *see also* constructive imagination (Collingwood)

aposiopesis, in Gayl Jones's "Persona," 128; in Larsen's *Passing*, 172

Apostolic Faith Gospel Mission, 6

Aptheker, Herbert, 37, 41, 247n. 11, 248n. 21, 248nn. 30–31, 249n. 37, 281

Archer-Straw, Petrine, 271n. 35, 271n. 39, 281

architextualité, Genette's concept of, 109, 259n. 26, 288

l'art nègre, 179, 185, 190, 269n. 7, 271n. 30; Josephine Baker's *danse sauvage* and, 200–201

Areopagitica (Milton), 145, 264n. 3, 294

Arnold, Matthew, 118, 260n. 11, 281